S0-ARO-241

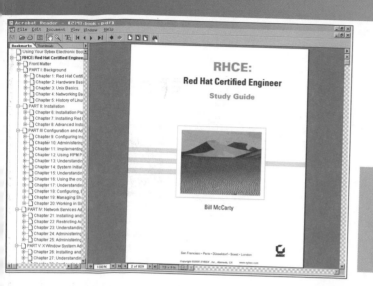

The CD also includes the entire text of RHCE: Red Hat Certified Engineer Study Guide! *The highly searchable PDF format makes it easy to find exactly what you're looking for. Adobe Acrobat Reader is also included, giving you all the tools you need to study when and where you want!*

✓ Take a break and study on your workplace desktop machine.

✓ Study anywhere with your laptop—airplanes, hotel rooms, even the coffee shop!

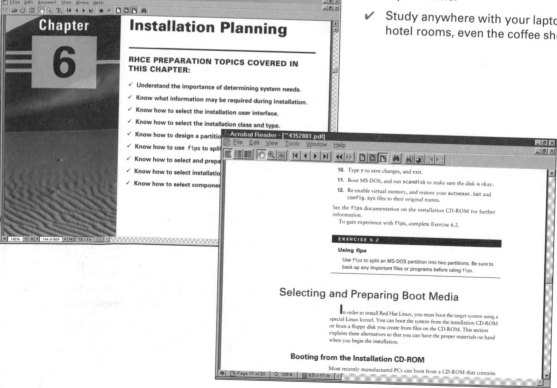

SYBEX

RHCE:
Red Hat Certified Engineer
Study Guide

RHCE:
Red Hat Certified Engineer
Study Guide

Bill McCarty

San Francisco • Paris • Düsseldorf • Soest • London

SYBEX

Associate Publisher: Jordan Gold
Contracts and Licensing Manager: Kristine O'Callaghan
Acquisitions and Developmental Editor: Ellen L. Dendy
Editors: Julie Sakaue, Suzanne Goraj, Sarah Lemaire
Production Editor: Dennis Fitzgerald
Technical Editor: Randolph Russell
Book Designer: Bill Gibson
Graphic Illustrator: Tony Jonick
Electronic Publishing Specialists: Susie Hendrickson, Judy Fung, Jill Niles
Proofreaders: Carol A. Burbo, Nanette Duffy, Mae Lum, Nathan Whiteside
Indexer: Ted Laux
CD Coordinator: Kara Eve Schwartz
CD Technician: Keith McNeil
Cover Designer: Archer Design
Cover Photograph: Tony Stone

Library of Congress Card Number: 00-106231

ISBN: 0-7821-2793-2

SYBEX and the SYBEX logo are trademarks of SYBEX Inc. in the USA and other countries.

Screen reproductions produced with FullShot 99. FullShot 99 © 1991-1999 Inbit Incorporated. All rights reserved. FullShot is a trademark of Inbit Incorporated.

The CD interface was created using Macromedia Director, COPYRIGHT 1994, 1997-1999 Macromedia Inc. For more information on Macromedia and Macromedia Director, visit http://www.macromedia.com.

SYBEX is an independent entity from Red Hat, Inc. and not affiliated with Red Hat, Inc. in any manner. This publication may be used in assisting students to prepare for a Red Hat Certified Engineer exam. Neither Red Hat, Inc. nor SYBEX warrants that use of this publication will ensure passing the relevant exam. Red Hat is a registered trademark or trademark of Red Hat, Inc. in the United States and/or other countries. Red Hat, RPM, Linux Library, PowerTools, and all Red Hat-based trademarks and logos are trademarks or registered trademarks of Red Hat, Inc. in the United States and other countries.

TRADEMARKS: SYBEX has attempted throughout this book to distinguish proprietary trademarks from descriptive terms by following the capitalization style used by the manufacturer.

The author and publisher have made their best efforts to prepare this book, and the content is based upon final release software whenever possible. Portions of the manuscript may be based upon pre-release versions supplied by software manufacturer(s). The author and the publisher make no representation or warranties of any kind with regard to the completeness or accuracy of the contents herein and accept no liability of any kind including but not limited to performance, merchantability, fitness for any particular purpose, or any losses or damages of any kind caused or alleged to be caused directly or indirectly from this book.

Manufactured in the United States of America

10 9 8 7 6 5 4 3 2

Acknowledgments

This is my tenth book, and I still find writing acknowledgments to be the hardest part of writing a book. This is doubly frustrating because they're so seldom read, or so it seems to me. I'm a teacher during the day, you see, and I find that my students are only dimly and rarely aware of the acknowledgments in books they've bought at my insistence. Perhaps the acknowledgments in works of fiction enjoy a gladder fate, but the pessimist in me doubts that this is so. I don't understand all this, because I'm the sort who watches the credits of a film until I see the copyright symbol go by. Okay, to be honest, I often skip out when I see the production accountants' names go by, but that's quite close to the end, isn't it?

Notwithstanding this conspiracy of obscurity that surrounds acknowledgments, I must insist that they're important. Yes, I concede that it's unlikely that more than a handful of people have ever purchased books on account of the acknowledgments. And, that seems to indicate that the acknowledgments are less important than what lies nearer the center of the book. But, not so.

After all, books are created by *people* and for *people*: It's people who are important, not books. And here, in the acknowledgments, I have an opportunity to pay a debt to the many people who worked on this book. In film, many people are sometimes given a prominent place in the credits—often above the title of the film itself—including producers, directors, actors, and actresses. But, in publishing, the cover of a book generally contains only the name of the publishing company and the author. (Gosh, come to think of it, I haven't seen the cover of this book: I'm merely presuming that my name will be on the cover.)

This is all wrong, and I'd like to give you the chance to help change it: I want you to copy this page—don't tear it out or anything crude like that—and tape it over the cover of your copy of this book. The result may not be very visually aesthetic, but my spirit soars when I consider this little act of rebellion against anonymity on behalf of the cast and crew of this book.

Now, I'd best get to the point or the names of all these folk will be on the back of this page, which would ruin the whole concept, wouldn't it? Let's start with Margot Maley-Hutchison, Literary Agent (think of her as the producer), and Ellen Dendy, Acquisitions and Developmental Editor (think of her as the director). Then, there's Randy Russell and Utilman, Technical Editors (think of them as the screenwriters who adapted my unfilmable novel, because that approximates the enormous scope of their contribution) and Ellen Bliss, Technical Editorial Coordinator (think of her as the screenwriting manager who had the wisdom to choose Randy and Utilman to write the screenplay). Stars include Dennis Fitzgerald, Production Editor (think of him as this year's best actor); Julie Sakaue, Editor (think of her as this year's best actress); and Sarah Lemaire and Suzanne Goraj, Editors (think of them as this year's best actresses in supporting roles). Each of these folks deserves an Oscar—or perhaps two Oscars—just for putting up with my idiosyncrasies and increasingly poor memory and lack of attention to detail.

Several others who didn't work directly on the book merit special mention. My home crew—Jennifer, Patrick, and Sara—seem by now to have become inured of my book writing habits. Thanks to them for handling the bills, the moving of furniture, and the household chores while I indulged my writing habit. Finally, and emphatically, I thank my Lord and Savior, Jesus Christ, who knows my many flaws and weaknesses better than any other and nevertheless patiently bears with me knowing that He—how, I don't know—can yet make something remarkable of me. I can't wait!

Contents at a Glance

Contents

Part III   **Configuration and Administration**   **201**

Chapter 9   **Configuring Install-Time Options after Installation**   **203**

Chapter 13	**Understanding the Red Hat Linux File System Layout**	**309**

Table of Exercises

How to Use This Book

This book has quite a few chapters—31, to be precise. Most of the chapters are small and focused so that you can quickly find and review topics. Small chapters also help you pace your study so that you avoid burn out. A few chapters, such as the chapter on installing Red Hat Linux, are longer than most, but, generally, their length is attributable to screen shots that will help you to stay oriented to the procedures those chapters explain. So, you probably won't find even the longer chapters overly tiring.

Be sure to read the inside front cover page of this book which discusses what's on the companion CD.

Because the chapters are small, the book is organized into parts that group related chapters:

Part I: Background   Chapters 1–5 explain RHCE certification and review basic material on PC hardware, Unix, TCP/IP networking, and Linux. You're probably familiar with much of this material already, so feel free to skim these chapters, using these chapters just to fill in gaps in your recollection and understanding.

Part II: Installation   Chapters 6–8 describe the procedure for installing Red Hat Linux, including pre-installation planning and advanced installation techniques.

Part III: Configuration and Administration   Chapters 9–20 describe and explain Red Hat Linux system administration, including such topics as user accounts, disk quotas, and RPM packages.

Part IV: Network Services Administration   Chapters 21–25 describe and explain the administration of network services. They include material on Apache, NFS, Squid, and a variety of other servers, plus material on network security and system logs.

Part V: X Window System Administration   Chapters 26–28 concern the X Window System, the Unix standard graphical user interface.

Part VI: Network Administration   Chapters 29 and 30 cover routers and firewalls.

Part VII: The RHCE Exam (RH302)   Chapter 31 describes the RHCE exam in detail and gives suggestions for performing well on the exam.

Appendix A Appendix A is a practice exam for you to take as you prepare for the RHCE exam.

Merely reading—or worse yet, skimming—this book won't suffice to prepare you for the RHCE exam. Instead, you should follow a methodical, organized process such as the following:

1. Take the assessment test to determine the areas in which you excel and those in which you should spend more time studying. Strive to learn from your mistakes as well as your successes.

2. Study a chapter. Studying, by the way, involves more than mere reading; it involves interacting with the text, asking yourself questions, and probing to discover the consequences of what you read.

3. Complete the exercises in the chapter. Bear in mind that the RHCE exam will require you to demonstrate skills, which are acquired only by practice, not by precept. The exercises are probably the closest experience to a real RHCE exam you'll find anywhere. They're worth doing, if you plan to pass the exam.

4. Answer the review questions at the end of the chapter. These questions closely resemble the experience of the written portion of the RHCE exam.

5. Review chapter topics related to any questions you missed. Be sure you know the right answer and why the other responses are wrong.

6. Work your way through the entire book in this fashion, one chapter at a time.

7. When you believe you're ready, take the practice exam in Appendix A, then assess your performance.

8. Take the bonus exam included on the CD to further test your readiness for the real thing. If you do well, sign up for the RHCE exam or the RHCE preparation course, according to your preference. If you don't do well, repeat steps 1–8 until you're able to pass the practice exam with confidence.

9. Use the Flashcard questions on the CD that accompanies this book to stay sharp while awaiting the RHCE exam.

31. Which of the following correctly pairs a virtual console with its installation program function?

   A. 2, shell prompt

   B. 3, install program messages

   C. 4, system messages

   D. 5, other messages

32. Which program is used by the installation procedure to configure X?

   A. Xcfg

   B. Xconfig

   C. Xconfigurator

   D. Xconfiguration

33. Which of the following are Apache configuration files that must exist?

   A. access.conf

   B. httpd.conf

   C. modules.conf

   D. srm.conf

34. To start a system in single-user mode without initial processes, what should be typed in response to the boot prompt?

   A. linux

   B. linux emergency

   C. linux s

   D. linux single

35. Which of the following programs is not PAM-aware?

   A. ftp

   B. login

   C. rlogin

   D. telnet

36. To permit a client host to access a printer remotely, the client host can be listed in:

   A. `/etc/hosts`

   B. `/etc/hosts.equiv`

   C. `/etc/hosts.lpd`

   D. `/etc/printcap`

37. Which of the following correctly specifies the location of a compiled Linux kernel?

   A. `/usr/src/linux/arch/i386/boot/bzImage`

   B. `/usr/src/linux/arch/i386/boot/kernel`

   C. `/usr/src/linux/arch/i386/boot/vmlinux`

   D. `/usr/src/linux/arch/i386/boot/vmlinuz`

38. To specify that members of the owning group can read the file data, which command do you enter?

   A. `chmod 727 data`

   B. `chmod 717 data`

   C. `chmod g+r data`

   D. `chmod uo+r data`

39. What does a LILO prompt of LIL indicate?

   A. LILO's first stage loaded.

   B. LILO's second stage loaded.

   C. LILO's second stage started.

   D. LILO's third stage loaded.

40. To update the shared library configuration, you must issue the command

   A. `ld`

   B. `ld.so`

   C. `ldconfig`

   D. `ldd`

37. A. The compiled Linux kernel is placed in /usr/src/linux/arch/
i386/boot/bzImage. See Chapter 17 for more information.

38. C. The command chmod g+r enables read permission for members of
the owning group. See Chapter 3 for more details.

39. A, B, C. LILO has no third stage. The LIL prompt indicates a problem
during execution of the second stage. See Chapter 8 for more information.

40. C. The ldconfig command rebuilds the loader's shared library cache.
See Chapter 19 for more information.

41. B, C. Neither kill nor vi is available in the standard rescue mode
environment. See Chapter 20 for more infromation.

42. B, C, D. The graphical mode installation procedure is generally easier
for beginners to use, but requires more resources, and therefore may not
run as quickly as the text mode installation procedure, particularly on
a system that has limited RAM. The text mode installation procedure is
more likely to recover from problems and requires fewer system
resources. See Chapter 6 for more information.

43. D. The /proc file system does not provide an option for disabling
gated and /etc/sysconfig/network-scripts is a directory, not a
file. See Chapter 29 for more information.

44. B, C. Although the file system type is reported as ncpfs, it can be specified
as either ncp or ncpfs. See Chapter 23 for more information.

45. C. It's generally best to specify the desired components. Selecting Everything installs unwanted packages, and selecting individual packages is too
tedious. See Chapter 6 for more information.

46. A. The cache file is /etc/ld.so.cache; the configuration file is
/etc/ld.so.conf. See Chapter 19 for more information.

47. C. The --kickstart flag specifies noninteractive operation to the extent
possible. The --expert flag lets you override probed information. See
Chapter 26 for more information.

48. B, D. The xvidtune and xf86config tools let you set invalid operating characteristics that can damage a monitor. In the case of xf86config, any damage will occur after the tool is run, since the tool itself operates only in text mode. See Chapter 26 for more information.

49. A. You can use a wildcard to specify the client hosts. The servers are specified following the CHOOSER keyword. See Chapter 28 for more information.

50. B, D. The clean argument deletes the results of previous builds and the dep argument propagates configuration information. Either may occur before the other; both should precede the bzImage. Option A fails to propagate the configuration through the source tree and Option C fails to remove the results of previous builds. Either A or C might work under special circumstances, but generally you should use the commands given in B or D. See Chapter 18 for more information.

Background

PART

I

Chapter 1

Red Hat Certification

RHCE PREPARATION TOPICS COVERED IN THIS CHAPTER:

✓ **Know and understand the benefits of certification.**

✓ **Know and understand the significance of certification as a Red Hat Certified Engineer (RHCE).**

✓ **Know and understand the RHCE certification process.**

- ▪ Know and understand the content of Red Hat's certification courses.

- ▪ Know and understand the general structure and content of the RHCE exam.

✓ **Know your readiness for the RHCE exam.**

✓ **Develop a strategy for passing the RHCE exam.**

Though the *Red Hat Certified Engineer* (RHCE) exam doesn't include questions on the material presented in this chapter, it is the most important chapter in this book. Here, you'll learn about *certification* and Red Hat certification in particular. You'll learn about the steps you must take and the options that are available along the path to Red Hat certification. You'll learn how to evaluate your readiness to sit for the RHCE exam. And, you'll learn how to plan a strategy for passing the RHCE exam.

Red Hat Certified Engineer

This section introduces *RHCE* certification. It briefly describes *Linux*, *Red Hat, Inc.* (Red Hat), and Red Hat Linux. RHCE certification is important because Linux is one of the most powerful and popular Internet operating systems, and Red Hat Linux is the leading Linux distribution in the United States. RHCEs are therefore in high demand.

Linux

Linux is an operating system, a software program that provides a standard environment in which application programs can run, that is closely related to *Unix*, an influential operating system developed at AT&T's Bell Laboratories during the 1970s. Although Unix continues to evolve and retain its popularity, particularly as an operating system for powerful network servers, many varieties of Unix are proprietary. Linux, on the other hand, is an open-source operating system and can be freely downloaded from Internet sites.

The source code for Linux is readily available and can be revised or improved by anyone having the requisite technical skill. Moreover, Linux is freely redistributable. You can make additional copies of Linux and give—or sell—them to others, so long as you observe several simple copyright restrictions. These qualities make Linux more attractive than Unix to many and explain its popularity as a leading Internet operating system.

Chapter 5, "History of Linux," describes the Linux operating system in more detail.

Red Hat and Red Hat Linux

Red Hat was founded in 1994 and provides the most popular distribution of Linux in the U.S., Red Hat Linux. Its Linux distribution, like those of other vendors, includes the Linux operating system, utilities to install and maintain it, and useful applications. Red Hat Linux has won many awards, including being named *Infoworld*'s Product of the Year three times. In addition to its Linux distribution, Red Hat provides Linux services, including support, consulting, and training.

Certification

The high demand for skilled technical workers has prompted many organizations to sponsor certification programs. Technical workers who seek to be certified sit for an exam, and if they perform sufficiently well, they're awarded a certificate that attests to their competency. Among the most popular technical certification programs are the Microsoft Certified Systems Engineer (MCSE) and Cisco Certified Internetwork Expert (CCIE) programs.

Three main groups may benefit from technical certification programs:

- Employees may benefit from the enhanced career opportunities that certification affords, because—other things being equal—a prospective employer may prefer a candidate who's certified over one who's not.

- Employers may benefit because they have access to an objective indicator of candidates' skills and can, therefore, make better hiring decisions.

- Sponsors may benefit from the revenue earned by offering certification training classes and certification exams. They may also benefit from increased name recognition within their industry.

Red Hat Certified Engineer Program

During 1998, Red Hat developed a certification program for Red Hat Certified Engineers (RHCE) called the RHCE program. In 1999, they began offering RHCE preparation courses and the certification exam. Like other technical certification programs, the RHCE program was designed to provide technical workers and employers with a useful metric of skills and knowledge. Red Hat also established the RHCE program as a screening device for companies who want to partner with Red Hat. These companies must have RHCEs on staff as a means of assuring that their technical staff possess the skills and experience necessary for successful collaboration with Red Hat.

An unusual aspect of the RHCE exam is that it is *performance-based*. Whereas other certification programs rely primarily on written exams to measure knowledge and skill, the RHCE exam includes a series of exercises that require the candidate to perform typical system and network administration tasks, such as software installation, configuration, and troubleshooting. The RHCE exam also includes a written component; however, it's common for a candidate who does well on the written component to perform poorly on—or even fail—the performance components. Red Hat believes that a *performance-based exam* measures the candidate's skills more reliably than the multiple-choice exams that compose most certification programs.

In addition to testing the candidate's general knowledge of Linux and networking, the RHCE exam assesses the candidate's ability to do the following:

- Install and configure Red Hat Linux

- Configure file systems and networking

- Configure X, the graphical user interface used on Unix and Linux systems

- Configure basic security

- Configure network services

- Perform routine maintenance

- Perform diagnostics and troubleshooting

Because Red Hat regularly updates its Linux distribution, RHCE certification is not valid indefinitely. However, according to Red Hat policy, RHCE certification remains valid for at least one year.

Red Hat has announced that it plans to offer a more advanced level of certification, RHCE II, focusing on server administration, networking, integration, and security. RHCE II will not replace RHCE. Instead, Red Hat expects that many candidates will use RHCE certification as a stepping stone to RHCE II certification. At the time of writing, further details on RHCE II have not yet been announced by Red Hat. You should check Red Hat's Web site, www.redhat.com, for the latest information on RHCE II.

RHCE Courses and Exam

As part of its RHCE program, Red Hat offers several courses designed to prepare candidates for the RHCE exam. Candidates must take course RH302, which is the exam itself. However, candidates can take none, some, or all of the other courses.

This section describes the RHCE courses offered by Red Hat, as well as the RH302 exam. The following sections help you assess your readiness to sit for the RHCE exam and help you to map out a strategy for exam success.

Red Hat offers courses at several locations throughout the U.S. and U.K. The current course schedule is available on their Web site, www.redhat.com, which also gives the current tuition for each course.

RH033: Introduction to Red Hat Linux I, II

RH033 is a four-day course intended for users who have no previous Unix or Linux experience. Students should, however, have previous experience with a computer, including use of a mouse and graphical user interface. Upon completion of the course, the student should be able to use and customize the GNOME desktop and be able to use the Linux command shell. At the time of writing, tuition for RH033 is $1,998.

RH133: Red Hat Linux System Admin I, II

RH133 is a four-day course intended for users who are familiar with Red Hat Linux. Before taking this course, students should complete RH033 or possess equivalent experience. Upon completion of the course, students should be able to install and configure Red Hat Linux, X, and various network services and clients, such as DHCP, NIS, NFS, and Samba. Students should also be able to perform basic troubleshooting and rebuild the Linux kernel from source code. At the time of writing, tuition for RH133 is $2,098.

RH253: Red Hat Linux Networking and Security Admin

RH253 is a four-day course intended for Unix or Linux system administrators. Before taking this course, students should complete RH133 or possess equivalent experience. Upon completion of the course, students should be able to install and configure network services such as Apache, DHCP, DNS, FTP, Samba, NFS, sendmail, and IMAP4/POP3 mail. Students should also be able to establish and administer a security policy that includes such elements as password security, kernel security, public/private key encryption, Kerberos, secure shell, and firewalls. At the time of writing, tuition for RH253 is $2,198.

RH300: RHCE

RH300 is a five-day course that includes RH302, the RHCE exam, as an integral part of the course. Before taking this course, students should complete RH253 or possess equivalent experience and have experience as a Unix or Linux system or network administrator.

The course consists of four days of instruction, and the fifth day is devoted to the RHCE exam. Upon completion of the course, students should be prepared to manage a Red Hat Linux system that offers common TCP/IP services, such as FTP and HTTP.

The course includes eight units of instruction, each of which has one or more hands-on labs associated with the following topics:

- Hardware and Installation (x86 Architecture)
- Configuration and Administration
- Alternate Installation Methods
- Kernel Services and Configuration

- Standard Networking Services

- X Window System

- User and Host Security

- Routers, Firewalls, Clusters, and Troubleshooting

At the time of writing, tuition for RH300 is $2,498, including the price of RH302, the RHCE exam.

RH302: RHCE Exam

Though styled by Red Hat as a "course," RH302 is not a course in the ordinary sense of the word. Instead, RH302 is the RHCE exam, which has a duration of one day. RH302 is the only course that RHCE candidates must take.

The exam consists of the following three closed-book components:

- Diagnosis and troubleshooting lab (2 1/2 hours)

- Installation and configuration lab (2 1/2 hours)

- Multiple choice exam (1 hour)

The components are not always presented in the same sequence. The course instructor, who acts as the exam proctor, will determine the sequence and announce it early in the day. The three components are equally weighted at 100 points each. The minimum passing score is 240 points, or 80 percent. However, a candidate must score at least 50 points (50 percent) on each exam component to pass the exam.

At the time of writing, tuition for RH302 is $749. However, for students taking RH300, the price of RH302 is included in the price of RH300. Red Hat advises candidates of their exam scores by e-mail within 10 business days of taking the exam.

Part VII of this book describes the RHCE exam in greater detail and gives specific advice on handling the exam and its three components.

Assessing Your Readiness

The CD-ROM that accompanies this book includes an Assessment Test that you can use to determine your readiness to sit for the RHCE exam. In addition to taking the Assessment Test, you can estimate your readiness before reading this book by considering the following questions.

1. Have you had classes in or read about Unix system administration?

2. Have you had classes in or read about TCP/IP networking?

3. Have you had classes in or read about Linux?

4. Have you installed, configured, and administered a Unix or Linux system?

5. Have you installed, configured, and administered a variety of Unix or Linux network services and applications, such as Apache, NFS, and Samba?

If your answer to each question is "yes," you're probably ready to sit for the RHCE exam. Nonetheless, this book will help you to refresh your recollection of important points and fill in any gaps in your knowledge.

If your answer to any of the first three questions is "no," you need to carefully read chapters of this book that present unfamiliar material. You may also need to supplement your study with the additional sources listed at the end of such chapters.

If your answer to either question 4 or 5 is "no," you need additional practice in order to successfully pass the performance-based components of the RHCE exam. The related chapters of this book include suggested hands-on exercises that you should perform in order to be prepared for the RHCE exam.

Developing Your Certification Strategy

You can prepare for the RHCE exam in one or more of the following ways:

- You can take courses from Red Hat or others.

- You can study this and other books and documentation by yourself.

- You can study this and other books and documentation as part of a group.

Let's take a closer look at each option.

Taking Red Hat Courses

One of the most effective ways to prepare for RHCE certification is to take the appropriate Red Hat courses. This approach is particularly attractive if your employer will cover all or most of the cost of the courses.

However, as Table 1.1 shows, if you're new to Unix and Linux, this approach can be quite expensive. And, unless you live near one of Red Hat's training locations, you must add the cost of travel, lodging, and food to the already considerable cost of the courses. For many, the time and cost of taking courses is prohibitive. Fortunately, other options exist.

TABLE 1.1 Approximate Tuition for Red Hat Courses

Course	Tuition
RH033	$1,998
RH133	2,098
RH253	2,198
RH300	2,498
Total	$8,792

In the U.S., you may be able to deduct some or all of the costs of taking certification courses from your taxable income. In some cases, you may even be eligible for a tax credit. Consult your tax advisor for details.

Self-Study

If you have the proper background and experience, you can prepare for the RHCE exam through self-study. This book is designed to help you learn or recall all you need to know to pass the RHCE exam. If you're uncertain of your ability to study effectively on your own, consider taking just the RH300 course, which includes the RHCE exam. By the end of the four-day course, you'll likely know exactly what topics you need to bone up on before the next day's exam.

See the Introduction for important information about this book's features and how to use them most effectively.

Study Group

Although you can prepare for the RHCE exam through self-study, you may find that your preparation is more efficient, effective, and fun if you prepare as part of a group. Members of a group usually have personal strengths that can be a resource to the group. For example, one member of a group may be particularly skilled in computer security. That member can brief other members of the group on computer security, clarify puzzling aspects of computer security, and help members assess their computer security expertise.

Even if the members of a group possess no distinctive expertise before coming together as a group, the group can divide the subject matter into segments. The group can then assign each segment to a group member, who instructs the group on that segment and oversees the progress of members with respect to that segment.

The accountability and friendly competition that accompany group work can spur members to greater achievement than may be likely as a result of self-study. So, if you can find others who share your interest in RHCE certification, form a study group.

Practice

Because the RHCE exam is performance-based, it's crucial that you have, or develop, experience in working with Unix or Linux and related network services. The chapters of this book present practical exercises. These exercises can be time-consuming, and you may feel that they're unnecessary. However, unless you have extensive practical experience, you should perform every exercise. Often, exercises will lead you to discover subtle points not evident merely from reading the exercise.

If your practical experience with Unix and Linux is small, you should construct and perform your own additional exercises. The RHCE exam tests for the equivalent of about two years of experience with Linux and networking. With diligent effort, you can accumulate that experience in a matter of weeks. However, doing so will require that you skimp nowhere.

Summary

In this chapter, you learned about Linux, certification, and RHCE certification. The following are the most important topics covered in this chapter:

The Benefits of Certification   As a technical worker, certification may lead to enhanced career opportunities.

Linux   Linux is a freely redistributable, open-source descendant of the Unix operating system.

Red Hat and Red Hat Linux   Red Hat markets Red Hat Linux, the most popular version of Linux in the United States. Red Hat also provides Linux support and consulting services and sponsors the RHCE certification program.

The Red Hat Courses   Red Hat offers several courses that train students to use and administer Red Hat Linux. One course, RH302, is the RHCE exam.

The RHCE Exam   The RHCE exam is a one-day exam that includes multiple-choice and performance-based components, measuring the candidate's knowledge and skills with respect to Red Hat Linux.

A Performance-Based Exam   A performance-based exam is an exam that requires candidates to demonstrate skills rather than mere recall and understanding.

Developing a Certification Strategy   You can take the exam, RH302, by itself, or you can take additional Red Hat courses as well. You can also study this book and other materials by yourself or as a member of a study group. Finally, you can do the practice exercises in this book to increase your experience and prepare for the performance-based components of the RHCE exam.

Key Terms

Before continuing on to the next chapter, be sure you're familiar with the following terms:

certification

Linux

performance-based exam

Red Hat Certified Engineer (RHCE)

Red Hat, Inc.

Unix

Additional Sources of Information

If you'd like further information about the topics presented in this chapter, you should consult the following sources:

- The official source for information about Red Hat's certification program is Red Hat's Web site, www.redhat.com.

- Global Knowledge is a Red Hat partner, providing RHCE training and other training throughout North America. See their Web site at www.globalknowledge.com.

- Red Hat is not the only company sponsoring a Linux certification program. Other companies and organizations offering Linux certification include:

  - Brainbench (www.brainbench.com)

  - Cyber Tech Institute (www.getcertified.com)

  - Linux Professional Institute (www.lpi.org)

  - Prosoft Training (www.prosofttraining.com)

  - Sair, Inc. (www.linuxcertification.org)

Review Questions

1. Certification benefits each of the following in the indicated way, EXCEPT:

   A. Employer, improved hiring decisions

   B. Sponsor, improved product quality

   C. Sponsor, increased revenue

   D. Worker, enhanced career opportunity

2. Which of the following is true of Linux?

   A. Linux is a relative of Unix.

   B. Linux is an open-source software system.

   C. Linux is an operating system.

   D. Linux is free.

3. Which of the following is the most popular Linux distribution in the U.S.?

   A. Caldera Open Linux

   B. Red Hat Linux

   C. Slackware Linux

   D. SuSE Linux

4. Which of the following Red Hat courses must an RHCE have completed?

   A. RH253

   B. RH300

   C. RH302

   D. RH310

5. The performance-based RHCE exam tests your ability by having you do which of the following?

   A. Answer essay questions.

   B. Answer multiple-choice questions.

   C. Demonstrate network administration skills.

   D. Demonstrate system administration skills.

6. To pass the RHCE exam, you should be able to do which of the following?

   A. Use Linux and X

   B. Install and configure Linux

   C. Install and configure network services

   D. Troubleshoot and repair Linux systems

Answers to Review Questions

1. B.   Certification of technical workers does not lead directly to improved quality of the products on which they're certified.

2. A, B, C, and D.   The architecture of Linux is based on that of Unix. The Linux kernel and the Red Hat Linux distribution are both freely downloadable from the Internet.

3. B.   Red Hat Linux is generally acknowledged as the most popular distribution in the U.S.; SuSE is popular in Europe and is becoming more popular in the U.S.

4. C.   RH302 is the RHCE exam, and RH300 is the exam preparation course that includes RH302. Every RHCE has completed RH302; however, some RHCEs have passed RH302 without taking RH300.

5. B, C, and D.   The RHCE exam does not include essay questions.

6. A, B, C, and D.   The RHCE exam requires you to be able to use and administer Linux and related services and to be able to troubleshoot their operation.

Chapter

2

Hardware Basics

RHCE PREPARATION TOPICS COVERED IN THIS CHAPTER:

✓ **Understand Linux support for computer systems.**

- Understand and use the Red Hat Hardware Compatibility List.
- Understand Red Hat's hardware detection tool, kudzu.
- Understand Linux support for CPUs and SMP.
- Understand Linux support for RAM.

✓ **Understand Linux support for character devices.**

- Understand device configuration and be able to configure devices.
- Understand Linux support for serial and parallel ports and be able to configure them.
- Understand Linux support for common peripherals and be able to configure them.
- Understand Linux support for video.

✓ **Understand Linux support for block devices.**

- Understand block device interfaces.
- Understand disk addressing.
- Understand disk partitioning and be able to choose an appropriate partition structure.
- Understand the boot process.

Linux supports a remarkable variety of computer systems and devices. Nevertheless, it doesn't support them all. Even if Linux supports a particular system or device, you must properly configure the device before Linux can access it.

This chapter deals with Linux support of hardware. In the Unix world, hardware devices are assigned to one of two categories:

Character Devices   *Character devices* read or write data not more than one character at a time.

Block Devices   *Block devices* read or write data several—perhaps many—characters at a time.

In the real world, these two categories sometimes overlap, but they're a useful way of organizing your thinking about devices.

This chapter begins by describing Linux support for systems. It then moves on to describe Linux support for character devices, and wraps up by describing Linux support for block devices.

Linux Support for Systems

Although Linux runs on a variety of platforms, Red Hat Linux currently supports only the following three:

- Compaq (formerly DEC) Alpha architecture

- Intel architecture

- Sun SPARC (scalable processor architecture)

The RHCE exam covers the administration of Red Hat Linux for only *Intel architecture* PCs, so this chapter describes only that architecture. Note that many companies other than Intel Corporation manufacture hardware that is compatible with the Intel architecture.

For more information on non-Intel architectures, see the Red Hat Hardware Compatibility List at www.redhat.com/support/hardware.

Hardware Compatibility

There are two main sources of information on hardware that is compatible with Linux. This section describes these sources.

The Linux Hardware Compatibility HOWTO

The Linux Documentation Project (www.linuxdoc.org) intends to "create the canonical set of free Linux documentation." Toward that end, they publish a useful series of HOWTOs, guides, and man pages. One of the most important and useful documents is the *Linux Hardware Compatibility HOWTO*, also known as the *Hardware-HOWTO*. This HOWTO identifies hardware devices and components that are compatible with Linux and gives hints and tips for choosing compatible hardware and getting it to work.

Beginning with the Red Hat Linux 6.2 distribution, the HOWTOs are available in over one dozen languages and several formats, including text, HTML, and PDF. You'll find the HOWTOs on the documentation CD-ROM, rather than on the installation CD-ROM. They're handy enough—and compact enough—that you should probably copy them to the /usr/doc/HOWTO directory of your system's hard disk. To do so, mount the CD-ROM and issue the following commands:

```
# mkdir /usr/doc/HOWTO
# cd /mnt/cdrom/HOWTOS
# cp -R *-HOWTO *.htm mini /usr/doc/HOWTO
```

If the /usr/doc/HOWTO directory exists, the mkdir command will fail; don't be concerned. If you mount the CD-ROM at a mount point other than /mnt/cdrom, you should revise the second command appropriately. You'll find non-English HOWTOs in the HOWTOS/translations directory and HTML and PDF HOWTOs in the HOWTOS/other-formats directory.

In subsequent chapters, it's assumed that you've installed the HOWTOs, so references to particular HOWTOs assume that the files are in /usr/doc/HOWTO. If you choose not to install the HOWTOs, you'll need to find them on the CD-ROM.

The Red Hat Hardware Compatibility List

Red Hat, Inc. maintains its own list of supported hardware, which is roughly a subset of the devices and components listed in the *Hardware-HOWTO*. *The Red Hat Hardware Compatibility List* is on the Web at www.redhat.com/support/hardware. When choosing hardware for a Red Hat Linux system or installing Red Hat Linux on an existing system, check the Red Hat Hardware Compatibility List to make sure that the devices you're installing are supported by Red Hat Linux.

The Red Hat Hardware Compatibility List classifies hardware devices according to the following four categories:

Tier 1 Hardware that Red Hat Linux can detect and reliably use.

Tier 2 Hardware that Red Hat Linux should be able to detect and use; however, some users experience problems using this hardware.

Tier 3 Hardware that is problematic or for which only experimental drivers currently exist. Red Hat, Inc. provides information concerning Tier 3 hardware but does not support it.

Incompatible Hardware known not to work with Red Hat Linux.

Red Hat Linux 6.1 and later include kudzu, a tool that runs at boot time and identifies newly installed hardware. When kudzu detects new hardware, it displays a convenient dialog box that lets you configure the new hardware or postpone configuration. The kudzu tool may not operate correctly with hardware that is not included on the Red Hat Hardware Compatibility List.

CPU Architectures and Symmetric Multiprocessing

Although originally implemented for the Intel *x*86 central processing unit (CPU) architecture, Linux now runs on a variety of architectures, including:

- Acorn
- ARM
- Compaq (DEC) Alpha
- Motorola 68k
- MIPS
- Power Mac
- PowerPC
- Sun SPARC

However, Red Hat Linux supports only the Compaq Alpha, Intel, and SPARC architectures.

Linux also supports *symmetric multiprocessing* (SMP) in which a single system includes multiple CPUs. However, the standard Red Hat Linux kernel is not SMP enabled. If your system is SMP-capable, the installation program will install both the standard kernel and a special SMP kernel; the SMP kernel will be enabled, even if only one CPU is present.

Linux SMP supports as many as 16 processors; however, the Intel architecture supports no more than 8. Figure 2.1 illustrates how SMP performance varies with the number of processors. As you can see, the performance increase slows after the addition of four processors.

FIGURE 2.1   SMP performance

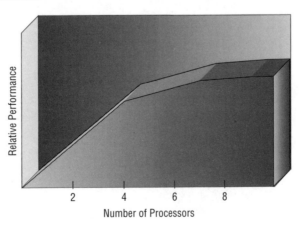

SMP doesn't increase the execution speed of processes; it merely lets multiple processes run concurrently. Single-threaded applications, which run on a single processor, do not benefit from SMP.

Memory

The Linux 2.2 kernel that ships with Red Hat Linux 6.2 generally auto-detects the amount of installed RAM (random access memory). However, the standard kernel cannot auto-detect or use more than 1GB of RAM. To enable support for more than 1GB of RAM, you must modify the `include/asm-i386/page.h` header file and recompile the kernel. You may also need to pass a `mem` parameter to `lilo`, instructing `lilo` to ignore the physical memory size reported by a system BIOS that is unable to detect and report more than 64MB of RAM.

When running on Intel-architecture CPUs, Red Hat Linux permits a system to access only 4GB of virtual memory, including both physical memory and swap memory. For example, a system that can access 2GB of physical memory can access only 2GB of swap memory.

CPUs and Buses

Red Hat Linux supports the Intel CPU family and Intel-compatibles, including those made by AMD, Cyrix, and Winchip. Table 2.1 summarizes the CPUs that are supported by Red Hat Linux.

TABLE 2.1 Supported CPUs

Support Level	CPU
Tier 1	Intel Celeron
	Intel Pentium
	Intel Pentium II
	Intel Pentium III
	Intel Pentium SMP
	AMD K6-2
	AMD K6-3

TABLE 2.1 Supported CPUs *(continued)*

Support Level	CPU
Tier 2	AMD Athlon
	Cyrix 6x86
	AMD K5
	AMD K6
	Winchip
Tier 3 (unsupported)	Cyrix MediaGX

The *bus* of a PC is used to connect devices to the CPU and memory, especially devices that are installed via expansion slots. The type of bus that's used determines the type of devices and expansion cards that a system can accommodate. Red Hat Linux supports the following bus interfaces:

AGP Accelerated Graphics Port, a high-performance video interface

EISA Extended Industry Standard Architecture bus, not commonly used today

ISA Industry Standard Architecture bus, the 16-bit bus found in older computers, such as the IBM PC-AT

PCI Peripheral Component Interconnect bus, the 32-bit bus found in most recently manufactured computers

PCMCIA Personal Computer Memory Card International Association bus, also known as the PC Card bus

VESA Video Electronics Standards Association bus, also known as the VL bus

Red Hat Linux does not support every PCMCIA controller, but it does support several popular controllers and a wide variety of cards. A convenient feature of PCMCIA cards is that they are hot swappable; they can be inserted or removed without powering down the system.

Red Hat Linux does not support the following bus interfaces:

IEEE 394 Also known as Firewire. This is a potential rival to the SCSI interface described later in this chapter.

MCA   Micro Channel Architecture. Although Linux is compatible with MCA, Red Hat Linux does not support it.

USB   Universal Serial Bus.

Linux kernel support for Firewire, MCA, and USB is not yet complete. The Linux 2.4 kernel will include additional support for USB, but USB device drivers may not be immediately available. Red Hat Linux support for Firewire, MCA, and USB is planned.

System Resources

Most devices require system resources in order to operate. Although some devices can share system resources, many cannot. An important part of configuring devices is assigning system resources in such a way that no conflicts occur. The three most important system resources are IRQs, I/O ports, and DMAs, which are explained in the following subsections.

IRQs

An *IRQ*, or hardware interrupt, is a signal that notifies the CPU of an important event, such as completion of an input/output (I/O) operation. Most devices require a dedicated IRQ, which must be assigned manually or by the system BIOS. A PC has a limited number of IRQs, most of which have standard assignments, as shown in Table 2.2.

TABLE 2.2   Standard IRQ Assignments

IRQ	Assignment
0	Reserved for nonmaskable interrupt (NMI), which flags parity errors
1	Reserved for system timer
2	Reserved for cascade to second interrupt controller (IRQ 8-15)
3	Serial ports ttyS1 and ttyS3 if enabled; otherwise, available
4	Serial ports ttyS0 and ttyS2 if enabled; otherwise, available
5	Parallel port lp1 if enabled; otherwise, available; often used for sound card or modem
6	Floppy disk drive controller

TABLE 2.2 Standard IRQ Assignments *(continued)*

IRQ	Assignment
7	Parallel port 1p0 if enabled; otherwise, available
8	Reserved for real-time clock
9	Available
10	Available: often used for network adapter
11	Available: often used for SCSI adapter
12	PS/2 mouse if enabled; otherwise, available
13	Reserved for floating-point processor
14	IDE hard disk controller 1 if enabled; otherwise, available
15	IDE hard disk controller 2 if enabled; otherwise, available

I/O Ports

As explained, most devices require an IRQ so that they can signal the CPU to notify it that an I/O operation has completed. Most devices also require a dedicated series of one-byte areas of memory, known as *I/O ports*, that are used to move data from the device to system memory or from system memory to the device. Some devices require more than one series of I/O ports.

A series of I/O ports is sometimes referred to as a device's *base I/O address*. I/O ports are identified by a hexadecimal (base 16) number in the range 0x0-0xFFFF.

DMAs

Most devices rely on the CPU to move data from memory to the device. However, some high-speed devices are capable of accessing memory directly. This leaves the CPU free to work on other tasks while I/O operations are in progress, a technique known as *direct memory access (DMA)*.

A system has a limited number of channels, known as DMA channels or simply DMAs, on which DMA can occur. Devices that use DMA must be assigned one—or sometimes two—DMA channels. Table 2.3 summarizes these channels and their standard assignments.

TABLE 2.3 Standard DMA Assignments

DMA	Assignment
0	Generally reserved for memory refresh
1	Available (8-bit)
2	Reserved for floppy drive
3	Available (8-bit)
4	Reserved for DMA controller 1
5	Available (16-bit)
6	Available (16-bit)
7	Available (16-bit)

Working with Adapter Cards

Configuring an adapter card involves specifying the IRQ, the I/O ports, and the DMA used by the device. Depending upon the type of adapter card you have, it can be configured in one or more of the following three ways:

Jumpered Cards   Older adapter cards often contain jumpers that let you physically set the configuration.

Jumperless Cards   More modern cards let you use a software program to set the configuration.

Plug-and-Play Cards   Some cards can be configured automatically by the BIOS or a plug-and-play–compatible operating system.

Configuring Jumpered Cards

Although configuring jumpered cards can be inconvenient, it is straightforward. You simply set the jumpers to specify the resources required by the card, making sure the resource assignments don't conflict with those of other cards. You may also need to specify the device driver options that identify the resources assigned to the card.

Configuring Jumperless Cards

Configuring jumperless cards is simple if the Linux device driver provides the proper options. Specify the desired options in the module configuration file, `/etc/conf.modules`. When the device's module is loaded, it obtains the options you specified and sets the card's configuration accordingly.

Some device drivers, however, may not support the configuration options you need. In that case, you can configure the system to boot either DOS or Linux. To configure the card, boot to DOS and run the DOS program that configures the card. Then, boot Linux by, for example, using the `loadlin` utility, which permits Linux to boot from DOS.

Configuring Plug-and-Play Cards

Most modern PCs use the PCI bus, which supports a feature known as *plug-and-play*. Plug-and-play is intended to simplify hardware configuration. All PCI cards support plug-and-play. Some ISA cards support plug-and-play, but only when inserted into a plug-and-play system.

In operation, plug-and-play first probes cards to determine what resource configurations they support. Then, it assigns resources so that each card has access to the resources it requires.

Plug-and-play configuration of PCI devices can be performed by BIOS or by an operating system. Currently, Linux does not fully support plug-and-play. Therefore, if your system BIOS supports plug-and-play, you should configure it to do so by setting the BIOS option PnP Aware OS or any similar option to No.

You can configure ISA plug-and-play devices by using the Linux `isapnp` utilities, which are explained in Chapter 15, "Understanding Configuration Files and Scripts."

Support for Character Devices

This section describes Red Hat Linux support for character devices. Character devices are devices that generally read or write data one character at a time. Most network adapters are block devices. However, their configuration more nearly resembles that of character devices than that of block devices. Consequently, they are included in this section, along with character devices.

Ports

Most PCs are equipped with both serial ports, which read or write one bit at a time, and parallel ports, which read or write one character at a time. This subsection explains Red Hat Linux support for serial and parallel ports.

Serial Ports

The standard Red Hat Linux kernel includes support for 192 serial ports. However, by default, only the device files /dev/ttyS0, /dev/ttyS1, /dev/ttyS2, and /dev/ttyS3 are created during the installation of Red Hat Linux. Linux documentation sometimes refers to devices such as /dev/cua0; however, this is an older, deprecated way of naming serial ports. You can increase the number of ports by modifying the file drivers/char/serial.c and recompiling the kernel.

You can generally use the BIOS to configure the IRQ and I/O port associated with serial ports ttyS0 and ttyS1. To configure additional ports, you can use the setserial command as follows:

```
setserial /dev/ttySn irq x port y skip_test autoconfig
```

where ttySn specifies the serial port, x specifies the IRQ to be assigned, and y specifies the I/O port to be assigned.

See the man page for the setserial command to learn about other options that set the baud rate and other operating parameters.

Parallel Ports

The standard Red Hat Linux kernel includes support for eight parallel ports. However, by default, only the device files /dev/lp0, /dev/lp1, and /dev/lp2 are created during installation of Red Hat Linux. You can increase the number of ports by modifying the header file drivers/char/lp.c and recompiling the kernel. You can generally use the BIOS to configure the IRQ and I/O port associated with serial ports lp0 and lp1. It is unusual to configure more than two parallel ports.

Peripherals

This subsection describes Red Hat Linux support for common peripherals, including keyboards, mice, modems, network adapters, sound cards, and video cards.

Keyboards

Red Hat Linux supports both AT-style and PS/2-style keyboards as Tier 1 devices.

Mice

Red Hat Linux includes support for standard serial and PS/2 mice, which are generally supported at Tier 1. Bus mice are generally supported at Tier 2. Recent Microsoft serial mice use a special protocol, which is not fully supported. Microsoft's IntelliMouse (wheel mouse) is listed as a Tier 3 device.

Modems

Red Hat Linux supports most external modems at Tier 1, along with internal PCI modems based on the Lucent Venus chipset. Unfortunately, an entire class of modems—known as *WinModems*—requires special software drivers for operation. Manufacturers bundle Win32 software with these modems, but they do not distribute software for other operating systems. Therefore, Red Hat Linux does not support such modems. Also listed as incompatible are plug-and-play internal modems, although these can be configured—even if somewhat inconveniently—by using isapnp or setserial.

Network Adapters

Red Hat Linux supports a variety of Ethernet cards and several Token Ring cards. Among the Ethernet cards listed as Tier 3 or incompatible devices are the following :

- 3Com 3C501
- 3Com 3C905B, 3C905C (though drivers recently provided by 3Com may alleviate the problem)
- 3Com ISA Etherlink XL (3Com 3C515)
- General Instruments SB1000
- Intel EtherExpress 100plus
- Intel EtherExpress Pro/10 PCI (incompatible)
- Intel EtherExpress Pro/100B
- Linksys Fast 10/100 tulip clones
- SeaLevel Systems 4012, 4021

- Silicon Integrated System Corporation Sis 900 PCI

- Macronix, Inc. cards that use the MX987x5 chipset

- Xircom Ethernet adapters (incompatible)

Sound Cards

The Red Hat Linux distribution's support for sound cards is among the best of any Linux distribution. However, support for sound cards remains a Linux weakness. No sound cards are currently supported at Tier 1. The following sound cards are supported at Tier 2:

- Acer Notebook Sound

- AdLib

- Advance Logic ALS-007

- Compaq Deskpro XL sound

- Creative/Ensoniq Audio PCI 1371

- Crystal CS423x sound chip

- Ensoniq Audio PCI 1370 (SoundBlaster 64/128 PCI)

- Ensoniq SoundScape

- ESS1688 AudioDrive

- ESS1868 AudioDrive

- ESS688 AudioDrive

- Gravis UltraSound

- Gravis UltraSound MAX

- Gravis UltraSound PnP

- Logitech SoundMan 16

- Logitech SoundMan Games (not SM16 or SM Wave)

- MAD16 Pro (OPTi 82C929/82C930)

- MediaTrix AudioTrix Pro (MT-0002-PC Control Chip)

- MediaVision Jazz16 (ProSonic, SoundMan Wave)

- miroSOUND PCM12

- Mozart/MAD16 (OPTi 82C928)

- OPL3-SA1 sound chip

- OPL3-SA2/3/x sound chip
- Pro Audio Spectrum/Studio 16
- PSS (Orchid SW32, Cardinal DSP16)
- S3 SonicVibes
- Sound Blaster
- Sound Blaster 16/PNP
- Sound Blaster 32/64 AWE
- Sound Blaster DS
- Sound Blaster Pro
- Turtle Beach MultiSound Classic/Monterey/Tahiti
- Turtle Beach MultiSound Pinnacle/Fiji
- Windows Sound System (AD1848/CS4248/CS4231)

Clones of these cards, or cards listed as compatible with these cards, are not necessarily supported.

Video Cards

The XFree86 Project provides a freely redistributable implementation of the X Window System (also known as X). The Red Hat Linux distribution uses the XFree86 implementation of X, and therefore generally supports the video cards supported by the XFree86 implementation of X. However, several exceptions exist, so you should consult the Red Hat Hardware Compatibility List (`www.redhat.com/support/hardware`) instead of the list of supported graphics cards published by the XFree86 Project. The list of supported and unsupported video cards is too lengthy to be summarized here. Among the notable cards with problematic Red Hat Linux support are laptop video cards, which manufacturers often customize for operation with the laptop's LCD.

WARNING

Laptops present special complications that affect Linux compatibility. For example, laptop manufacturers often employ a variety of hardware components in laptops that bear an identical model number. In general, the only way to determine that a laptop is compatible with Red Hat Linux is to successfully install, configure, and run Linux on the laptop. This confusing situation has begun to improve because a handful of manufacturers are now shipping laptops with Linux pre-installed. However, such laptops are not necessarily officially supported by Red Hat Linux.

Other Peripherals

Among other character devices supported by or compatible with Red Hat Linux are such devices as the following:

- Infrared devices
- Joysticks
- Multi-port serial devices
- Printers
- Radio cards
- Scanners
- Various devices that connect via the parallel port, such as Iomega zip drives

See the Red Hat Hardware Compatibility List for more details about these peripherals.

Support for Block Devices

Block devices are devices that read or write more than one character at a time. Examples of block devices include floppy disk drives, hard disk drives, CD-ROM drives, CD-R drives, and other devices. This section describes Red Hat Linux support for block devices.

Drives and Drive Interfaces

Block devices can be connected to a system in a variety of ways. However, the most common ways are by means of a floppy disk interface, an IDE or EIDE interface, or a SCSI interface. This subsection describes the Red Hat Linux support for these interfaces.

Floppy Disk Drives

Floppy disk drive interfaces present few problems. Except for a handful of motherboards that have quirky floppy disk controllers, you shouldn't anticipate difficulties with floppy drives. They're generally auto-detected by the kernel without special configuration.

IDE and EIDE Interfaces

Most on-board IDE controllers on Pentium motherboards are fully supported. UDMA/66 controllers are supported when configured for UDMA/33 operation. Most other IDE and EIDE controllers are supported at Tier 2. A maximum of eight IDE devices are supported, though only two interfaces (up to four drives) are automatically probed. Additional interfaces can be probed by specifying boot-time parameters such as

```
ide2=0x1e8,0x3ee,11 ide3=0x168,0x36e,10
```

UDMA/66 controllers are not fully supported by the Linux 2.2 kernel and, thus, are not supported by Red Hat Linux. The Promise Ultra/66 and HPT66 are likewise not supported by the Linux 2.2 kernel.

The Linux 2.4 kernel is expected to support UDMA/66 and the Promise Ultra/ 66 and HPT66 controllers.

IDE and EIDE Drives

Red Hat Linux fully supports almost all internal IDE/EIDE drives, including IDE drives that have a capacity greater than 33.8GB, which are supported by Red Hat Linux kernels 2.2.14-5 and later. Some drives require that their geometry be specified to the kernel via a boot-time parameter such as:

```
linux hda=1023,63,255
```

A few drives are compatible with Linux but not supported. These include the following:

- Internal Iomega IDE Zip drives

- SuperDisk LS-120 removable media drives, which don't function properly during Linux installation but can be configured later

A few drives are incompatible with Linux. These include most removable media IDE drives, including those made by Syquest.

SCSI Interfaces

Red Hat Linux supports a variety of SCSI (and RAID) controllers. However, some controllers are supported at Tier 2, and several controllers are not supported by Red Hat Linux at all. The list of SCSI controllers is too lengthy to be summarized here. See the Red Hat Hardware Compatibility List for details (`www.redhat.com/support/hardware`).

SCSI Drives

Red Hat Linux fully supports all SCSI devices when they are attached to a supported controller. This includes removable media drives, such as the Iomega SCSI Zip and Jaz drives, and drives made by Syquest. Note that the Iomega parallel port Zip drive uses a SCSI interface and is fully supported by Red Hat Linux.

Hard Disks

The technique used to access a hard drive may impose restrictions on the amount of data that the drive can store. Likewise, the way in which a hard drive is divided into *partitions* has implications for the ways in which it can be used. This subsection explains these considerations.

Disk Geometry

The *disk geometry* of a hard drive describes the possible addresses at which data can be stored and accessed. Disk addresses can take either of the two following forms:

Physical Address The data is addressed by the cylinder, head, and sector that contain them.

Logical Block Address (LBA) The data is addressed by a relative sector number.

Each addressing scheme imposes its own restrictions. Many BIOS drivers can access only the first 1024 cylinders (cylinders 0–1023) of a hard disk that is accessed via the physical address. The Linux loader, lilo, uses BIOS to access a hard disk only during bootup. But a BIOS that can't access cylinder 1024 or beyond cannot boot a kernel stored, for example, on cylinder 1025. A simple way to avoid this problem is to ensure, through partitioning, that the Linux kernel is stored below cylinder 1024.

Logical block addressing carries a similar restriction. The maximum relative sector number is such that only about 8GB of disk space is addressable. Again, this restriction affects Linux only during the boot process, because the BIOS is not used after bootup.

Partitions

It's generally best—though not strictly necessary—to divide a hard disk's space into several partitions. The main benefit of partitions is that damage or corruption may often be confined to a single partition, making it simple to recover data from the remaining partitions.

IDE disk drives have device names such as /dev/hda, /dev/hdb, and so on. SCSI disk drives have device names such as /dev/sda, /dev/sdb, and so on. Partitions are designated with a number, beginning with 1, that is appended to the drive name. Thus, the first partition on the first IDE drive is named /dev/hda1, and the third partition on the second SCSI drive is named /dev/sdb3.

Primary, Extended, and Logical Partitions

A hard disk can have only four ordinary partitions, known as *primary partitions*. However, one of the primary partitions can be designated as an *extended partition*. An extended partition does not contain a file system; instead, it contains as many as 12 other partitions, known as *logical partitions*. The first logical partition is always designated as partition 5, even if fewer than four primary partitions are defined. Figure 2.2 shows a typical hard disk partition structure.

FIGURE 2.2   A typical hard disk partition structure

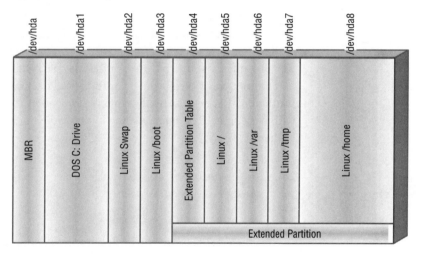

Partition Types

Partitions used by Linux are one of the following two main types:

Linux Native   Used to hold a standard Linux file system containing programs and data files.

Linux Swap   Used to hold memory contents temporarily swapped from physical memory to the hard drive.

Red Hat Linux also supports a variety of other *partition types*, including MS-DOS, VFAT, HPFS, and NTFS. However, the standard Red Hat Linux kernel cannot access the HPFS and NTFS file systems; you must recompile the kernel if you require this support.

The Linux kernel supports a swap partition as large as 2GB. Up to eight swap partitions can be defined.

Mount Points

Like UNIX, Linux mounts partitions of block devices as subdirectories within a unified file system. The directory that holds the contents of a partition is called its *mount point*. The following two partitions, known by their mount points, are particularly important:

/ The root file system

/boot The boot partition, which contains the Linux kernel

The root partition is mounted at the beginning of the system initialization process, after the kernel itself has been loaded into memory. Its identity must be known to the kernel and is typically passed to the kernel by the lilo bootloader on Red Hat Linux systems. Other partitions are integrated into the system by being mounted as subdirectories of the root file system.

The boot partition is a small partition used to circumvent the 1024-cylinder restriction affecting the BIOS of many systems. By locating the boot partition within the first 1024 cylinders, the Linux kernel is guaranteed to be available to the BIOS.

Summary

In this chapter, you learned about Linux support for a wide variety of hardware devices. The following are the most important topics covered in this chapter:

Hardware Compatibility Red Hat, Inc. publishes a list of hardware that is compatible with and supported by Red Hat Linux.

Hardware Configuration A hardware device must generally be assigned a unique IRQ and base I/O address. Some devices must also be assigned a unique DMA.

Adapter Cards Configuring most PCI adapter cards is straightforward. Configuring other types of cards, especially ISA plug-and-play cards, can be more difficult.

Device Support   Red Hat Linux supports devices at one of several levels. Tier 1 devices are fully supported. Tier 2 devices are partially supported. Tier 3 devices are compatible, but unsupported. Other devices may be incompatible with Red Hat Linux.

Hard Disks   BIOS can access a hard disk by physical address or logical block address. Each method imposes restrictions on the location of the Linux kernel.

Partitions   A maximum of four primary partitions can be defined. In addition, one primary partition may be designated as an extended partition and be used to hold as many as 12 logical partitions.

Partition Types   The most important Linux partition types are Linux native, which holds programs and data files, and Linux swap, which holds the physical memory contents temporarily swapped to the hard disk.

Mount Points   Linux integrates partitions within a single file system by associating each partition with a mount point.

Key Terms

Before going on to the next chapter, be sure you're familiar with the following terms:

base I/O address

Block devices

bus

Character devices

direct memory access (DMA)

disk geometry

extended partition

Intel architecture

I/O ports

IRQ

Logical block addressing

logical partitions

mount point

partitions

partition types

plug-and-play

primary partitions

Red Hat Hardware Compatibility List

symmetric multiprocessing

WinModems

Additional Sources of Information

If you'd like further information about the topics presented in this chapter, you should consult the following sources:

- *The Complete PC Upgrade & Maintenance Guide*, 11th Edition, by Mark Minasi (Sybex, 2000)
- Linux HOWTOs
    - *Busmouse-HOWTO*, by Chris Bagwell
    - *Ethernet-HOWTO*, by Paul Gortmaker
    - *Ftape-HOWTO*, by Claus-Justus Heine
    - *IR-HOWTO*, by Werner Heuser
    - *Modem-HOWTO*, by David S. Lawyer and Greg Hankins
    - *Multi-Disk-HOWTO*, by Stein Gjoen
    - *PCMCIA-HOWTO*, by David Hines
    - *Plug-and-Play-HOWTO*, by David S. Lawyer
    - *Serial-HOWTO*, by David S. Lawyer and Greg Hankins
    - *Sound-HOWTO*, by Jeff Tranter
    - *UPS-HOWTO*, by Harvey J. Stein
- Linux mini-HOWTOs, such as the *Alsa-sound* and *Cable-Modem mini-HOWTOs*

Review Questions

1. Which of the following must generally be assigned when configuring a device?

   A. Bus

   B. DMA

   C. I/O port

   D. IRQ

2. Which of the following adapter card types is the easiest to configure?

   A. EISA

   B. ISA

   C. ISA plug-and-play

   D. PCI

3. Which addressing method generally requires the Linux kernel to reside within the first 1024 cylinders of the hard disk?

   A. Logical block

   B. Logical byte

   C. Physical

   D. Virtual

4. Which of the following are associated with devices supported by Red Hat, Inc.?

   A. Tier 1

   B. Tier 2

   C. Tier 3

   D. Incompatible

5. What is the maximum amount of physical memory that can be accessed by Red Hat Linux running on a 32-bit Intel architecture system?

   A. 2GB

   B. 4GB

   C. 8GB

   D. 64GB

6. What is the maximum amount of swap memory that can be accessed by a Linux system?

   A. 2GB

   B. 4GB

   C. 16GB

   D. 64GB

Answers to Review Questions

1. B, C, and D. A device is connected to a bus, but the bus does not have to be assigned to the device.

2. D. PCI cards are plug-and-play and can generally be configured automatically by the BIOS.

3. C. Logical block addressing (LBA) requires the kernel to reside within the first 8GB of the hard disk. Logical byte and virtual are not forms of disk addressing.

4. A and B. Tier 3 devices are compatible with Linux, but they are not supported by Red Hat, Inc. Incompatible devices are not supported by Red Hat Linux.

5. B. When Red Hat Linux is running on a 32-bit Intel architecture system, it can access a maximum of 4GB of RAM.

6. A. A swap partition can be as large as 2GB, and a Linux system can have as many as eight swap partitions. When, however, Red Hat Linux is running on a 32-bit Intel architecture system, it can access a maximum of 4GB of virtual memory. Since some virtual memory must represent physical memory, the best answer is 2GB.

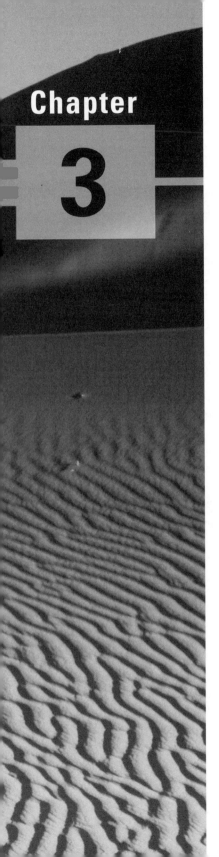

Chapter 3

Unix Basics

RHCE PREPARATION TOPICS COVERED IN THIS CHAPTER:

✓ **Use the Unix command line.**

- Use the basic Unix commands effectively.
- Understand and use file ownership and permissions.
- Understand the Linux file system structure.
- Use and manipulate the path.
- Edit text files.
- Print files.

✓ **Administer file systems.**

- Back up and restore files.
- Mount and unmount a file system.
- Use removable media, such as floppy disk.
- Create a file system.
- Partition a hard disk.
- Check a file system.

✓ **Use Unix command facilities.**

- Use stream redirection and filters.
- Use regular expressions to specify command options and arguments.
- Write shell scripts that employ environment variables and control structures.

The installation and troubleshooting components of the RHCE exam don't specifically test your knowledge and skill in the use of the Unix command line. However, you will not be able to complete those exam components unless you are proficient in using the Unix command line. This chapter reviews the basics of using Unix commands and then moves on to special topics that are important to system administrators, including file system administration and shell scripts.

If you lack previous experience with Unix, you should study Unix beyond this chapter. Although this chapter covers many important Unix topics, a single chapter cannot describe every feature of the Unix commands or even every important feature.

On the other hand, those who are familiar with varieties of Unix other than Linux will probably not find this chapter particularly demanding. For example, many Unix systems use the standard Linux shell, the bash shell, which is a derivative of the original Bourne shell. Consequently, this chapter often refers to Unix rather than Linux, because its material is widely applicable and is available even if X is not.

Using the Unix Command Line

Those who've worked only with graphical user interfaces (GUIs) are sometimes shocked to discover that the Unix graphical user interface, X, is not always available. Some Unix systems, especially network servers, may not have X installed at all. Moreover, even if X is installed, X may not operate if the system is misconfigured. Consequently, Red Hat Linux administrators must be familiar with the Unix command line.

The Basic Unix Commands

Although Red Hat Linux provides over 1,000 commands, you don't need to know them all. Knowing a dozen or so commands is enough to enable you to perform the most common tasks. Table 3.1 summarizes the most important Unix commands. The following subsections explain these commands in greater detail.

TABLE 3.1 Basic Unix Commands

Command	Function
cd	Changes the current working directory.
cp	Copies files.
find	Finds a file.
less	Scrolls through a text file one page at a time.
ls	Lists files and their characteristics.
man	Describes commands and configuration files.
mkdir	Creates directories.
mv	Moves files to another folder or renames files.
pwd	Displays the name of the current working directory.
rm	Deletes files.
rmdir	Deletes directories.
touch	Adjusts the modification date of files.

cd

Unix directories resemble the folders used in GUIs. Directories can contain files and other directories.

Every Unix user or process is associated with a directory, called the *current working directory* or, more simply, the *current directory*. When a file is referenced, the file is assumed to reside in the current working directory unless path information is explicitly specified. This feature makes it convenient to reference files in the current directory.

You can change the current directory by issuing the `cd` command. For example, the command

```
cd /home/fred
```

makes the directory `/home/fred` the current directory.

Notice that Unix directories are named by using a forward slash (/) to separate the components of the path. You'll learn more about Unix directories shortly.

If you issue the `cd` command without an argument, your home directory becomes the current working directory.

cp

The `cp` command copies files. You can use it to copy a single file. For example, the command

```
cp filex filey
```

copies `filex` to `filey`. You can also use the `cp` command to copy a set of files. For example, the command

```
cp filex filey folder1
```

copies `filex` and `filey` to `folder1`.

find

The `find` command helps you locate a file. The `find` command provides many ways of finding files, but it's most often used to find a file by name. This is helpful when you have many directories, and you're unsure which directory contains the file. For example, the command

```
find /home/fred -name filex
```

will tell you what folder within the directory `/home/fred` contains the file `filex`.

If you don't know the name of the file, but you know a string contained within the filename, you can use a command such as this:

```
find /home/fred -name '*ile*'
```

This command will find all the files whose filenames contain the characters `ile` that reside in `/home/fred` and its subdirectories.

less

The less command lets you page through a text file much as the man command lets you page through a man page. You use the same characters to control both programs. For example, to page through the file /etc/hosts, issue the command

    less /etc/hosts

ls

The ls command lists files and their characteristics. It has many options and arguments; this section describes only the most commonly used ones.

Used without any options or arguments, the ls command lists the names of files residing in the current directory. If you want to list some other directory, issue a command such as

    ls /home/bob

which lists the names of files residing in the directory /home/bob. You might, for example, see output like this:

    Desktop My Documents Sara.wab WAB.EXE sara.blt sounds

As explained later, this command will give you an error message if you lack the appropriate permissions to access the specified directory.

An important option of the ls command causes it to list the characteristics of the files along with their names. For example, the command

    ls -l /home/bob

might produce output like this:

```
total 137
drwxr-xr-x   5 bob      bob        1024  Nov 26 10:35 Desktop
drwxr-xr-x  14 bob      bob        1024  Nov 26 10:38 My Documents
-rwxr-----   1 bob      bob      115030  Nov 26 13:15 Sara.wab
-rwxr-----   1 bob      bob       14768  Mar 13  1997 WAB.EXE
-rwxr-----   1 bob      bob        2089  Nov 26 10:36 sara.blt
drwxr-xr-x   2 bob      bob        2048  Nov 26 10:39 sounds
```

The first line tells you that the files in the /home/bob directory occupy a total of 137 blocks of disk space. Each subsequent line describes one of the files.

The first column, which is 10 characters wide, specifies the file permissions for that particular file. You'll learn more about them shortly. For now, it's enough to know that if the file permissions begin with d, the line describes a directory; otherwise, it describes a file. For example, `Desktop` is a directory and `Sara.wab` is a file.

The second column gives the number of directory blocks (inodes) used by the file or directory. For example, the directory `Desktop` uses five blocks.

The third column gives the name of the user who owns the file. This is generally the user who created the file. The user **bob** owns all the files listed.

The fourth column gives the name of the user group that owns the file. Red Hat Linux establishes a group for each user, with the user as its only member. As a system administrator, you can establish additional groups and assign members as desired. The group **bob** owns all the files listed.

The fifth column gives the size of the file in bytes or the size of the directory entry in bytes. For example, the size of the file `Sara.wab` is 115030 bytes.

The sixth through eighth columns give the date and time at which the file was last modified. If the file has not been modified for a long period of time, only the date is shown. For example, the file `Sara.wab` was modified at 1:15 p.m. last November 26.

The rightmost column provides the name of the file that the line describes.

man

The man command describes commands and configuration files. You can use this command to learn about command options and arguments. To view a command's man page, issue a command such as the following:

```
man find
```

This command displays the options and arguments of the `find` command and describes the operation of the command.

When a man page is long, the man command helps you by providing a simple paging facility that you can use to scroll through the output pages. By typing one of the following characters, you can control the output of the man command:

Space   Move forward one page.

b   Move backward one page.

q   Terminate the command.

mkdir

The `mkdir` command creates a directory. For example, the command

    mkdir newfolder

creates a directory named `newfolder`. The new directory is a subdirectory of the current directory. If you want to place the new directory somewhere else, use a command such as

    mkdir /tmp/newfolder

which creates the new directory as a subdirectory of /tmp, which must already exist.

mv

You can use the `mv` command to rename a file. For example, the command

    mv filex filey

renames `filex` to the new filename `filey`. You can also use the `mv` command to move a file or a set of files from one directory to another. For example, the command

    mv filex filey /home/bob

moves the files `filex` and `filey` from the current working directory to the directory /home/bob.

pwd

The `pwd` command displays the name of the current working directory. This command requires no options or arguments.

rm

The `rm` command deletes files. For example, the command

    rm filex filey

deletes `filex` and `filey`. Generally, there is no way to recover a file once it has been deleted, so you should be very careful when using the `rm` command. You can delete a directory and all the files it contains by specifying a command such as:

    rm -rf dir

rmdir

The rmdir command deletes directories. For example, the command

    rmdir folderx foldery

deletes the directories folderx and foldery, which reside in the current directory. The directories must be empty or the command will fail. To delete a directory that contains files, use the rm -rf command.

touch

The touch command updates the file access and modification times associated with a file. For example, the command

    touch mydata

sets the access and modification times of the file mydata to the current time. If you touch a file that does not exist, Unix creates an empty file having the specified filename.

Now try Exercise 3.1 to see if you now know how to use some of the basic Unix commands just covered.

EXERCISE 3.1

Basic Unix Commands

1. Log in as a user other than root.

2. Change the current working directory to /tmp.

3. Change the current working directory to your home directory.

4. Create the file ex3.1 by issuing the following command:

   touch ex3.1

5. Copy the file to the file ex3.1.SAVE.

6. Rename the file ex3.1.SAVE to ex3.1.BACKUP.

7. Create a directory named testdir.

8. Move the file ex3.1 into the testdir directory.

9. Delete the file ex3.1.BACKUP.

10. Delete the directory testdir and its contents.

11. Find the location of the file /passwd.

File Ownership and Permissions

The ls command displays the *file ownership* and *file permissions* of the files in the specified directory or the current directory if one is not specified. You can manipulate these file characteristics by issuing several commands.

You can change the owner of a file or a set of files by issuing the chown command. For example, the command

```
chown bill filex filey
```

makes the user bill the owner of the files filex and filey. Only the system administrator root can use the chown command to change the ownership of files; ordinary users can use the command to change the group ownership of files they own.

Similarly, you can change the group ownership of a file by issuing the chgrp command. For example, the command

```
chgrp bill filex filey
```

makes the group bill the new group owner of the files filex and filey. You don't have to be the system administrator to use the chgrp command. You can change group ownership of files you own to any group of which you're a member.

The system administrator can change the ownership and group ownership of a file by issuing the chown command. For example, the command

```
chown bill.bob filex
```

makes bill the owner and bob the group owner of the file filex.

File permissions determine who can read, write, and execute a file. Directory permissions also determine who can add and remove files from a directory, list the names of files in a directory, and access files in a directory. Each of these operations is associated with a character, as shown in Table 3.2.

TABLE 3.2   File and Directory Access Permissions

Permission	File Permission	Directory Permission
r	Permitted to read the file	Permitted to list the directory
w	Permitted to write the file	Permitted to create and delete files within the directory

TABLE 3.2 File and Directory Access Permissions *(continued)*

Permission	File Permission	Directory Permission
x	Permitted to execute the file	Permitted to access files within the directory
-	No access permitted	No access permitted

Unix assigns a separate set of permissions to the file's owner, group owner, and to other users. The ls command displays permissions in that order. For example, the permissions rw-r----- allow the following actions on a file:

owner (rw-)   The owner of the file can read and write, but not execute, the file.

group (r--)   Members of the group who own the file can read, but not write or execute, the file.

other (---)   Other users cannot access the file.

You can manipulate file or directory permissions by using either of two forms of the chmod command. The first form represents permissions as numbers, as shown in Table 3.3.

TABLE 3.3 Numerical File and Directory Access Permissions

Permission	Number
r	4
w	2
x	1
-	0

To form a permission value, the numbers are summed. For example, permissions rwx have the value 7, and permissions r-x have the value 5. The permission sums are then specified in the following order: user, group, other. For example, the permissions `rw-r----` would be specified as 640. The following `chmod` command uses the numbers to specify file permissions:

`chmod 640 filex`

This command sets the permissions of the file `filex` to `rw-r-----`. The `chmod` command supports an alternative way of specifying permissions, which associates letters with the users, as listed in Table 3.4.

TABLE 3.4   User Designations Used to Specify Permissions

User	Designation
owner	u
group owner	g
other	o

These designations are used with the letters shown in Table 3.2 to add or subtract permissions from a file or directory. For example, to ensure that group members can read a file, issue a command such as

`chmod g+r filex`

This command enables the owner of the file and members of the group that owns the file to read the file. To assure that others cannot access the file, issue a command such as

`chmod o-rwx filex`

This command disables the read, write, and execute permissions of users other than the owner and members of the group that own the file.

When you create a file, its access permissions are set according to the complement of the value specified by the `umask` command. You can compute the complement by subtracting each digit from 7. For example, if you issue the command

`umask 027`

the complement of the `umask` value is 750. However, a newly created file is never automatically set to be executable, so the effective value is 640. Thus, given a `umask` value of 027, you will be able to read and write any files that you create, members of your default group will be able to read the files, and others won't be able to access the files in any way. Of course, after creating a file, you can issue a chmod command to establish exactly the permissions you want on that specific file.

See Exercise 3.2 to confirm that you understand how to assign file and directory ownership and permissions.

EXERCISE 3.2

File and Directory Ownership and Permissions

1. Log in as root.

2. Create the file ex3.2 by issuing the command

   touch ex3.2

3. Use the ls command to determine who is allowed to read the file, who is allowed to write the file, and who is allowed to execute the file.

4. Change the owner of the file to bin.

5. Change the group owner of the file to nobody.

6. Set the file permissions to enable bin to read and execute the file.

7. Set the file permissions to allow members of the group nobody to execute the file.

8. Set the file permissions to allow other users to read the file.

Understanding the Red Hat Linux File System

Table 3.5 summarizes the main directories that compose the Red Hat Linux *file system*. Be sure you're familiar with each directory and its contents.

TABLE 3.5 Important Red Hat Linux Directories

Directory	Contents
/	System root directory
/bin	Common commands and programs
/boot	Linux kernel and boot-related files
/dev	Device files
/etc	Configuration files

TABLE 3.5   Important Red Hat Linux Directories *(continued)*

Directory	Contents
/home	Users' home directories
/lib	Shared libraries
/lost+found	Damaged files
/mnt	Mount points for file systems
/proc	System status information
/root	The root user's home directory
/sbin	System commands and programs
/tmp	Temporary files
/usr/X11R6	X commands and programs
/usr/bin	Common commands and programs
/usr/doc	Documentation
/usr/games	Games
/usr/include	Header files
/usr/info	Online documentatioı
/usr/lib	Shared libraries
/usr/local	Locally installed files
/usr/man	Manual pages
/usr/sbin	System commands and programs
/usr/share	Shared information
/usr/src	Source code
/var	Log files, spool files, and other dynamic files

Follow the steps in Exercise 3.3 to learn what kinds of files and subdirectories are in each of the directories listed in Table 3.5.

EXERCISE 3.3

Touring the Linux File System

1. Begin at the root directory of your computer system.

2. Referring to Table 3.5, move to each of the listed directories and use the `ls -l` command to list their contents.

3. Notice the kinds of files and subdirectories that are present.

Using and Manipulating the Path

Unix commands are stored in several directories. The shell has a list of directories, known as the *path*, which are stored in the PATH environment variable. When you issue a Unix command, the shell searches the path for the command you invoked and runs the command.

You can view the path by issuing the command

```
echo $PATH
```

You'll see output that resembles the following:

```
/usr/bin:/bin:/usr/X11R6/bin
```

In this case, the path consists of three directories: `/usr/bin`, `/bin`, and `/usr/X11R6/bin`. An entry is separated from an adjacent entry by a colon (`:`).

You can add a directory to the path by issuing a command such as

```
export PATH=/sbin:$PATH
```

which adds the directory `/sbin` to the front of the path, so that it will be searched first. To add a directory to the back of the path, issue a command such as

```
export PATH=$PATH:/sbin
```

You can find the directory in which a command resides—assuming that it resides in a directory on the path—by issuing a command such as

```
which ls
```

The `which` command reports the location of the `ls` command.

See Exercise 3.4 to verify that you understand how to view the contents of a path and find what directories are present.

Viewing the Path

1. View the contents of your path. What directories are present?

Editing Files

To edit a text file, you use a text editor. Two popular Unix editors are vi and pico. Both of these text editors are relatively compact, which means they can be used even when your system has access to little or no hard disk space. The vi editor is the more sophisticated editor, but mastery of vi requires considerable practice.

The pico editor, used with the popular e-mail client pine, is much simpler to learn and use. To edit a file by using pico, issue a command such as

    pico filex

Or, to create a new file, simply issue the pico command without arguments

    pico

Once pico has launched, you'll see a screen like that shown in Figure 3.1.

FIGURE 3.1 The pico user interface

Most pico commands require you to press and hold the Ctrl key and type a letter indicating the operation you want to perform. The menu at the bottom of the screen reminds you of the most commonly used commands; the caret (^) denotes the use of the Ctrl key. Table 3.6 summarizes the most important pico commands. The cursor navigation keys, the Enter key, the Backspace key, and the Delete key have their familiar meanings.

TABLE 3.6 Important pico Commands

Command	Function
^G	Get help.
^J	Justify a paragraph of text.
^K	Cut text.
^O	Write the edit buffer to a file.
^R	Read a file and insert its contents into the edit buffer.
^U	Insert cut text.
^V	Page down.
^X	Exit the program.
^Y	Page up.

See Exercise 3.5 to check whether you now understand how to use a text editor to view the contents of a file and create new files.

EXERCISE 3.5

Using a Text Editor

1. Use a text editor to view the contents of the file /etc/passwd. Do not change the contents of this file.

2. Use a text editor to create a file named ex3.5. Enter your current to do list into the file.

Printing Files

To print a file, issue a command such as

```
lpr filex
```

which prints the file filex. To print a file to a specific printer, issue a command such as

```
lpr -P lj4 filex
```

where lj4 is the name of a configured printer.

See Exercise 3.6 to check whether you now understand how to print files.

EXERCISE 3.6

Printing Files

1. Print the file you created in step 2 of Exercise 3.5.

Administering File Systems

System administrators must be able to perform a variety of operations not generally performed by ordinary users. These include backing up and restoring files, mounting and unmounting file systems, partitioning disks, creating file systems, and checking file systems. This section explains how to perform these operations. Most commands in this section can be performed only by root. If a command fails to work, check to make sure you've specified it correctly. If so, retry the command as root.

Backing Up and Restoring Files

Several Unix commands can back up and restore files. The most popular backup and restore command is tar. To back up a file or directory by using tar, issue a command such as

```
tar cvf tarfile.tar filex filey dirz
```

This command backs up the files filex and filey and the directory dirz, storing the backup in the file tarfile.tar.

To restore the backup, issue a command such as

```
tar xvf tarfile.tar
```

You can compress the backup file to reduce the amount of disk space required to store it. To specify compression when creating a backup, issue a command such as

```
tar zcvf tarfile.tgz filex filey dirz
```

where the z denotes compression. If a backup file is compressed, the z option must be used when restoring the files:

```
tar zxvf tarfile.tgz
```

Now test your understanding of the steps involved in backing up and restoring files by completing Exercise 3.7.

EXERCISE 3.7

Backing Up and Restoring Files

1. Use the tar command to back up the files and directories in your home directory.

2. Move to the /tmp directory and restore the backup, thereby duplicating the files of your home directory.

3. Delete the restored files by using the rm −rf command.

Mounting and Unmounting File Systems

You must mount a file system before you can access the files it contains. To mount a file system, issue a command such as

```
mount −t ext2 /dev/hdb1 /mnt/data
```

This command mounts the ext2 file system residing on the partition /dev/hdb1 as the directory /mnt/data, which exist before the command is issued. File system types other than ext2 can be specified; for example, to mount an MS-DOS (FAT-16) file system, specify msdos as the file system type.

You can mount a file system for reading only by specifying the ro option

```
mount −t ext2 /dev/hdb1 /mnt/data −o ro
```

When you're done accessing a file system, you can unmount it by issuing a command such as

```
umount /dev/hdb1
```

or

```
umount /mnt/data
```

You won't be able to unmount the file system if it is in use. If your current working directory—or that of another user—is a directory of the mounted file system, then the file system is in use and you won't be able to unmount it. Change your current working directory to a directory outside the file system before attempting to unmount it.

Now complete Exercise 3.8 to mount and unmount file systems on your own.

EXERCISE 3.8

Mounting and Unmounting File Systems

1. If a CD-ROM is mounted, unmount it.

2. Mount a Red Hat Linux CD-ROM disk at the directory /redhat.

3. Copy a file from the CD-ROM disk to your home directory.

4. Delete the copied file.

5. Unmount the CD-ROM disk.

Using Removable Media

Users familiar with MS-DOS may be accustomed to inserting and removing removable media—such as floppy disk—at will. However, under Unix, the file system on the removable media must be mounted in order to be accessible. Conversely, the file system should be unmounted before the media is removed. Failure to unmount the file system may result in corrupted data or a corrupted file system.

The GNOME and KDE environments provide convenient ways to work with removable media. You may prefer working in a graphical environment when mounting and unmounting media.

Creating File Systems

To create a Linux file system, issue the mke2fs command

```
mke2fs /dev/hdb2
```

specifying the partition (for example, /dev/hdb2) on which the file system is to reside.

To initialize a swap partition, issue the command

```
mkswap /dev/hdb3
```

specifying the swap partition (for example, /dev/hdb2).

Creating a file system or initializing a swap partition destroys any existing file system on the partition. Be certain to specify the proper partition.

See Exercise 3.9 to check whether you now understand how to create a file system.

EXERCISE 3.9

Creating File Systems

1. Place an MS-DOS formatted floppy disk in the floppy drive.

2. Create an ext2 file system on the floppy.

3. Mount the file system at a mount point of your choosing.

4. Copy the file /etc/passwd to the file system on the floppy disk.

5. Unmount the floppy disk.

Partitioning Hard Disks

The Red Hat Linux installation program provides a text-based interface that lets you divide a hard disk into *partitions*, which are contiguous regions of disk space on which you can make file systems. This process is called *disk partitioning*. Alternatively, during and after installation, you can use the fdisk command to partition a hard disk. To launch the fdisk utility, issue the fdisk command and specify as an argument the hard disk you wish to partition. For example, the command

```
fdisk /dev/hdb
```

lets you partition the second IDE hard disk.

Once fdisk has started, it presents a prompt that lets you know it's ready

```
Command (m for help):
```

Table 3.7 summarizes the most important fdisk commands.

TABLE 3.7   Important fdisk Commands

Command	Action
a	Toggles the active partition flag.
d	Deletes a partition.
l	Lists known partition types.
n	Adds a new partition.
o	Creates a new empty partition table.
p	Prints (displays) the partition table.
q	Quits without saving changes.
t	Sets the partition type.
u	Toggles display units from cylinders to sectors or the reverse.
v	Verifies the partition table.
w	Writes the partition table to disk and exits.

Usually, your first step after starting fdisk is to issue the p command to display the partition table. The result should resemble the following output:

```
Disk /dev/hda: 255 heads, 63 sectors, 2489 cylinders
Units = cylinders of 16065 * 512 bytes

     Device Boot     Start       End     Blocks   Id  System
/dev/hda1      *         1       127    1020096    6  FAT16
/dev/hda2              128      2489   18972765    5  Extended
/dev/hda5              128       132      40131   83  Linux
```

```
/dev/hda6        133    387   2048256   83 Linux
/dev/hda7        388    898   4104576   83 Linux
/dev/hda8        899    962    514048+  83 Linux
/dev/hda9        963   1090   1028128+  83 Linux
/dev/hda10      1091   1157    538146   82 Linux swap
/dev/hda11      1158   2489  10699258+  83 Linux
```

The data in this output is as follows:

- The Device column indicates the name of the Linux partition that a particular row of data describes.

- The Boot column contains an asterisk that indicates the active partition, that is, the partition that will be booted by the MS-DOS loader.

- The Start and End columns give the starting and ending cylinder numbers of the partition.

- The Blocks column gives the size of the partition in 1024-byte blocks.

- The Id and System columns specify the type of the partition, the former giving the numerical code and the latter giving the descriptive name.

You can toggle the display to show sectors instead of cylinder numbers, which is appropriate if you're using logical block addressing (LBA) rather than physical addressing, by issuing the u command.

To delete a partition, issue the d command and then specify the number of the partition you wish to delete.

To create a new partition, issue the n command and specify the type of partition (primary, extended, or logical) and the start and end values. Then, issue the t command and specify the numerical type of the partition. Use type 82 for a swap partition and type 83 for a regular partition.

When you've specified all of the partitions, issue the w command to write the revised partition table and exit the program. Sometimes, changes to the partition table require you to reboot the system. If instructed to do so, reboot the system.

Checking File Systems

To check the integrity of a Linux file system, issue a command such as

```
e2fsck -f /dev/hdb2
```

specifying the partition (for example, /dev/hdb2) that you want to check. To specify that the check should include a test for bad blocks and that errors should be repaired automatically, add the –c and –p options (respectively) as in the following command:

```
e2fsck -f -c -p /dev/hdb2
```

Unix Command Facilities

This section surveys important Unix command facilities, including stream redirection, regular expressions, and shell scripts. Several entire books have been written on Unix command facilities, so it's not possible to cover every detail here. This section focuses on the most useful aspects of these facilities. If you're unfamiliar with the material in this section, you should consult the reference given at the end of this chapter.

Using Stream Redirection

Every Unix process has the following three standard streams:

Standard Input   Command input

Standard Output   Command output

Standard Error   Error messages

Table 3.8 summarizes important stream redirection operators, which let you redirect these input and output streams. For example, the command

```
ls -l > filelist
```

sends the output of the ls command to the file filelist.

TABLE 3.8   Important Redirection Operators

Operator	Meaning
< *file*	Take standard input from *file*.
> *file*	Write standard output to *file*.
>> *file*	Append standard output to *file*.

TABLE 3.8   Important Redirection Operators *(continued)*

Operator	Meaning
>&2	Write standard output stream to standard error stream.
2> *file*	Write standard error stream to *file*.
2>&1	Write standard error stream to standard output stream.
x | *y*	Process *y* takes as its input the output of process *x*.

Using Regular Expressions

The Unix filename globbing facility is more powerful than DOS wildcards, because Unix employs more powerful expressions, known as *regular expressions*, to specify a set of files. Table 3.9 summarizes important Unix filename metacharacters.

TABLE 3.9   Important Filename Metacharacters

Metacharacter	Matches...
*	Any string of zero of more characters.
?	Any single character.
[abc...]	Any specified character. You can use a hyphen to specify a range of characters. For example, 0-9 matches any digit.
[!abc...]	Any character except those specified.
~*user*	The home directory of the specified user.

If you prefix a backslash (\) to a metacharacter, the special meaning of the metacharacter is ignored. Likewise, if you enclose text containing a metacharacter within single quotes, the special meaning of the metacharacter is ignored. However, a metacharacter that appears within double quotes retains its special meaning.

Creating and Using Shell Scripts

Perhaps the most important aspect of the Unix command line is that its command language is extensible: You can write your own shell scripts that can be executed just as any other Unix command. This subsection surveys several important topics related to shell scripts, including the structure of shell scripts, shell script control structures, and environment variables.

Structure of a Shell Script

Shell scripts are ordinary text files that contain shell commands. One of the most important shell commands is the comment. Any shell script line beginning with a hash mark (#) is considered a comment.

The first line of a shell script should be a special comment that consists of the comment character (#), followed immediately by an exclamation mark (!), followed by the path name of the program that Unix should use to process the commands in the shell script, usually /bin/bash. The bash shell is the most commonly used Linux shell.

Table 3.10 summarizes important command forms that are used within shell scripts.

TABLE 3.10   Important Command Forms

Form	Meaning
cmd &	Execute *cmd* in the background.
cmd1 ; *cmd2*	Execute *cmd1* followed by *cmd2*.
(*cmd1* ; *cmd2*)	Execute *cmd1* followed by *cmd2*, treating them as a command group.
cmd1 \`*cmd2*\`	Use the output of *cmd2* as the arguments of *cmd1*.
cmd1 && *cmd2*	Execute *cmd1*; execute *cmd2* only if *cmd1* succeeds.
cmd1 || *cmd2*	Execute *cmd1*; execute *cmd2* only if *cmd1* fails.
{ *cmd1* ; *cmd2* }	Execute *cmd1* followed by *cmd2* in the current environment.

Environment Variables

In shell scripts, you can use variables known as *environment variables*. To assign a value to an environment variable, use a command such as

    x=y

This assignment puts the value *y* in the environment variable *x*. You can assign the value of an environment variable to another environment variable by using a command such as

    x=${y}

This assignment puts the value of the environment variable *y* in the environment variable *x*. The curly braces delimit the name of the environment variable and can sometimes be omitted:

    x=$y

As an example of an occasion where the braces are important, consider the command

    x=${y}es

This assignment concatenates the value of the environment variable *y* with the string **es** and places the result in the environment variable *x*. Writing the command as

    x=$yes

places the value of the environment variable *yes* in the environment variable *x*.

To negate the special meaning of the syntax used to reference an environment variable, enclose the expression in single quotes as follows:

    x='$y'

This assignment puts the value *$y* in the environment variable *x*. Alternatively, you can prefix the metacharacter *$* with a backslash as follows:

    x=\$y

By default, an environment variable is available only as a part of the immediate local environment. To make an environment variable accessible to programs and processes started from a local environment, specify the name of the variable in an export command, such as

```
export x,y,z
```

or

```
export x=$y
```

Control Constructs

Several commands can be used to alter the standard top-to-bottom sequence of the execution of shell script commands. The most important of these is the if command. This subsection explains the if command and several other important control constructs.

The *if* Command

Every Unix command posts an exit code when it completes, whether it terminates normally or abnormally. The value 0 signifies successful completion; other values signify various error conditions. The if command tests the completion value of a command. In its simplest form, the if command executes a series of commands only if the tested command succeeded

```
if test-command
then
  commands
fi
```

Another form of the if command chooses between two series of commands based on success or failure of the tested command

```
if test-command
then
  commands
else
  commands
fi
```

Often the test command is used as the subject command of the if command. For example, the following command

```
if test -e /etc/hosts
```

tests whether the file /etc/hosts exists. Table 3.11 summarizes important arguments of the test command.

TABLE 3.11 Important *test* Command Arguments

Condition	Meaning
-d *file*	*file* is a directory.
-e *file*	*file* exists.
-f *file*	*file* is a regular file.
-r *file*	*file* is readable.
-s *file*	*file* has size greater than 0.
-w *file*	*file* is writable.
-x *file*	*file* is executable.
file1 -nt *file2*	*file1* is newer than *file2*.
file1 -ot *file2*	*file1* is older than *file2*.
s1 = *s2*	String *s1* is identical to string *s2*.
s1 != *s2*	String *s1* is not identical to string *s2*.
n1 -eq *n2*	Integer *n1* is equal to integer *n2*.
n1 -ge *n2*	Integer *n1* is greater than or equal to integer *n2*.
n1 -gt *n2*	Integer *n1* is greater than integer *n2*.
n1 -le *n2*	Integer *n1* is less than or equal to integer *n2*.
n1 -lt *n2*	Integer *n1* is less than integer *n2*.
n1 -ne *n2*	Integer *n1* is not equal to integer *n2*.
! *cnd*	True if and only if condition *cnd* is false.

TABLE 3.11   Important *test* Command Arguments *(continued)*

Condition	Meaning
cnd1 -a *cnd2*	True if condition *cnd1* and condition *cnd2* are both true.
cnd1 -o *cnd2*	True if either condition *cnd1* or condition *cnd2* is true.

The *case* Command

Whereas the if command provides a one-way branch and the combination of an if command and an else command provides a two-way branch, the case command provides a multi-way branch:

```
case string
in
  pattern1)
    commands
    ;;
  pattern2)
    commands
    ;;
  (etc.)
esac
```

The *while* and *until* Commands

The while command executes a series of commands until an associated test command is tested and found to be false:

```
while
    test-command
do
    commands
done
```

The similar until command executes a series of commands until an associated test command is tested and found to be true:

```
until
    test-command
```

```
do
     commands
done
```

The *for* Command

The for command executes a series of commands iteratively, once for each member of a specified list:

```
for list
do
     commands
done
```

Another form of the for command assigns the value of the current list member to a specified variable:

```
for x in list
do
     commands
done
```

During each iteration, the variable *x* holds the value of the current list member.

The *break* Command

The break command can be used in the body of a for, while, or until command. When executed, it immediately terminates the loop.

The *continue* Command

The continue command can be used in the body of a for, while, or until command. When executed, it immediately ends the current iteration of the loop.

The *exit* Command

The exit command terminates the execution of a shell script and sets the exit code to the value specified as its argument:

```
exit 0
```

Summary

In this chapter, you learned about the most commonly used Unix commands. The most important topics covered are:

Basic Unix Commands   Although Linux boasts over one thousand commands, you need to know only a dozen or so commonly used commands.

File Ownership and Permissions   Files have owners and group owners. Owners, group owners, and others are assigned access permissions to read, write, or execute a file.

Red Hat Linux File System   Red Hat Linux establishes about two dozen standard directories, each containing a specific type of programs or files.

The PATH Environment Variable   The PATH environment variable specifies directories that the shell searches to locate programs.

Editing Files   The `pico` editor is a simple editor suitable for use in system administration.

Backing Up and Restoring Files   The `tar` command is useful for backing up and restoring files.

File Systems   The `mke2fs` command creates a Linux file system. The `mount` and `umount` commands mount and unmount (respectively) file systems.

Partitions   The `fdisk` program lets you establish hard disk partitions.

Redirection   You can redirect the input and output of Unix commands.

Regular Expressions   You can use regular expressions to specify filenames and sets of filenames.

Environment Variables   You can use environment variables to store values.

Control Structures   Shell scripts can include commands that conditionally or iteratively execute series of commands.

Key Terms

Before going on to the next chapter, be sure you're familiar with the following terms:

current directory

current working directory

environment variables

file ownership

file permissions

file system

partitions

path

regular expressions

Additional Sources of Information

If you'd like further information about the topics presented in this chapter, you should consult the following source:

- *Unix Complete*, Peter Dyson, Stan Kelly-Bootle, John Heilborn (Sybex, 1999)

Review Questions

1. Which Unix command renames a file?

   A. cp

   B. mv

   C. rename

   D. rn

2. What operations can be performed on a file that has permissions rwxr-----?

   A. Can be read by any user

   B. Can be read by its owner

   C. Can be read by its owner and members of its owning group

   D. Cannot be read

3. Which command is used to restore files from a compressed backup?

   A. tar cvf

   B. tar xvf

   C. tar zcvf

   D. tar zxvf

4. Which command is used to create a Linux file system?

   A. fdisk

   B. mke2fs

   C. mkswap

   D. mount

5. To redirect the output of command x as the input of command y, which command do you use?

    A. x < y

    B. x > y

    C. x >> y

    D. x | y

6. To set the value of environment variable x to that of environment variable y, which command do you use?

    A. x=y

    B. x=$y

    C. x=${y}

    D. export x=$y

Answers to Review Questions

1. B. The mv command moves files from one name or directory to another. The mv command can also be used to rename a file.

2. B and C. The file can be read, written, and executed by its owner; it can be read by members of its owning group.

3. D. The tar zxvf extracts (*x*) files from a compressed (*z*) backup.

4. B. The mke2fs command creates a standard Linux file system.

5. D. The pipe operator (|) joins the output stream of one command to the input stream of another.

6. B, C, and D. The command *x=y* sets the value of environment variable *x* to *y*, not the value of the environment variable *y*.

Chapter 4

Networking Basics

RHCE PREPARATION TOPICS COVERED IN THIS CHAPTER:

✓ **Understand IP addressing for hosts and networks.**

✓ **Understand the TCP/IP networking model and its primary protocols and services.**

✓ **Understand TCP/IP routing.**

✓ **Understand the function of common Linux services.**

- Understand well-known TCP/IP ports and the associated TCP/IP services.
- Understand how Red Hat Linux starts and stops services.
- Know how to start and stop common Linux services.

To pass the RHCE exam, you must be familiar with TCP/IP networking and common TCP/IP network services. This chapter reviews the fundamentals of TCP/IP networking and services.

If the material in this chapter is unfamiliar to you, you should consult additional sources in order to adequately prepare for the RHCE exam. A couple of recommended books are listed at the end of this chapter.

TCP/IP Networking

At one time, a variety of protocols vied for ascendancy as the preeminent protocol. The advent of the Internet, which is based on the TCP/IP (Transmission Control Protocol/Internet Protocol) protocol family, has essentially ended the contest. Except for closed, private networks, most networks today use TCP/IP as their primary protocol.

This section describes how TCP/IP hosts and networks are addressed. The subsequent section describes how TCP/IP networks function and the services that TCP/IP networks provide.

IP Addresses

TCP/IP networks are made up of interconnected computer systems called hosts. Each host has one or more *IP addresses*, usually one address for each network interface installed on the host. TCP/IP addresses are 32-bit numbers, which are commonly written as a series of four *octets* (8-bit values) in dotted quad notation. For example, a TCP/IP host might have an IP address such as 192.168.1.1, which is equivalent to the 32-bit integer 3,232,235,777 ($192 \times 256^3 + 168 \times 256^2 + 1 \times 256 + 1$).

Some hosts have a more or less permanently assigned IP address, called a *static IP address*. Other hosts are assigned a temporary IP address, called a *dynamic IP address*. Dynamic IP addresses are commonly used for mobile hosts, such as laptops, and for dial-in clients. Hosts that provide services to other hosts are generally assigned a static IP address so that clients will be able to refer to them using a consistent IP address. As you'll see later in the chapter, IP addresses are a somewhat scarce commodity. Dynamic IP addresses require an IP address pool only as large as the number of active hosts rather than the total number of hosts.

Network Classes

Organizations don't ask the Internet authorities to assign them a single IP address. Instead, they request a consecutive series of IP addresses that can be assigned to hosts within their network. The IP addresses are chosen from one of three classes, distinguished by the value of the first octet:

1.0.0.0–126.0.0.0   Class A network addresses

128.0.0.0–191.0.0.0   Class B network addresses

192.0.0.0–223.0.0.0   Class C network addresses

An IP address consists of two parts: a *network address* and a *host address*. The network address is common to all directly connected hosts that compose a network. The host address distinguishes an individual host from the other hosts on its network. The network address is taken from the high-order bits of the IP address, and the host address is taken from the low-order bits. The size of the network address varies according to the network class:

Class A   8 bits (1 octet)

Class B   16 bits (2 octets)

Class C   24 bits (3 octets)

Because the network address of a class A address is only 8 bits long, 24 bits are available to specify host addresses. Thus, a class A network can include over 16 million hosts. In contrast, the network address of a class C network is 24 bits long; only 8 bits are available to specify host addresses. Thus, a class C network can include only 254 hosts (the IP addresses and *xxx. xxx. xxx*.255 assigned to the network, so only IP addresses *xxx. xxx . xxx*.1- *xxx. xxx. xxx*.254 are available for hosts).

Class C networks may appear less desirable than class A networks. However, because the network address of a class A network consists of only 8 bits, only 126 class A network addresses are possible. All such addresses have long been assigned, so, although you might prefer a class A address, you're not likely to receive one. The 24-bit network address of a class C address yields over 16 million possible network addresses. Unfortunately, even class C addresses are becoming scarce.

A new TCP/IP standard, IPv6, will provide 128-bit IP addresses. The Linux kernel already provides experimental support for IPv6. However, it will be several years before IPv6 is widely supported and used.

Several IP address ranges are specially allocated:

127.0.0.0–127.255.255.255   Used to refer to the local host and network (*loopback addresses*).

224.0.0.0–239.0.0.0   Reserved for use by multicast protocols.

240.0.0.0–255.0.0.0   Reserved (do not use).

10.0.0.0–10.255.255.255   Reserved for private networks.

172.16.0.0–172.31.255.255   Reserved for private networks.

192.168.0.0–192.168.255.255   Reserved for private networks.

You can freely assign IP addresses from ranges allocated to private networks. However, you must take special steps (such as implementing IP masquerading or network address translation, which are described in Chapter 30, "Configuring a Firewall Using `ipchains`") to enable a host with a private IP address to access hosts outside its local network.

Subnetting

Suppose you have two small networks, each consisting of about one dozen hosts. You could request a class C network address for each network. However, a class C network address provides many more IP addresses than you need. If you could somehow have a network address of, say, 26 bits instead of 24, you could host several networks within the range of IP addresses that compose a single class C network address. The remaining 6 bits of the IP address would let you assign as many as 31 hosts to each network.

Subnetting lets you split an IP address into its network and host address components anywhere you like, rather than only at an octet boundary. You designate the part of an IP address that composes the network address by specifying a *netmask*, a 32-bit string that has a 1 bit in each position that's part of the network address and a 0 bit elsewhere. You write a netmask using the same dotted quad notation used for IP addresses. For example, a standard class C address has a netmask of 255.255.255.0: The first three octets have all 1 bits and the final octet has all 0 bits. To specify a 26-bit network address, you use a netmask of 255.255.255.192 in which the final octet has 1 bits in its two highest order positions.

To understand the significance of a host's IP address, you must know the associated netmask. Otherwise, you won't be able to determine which hosts are on the same local network as the host.

Some programs allow you to specify an IP address and netmask as a pair. You write the IP address, follow it with a slash, and then write the number of bits in the netmask. For example, 192.168.1.100/24 specifies a host with IP address 192.168.1.100 on a network having a 24-bit (class C-like) netmask. A subnetted IP address is one in which the number of netmask bits is not an even multiple of 8, for example, 192.168.1.100/26.

Supernetting

As you might expect, *supernetting* is related to subnetting. Whereas subnetting lets you split a network into several smaller networks, supernetting lets you join consecutively numbered networks into a larger network. For example, suppose you have been assigned 256 class C network addresses that span the entire range from 192.192.0.0 to 192.192.255.255. By specifying a netmask of 255.255.0.0, you can treat these class C network addresses as though they are a single class B address: 16 bits for the network address and 16 bits for the host address.

Host and Domain Names

Most people find it cumbersome to recall IP addresses. Therefore, hosts are generally assigned host names as well as IP addresses. It's much easier to point your Web browser to `www.redhat.com` than to 206.132.41.202.

Just as organizations apply to the Internet authority for a network address rather than individual host addresses, they apply for a domain name rather than individual host names. A domain name consists of at least two parts: a top-level domain and a subdomain. The parts are separated by a dot (.).

Sometimes, additional subdomains are used, each separated by a dot. Several top-level domains have been established, including the following:

com Networks operated by businesses

edu Networks operated by schools

gov Networks operated by U.S. government agencies

mil Networks operated by the U.S. military

net Networks operated by Internet service providers (ISPs)

In addition, most countries around the world have a designated top-level domain. For example, the UK has the domain uk.

An organization registers its domain name (or names) with the Internet authority. Then, it assigns host names that include the domain name. As a simple example, the host name www.redhat.com consists of

- a host name, www

- a domain name, redhat.com, which consists of:

    - a subdomain, redhat

    - a top-level domain, com

It's common for hosts within a network to refer to one another by host name, without reference to their implied common domain name. The combination of a host name and domain name is called a *fully qualified domain name* (*FQDN*).

TCP/IP Model

The previous section described how TCP/IP hosts are named and numbered. This section describes how TCP/IP networks function and the types of services they typically provide.

It's common to explain a protocol suite by referring to the Open Systems Interconnection (OSI) reference model, which groups network functions into seven layers. However, the TCP/IP family of protocols does not closely conform to the OSI model. It's more convenient to think of TCP/IP as consisting of four protocol layers, as shown in Figure 4.1. The following subsections explain each of these layers in detail.

FIGURE 4.1   The TCP/IP protocol layers

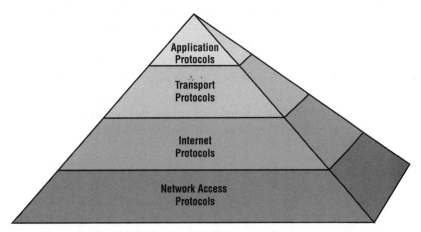

Network Access Protocols

The bottommost layer of protocols, the network access protocols, includes all functions necessary to access the physical network medium and transmit data to hosts on the local network. Commonly, TCP/IP is used in conjunction with Ethernet, a protocol that provides these functions.

Network access protocols tend to be implemented in hardware. For example, typical network adapter cards understand the Ethernet protocol. Consequently, the network access layer is seldom a major concern of the Linux systems administrator.

Internet Protocols

The Internet protocols layer establishes IP addresses as the standard means of addressing TCP/IP hosts. This layer also handles the routing of messages that are destined for hosts outside of the local network.

A host can send data to another host on the local network by directing the data to the IP address of the destination host. Alternatively, a network host can send a *broadcast message* that reaches every host on the local network.

A host that is connected to more than one network can be configured to pass data from one network to the other. Such a host is known as a *router*.

Each host that can access hosts beyond the local network must be configured with a *default route* that designates a special router host—called a *gateway*—that passes information to and from the local network. Hosts may also be configured with additional routes for accessing specific networks or hosts.

Routing information can be specified by means of *static routes*, which are hard-coded in configuration files. Alternatively, a host can use *dynamic routing*. A router capable of dynamic routing sends broadcast messages that advertise its ability to route data to specific networks. Hosts configured for dynamic routing listen for such messages and automatically update their configuration when the status of a router changes.

The Internet protocols layer includes two main protocols: IP (Internet Protocol) and ICMP (Internet Control Message Protocol).

IP

The IP protocol is responsible for the routing and delivery of data. It is a *connectionless protocol*, meaning that no handshake occurs between hosts before an exchange of data occurs.

The IP protocol is called an *unreliable protocol*. This doesn't mean that it cannot be trusted to deliver data. It merely refers to IP's lack of error detection and recovery mechanisms. These functions are not missing from TCP/IP; they are provided by transport layer protocols.

ICMP

The ICMP protocol passes control messages from host to host. These control messages perform the following functions:

- They regulate the flow of data, so that a receiving host is not overwhelmed.

- They inform the sending hosts of unreachable destinations.

- They inform hosts of new and closed routes.

- They enable hosts to check the status of remote hosts.

Transport Protocols

The transport layer protocols are used to pass application data from host to host, using the services provided by protocols of the network access and Internet layers. The two main transport protocols are the User Datagram Protocol (UDP) and the Transmission Control Protocol (TCP).

UDP

The UDP enables applications to send finite-length messages from one host to another. Like IP, UDP is a connectionless, unreliable protocol. Its main virtue is low overhead, which makes it suitable for short, infrequent host-to-host interactions and interactions in which dropping a message now and again is less important than sending data quickly. When error detection and recovery are needed, TCP is used.

TCP

The TCP enables applications to send streams of data from one host to another. Unlike IP and UDP, TCP is a *connection-oriented protocol*. Before hosts exchange data via TCP, a session is initiated. The session provides error control by such means as sequence-checking of the discrete messages that compose the data stream. Creating a session and performing error-checking and recovery entails some overhead; consequently, TCP is preferred over UDP only when these considerations are important.

Application Protocols

TCP/IP provides many application protocols, known as *services*. Moreover, programmers can easily create new services based on the UDP or TCP protocols. A service is associated with a *port*, a 16-bit number that identifies the service. UDP and TCP ports are distinct; a service based on UDP can have the same port as one based on TCP without confusion.

Accessing ports 0–1023 under UNIX requires root privileges. Consequently, these ports are known as *privileged ports*. The remaining ports are known as *non-privileged ports*.

Certain ports are associated by long standing practice with specific services. For example, port 7 is associated with the echo service (used by the ping command). Such ports are called *well-known ports*. Under UNIX, the file /etc/services identifies the well-known ports. Table 4.1 summarizes important TCP/IP services and their port numbers. You'll find additional services listed in the /etc/services file distributed with Red Hat Linux.

Not all these services, nor the services listed in Table 4.1, are likely to be available on a given host.

TABLE 4.1 Important TCP/IP Services and Their Port Numbers

Port	Underlying Protocol	Service	Description
7	UDP/ TCP	echo	Determines if a remote host is accessible.
9	UDP/ TCP	discard	Provides access to a service that discards its input.
11	TCP	systat	Shows active users.
13	UDP/ TCP	daytime	Provides local time as an ASCII string.
15	TCP	netstat	Provides network performance statistics.
17	TCP	qotd	Provides a "quote of the day."
18	UDP/ TCP	msp	Sends a simple message to a user.
19	UDP/ TCP	chargen	Sends a stream of characters.
20	TCP	ftp-data	Used by the File Transfer Protocol (FTP) service to send data.
21	TCP	ftp	Used by the FTP service to send control information.
22	UDP/ TCP	ssh	Provides access to the secure shell service.
23	TCP	telnet	Provides access to the telnet remote shell service.

TABLE 4.1 Important TCP/IP Services and Their Port Numbers *(continued)*

Port	Underlying Protocol	Service	Description
25	TCP	smtp	Provides access to the Simple Mail Transfer Protocol (SMTP).
37	UDP/ TCP	time	Provides time as a binary value.
43	TCP	whois	Provides name and address information.
53	UDP/ TCP	domain	Provides access to the domain name service (DNS).
67	UDP/ TCP	bootps	Used by the bootstrap protocol (bootp) server.
68	UDP/ TCP	bootpc	Used by bootstrap protocol (bootp) client.
69	UDP	tftp	Provides access to the Trivial File Transfer Protocol (TFTP) service.
70	UDP/ TCP	gopher	Provides access to the Gopher information retrieval service.
79	TCP	finger	Provides access to the finger service, which describes users.
80	UDP/ TCP	www	Provides access to the HTTP (Web) service.
88	UDP/ TCP	kerberos	Provides access to the Kerberos authentication service.
109	UDP/ TCP	pop-2	Provides access to the post office service (version 2).
110	UDP/ TCP	pop-3	Provides access to the post office service (version 3).
111	UDP/ TCP	sunrpc	Provides access to the remote procedure call (RPC) service.

TABLE 4.1 Important TCP/IP Services and Their Port Numbers *(continued)*

Port	Underlying Protocol	Service	Description
113	TCP	auth	Provides access to the BSD identd authenticated service.
119	TCP	nntp	Provides access to the Network News Transfer Protocol (NNTP) service.
123	UDP/ TCP	ntp	Provides access to the Network Time Protocol (NTP) service.
137	UDP/ TCP	netbios-ns	Provides access to the NetBIOS name service.
138	UDP/ TCP	netbios-dgm	Provides access to the NetBIOS datagram service.
139	UDP/ TCP	netbios-ssn	Provides access to the NetBIOS session service.
143	UDP/ TCP	imap2	Provides access to the interactive mail access service (version 2).
161	UDP	snmp	Provides access to the Simple Network Management Protocol (SNMP) service.
162	UDP	snmp-trap	Provides access to the SNMP service.
177	UDP/ TCP	xdmcp	Provides access to the X Display Manager Control Protocol (XDMCP) service.
179	UDP/ TCP	bgp	Provides access to the Border Gateway Protocol (BGP) service.
194	UDP/ TCP	irc	Provides access to the Internet Relay Chat (IRC) service.
213	UDP/ TCP	ipx	Provides access to the IPX (Novell's Networking protocol family) service.
220	UDP/ TCP	imap3	Provides access to the interactive mail access service (version 3).

TABLE 4.1   Important TCP/IP Services and Their Port Numbers *(continued)*

Port	Underlying Protocol	Service	Description
443	UDP/ TCP	https	Provides access to the secure HTTP (Web) service.
512	UDP	biff	Provides access to the service that notifies the user of the arrival of mail.
512	TCP	exec	Provides access to the remote execution (REXEC) service.
513	UDP	who	Provides access to a service that maintains a database of users.
513	TCP	login	Provides access to the remote login (rlogin) service.
514	UDP	syslog	Provides access to the system logging (SYSLOG) service.
514	TCP	shell	Provides access to the remote shell (RSH) service.
515	TCP	printer	Provides access to the remote printing (LPR/LPD) service.
517	UDP	talk	Provides access to a chat service.
518	UDP	ntalk	Provides access to a chat service.
749	TCP	kerberos -adm	Provides access to the administration services of the Kerberos authentication server.

Daemons

Under UNIX, TCP/IP services can be supported in any of three ways:

- By the UNIX kernel
- By a continuously running process
- By a process started by the inetd process whenever a client requests service

Only a few services are supported directly by the kernel. Most are supported by processes that run continuously or are started when needed by the inetd process. Such processes are called *daemons*, because they run without being associated with a console terminal. Sometimes daemons are called *background processes*. Table 4.2 describes important Linux daemons that generally run continuously, and Table 4.3 describes important Linux daemons that generally run only when started by inetd, which is sometimes called the *Internet super server*.

TABLE 4.2 Important Linux Daemons

Daemon	Description
amd	Automatically mounts and unmounts NFS file systems.
apmd	Manages the interface between the operating system's Advanced Power Management (APM) features and the BIOS.
arpwatch	Tracks IP address and Ethernet address pairings.
atd	Queues jobs for scheduled execution.
autofs	Automatically mounts and unmounts file systems.
bootparamd	Provides booting information to diskless clients.
crond	Executes scheduled commands.
dhcpd	Provides hosts with dynamic IP addresses and information about the network.
diald	Automatically establishes and breaks remote IP connection via phone line.
gated	Manages network routes.
gpm	Enables mouse cut-and-paste operations on consoles.
httpd	Web server.
innd	Handles incoming USENET news feeds.
linuxconf	Red Hat Linux system administration utility.
lpd	Spools and submits local and remote print jobs.

TABLE 4.2 Important Linux Daemons *(continued)*

Daemon	Description
mars-nwe	Novell NetWare-compatible file and print server.
mcserv	Provides remote access to the Midnight Commander file manager.
named	Provide domain name services.
nmbd	NetBIOS name server.
nfs	Provides remote access to files.
nscd	Caching service for authentication facility.
pcmcia	Manages PC card devices.
portmap	Manages remote procedure call (RPC) connections.
postgresql	Provides access to Postgres databases.
routed	Manages network routes of small, simple networks.
rstatd	Provides system performance measures.
rusersd	Locates users on other network hosts.
rwalld	Displays messages on active terminals.
rwhod	Provides a list of active users.
sendmail	Mail transport agent.
smbd	SMB-compatible file, print, and login server.
snmpd	Provides network management services.
squid	Internet object (HTTP, FTP, and Gopher) cache.
sshd	Secure shell service.
syslog	Provides access to the system log.
xfs	Provides fonts for X.

TABLE 4.2 Important Linux Daemons *(continued)*

Daemon	Description
xntpd	Provides time synchronization services.
ypbind	Binds an NIS client to its domain.
yppasswd	Enables NIS users to change their password.
ypserv	Provides a networkwide database of host, user, and other information.

TABLE 4.3 Important Linux Daemons Using inetd

Daemon	Description
auth	Identifies users (identd).
bootps	Provides IP address and other boot information.
comsat	Notifies users of incoming mail.
exec	Executes commands submitted remotely.
finger	Provides remote access to the finger command.
ftp	Transfers files to and from remote hosts.
imap	Provides interactive access to mail.
linuxconf	Linux system administration utility.
login	Provides remote login.
netbios-ns	Provides NetBIOS name service.
netbios-ssn	Provides NetBIOS session service.
netstat	Provides network performance data.
ntalk	Provides remote user communication.
pop-2	Provides remote access to mail.
pop-3	Provides remote access to mail.

TABLE 4.3 Important Linux Daemons Using `inetd` *(continued)*

Daemon	Description
shell	Provides remote shell service.
swat	Provides Web-based administration for the Samba package.
systat	Provides process performance data.
talk	Provides remote user communication.
telnet	Provides remote login.
tftp	Transfers files to and from remote hosts with minimal authentication and overhead.

You can determine what daemons are currently running by issuing the command

```
ps x
```

The output of this command includes the process ID (PID) and the command associated with each daemon:

```
PID TTY       STAT    TIME COMMAND
  1 ?          S      0:03 init
391 ?          S      0:17 syslogd -m 0
402 ?          S      0:00 klogd
430 ?          S      0:00 crond
444 ?          S      0:00 inetd
458 ?          S      2:37 arpwatch -i eth1
472 ?          S      0:18 named
478 ?          S      0:28 /usr/sbin/sshd -p 23
491 ?          SL     0:14 xntpd -A
506 ?          S      0:00 lpd -l
521 ?          S      0:06 /usr/sbin/dhcpd
556 ?          S      0:00 sendmail: accepting connections
➥on port 25
571 ttyS0      S      0:00 gpm -t MouseMan
585 ?          S      0:00 httpd
602 ?          S      0:00 logger
```

```
  685 tty3    SW    0:00 [mingetty]
  686 tty4    SW    0:00 [mingetty]
  688 tty6    S     0:00 /sbin/mingetty tty6
  690 ?       S     0:04 update (bdflush)
  723 tty2    S     0:00 /sbin/mingetty tty2
  726 tty1    S     0:00 /sbin/mingetty tty1
 1110 ?       S     0:00 [smbd]
 1121 ?       S     0:09 nmbd -D
 1124 ?       S     0:00 [nmbd]
 2803 ?       SW    0:00 [rpciod]
 2804 ?       SW    0:00 [lockd]
 5873 tty5    S     0:00 /sbin/mingetty tty5
15739 pts/1   R     0:00 ps x
```

To determine which daemons are currently running or which daemons will be started by inetd, issue the command

```
netstat -ap --inet | grep LISTEN
```

This command reports the port number or name of the associated service and the process number and name of the process currently listening on the port. If the listening process is inetd, this indicates that the service will be started by inetd when needed, as in the following output from the netstat command:

```
tcp 0 0 *:1047              *:*    LISTEN    -
tcp 0 0 *:netbios-ssn       *:*    LISTEN    1110/
tcp 0 0 *:www               *:*    LISTEN    585/httpd
tcp 0 0 *:smtp              *:*    LISTEN    556/
➥sendmail: accep
tcp 0 0 *:printer           *:*    LISTEN    506/lpd
tcp 0 0 *:telnet            *:*    LISTEN    478/sshd
tcp 0 0 router:domain       *:*    LISTEN    472/named
tcp 0 0 www:domain          *:*    LISTEN    472/named
tcp 0 0 localhost:domain    *:*    LISTEN    472/named
tcp 0 0 *:linuxconf         *:*    LISTEN    444/inetd
tcp 0 0 *:imap2             *:*    LISTEN    444/inetd
tcp 0 0 *:pop-3             *:*    LISTEN    444/inetd
tcp 0 0 *:ftp               *:*    LISTEN    444/inetd
tcp 0 0 *:sunrpc            *:*    LISTEN    344/portmap
```

Now complete Exercise 4.1 to gain experience monitoring running daemons.

EXERCISE 4.1

Listing Daemons

To see what a daemons are running in your system, perform the following steps:

1. Run the ps command on a Linux system, and identify the running daemons.

2. Run the netstat command on a Linux system, and identify the running daemons and those that will be started by inetd.

Most services can be configured to run either continuously or only when started by inetd. However, performance considerations dictate that some services should run continuously. For example, the secure shell service (SSH) must compute a cryptographic key when started. Running SSH under the control of inetd entails running this lengthy computation every time a client connects. It's generally better to run SSH continuously so that clients will obtain speedy service.

Controlling Daemons

Red Hat Linux includes a script for each installed daemon. The script can do the following:

- start the daemon

- stop the daemon

- restart the daemon

- display status information pertaining to the daemon

The scripts that perform these functions are stored in the /etc/rc.d/init.d directory. Not all scripts in that directory pertain to continuously running daemons. For example, some daemons that are started by inetd may have scripts in that directory. Similarly, some scripts in the directory pertain to system startup tasks rather than daemons. You can generally distinguish scripts that control daemons by their names, which are similar to the names of daemons listed in Tables 4.2 and 4.3. You can also inspect the script for comments that explain its purpose.

Starting a Daemon

To start a daemon, take the following steps:

1. Move to the /etc/rc.d/init.d directory.

2. Issue the command

   ./*xxx* start

   where *xxx* is the name of the file associated with the daemon.

3. Check the system log, /var/log/messages, for error messages.

Stopping a Daemon

To stop a daemon, take the following steps:

1. Move to the /etc/rc.d/init.d directory.

2. Issue the command

   ./*xxx* stop

   where *xxx* is the name of the file associated with the daemon.

3. Check the system log, /var/log/messages, for error messages.

Restarting a Daemon

To restart a daemon, take the following steps:

1. Move to the /etc/rc.d/init.d directory.

2. Issue the command

   ./*xxx* restart

   where *xxx* is the name of the file associated with the daemon.

3. Check the system log, /var/log/messages, for error messages.

Some daemons, such as nfsd, may sometimes not restart properly. In such a case, you may prefer to stop and then start the daemon.

Displaying a Daemon's Status

To display a daemon's status information, take the following steps:

1. Move to the /etc/rc.d/init.d directory.

2. Issue the command

   ./*xxx* status

   where *xxx* is the name of the file associated with the daemon.

Now, complete Exercise 4.2 to explore the status of running daemons.

EXERCISE 4.2

Controlling Daemons

To gain experience controlling daemons, perform the following steps:

1. Use the instructions in the previous sections to display the status of daemons running on a Linux system.

2. If the Linux system provides non-critical services, then stop, start, and restart a service that no one is using.

In Red Hat Linux 6.2, it's no longer necessary to move to the /etc/rc.d/init.d directory to issue a command to control a service. Instead, issue a command of the form: service *daemon operation*. The argument daemon identifies the /etc/rc.d/init.d file associated with the daemon and the argument operation specifies the operation you want to perform, such as start or stop.

Summary

In this chapter, you learned the fundamentals of TCP/IP networking and services. The most important topics covered are:

IP Addresses TCP/IP hosts are known by IP addresses, which are normally expressed using dotted quad notation. IP addresses consist of a network address and a host address.

Network Classes The Internet authority assigns blocks of IP addresses based on a requested network class that reflects the number of hosts in the network.

Subnetting and Supernetting A netmask can be used to specify a network address that is not an even multiple of eight bits in length.

Host Names TCP/IP hosts are generally referred to by their host names, which are easier to recall than IP numbers. A host name that includes a domain name is said to be a fully qualified domain name (FQDN).

The TCP/IP Family of Protocols   TCP/IP can be thought of as consisting of four protocol layers: network access, Internet, transport, and application. The most important Internet protocols are IP and ICMP. The most important transport protocols are UDP and TCP.

TCP/IP Services   Services are associated with ports, which can be privileged or nonprivileged. Certain ports are well-known and listed in the file `/etc/services`. Services can be provided by the kernel or by a daemon, which can run continuously or be started on demand by the `inetd` service. You can control Red Hat Linux TCP/IP services by using scripts that reside in `/etc/rc.d/init.d`.

Key Terms

Before going on to the next chapter, be sure you're familiar with the following terms:

background process

broadcast message

connection-oriented protocol

connectionless protocol

daemons

default route

domain name

dotted quad notation

dynamic IP address

dynamic routing

fully qualified domain name (FQDN)

gateway

host address

host name

hosts

Internet super server

IP address

loopback address

netmask

network address

network class

non-privileged ports

octets

port

privileged port

router

service

static IP address

static routing

subnetting

supernetting

TCP

top-level domain name

UDP

unreliable protocol

well-known ports

Additional Sources of Information

If you'd like further information about the topics presented in this chapter, you should consult the following sources:

- *TCP/IP 24seven*, Gary Govanus (Sybex, 1999)

- *Network+ Study Guide*, David Groth, with Ben Bergersen and Tim Catura-Houser (Sybex, 1999)

Review Questions

1. Why is IP considered an unreliable protocol?

   A. Because higher-level protocols perform error control.

   B. Because it includes no error checking.

   C. Because it includes no error recovery.

   D. Because it uses unreliable hardware protocols.

2. Which of the following apply to a dynamic IP address?

   A. It is always assigned at boot time.

   B. It is assigned to a host by the Internet authority.

   C. It may belong to one host today and another tomorrow.

   D. It overcomes routing obstacles.

3. What is the combination of a host name and domain name known as?

   A. A full host name

   B. A fully qualified domain name

   C. A fully qualified host name

   D. A host name

4. Which of the following network classes provides the largest number of hosts in a single network?

   A. Class A

   B. Class B

   C. Class C

   D. Class D

5. Which statement applies to port 23?

   A. It is a dynamic port.

   B. It is a nonprivileged port.

   C. It is a privileged port.

   D. It is a well-known port.

6. Which of the following can provide a TCP/IP service?

   A. A continuously running daemon

   B. A daemon started when needed

   C. The kernel

   D. A pseudo-tty

Answers to Review Questions

1. A, B, C. IP has no error checking or recovery; TCP adds these functions.

2. C. A dynamic IP address is generally assigned when a network connection is made. It is taken from a pool of IP addresses designated by a system administrator.

3. B, D. A host name with an explicit domain name is known as a fully qualified domain name or a host name.

4. A. A class A network has an 8-bit network address and supports over 16 million network hosts.

5. C, D. Port 23 is a privileged port associated with the `telnet` service.

6. A, B, C. A service can be provided by the kernel, a continuously running daemon, or a daemon started by `inetd` when needed.

Chapter

5

History of Linux

RHCE PREPARATION TOPICS COVERED IN THIS CHAPTER:

✓ Know the history of Linux.

✓ Know the history of the GNU project.

✓ Understand the characteristics of Open Source Software.

✓ Know the history of Red Hat Linux.

✓ Understand the main characteristics of Red Hat Linux.

✓ Know how to locate and use important Linux resources.

his chapter describes the history of Unix and Linux, the GNU project, Open Source Software, and Red Hat Linux. It explains the nature and characteristics of Open Source Software. It also describes important Linux resources and explains how to access them. Some folks find history boring. If you're one of them, you're welcome to skip this chapter. But, bear in mind that the RHCE exam is likely to include some questions on the history of Linux. If you plan on taking the RHCE exam, you should be familiar with the history of Linux and the history of Red Hat Linux in particular.

Unix

Though a recent arrival to the operating system scene, Linux has a sterling pedigree as a child of Unix, perhaps the most influential operating system. To fully understand Linux, you need to know something of the history of its parent.

In the 1960s, AT&T's Bell Labs partnered with the Massachusetts Institute of Technology (MIT) and General Electric in developing a multiuser computer operating system known as Multics. Two Bell Labs researchers—Dennis Ritchie and Ken Thompson—worked on this project until Bell Labs withdrew from the project.

During the Multics project, Ritchie and Thompson had amused themselves by playing Space Travel, an early multiuser computer game that ran under Multics. Following Bell Labs' withdrawal from the project, they could no longer relieve job stress by hopping around the galaxy. They determined to resolve this by rehosting Space Travel to run on a little-used DEC PDP-7 computer available to them.

This new project required them to implement a new operating system for the PDP-7, which they called *Unics* as a pun on *Multics*. Not being the most careful spellers, they somehow eventually changed the name of the operating system to Unix. One of the unique features of Unix was that Ritchie and Thompson had implemented it using Ritchie's new programming language, C. Implementing Unix in C made it possible to port Unix to other computers more easily than previous operating systems, which were usually written in assembly language.

When word of their work reached others, Ritchie and Thompson began to receive requests for copies of Unix. Whether the requestors were primarily interested in operating system research or Space Travel is an open question. In any case, Unix was widely distributed, especially to universities. Computer scientists and students the world over studied Unix, found ways to improve it, and sent their code back to Ritchie and Thompson, who incorporated it into Unix. As a result, Unix rapidly grew and improved, becoming one of the most important computer operating systems.

The GNU Project and the Free Software Foundation

In the early 1980s, AT&T began to recognize the commercial value of Unix. Consequently, they asserted proprietary rights to it and began charging a substantial license fee. Many who had contributed code to Unix believed that AT&T had unfairly appropriated their contributions. Not content merely to whine, MIT researcher Richard Stallman launched the *GNU* (GNU is not Unix) project, which focused on creating a Unix-like operating system that could be freely distributed. As a vehicle in support of the GNU, Stallman and others created the *Free Software Foundation (FSF)* in 1984.

The FSF promotes free software, but free software is not necessarily cost free software. The FSF intends the word *free* in the sense of *freedom*. Free software is software with which you can do the following:

- Use for any purpose

- Study to learn how it works, and adapt to meet your needs

- Copy and redistribute

- Distribute as part of an improved software system

As a practical matter, these freedoms require access to the software's source code, which is why some refer to *Open Source Software (OSS)*, rather than free software. The Apache Web server and Linux are, in the opinion of many, the most significant OSS products created to date.

The GNU General Public License (GPL)

Perhaps the most significant contribution of the GNU project is a license known as the GNU General Public License or simply the *GNU Public License (GPL)*. The GPL is a form of copyright, known as *copyleft*, designed to protect—not preclude—rights to use, study, copy, and distribute software. Essentially, the GPL provides that a user has the right to use a software program as long as the user doesn't attempt to impair others' rights to use it. The full text of the current version of the GPL is on the companion CD.

The Linux Kernel

In the early days of Unix, universities used Unix as a vehicle for teaching computer science students about operating systems. When AT&T asserted its proprietary claim to Unix, universities needed a replacement. Andrew Tannenbaum created a Unix-like operating system called *MINIX*, which became popular as a teaching tool. However, unlike Unix, MINIX was designed primarily as a pedagogical tool and performed relatively poorly.

In 1990, Finnish computer science student Linus Torvalds began work on a memory manager for Intel-architecture PCs. At some point he realized that his work could be extended to operate as a Unix *kernel*. In August 1991, he posted his work-in-progress to the Internet newsgroup comp.os.minix, inviting others to request features to be considered for implementation:

```
From: torvalds@klaava.Helsinki.FI (Linus Benedict Torvalds)
    Newsgroups: comp.os.minix
    Subject: What would you like to see most in minix?
    Summary: small poll for my new operating system
    Message-ID: <1991Aug25.205708.9541@klaava.Helsinki.FI>
    Date: 25 Aug 91 20:57:08 GMT
    Organization: University of Helsinki
```

```
Hello everybody out there using minix -
I'm doing a (free) operating system (just a hobby, won't be big
and professional like gnu) for 386(486) AT clones. This has been
brewing since april, and is starting to get ready. I'd like any
feedback on things people like/dislike in minix, as my OS
resembles it somewhat(same physical layout of the file-system (due
to practical reasons)among other things).
I've currently ported bash(1.08) and gcc(1.40), and things seem to
work. This implies that I'll get something practical within a few
months, and I'd like to know what features most people would want.
Any suggestions are welcome, but I won't promise I'll implement
them :-)
Linus (torvalds@kruuna.helsinki.fi)
PS. Yes - it's free of any minix code, and it has a multi-threaded fs.
It is NOT protable [sic](uses 386 task switching etc), and it
probably never will support anything other than AT-harddisks, as
that's all I have :-(.
```

Torvalds called his operating system kernel Linux, for Linus's Minix. Unix programmers eagerly offered help in developing Linux. Because Stallman's GNU project had completed almost all of the components needed for its Unix-like operating system except the kernel, Linux and GNU were a natural marriage. In 1994, about three years after Torvalds's posting, Linux 1.0 was released under the terms of the GPL. Already, Linux had about 100,000 users.

NOTE Because GNU was—and remains today—important to the development of Linux, many like to refer to Linux as *GNU/Linux.*

Linux kernels are numbered using an even/odd system. An even-numbered kernel—for example, Linux 2.2—is called a called *stable kernel.* Changes are generally made to a stable kernel only to fix bugs and problems. An odd-numbered kernel—for example, Linux 2.3—is called a *development kernel.* Development kernels are works-in-progress and sometimes contain bugs, some of which are serious. Most Linux users work with stable kernels, reserving spare computers for testing development kernels. At the time of the writing of this book, Linux 2.2 is the latest stable kernel.

Red Hat Linux

When Linux was first made available, setting up a working Linux system was quite a chore. However, Linux fans soon created *Linux distributions*, suites of software that made it relatively easy to install, configure, and use Linux. Two of the most popular early distributions were Soft Landing Systems (SLS) and Slackware; Slackware is still available today.

Red Hat, Inc. was founded in 1994 by Bob Young and Marc Ewing. Soon thereafter, in 1995, Red Hat, Inc. created a Linux distribution called Red Hat Linux. Unlike other distributions at that time, Red Hat Linux was a package-based distribution, meaning that component programs were contained in package files that also contained information describing the programs. A utility program called the Red Hat Package Manager (RPM) was used to install packages. Because it maintained a database describing installed packages, RPM made it simple to update a Linux system, a crucial capability in view of the rapid rate of change of Linux software. Today, almost every Linux distribution is package based; the majority of Linux distributions use RPM as their package manager.

Red Hat Linux is the dominant Linux distribution. It has won *Infoworld* awards for three consecutive years, an unprecedented achievement. Red Hat, Inc., the company founded by Young and Ewing, is now a publicly traded corporation with a capitalized value in the billions. In addition to Red Hat Linux, the company offers services such as telephone support, on-site consulting, developer training, certification programs, and priority access updates.

Linux Resources

Linux improves daily, so keeping up with Linux requires having—and using—access to information that's updated daily. This section lists some Web sites and newsgroups that will help you stay current with the Linux scene.

Linux Information

- Groups of Linux Users Everywhere (GLUE), `www.linuxjournal.com/glue`

- Linux Documentation Project, `metalab.unc.edu/LDP`

- Linux HOWTOs, `howto.tucows.com`

- Linux International, `www.li.org`

- Linux Knowledge Base, `linuxkb.cheek.com`
- Linux OnLine, `www.linux.org`
- Linux Start, `www.linuxstart.com`
- Linux.com, `www.linux.com`
- Red Hat, Inc., `www.redhat.com`

Major Linux Distributors

- Caldera Systems, Inc., `www.caldera.com`
- Corel, `www.corellinux.com`
- Debian GNU-Linux, `www.debian.org`
- Linux Mandrake, `www.mandrake.com`
- Red Hat, Inc., `www.redhat.com`
- Slackware, `www.cdrom.com`
- Storm Linux, `www.stormlinux.com`
- SuSE, `www.suse.com`
- TurboLinux, `www.turbolinux.com`

Other Linux Vendors

- ASL, Inc., `www.aslab.com`
- Cheap Bytes, `www.cheapbytes.com`
- Infomagic, `www.infomagic.com`
- Linux Central, `www.linuxcentral.com`
- Linux General Store, `www.linuxgeneralstore.com`
- Linux Mall, `www.linuxmall.com`
- Linux System Labs, `www.lsl.com`
- LinuxCare, `www.linuxcare.com`
- VA Linux Systems, `www.valinux.com`

Linux News

- FileWatcher, filewatcher.org
- Freshmeat, www.freshmeat.net
- Kernel Traffic, kt.linuxcare.com
- Linux Gazette, www.ssc.com/lg
- Linux Information HQ, www.linuxhq.com
- Linux Journal, www.linuxjournal.com
- Linux Kernel, www.kernel.org
- Linux Magazine, www.linux-mag.com
- Linux Radio Show, www.linuxradio.net
- Linux Show, www.thelinuxshow.com
- Linux Today, linuxtoday.com/index.html
- Linux Weekly News, www.lwn.net
- Linux World, www.linuxworld.com
- Linux-2000 Online, www.linux-2000.org
- Slashdot, www.slashdot.org

Linux Newsgroups

- comp.os.linux.announce (moderated)
- comp.os.linux.answers
- comp.os.linux.hardware
- comp.os.linux.misc
- comp.os.linux.setup
- comp.os.linux.x

Summary

In this chapter, you learned about the history of Linux, the GNU project, and Open Source Software. You also learned about the features of Red Hat Linux and where to go to get more information about Linux. The most important topics covered are:

Unix   Linux is based on concepts originally implemented by Dennis Ritchie and Ken Thompson of AT&T in their Unix operating system.

GNU and FSF   Richard Stallman founded the FSF and the GNU Project to ensure software freedom. The goal of the GNU project was to create a free, Unix-like operating system.

GPL   The GNU General Public License is a form of copyright that protects software freedoms, including the rights to use, modify, and distribute software.

Linux   Linux is a Unix-like operating system distributed under terms of the GPL. Linux includes a kernel originally created by Linus Torvalds and utilities and programs originally created by the GNU Project.

Red Hat Linux   Red Hat, Inc. distributes Red Hat Linux, the leading Linux distribution.

Key Terms

Before going on to the next chapter, be sure you're familiar with the following terms:

copyleft

development kernel

FSF (Free Software Foundation)

GNU

GPL (General Public License)

kernel

Linux distributions

OSS (Open Source Software)

stable kernel

Review Questions

1. Which of the following is an operating system ancestor of Linux?

   A. C

   B. GNU

   C. Solaris

   D. Unix

2. Which of the following was the principal author of the Linux kernel?

   A. Dennis Ritchie

   B. Andrew Tannenbaum

   C. Ken Thompson

   D. Linus Torvalds

3. Which of the following was the founder of the Free Software Foundation and the GNU project?

   A. Marc Ewing

   B. Richard Stallman

   C. Linus Torvalds

   D. Bob Young

4. Which of the following version numbers would denote a stable Linux kernel?

   A. 1.1

   B. 1.2

   C. 2.1

   D. 2.2

5. Which of the following characteristics made Red Hat Linux superior to other Linux distributions?

A. Cost

B. Efficiency

C. Maintainability

D. Scalability

6. Linux was originally implemented for what type of computer?

A. Intel 286

B. Intel 386/486

C. Intel Pentium

D. Motorola 68000

Answers to Review Questions

1. D. C and GNU are not operating systems, although GNU is intended to someday be one. Solaris is not an ancestor of Linux.

2. D. Linus Torvalds, a Finnish computer science student, wrote the original Linux kernel.

3. B. Richard Stallman, a former MIT researcher, founded the FSF and the GNU project.

4. B, D. The decimal part of the version number is even for a stable kernel and odd for a development kernel.

5. C. Packages made Red Hat Linux more maintainable than other Linux distributions, because it was simpler to update the system.

6. B. Linus Torvalds implemented Linux for the Intel 386/486.

Installation

PART

II

Chapter

6

Installation Planning

RHCE PREPARATION TOPICS COVERED IN THIS CHAPTER:

- ✓ Understand the importance of determining system needs.
- ✓ Know what information may be required during installation.
- ✓ Know how to select the installation user interface.
- ✓ Know how to select the installation class and type.
- ✓ Know how to design a partition structure.
- ✓ Know how to use fips to split an MS-DOS partition.
- ✓ Know how to select and prepare installation media.
- ✓ Know how to select installation media.
- ✓ Know how to select components and packages.

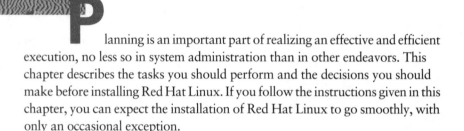

Planning is an important part of realizing an effective and efficient execution, no less so in system administration than in other endeavors. This chapter describes the tasks you should perform and the decisions you should make before installing Red Hat Linux. If you follow the instructions given in this chapter, you can expect the installation of Red Hat Linux to go smoothly, with only an occasional exception.

Determining Needs

The first step in installation planning is to determine the needs that the system must satisfy. For example, a worker who will use the system as a workstation for preparing graphics will have a different set of needs than a system administrator who plans to use the system primarily as an FTP server. Once you know what the system must do, you're ready to decide what hardware is needed and how Red Hat Linux should be installed and configured.

Gathering Information

Installation will go more smoothly if you've collected information about the hardware on the target system. If you have the flexibility to choose the hardware, choose hardware that's listed in the Red Hat Hardware Compatibility List (HCL) over other hardware. Be wary of devices, such as CD-ROM drives, that have proprietary interfaces. Also be wary of WinModems and WinPrinters.

Before beginning the installation, have the following information handy:

- CPU: type and speed.

- Motherboard: bus types (ISA, EISA, VESA, PCI, MCA, and so on).

- Drive controllers: the type of interface and the chipset used.

- Drives: the make and model of each drive and its drive number or SCSI ID on the controller.

- System RAM: size.

- Network adapters: the make and model. For non-PCI cards, know the IRQ, DMA, and I/O ports used.

- Modems: the IRQ, DMA, and I/O ports used by an internal modem or the number of the serial port to which an external modem is connected.

- Sound cards: make and model, the IRQs, DMAs, and I/O ports used.

- Serial and parallel ports: the IRQs and I/O ports used.

- Mouse: type (serial, PS2, or bus) and number of buttons. For a serial mouse, know the number of the serial port to which it's connected.

- Video card: make, model, chipset, amount of RAM, and color depths supported.

- Monitor: make, model, horizontal sync range, and vertical sync range.

You should have similar information for any other hardware devices installed in the system.

If your system will be attached to a network, you should have the following information available:

- Method of IP address assignment: static, DHCP, BOOTP.

For statically defined hosts, you should have the following information available:

- IP address

- Netmask

- Gateways

- Fully qualified domain name (FQDN)

In some circumstances, additional information will be needed. But, generally, this information will be enough to let you complete the installation procedure. Once the installation procedure is complete, you can configure special options as needed.

In addition to information on the hardware of the target system, you should have available the *Red Hat Linux Installation Guide* and other Linux documentation, particularly the HOWTOs. If necessary, you can use another Linux system or a Microsoft Windows system to read documentation stored on the documentation CD-ROM or to access Web sites and newsgroups that provide pertinent information. Having this information available will help you complete the installation procedure; otherwise, you may find it necessary to terminate the installation procedure, obtain the needed information, and then restart the installation.

Selecting the Installation User Interface

Red Hat Linux supports two *installation types*: Install and Upgrade. You should choose Install when installing Linux on a target system that doesn't currently host Red Hat Linux. Choose Upgrade when the target system already hosts an earlier version of Red Hat Linux. The Upgrade procedure saves the existing configuration files, rather than overwriting them. The existing files are renamed with the extension `.rpmsave`.

Red Hat Linux 6.1 introduced a *graphical mode installation procedure* based on X. The initial screen of the installation procedure lets you choose the new graphical mode installation procedure or a *text mode installation procedure*.

Beginners generally find the graphical mode installation procedure easier to use. However, you may prefer the text mode installation for the following reasons:

- The graphical mode installation procedure may fail if the target system has unusual video characteristics, such as an old or uncommon video adapter.

- The text mode installation procedure can recover from some errors—such as running out of disk space—that cause the graphical mode installation procedure to fail.

- The text mode installation will run better and faster than the graphical mode installation on computers having a slow processor or a small amount of RAM.

- The graphical mode installation supports only media mounted as a file system, such as an existing hard drive partition, a CD-ROM, or media made available via NFS.

Selecting the Installation Class

The Red Hat Linux installation procedure provides three default *installation classes* or configurations:

- GNOME Workstation
- KDE Workstation
- Server

The workstation classes are a quick way to get a Red Hat Linux system up and running. Both workstation classes install the most commonly used packages. In addition, the GNOME Workstation class installs the GNOME desktop manager, and the KDE Workstation class installs the KDE desktop manager.

The workstation classes are particularly useful for building a dual-boot system, because they disturb no non-Linux partitions as long as sufficient unallocated disk space is available. They do, however, delete all existing Linux (`ext2`) partitions. They establish three standard partitions:

- A 64MB swap partition
- A 16MB boot partition (`/boot`)
- A *root partition* (`/`) that uses the remaining free disk space

Both workstation installation classes require about 600MB of free disk space.

In contrast to the workstation classes, the Server installation class deletes all existing partitions, including DOS/Windows partitions. The Server installation class requires about 1.6GB of disk space. By default, a Server installation lacks the following components, which are included in one or the other of the workstation installations:

- Author/Publishing
- DOS/Windows connectivity
- GNOME or KDE
- Graphics manipulation
- Multimedia support
- X Window system

However, a Server installation includes the following components, which are not included in one or the other of the workstation installations:

- Anonymous FTP server
- DNS name server
- IPX/NetWare connectivity
- NFS server
- Network management workstation
- News server
- Postgres (SQL) server
- SMB (Samba) server
- Web server

A Server installation creates a more elaborate partition structure, including:

- A 64MB swap partition
- A 16MB boot partition (`/boot`)
- A 256MB root partition (`/`)
- A 256MB `/var` partition

Two further partitions split the remaining free disk space equally:

- `/home`
- `/usr`

If neither the workstation classes nor the Server installation class meets your needs, you can specify a Custom installation. The Custom installation class has no predefined characteristics. You can partition hard disk drives and install components and packages as you choose.

Partitioning the Hard Disk

If you select either of the workstation installation classes or the Server installation class, the installation procedure partitions your hard disk drive automatically. However, if you select the Custom installation class, you must partition the hard disk.

Partitions improve system data integrity and can improve system data security. If a hard disk suffers damage, the damage is often confined to a single partition. Recovery of a single partition may be simpler and quicker than recovery of an entire drive. It's also possible to mount partitions as read only. By organizing data that need not be changed as a partition and mounting the partition as read only, data integrity and security can be improved. A partition that cannot be written is less vulnerable to corruption than one mounted for reading and writing. And, it's more difficult for a hacker to surreptitiously modify data on a read-only partition than on a read-write partition.

In designing a partition structure, the following directories should be kept in a single partition:

- /
- /etc
- /lib
- /bin
- /sbin
- /dev

These directories—and their subdirectories—contain programs and files essential to proper system operation. They should always be present and therefore should be part of the so-called root partition, mounted as /.

The non-Custom installation classes create a 16MB boot partition, mounted as /**boot**. Generally, your design should include such a partition. By locating a boot partition within the 1024-cylinder region that is addressable by the system's BIOS, you ensure that the kernel will be accessible at boot time.

Generally, you should include one or more swap partitions. As a rule of thumb, the swap partitions should have a total size that is 2–3 times that of the installed RAM. For example, a system having 16MB of RAM should have 32–48MB of swap space. No more than eight swap partitions can be defined; the total swap space cannot exceed 4GB.

Directories that are often made mount points of separate partitions include:

- /home
- /opt
- /tmp

- /usr

- /usr/local

- /var

To apply your understanding of partitions to a practical problem, complete Exercise 6.1.

EXERCISE 6.1

Designing a Partition Structure

Design a partition structure for a system having two disk drives, each with a 5GB capacity. Provide at least 1GB of space for users' home directories and 2GB of space for commercial applications installed under the /opt directory.

Using *fips*

Often, a target system has insufficient free disk space for installing Linux. If an MS-DOS (FAT or FAT32) partition contains unused space, you can use fips to split the partition, creating an empty partition into which you can install Linux.

To use fips, follow these steps:

1. Use scandisk to check the partition for errors.

2. Use defrag to move the files to the low end of the partition.

3. Disable virtual memory by using the System Control Panel applet.

4. Create an MS-DOS boot floppy by using the Add/Remove Programs Control Panel applet.

5. Copy the following files from the installation CD-ROM to the floppy disk:

   - \dosutils\fips20\restorrb.exe

   - \dosutils\fips20\fips.exe

   - \dosutils\fips20\errors.txt

6. Rename `autoxec.bat` and `config.sys` to `autoexec.fips` and `config.fips`, respectively, so that no startup programs will write to the hard disk.

7. Boot from the floppy, and run `fips`.

8. Let `fips` create a backup of the partition table on the floppy.

9. Specify the number of the partition you want to split and the number of the cylinder on which the new partition should begin.

10. Type y to save changes, and exit.

11. Boot MS-DOS, and run `scandisk` to make sure the disk is okay.

12. Re-enable virtual memory, and restore your `autoexec.bat` and `config.sys` files to their original names.

See the `fips` documentation on the installation CD-ROM for further information.

To gain experience with `fips`, complete Exercise 6.2.

EXERCISE 6.2

Using *fips*

Use `fips` to split an MS-DOS partition into two partitions. Be sure to back up any important files or programs before using `fips`.

Selecting and Preparing Boot Media

In order to install Red Hat Linux, you must boot the target system using a special Linux kernel. You can boot the system from the installation CD-ROM or from a floppy disk you create from files on the CD-ROM. This section explains these alternatives so that you can have the proper materials on hand when you begin the installation.

Booting from the Installation CD-ROM

Most recently manufactured PCs can boot from a CD-ROM that contains appropriate boot information, such as that contained on the Red Hat Linux installation CD-ROM. To boot from a CD-ROM, the system BIOS must specify that the system will attempt to boot from the CD-ROM before attempting to boot from a hard disk drive or a floppy disk drive. Generally, this BIOS setting is labeled Boot Sequence or something similar.

If the system is set up to boot DOS, you may be able to boot by using the files on the CD-ROM, even if the system cannot boot from its CD-ROM. The file `dosutils/autoboot.bat` invokes the Linux `loadlin` program, which uses DOS system calls to boot a Linux kernel residing on a hard disk or CD-ROM drive.

To use `autoboot.bat`, boot the system into DOS, not Microsoft Windows. If the system runs Microsoft Windows, restart the system in MS-DOS mode by using the Shut Down dialog box. When the system enters DOS, move to the drive associated with the CD-ROM. Then, launch the boot sequence by issuing the command

```
dosutils/autoboot.bat
```

The system should load and execute the Linux kernel.

DOS must be set up to allow access to the CD-ROM or this procedure will fail. Sometimes Microsoft Windows systems have driver problems or virus infections that prevent access to the CD-ROM. You must correct such a condition in order to initiate the boot sequence.

To gain experience booting Red Hat Linux, complete Exercise 6.3.

EXERCISE 6.3

Booting from a CD-ROM

1. Boot a system from the Red Hat Linux CD-ROM.

2. Boot a system using the `autoboot.bat` file.

Booting from a Boot Floppy Disk

If you can't boot the system from a CD-ROM, and the system isn't set up to boot DOS, you must prepare a boot floppy disk from which to boot the system. This is most easily done using a Linux system to copy the *image file* on the CD-ROM to a floppy disk. An image file contains an exact replica of a floppy disk. By copying the image file to a disk, you create a duplicate of the disk that was used to make the image file.

Mount the Red Hat Linux installation CD-ROM by issuing the command

`mount -t iso9660 /dev/cdrom /mnt/cdrom -o ro`

Place a formatted floppy disk in the floppy drive and issue the command

`dd if=/mnt/cdrom/images/boot.img of=/dev/fd0H1440 obs=18k`

It may take a minute or so to write the image to the floppy disk. When activity ceases, remove the disk, which can now be used to boot the target system.

If you plan to install Linux via the network rather than from a CD-ROM, copy the image file bootnet.img, rather than boot.img.

If you need to access PCMCIA devices during installation, you'll need a second floppy disk. Use a similar command to create a floppy disk from the file pcmcia.img.

If you don't have handy access to a Linux system, you can make a floppy from an image file by using the DOS program rawrite, which resides in the dosutils directory of the CD-ROM. The rawrite program can be run from DOS or from a Microsoft Windows MS-DOS Prompt window. The program prompts for the letter of the drive containing the floppy disk (usually a:) and for the path of the image file (usually d:\images\boot.img).

To gain experience creating boot floppies, complete Exercise 6.4.

EXERCISE 6.4

Making Boot Floppies

1. Use the dd command to make a boot floppy.

2. Use rawrite to make a boot floppy.

Selecting Installation Media

Most users install Red Hat Linux from an installation CD-ROM. However, if you frequently install Linux, you may prefer to set up a server that makes the installation files available via a network. You can access Red Hat Linux installation files via the following methods:

- FTP

- NFS

- HTTP

You can also access installation files residing on a local hard drive. However, Red Hat Linux does not currently support installation via files shared by a Samba server.

Selecting Components and Packages

Red Hat Linux combines related programs, configuration files, and data files into a unit known as a *package*, which is contained in a single file. By treating a package as a unit, Red Hat Linux makes it relatively simple to install, update, or uninstall programs. Packages contain *dependency information* that identifies programs or libraries that are needed for proper operation. In general, Red Hat Linux will not let you install a package unless the package's dependencies are satisfied. This helps ensure that installed programs operate correctly.

During the installation procedure, specify the packages to be installed on the target system. You can specify the packages in one of several ways:

- By choosing the option Everything, which specifies that every available package should be installed. If you're installing from the installation CD-ROM, you should not generally choose this option because it will install many packages that you're unlikely to use.

- By choosing components from a list. A *component* is a set of related packages. For example, the GNOME component consists of over three dozen packages that are necessary or useful to the GNOME desktop manager.

- By choosing individual packages from a list. This gives you a high level of control over the packages that are installed.

Generally, the most convenient approach is to choose desired components, then select or deselect individual packages as desired. Components are defined only within the installation procedure. Red Hat Linux provides no mechanism for installing components after completing the installation procedure. Once the installation procedure is complete, you must install individual packages rather than components. However, you can discover the packages that compose a component by inspecting the file `RedHat/base/comps` on the installation CD-ROM. Following is a list of the components defined by Red Hat Linux 6.2.

- Anonymous FTP server
- Authoring/Publishing
- Base
- Development
- Dial-up workstation
- DNS name server
- DOS/Windows connectivity
- Emacs
- Games
- GNOME
- Graphics manipulation
- IPX/NetWare compatibility
- KDE
- Kernel development
- Mail/WWW/News tools
- Multimedia support
- Network management workstation
- Networked workstation
- News server
- NFS server
- Postgres (SQL) server

- Printer support

- SMB (Samba) server

- Utilities

- Web server

- X Window system

The `rpm` program makes it easy to install packages after installation is complete. So, it's not crucial to select exactly the right components or packages during installation.

Summary

In this chapter, you learned everything you need to know to prepare to install Linux on your system. The most important topics covered are:

Installation Planning Installation will be more effective and efficient if you collect the proper information before beginning the installation.

Installation User Interface Experienced users may prefer the text mode installation user interface to the graphical mode installation user interface, because the text mode installation user interface is more reliable and requires fewer system resources.

Installation Class Red Hat Linux lets you easily create a GNOME or KDE workstation or a server. In addition, you can specify a Custom installation.

Partition Structure You should generally define a swap partition, a boot partition, and a root partition. Defining additional partitions may be useful.

The `fips` Program You can use `fips` to split an MS-DOS partition, gaining free space for the installation of Linux.

Booting Linux You can boot the Linux installation procedure by using the Red Hat Linux installation CD-ROM or by creating a boot floppy from files on the CD-ROM.

Installation Files   The installation procedure can access installation files stored on a CD-ROM disk or hard drive. It can also access files via FTP, HTTP, or NFS.

Selecting Components and Packages   You can select components, which are sets of packages, for installation on the target system. In addition, you can select or deselect individual packages.

Key Terms

Before going on to the next chapter, be sure you're familiar with the following terms:

component

dependency information

graphical mode installation procedure

image file

installation classes

installation types

`loadlin`

package

`rawrite`

root partition

text mode installation procedure

Additional Sources of Information

If you'd like further information about the topics presented in this chapter, you should consult the following sources:

- The *Red Hat Linux Installation Guide,* included on the Red Hat Linux installation CD-ROM

- Documentation files for `fips` and `rawrite`, included on the Red Hat Linux installation CD-ROM

- The *Linux Partition mini HOWTO,* located in the `/usr/doc/HOWTO /mini` directory

Review Questions

1. Which of the following should generally be avoided when choosing hardware for a Red Hat Linux system?

   A. CD-ROM drives with unusual proprietary interfaces

   B. Devices not listed in Tier I or Tier II of the Hardware Compatibility List

   C. WinModems

   D. WinPrinters

2. Which of the following sources of installation media is supported by the installation procedure's graphical mode installation user interface?

   A. FTP

   B. HTTP

   C. NFS

   D. SMB (Samba)

3. Which of the following components is installed by the Server installation class but not by workstation installation classes?

   A. Anonymous FTP

   B. Multimedia Support

   C. NFS Server

   D. SSH Server

4. What is the maximum amount of swap space usable by a Linux system?

   A. 512MB

   B. 1GB

   C. 4GB

   D. 8GB

5. Which of the following servers can provide files needed by the Red Hat Linux installation procedure?

   A. FTP

   B. HTTP

   C. NFS

   D. SMB (Samba)

6. Which command should you use to create a Linux boot floppy?

   A. autoboot

   B. dd

   C. pcmcia

   D. rawrite

Answers to Review Questions

1. A, B, C, D. Problematic CD-ROM drives, WinModems, and WinPrinters will not be listed at Tier 1 or 2 of the Red Hat Linux Hardware Compatibility List.

2. C. Only NFS is supported by the graphical mode installation user interface.

3. A, C. The Server installation class does not install an SSH server; neither does it install Multimedia, which is installed by the workstation classes.

4. C. No more than 4GB of swap space can be accessed by a Linux system.

5. A, B, C. Red Hat Linux does not currently support access to installation files via Samba.

6. B, D. Under Linux, you create the boot floppy using the dd command; under DOS, you create the boot floppy using the rawrite command.

Chapter

7

Installing Red Hat Linux

RHCE PREPARATION TOPICS COVERED IN THIS CHAPTER:

✓ Understand and be able to perform the Red Hat Linux installation procedure.

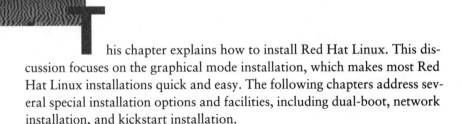

This chapter explains how to install Red Hat Linux. This discussion focuses on the graphical mode installation, which makes most Red Hat Linux installations quick and easy. The following chapters address several special installation options and facilities, including dual-boot, network installation, and kickstart installation.

Installation Overview

This section presents an overview of the Red Hat Linux installation procedure. It explains how to use the installation program's user interfaces, how to view logs that report installation progress, and the sequence of operations performed by the installation procedure.

Installation User Interfaces

The installation program lets you choose between two user interfaces: a graphical mode user interface and a text mode user interface.

Graphical Mode User Interface

The operation of the graphical mode user interface resembles that of familiar point-and-click interfaces:

- You can use the mouse to select a control, such as a button or text field, and to manipulate check boxes and radio buttons.

- If you prefer, you can use the Tab key to move from control to control until you arrive at the control you would like to select.

- You use the keyboard to enter text.

Text Mode User Interface

The text mode user interface is not a command-line interface, but a mouse-less, low-resolution graphical user interface. It includes familiar controls such as text boxes, check boxes, scroll bars, and buttons. Since the text mode interface is mouse-less, you use it somewhat differently from more familiar graphical user interfaces. This interface works in the following ways:

- You use Tab and Alt+Tab to move from control to control.

- You press the spacebar to select or deselect check boxes.

- You use the Left, Right, Up, and Down keys to move the cursor.

- You press Enter or the spacebar to press a highlighted button.

- You press Enter to select an item from a list.

Consoles and Message Logs

The installation program uses the Linux virtual consoles to display a variety of information. Virtual consoles let you associate the keyboard and monitor with any of several tasks, performing in text mode a function that's analogous to using windows in graphical mode. Virtual consoles are handier than having several physical consoles, because they don't require extra desk space and it's easy to switch from one to the other. Table 7.1 summarizes the virtual consoles used during installation.

TABLE 7.1 Virtual Consoles Used during Installation

Console	Keystrokes	Contents
1	Ctrl+Alt+F1	Text-based installation procedure
2	Ctrl+Alt+F2	Shell prompt
3	Ctrl+Alt+F3	Messages from installation program
4	Ctrl+Alt+F4	Kernel messages
5	Ctrl+Alt+F5	Other messages, including file system creation messages
7	Ctrl+Alt+F7	Graphical installation procedure

The indicated keystrokes let you switch to a given console. By switching to a console, you can view messages that can help you diagnose and trouble-shoot installation problems. Console 2 provides a shell prompt that you can use to issue commands to resolve problems.

Overview of the Installation Process

The operations performed by the installation procedure are as follows:

- Starting the installation process

    - Installation mode

    - Language

    - Keyboard

    - Mouse

    - Install media (optional)

    - Install path

- Partitioning and LILO installation (optional)

- Network configuration (optional)

- Setting the time zone

- Specifying authentication options (optional)

- Specifying user accounts

- Selecting packages (optional)

- Configuring the X Windows system (optional)

- Installing packages

- Creating a boot disk (optional)

As you can see, several of these operations are optional. The execution of the optional operations is determined by user choices, detected hardware, and detected installation media. The remaining sections of this chapter describe the installation procedure in detail.

Starting the Installation Process

To start the installation process, you must boot the target system using a special Red Hat Linux installation kernel. You can boot the system in any of several ways, as described in the previous chapter. In order to boot the system, you must provide the proper boot medium (for example, a boot floppy disk).

You must also configure the target system's BIOS to boot from the boot medium. Often, the BIOS is set to boot the system from its internal hard drive and must be reconfigured to boot from a floppy or CD-ROM.

Installation Mode

When the system boots, it displays the Welcome to Red Hat Linux screen, shown in Figure 7.1 This screen lets you select the installation mode: graphical, text, or expert. The graphical mode installation is the easiest to use. The text mode installation is more robust, but somewhat clumsier to use. The expert mode installation suppresses automatic device probes and gives you almost complete control over the installation process. Expert mode is useful primarily when automatic device probes hang a system. Otherwise, it's generally more convenient to use graphical or text mode.

FIGURE 7.1 The Welcome screen

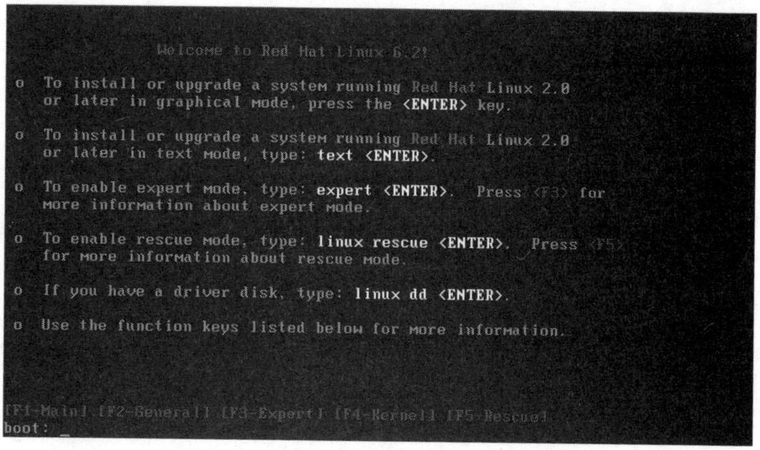

Language

If you selected the graphical mode installation and the installation program detects a Red Hat Linux CD-ROM, it immediately enters graphical mode. Otherwise, the next several screens are presented in text mode even if you selected graphical mode.

The Language Selection screen lets you specify the language in which the installation program displays instructions. Figure 7.2 shows the graphical mode version of this screen; the text mode version is similar in function, even though it differs in appearance.

FIGURE 7.2 The Language Selection screen

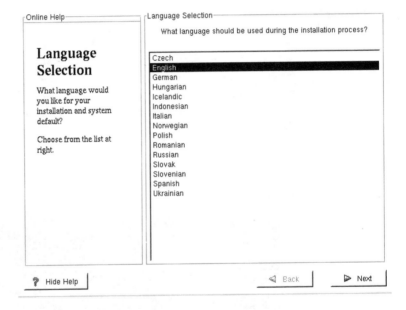

The selected language also becomes the default language used by the target system. Installation options, including the language, can be changed after the installation is complete. Chapter 9, "Configuring Install-Time Options after Installation," explains how to change installation options.

Keyboard

The Keyboard Configuration screen lets you select the system's keyboard type. The graphical mode version of this screen is shown in Figure 7.3. The graphical mode screen lets you test your choice by typing characters in the text box at the bottom of the screen.

FIGURE 7.3   The Keyboard Configuration screen

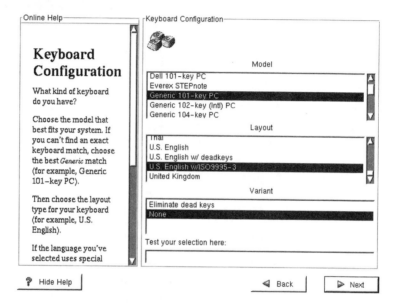

Mouse

The Mouse Configuration screen lets you specify the system's mouse type. The graphical mode version of this screen is shown in Figure 7.4. The Port and Device options are required only for a serial mouse; do not specify them for a PS/2 or bus mouse. If the mouse has two buttons, you should generally specify the Emulate 3 Buttons option. The *three-button mouse emulation* lets you simultaneously press both mouse buttons of a two-button mouse to emulate the pressing of the missing middle mouse button. Use the Generic mouse type if you find no closer match.

FIGURE 7.4 The Mouse Configuration screen

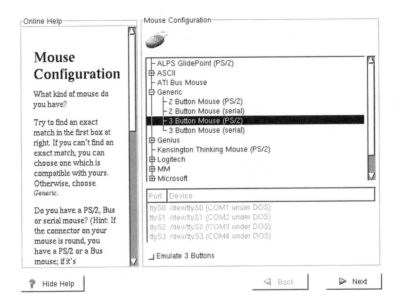

Installation Media

If you selected an installation mode other than graphical or the installation program failed to detect a Red Hat Linux CD-ROM, the Installation Method screen, shown in Figure 7.5, will appear. This screen lets you specify the installation media, which can be a CD-ROM or files on a local hard drive. You can also install Red Hat Linux via FTP, HTTP, or NFS. However, you must use a special boot floppy that supports network installation; Chapter 8, "Advanced Installations," explains network installations.

FIGURE 7.5 The Installation Method screen

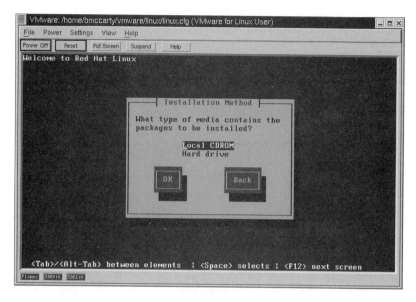

If you selected the graphical mode installation, a second welcome screen, like that shown in Figure 7.6, will appear. This screen contains no options; it merely explains where to find documentation that explains the installation procedure and how to register Red Hat Linux.

FIGURE 7.6 The Welcome to Red Hat Linux screen

Installation Path

Next, you're prompted to select the *installation path*, which defines the type—*Installation* or *Upgrade type*—and class—*GNOME Workstation*, *KDE Workstation*, *Server*, or *Custom*—of the installation. Figure 7.7 shows the graphical version of the Install Path screen, which lets you specify the installation path.

FIGURE 7.7 The Install Path screen

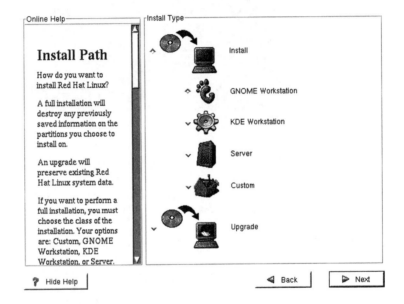

WARNING   If you specify Install rather than Upgrade for the installation type, the installation program will erase all Linux partitions present on the system.

WARNING   If you specify Server for the installation class, the installation program will erase all partitions present on the system, including non-Linux partitions.

TIP   Neither the GNOME Workstation nor KDE Workstation class will overwrite existing non-Linux partitions, unless there is insufficient free disk space available.

Partitioning Hard Disks

If you selected the GNOME Workstation, KDE Workstation, or Server installation class, the installation procedure offers to perform automatic partitioning of the system's hard disks. The graphical mode version of the Automatic Partitioning screen is shown in Figure 7.8.

FIGURE 7.8   The Automatic Partitioning screen

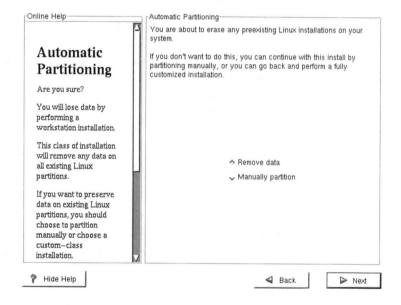

If you prefer to partition the disks manually, check the Manually Partition check box. If you do so, the installation program displays the Partitions screen, which lets you access Disk Druid, Red Hat Linux's partitioning program, or `fdisk`, the standard Linux partitioning program. The graphical version of the Disk Druid screen is shown in Figure 7.9.

FIGURE 7.9 The Partitions screen

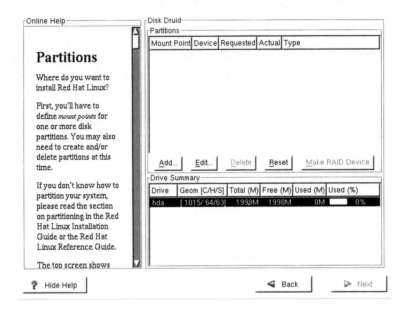

The Partitions screen displays the existing partitions, if any, giving the following information:

Mount Point The directory name at which the device will be mounted. Use the Edit button to specify the mount point. Swap partitions have no mount point.

Device The name of the device on which the partition resides.

Requested The partition's original size. You cannot change the size of a partition; you must delete the partition and add a new one.

Actual The amount of space allocated to the partition.

Type The type of the partition.

The Partitions screen also summarizes the status of each hard disk drive, giving the drive's geometry, total space, free space, and allocated space.

There are buttons that let you add, edit, and delete partitions. Clicking the Reset button returns Disk Druid to its original state. You can use the Make RAID Device button, shown in Figure 7.9 at the bottom right of the Partitions pane, to create a software RAID device.

Clicking the Add button opens a dialog box that lets you add a new partition. The graphical version of this dialog box is shown in Figure 7.10. The dialog box contains the following fields:

Mount Point   Lets you specify the directory at which the partition will be mounted. You shouldn't specify a mount point for a swap partition.

Size   The size of the partition, in MB.

Grow to Fill Disk   Specifies that the partition size should be increased until all available free space is allocated.

Partition Type   The partition type.

Allowable Drives   The drive or drives from which you're willing to let Disk Druid choose in placing the partition.

FIGURE 7.10   The Add Partition dialog box

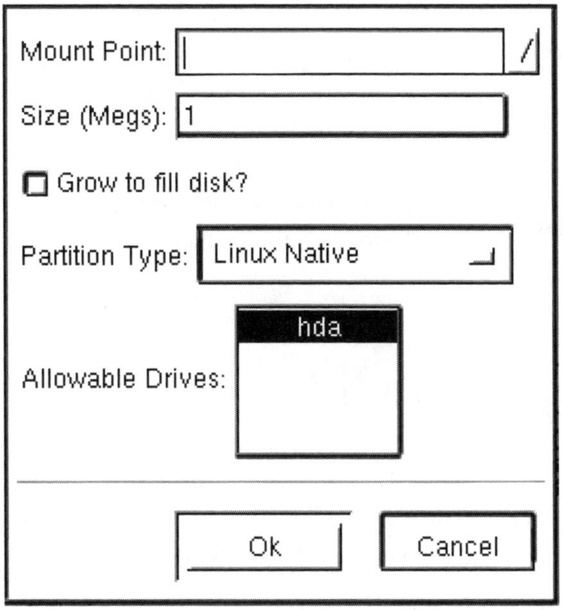

Once the partitions have been automatically or manually established, the installation program displays the Choose Partitions to Format screen, which lets you specify which partitions should be formatted. Figure 7.11 shows the graphical mode version of this screen.

FIGURE 7.11 The Choose Partitions to Format screen

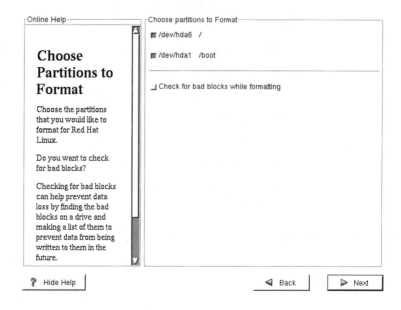

Formatting a partition destroys all the data on the partition. Be sure not to format partitions that contain useful data or programs.

Configuring LILO

If you specified the Custom installation class, the installation program displays the LILO Configuration screen. The graphical mode version of this screen is shown in Figure 7.12.

FIGURE 7.12 The LILO Configuration screen

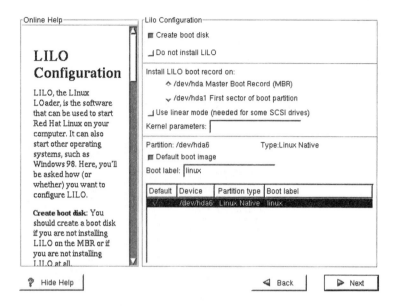

You can use the LILO Configuration screen to specify that the installation program should skip the creation of a boot disk or the installation of LILO. You can also specify whether LILO should be installed on the master boot record (MBR) or on the first sector of the boot partition. Unless the system has a boot manager installed, such as the Windows NT loader or OS/2 boot manager, and you wish to use the boot manager to boot Linux, you should install LILO on the MBR.

The LILO Configuration screen lets you disable use of linear block addressing (LBA); to do so, uncheck the Use Linear Mode check box. The screen also lets you specify parameters to be passed to LILO or the kernel. You might use this capability, for example, if you know that one or more system devices cannot be automatically probed and therefore require kernel parameters.

The LILO Configuration screen lists bootable partitions, and lets you associate a boot label with a partition so that you can boot the partition by using LILO. You can also specify a default partition, which is booted if no partition is specified at boot time.

Network Configuration

If the installation program determines that the system has a network adapter, the installation program displays the Network Configuration screen. The graphical mode version of this screen is shown in Figure 7.13.

FIGURE 7.13 The Network Configuration screen

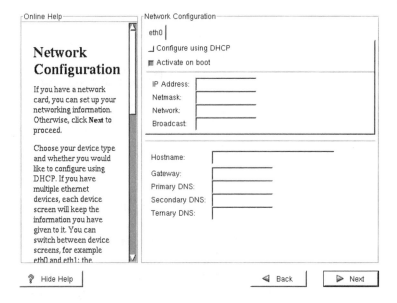

If the system has multiple network adapters, the Network Configuration screen includes tabs that let you choose each adapter. The screen lets you specify the following network configuration information:

Configure Using DHCP   Specifies that network configuration will be obtained from a DHCP server at system startup. If you enable this option, you don't need to specify other network configuration options or parameters.

Activate on Boot   Specifies that networking is enabled on system startup.

IP Address   The static IP address of the system.

Netmask   The static network mask of the system.

Network Address   The static network address of the system.

Broadcast Address   The static broadcast address of the system.

Hostname   The fully qualified domain name (FQDN) of the system.

Gateway   The default gateway used by the system.

Primary, Secondary, and Ternary DNS Servers   One or more DNS servers to be used to resolve host names to IP addresses.

Setting the Time Zone

The Time Zone Selection screen, shown in Figure 7.14, lets you specify the time zone associated with the system's location. You can specify the time zone by using a world map or by specifying an offset from Universal Time (UTC).

FIGURE 7.14   The Time Zone Selection screen

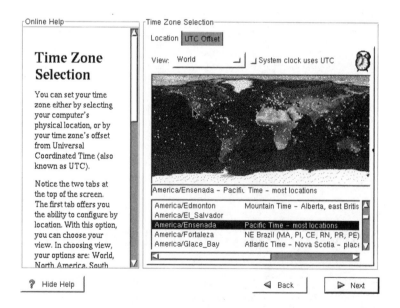

You can specify that the system's clock is set to UTC. However, other operating systems may not support this capability, so be careful about specifying this option if the system is to be configured for dual-booting.

Creating User Accounts

The Account Configuration screen lets you specify the password for the root user. The graphical version of the screen is shown in Figure 7.15. This screen also lets you add other user accounts. For each account, you specify the user id, password, and full name.

FIGURE 7.15 The Account Configuration screen

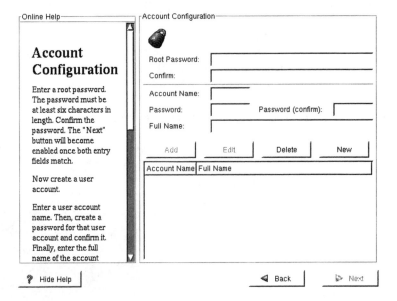

Specifying Authentication Options

If you specified the Custom installation class, the Authentication Configuration screen appears. The graphical mode version of this screen is shown in Figure 7.16.

FIGURE 7.16 The Authentication Configuration screen

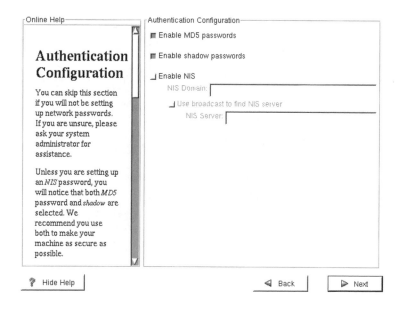

Unless you plan to use network passwords, you can take the default values proposed by the installation program. Otherwise, you must enter an NIS domain. You may also enter an NIS server. You should generally enable MD5 and shadow passwords, as these options improve system security.

Selecting Packages

If you selected the Server or Custom installation class, the Package Group Selection screen appears. The graphical mode version of this screen is shown as Figure 7.17.

FIGURE 7.17 The Package Group Selection screen

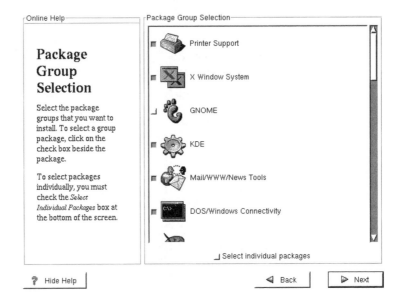

This screen lets you select *package groups* (also known as *components*) for installation. You can also deselect package groups that you don't want to install. To gain greater control over package selection, you can specify the Select Individual Packages option. This causes the Individual Package Selection screen to appear. The graphical version of this screen is shown in Figure 7.18.

FIGURE 7.18 The Individual Package Selection screen

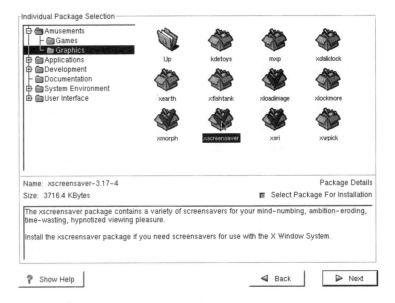

The Individual Package Selection screen lets you select packages to be installed. You can also deselect specific packages. Clicking a package icon causes the installation program to display information about the selected package. The installation program uses the Red Hat Package Manager (RPM) to determine whether the selected packages require support provided by unselected packages. If so, the installation program displays the Unresolved Dependencies screen. The graphical version of this screen is shown in Figure 7.19.

FIGURE 7.19 The Unresolved Dependencies screen

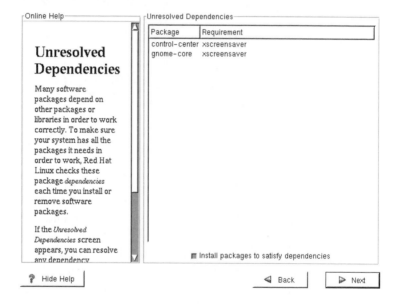

The Unresolved Dependencies screen lets you specify whether the installation program will automatically install the required packages, even though you did not select it.

Configuring the X Window System

If you selected packages that are part of the X Window system, the installation program display the X Configuration screen, which lets you configure X. The graphical version of this screen is shown in Figure 7.20.

FIGURE 7.20 The X Configuration screen

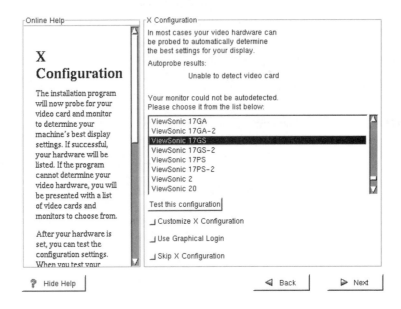

The installation program uses Xconfigurator to probe and determine the type of video card and monitor on the system. If Xconfigurator cannot identify your card or monitor, it displays a list of hardware from which you can choose. Hundreds of cards and monitors are listed; scroll down the list to find your card and monitor. If your hardware is not listed, you may nevertheless be able to configure X. Select Unlisted Card, and specify the characteristics of your video card. Alternatively, select Custom Monitor, and specify the horizontal and vertical sync ranges of your monitor.

You can test the configuration to see that it works. To do so, click Test This Configuration. You can also select a custom resolution or color depth. To do so, click Customize X Configuration.

Enable the Use Graphical Login check box to cause Linux to display an X login when the system starts. If you prefer a text-based login, disable the Use Graphical Login check box.

If you cannot configure X or you prefer not to try, you can postpone the configuration by selecting Skip X Configuration.

Installing Packages

Finally, the installation program will present the About to Install screen. The graphical mode version of this screen is shown in Figure 7.21. Up to this point, the configuration changes that you specified have been stored in RAM memory. You can reboot at this point without affecting the configuration of the target system. However, clicking Next commits the changes.

FIGURE 7.21   The About to Install screen

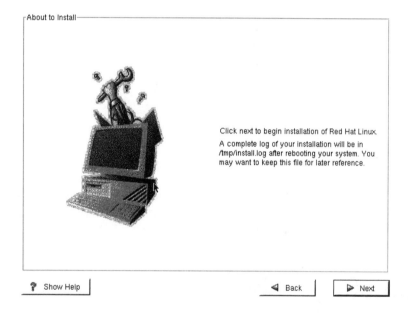

When you click Next, the installation program displays the Installing Packages screen. The graphical mode version of this screen is shown as Figure 7.22.

FIGURE 7.22 The Installing Packages screen

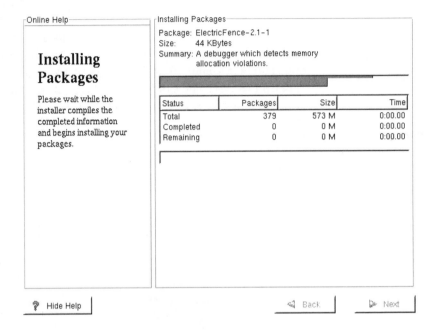

The Installing Packages screen lets you monitor the progress of package installation. The Next button is disabled until the package installation is complete.

Creating a Boot Disk

Unless you specified that no boot disk is needed, the installation program will display the Boot Disk Creation screen. The graphical version of this screen is shown in Figure 7.23.

FIGURE 7.23 The Boot Disk Creation screen

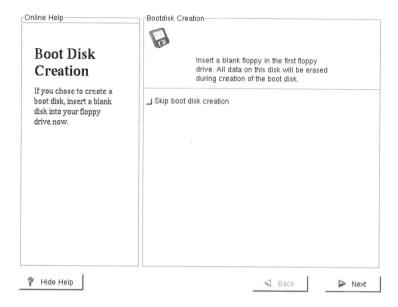

You can skip creation of the boot floppy disk by clicking Skip Boot Disk Creation and then clicking Next. However, in most cases, you should not do this; the book disk is useful if you find that you're unable to boot Linux from the hard drive. To create the boot diskette, place a blank floppy disk in the floppy drive, and click Next.

Completing the Installation

Next, the installation program will display the Congratulations screen, which signals the completion of installation. The graphical version of this screen is shown in Figure 7.24.

FIGURE 7.24 The Congratulations screen

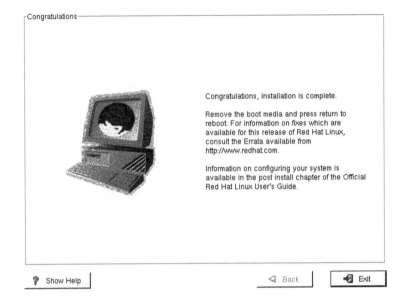

You should remove the boot disk—if you created one—from the floppy drive, and click Exit. The computer will automatically restart. However, you may need to set the system's BIOS so that the system will boot from its hard disk. Now, practice installing Red Hat Linux by completing Exercise 7.1.

EXERCISE 7.1

Installing Red Hat Linux

Perform the following installations, exercising a variety of options so that you can see what they do:

- A graphical mode installation of a GNOME workstation

- A text mode installation of a server

- A graphical mode Custom installation

- An expert mode installation

When you're done with each installation, examine the installation log and become familiar with its typical contents. Knowing how the log should look will help you spot problems with actual installations.

Summary

In this chapter, you learned how to install Red Hat Linux. The most important topics covered are:

Installation Modes   You can install Linux using graphical, text, or expert mode.

Virtual Consoles   You can use Linux virtual consoles to monitor the installation procedure.

Sequence of Operations   Several steps of the installation procedure are optional. They may be skipped based on user input, detected hardware, and detected installation media.

Installation Path   The installation path defines the installation type and class.

Partitioning   Hard disks can be partitioned automatically or manually.

Network Configuration   By configuring the system to use a DHCP server (when available), network configuration can be automatically performed at boot time.

Selecting Packages   You can select packages by component. You can also select individual packages. The GNOME Workstation, KDE Workstation, and Server installation classes automatically choose packages for you.

X Configuration   The installation procedure can generally identify and automatically configure X for your video hardware. If you prefer, you can postpone configuring X.

Boot Disk   You should generally create a boot disk, which is handy if your Linux system cannot be booted from the hard drive.

Key Terms

Before sitting for the RHCE exam, be sure you're familiar with the following terms:

components

Custom installlation class

GNOME Workstation installation class

installation path

Install installation type

KDE Workstation installation class

package groups

Server installation class

three-button mouse emulation

Upgrade installation type

Additional Sources of Information

If you'd like further information about the topics presented in this chapter, you should consult the following sources:

- *The Official Red Hat Linux Installation Guide*
- *The Official Red Hat Linux Getting Started Guide*
- *The Official Red Hat Linux Reference Guide*

These documents are available on the Web, at `www.redhat.com /support/manuals`.

Review Questions

1. Which of the following are Red Hat Linux installation modes?

    A. Expert

    B. Graphical

    C. Text

    D. Upgrade

2. Which of the following is true of graphical mode installation?

    A. You can use the Tab key to select controls.

    B. You can use the keyboard to enter text.

    C. You can use the mouse to select an item from a list.

    D. You can use the mouse to select controls.

3. Which of the following is true of the text mode installation?

    A. You can use the Tab key to select controls.

    B. You can use the keyboard to enter text.

    C. You can use the mouse to select an item from a list.

    D. You can use the mouse to select controls.

4. What is the primary purpose of the expert mode?

    A. To impress colleagues and friends

    B. To omit device probes

    C. To specify boot parameters

    D. To support network installation

5. Which of the following correctly pairs a virtual console with its installation program function?

    A. 1, text-based install program

    B. 2, shell prompt

    C. 3, install program messages

    D. 4, kernel messages

6. Which of the following installation functions are optional?

A. Partitioning

B. Network configuration

C. Setting the time zone

D. Authentication configuration

7. Which of the following is true of a two-button mouse?

A. It is a bus mouse.

B. It is a PS/2 mouse.

C. It is a serial mouse.

D. You should generally enable three-button emulation for a two-button mouse.

8. Which installation class is automatic partitioning performed for?

A. The Expert installation class

B. The GNOME Workstation installation class

C. The KDE Workstation installation class

D. The Server installation class

9. What is a mount point?

A. The device file associated with a removable device

B. The directory associated with a mountable device

C. The side of a floppy diskette inserted into the drive

D. The time at which you insert the installation media

10. What should you do to make a partition as large as possible, given that other partitions have already been allocated?

A. Enter a big number as the size of the partition.

B. Enter a negative number as the size of the partition.

C. Enable the Allowable Type option.

D. Enable the Grow to Fill option.

11. If you plan to dual-boot OS/2 and Linux, where should you install LILO?

A. In memory

B. On a CD-ROM

C. On the first sector of the Linux boot partition

D. On the master boot record

12. What happens when you configure the system to use DHCP?

A. Authentication is performed at boot time.

B. LILO installation is performed at boot time.

C. Network configuration is performed at boot time.

D. Partitioning is performed at boot time.

13. What will happen if you use the Time Zone screen to specify that the system clock be set to UTC?

A. A dual-boot operating system may malfunction.

B. Time will be kept more accurately.

C. Time will be kept somewhat less accurately.

D. You don't need to specify a time zone.

14. Which of the following authentication options should normally be set?

A. MD5 passwords

B. NIS domain

C. NIS server

D. Shadow passwords

15. When will the Unresolved Dependencies screen appear?

A. When disk geometry is unsuitable.

B. When packages you specify for installation require additional packages.

C. When you enter ambiguous information.

D. When you run low on system resources.

16. Which program is used by the installation procedure to configure X?

    A. Xconfig

    B. Xconfigurator

    C. XF86Config

    D. XF86Setup

17. Which of the following is an appropriate response if you can't boot the installation procedure by using the system's CD-ROM drive?

    A. Revise the BIOS settings to permit booting from CD-ROM.

    B. Install a memory upgrade.

    C. Boot from a boot floppy.

    D. Boot using `autoboot.bat`.

18. Why should you create a boot disk?

    A. Creating the boot disk proves Linux is properly installed.

    B. You can use it to boot your system.

    C. You can't boot the system from the hard drive until installation is complete.

    D. You can't create one after installation is complete.

Answers to Review Questions

1. A, B, C. Upgrade is an installation type, not an installation mode.

2. A, B, C, and D. You can use a variety of techniques during a graphical mode installation.

3. A, B. You cannot use the mouse during a text mode installation.

4. B. Expert mode installation lets you avoid device probes that might hang the system.

5. A, B, C, D. Table 7.1 summarizes the installation program's use of virtual consoles.

6. A, B, D. Partitioning may be performed automatically. Network configuration is performed only if a network adapter is present. Authentication configuration occurs only during Custom installations.

7. D. A three-button mouse is preferred for use with X. If you have a two-button mouse, you should generally enable three-button emulation.

8. B, C, D. There is no Expert installation class. Installation classes other than Custom are automatically formatted.

9. B. A mount point is a directory bound to a mounted device by the `mount` command.

10. D. When you enable the Grow to Fill option, the installation program makes the partition as large as possible.

11. C. You should use the OS/2 boot manager to load Linux by fetching LILO from the boot partition.

12. C. A DHCP server can supply network configuration information to a system at boot time.

13. A. Another operating system may not support setting the system clock to UTC. Setting the clock to UTC has no effect on accuracy. The local time zone must be known to the system, so the time zone must be set.

14. A, D. Specify an NIS domain or server only if you plan to use network passwords.

15. B. The Unresolved Dependencies screen tells you that additional packages may need to be installed.

16. B. The installation program uses `Xconfigurator` to configure X.

17. A, C, D. Many systems—especially older systems—cannot boot from a CD-ROM drive.

18. B. The boot disk is handy if your system's boot information becomes damaged.

Chapter
8

Advanced Installations

RHCE PREPARATION TOPICS COVERED IN THIS CHAPTER:

- ✓ Understand how and be able to install Red Hat Linux on a compatible laptop computer.

- ✓ Understand how and be able to install Red Hat Linux in a multi-boot configuration.

- ✓ Understand how and be able to configure and troubleshoot the Linux loader, LILO.

- ✓ Understand how and be able to install Red Hat Linux on a computer that requires PCMCIA support during installation.

- ✓ Understand how and be able to install Red Hat Linux using a network server to provide access to installation media.

- ✓ Understand how and be able to perform an automated (kickstart) installation of Red Hat Linux.

his chapter covers some odds and ends related to installation. It explains how to cope with several unusual types of installations, how to configure and troubleshoot several Linux facilities, and how to perform installations by using network servers. Although some of these topics may seem to be of minor importance, examination questions are apt to address these topics. Be sure you invest sufficient time to master this chapter, paying special attention to unfamiliar topics.

Installing Linux on Laptops

Installing Linux on a laptop often presents complications. The biggest obstacle is that laptop manufacturers generally do not standardize the components used in a given model laptop. For example, laptops manufactured at one time or location may have a different sound card than units manufactured at another time or location. Thus, one laptop owner may have little difficulty installing Linux, but someone else who owns the same model laptop and follows the same installation procedure as the first owner may be unable to properly configure Linux. To further complicate matters, laptop technology advances at a more rapid pace than desktop technology. Manufacturers introduce new models every several months.

A second obstacle is that laptops are more likely than desktop computers to use integrated components and chipsets that are not widely used. Linux drivers supporting such components and chipsets are sometimes not available. For example, many laptops use video hardware that is not supported by

XFree86 or sound hardware that is not supported by the standard Linux kernel and drivers. You may be able to obtain a commercial X server or sound card driver to support unusual hardware. For example, see Metro Link's Metro-X X Server (`www.metrolink.com`) and 4Front Technologies' Open Sound System (`www.opensound.com`).

Laptops are also more likely than desktops to use PCMCIA and Advanced Power Management (APM). Red Hat Linux supports PCMCIA and APM, but you may need to configure these facilities in order to use all available devices and optimize system performance; this adds a few steps to the installation and configuration process. A subsequent section of this chapter explains how to access PCMCIA devices during installation. Chapter 15, "Understanding Configuration Files and Scripts," explains how to configure and use PCMCIA and APM.

Several laptop manufacturers have begun offering laptops with Red Hat Linux preinstalled. If you're able to choose your laptop, you may find it convenient to pick one of these. Otherwise, consult the Linux on Laptops Web page, at `www.cs.utexas.edu/users/kharker/linux-laptop`. This Web page includes a wealth of resources, including:

- Links to notes on running Linux on specific laptop models

- Links to information on configuring XFree86 to work with an LCD display

- Links to information on typical notebook components, such as PCMCIA

- Links to articles and presentations on running Linux on a laptop

- Links to special Linux software that is useful when running Linux on a laptop

- Links to forums for discussing Linux laptop issues

You should also consult the Linux Laptop HOWTO, `home.snafu.de/wehe/howtos.html`. This HOWTO also includes information on using Linux on or with palmtops and other devices, such as cellular phones and calculators.

Performing Multi-Boot Installations

Many Linux users want to use a single computer to host multiple operating systems in what is called a *multi-boot* configuration. A computer configured for multi-boot operation does not generally boot an operating system. Instead, it boots a special program called a *boot loader* that lets the user choose an installed operating system and then loads the user's choice. Desktop users often configure their systems to boot Microsoft Windows or

Linux. However, it's possible to configure multi-boot configurations that support Windows NT and other operating systems, such as IBM's OS/2.

In a multi-boot configuration, each time you start the system, you choose the operating system you want to boot. However, instead of configuring a system for multi-boot operation, you can install special software that lets you use Windows programs and Linux at the same time. For example, the WINE project (`www.winehq.com`) is implementing the Win32 API under Linux. Already, you can use WINE to run many common Windows programs under Linux.

Another approach to running Windows programs under Linux is VMware, Inc.'s product called VMware, which lets you run the Windows 9x or the Windows NT operating system under Linux. Alternatively, a Windows NT version of VMware lets you run Linux under Windows NT. The company's Web site is `www.vmware.com`. One of the most useful features of VMware is its ability to simultaneously run multiple versions of Linux on a single computer. By doing so, you can install, configure, and test new versions of Linux and Linux software without disturbing a running server.

This section explains a *multi-boot installation* for configuring a multi-boot system. The first several subsections describe the use, configuration, and troubleshooting of the Linux loader, LILO. Subsequent subsections explain the procedure for installing Linux in a multi-boot configuration.

Using and Configuring LILO

The Linux loader, LILO, can act as a *primary boot loader* or a *secondary boot loader*. When used as a primary boot loader, LILO is installed on the master boot record (MBR) of a hard disk so that the system's BIOS loads LILO when the system is booted. LILO then controls the booting of Linux and other installed operating systems.

Some operating systems have an associated boot loader. For example, Windows NT has a boot loader known as the NT Loader, and IBM's OS/2 has a boot loader known as the Boot Manager. Often, it's easier to boot an operating system by using its associated boot loader. Common boot loaders can also be configured to boot Linux. To do so, install LILO on the boot sector of the /`boot` partition, and create a boot loader entry for Linux that points to the /`boot` partition. In this configuration, LILO acts as a secondary boot loader: It provides the means to boot Linux, but it does not boot any other operating system.

When configured as a primary boot loader, LILO generally displays a LILO: prompt as soon as it's loaded. This prompt is called a *boot prompt*, and it provides an opportunity to choose the boot image to boot or to enter Linux boot parameters that control the boot and startup process. If LILO has been configured to display no prompt, pressing Shift or Caps Lock will force the LILO: prompt to be displayed.

If you press the Tab key in response to LILO's prompt, LILO displays the boot images it is configured to boot. To boot an image, type the label displayed by LILO and press Enter. Typically, the label dos refers to Microsoft Windows, and the label linux refers to Linux. However, you can configure LILO to display a label you choose, as described in the next subsection. For example, you may prefer to associate the label Win95 with the Microsoft Windows 95 operating system.

Often, LILO is configured to automatically boot a default boot image if the user fails to choose one within a defined time period. The default boot image, if any, is the one listed first when you press Tab in response to the prompt. You can disable the automatic boot feature by pressing Shift or Caps Lock. If you want to boot the default boot image immediately, press Enter in response to LILO's prompt. However, you can configure LILO to ignore these Shift and Caps Lock functions, if you prefer.

Boot arguments let you control the boot and startup processes. Many boot arguments have a *name=value* form. LILO recognizes and processes several such arguments, but if LILO doesn't recognize a *name=value* argument or if an argument has some other form, LILO passes the argument to the kernel. In turn, the kernel will try to recognize and process the argument. If the kernel doesn't recognize an argument, it passes the argument to the first process, usually init. The kernel passes *name=value* arguments as environment variables, and it uses arguments that have some other form to invoke the first process.

The most common use of a boot argument is to start the system in single-user mode. When booted in single-user mode, the system mounts only the root file system and starts only those system processes associated with run level 1. Booting a system in single-user mode may facilitate troubleshooting and repair.

To start a system in single-user mode, type S, **single**, or **1** after the name of the operating system. For example, you might start Linux in single-user mode as follows:

```
LILO: linux S
```

See Exercise 8.1 for hands-on experience with the LILO prompt.

EXERCISE 8.1

Using the LILO Prompt

To become better acquainted with multiple boot images and booting Linux in single-user mode, do each of the following steps using a system configured for multi-boot operation.

1. Use the Tab key to see what boot images are available.

2. Boot each available operating system.

3. Boot Linux in single-user mode.

Configuring LILO

The installation program generally configures LILO correctly on your behalf. However, when configuring a system for multi-boot operation, you may find it necessary to tweak the LILO configuration after installation. To do so, you can use the `linuxconf` program. However, the RHCE exam is likely to include questions or exercises that test your ability to configure LILO manually. This subsection explains LILO's configuration file and how to use it.

LILO's configuration file is `/etc/lilo.conf`. To install a new LILO configuration, modify the configuration file using a text editor, and then run the LILO map installer, `/sbin/lilo`. Here's a sample LILO configuration file that illustrates the most important configuration options:

```
boot=/dev/hda
map=/boot/map
install=/boot/boot.b
prompt
delay=50
timeout=3000
default=dos

image=/boot/vmlinuz-2.2.12-20
    label=old
    root=/dev/hda4
    read-only
```

```
image=/boot/vmlinuz-2.2.12-20b1
    label=linux
    root=/dev/hda4
    read-only

other=/dev/hda1
    label=dos
```

This configuration file includes four stanzas. The first, consisting of the first six lines, specifies global parameters. Table 8.1 describes the global parameters that appear in the same configuration. Each remaining stanza describes a boot image that LILO should offer for booting. The first two boot images are associated with Linux, and the final boot image is associated with Microsoft Windows. Table 8.2 describes the parameters used to specify a boot image.

Note that both Linux boot images refer to the same partition. This arrangement lets you choose the kernel used to boot the system and is helpful when installing a new kernel. If the new kernel fails to work properly, you can use the LILO prompt to load the old kernel.

TABLE 8.1 LILO Global Parameters

LILO Global Parameter	Description
boot	Specifies the device or partition to which boot information will be written. To install LILO to the MBR, where it will act as the primary boot loader, specify a device (for example, /dev/hda). Alternatively, to install Linux to the boot sector of the partition, where it will act as a secondary boot loader, specify a partition (for example, /dev/hda3).
default	Specifies the default boot image.
delay	Specifies the amount of time (in tenths of a second) that LILO will wait before booting the default boot image.
install	Specifies the file installed as the new boot sector.

TABLE 8.1 LILO Global Parameters *(continued)*

LILO Global Parameter	Description
map	Specifies the name of the map file, which contains the names and locations of boot images.
prompt	Specifies that LILO will display a boot prompt.
timeout	Specifies the amount of time (in tenths of a second) that LILO will wait for keyboard input before booting the default boot image.

TABLE 8.2 LILO Boot Image Parameters

LILO Global Parameter	Description
image	Specifies the Linux kernel associated with the boot image (required for Linux boot images).
label	Specifies the label associated with the boot image.
other	Specifies the partition that contains the bootable non-Linux image (required for non-Linux boot images).
read-only	Specifies that the root partition is initially to be mounted as a read-only partition.
root	Specifies the root partition associated with the Linux boot image (required for Linux boot images).

Now try Exercise 8.2 to see if you understand how to configure LILO.

EXERCISE 8.2

Configuring LILO

1. Create a boot disk for your system, so you can boot your system even if LILO is badly configured.

2. Revise the LILO configuration to specify a different timeout, delay, and default.

3. Revise the labels associated with boot images.

EXERCISE 8.2 *(continued)*

4. Run /sbin/lilo to update the boot map and install the boot sector.

5. Boot the system, and verify that your changes work as planned.

LILO Error Messages

LILO actually loads in two stages. LILO's first stage resides in the MBR or boot sector of a partition, depending on whether LILO is installed as the primary or a secondary boot loader. LILO's second stage resides in the file /boot/boot.b. LILO displays its prompt letter by letter as it loads. So, an incomplete LILO prompt provides useful information about what went wrong. LILO sometimes displays a modified prompt that indicates an error condition. Table 8.3 describes the LILO error messages.

TABLE 8.3 LILO Error Messages

Prompt	Meaning
nothing	LILO did not load.
L	First stage loaded.
LI	Second stage loaded.
LIL	Second stage started.
LIL?	Second stage loaded at incorrect address.
LIL-	Descriptor table is corrupt.
LILO	LILO loaded correctly.

Windows 9*x*

Configuring a multi-boot system that boots Microsoft Windows 9*x* and Linux is straightforward. If possible, you should install Microsoft Windows before installing Linux. If you then perform a Workstation or Custom installation of Red Hat Linux, the installation program can automatically configure the system to boot both operating systems. Simply ensure that the installation program's LILO Configuration dialog box lists the partition containing Microsoft Windows.

If you must install Linux first and then install Microsoft Windows, be sure to leave room for the Windows partition, which must be located in a bootable region of the hard disk (generally, below cylinder 1024). Also, be sure to create a Linux boot disk, because the Windows installation procedure overwrites the MBR, destroying LILO. After the Windows installation is complete, use the boot disk to boot Linux, revise the LILO configuration to include the Windows boot image, and run /sbin/lilo to reinstall LILO.

You may find it helpful to use the BIOS to turn off plug-and-play for ISA slots. Otherwise, Windows may use plug-and-play to change the system resources associated with a device, rendering it unusable in Linux until you reconfigure the device.

See Exercise 8.3 to confirm that you understand how to configure a multi-boot system that boots both Linux and Windows 9x.

EXERCISE 8.3

Configuring a System to Boot Linux and Windows 9x

1. Configure a system for multi-boot operation, using Windows 9x and Linux.

2. If you have a Windows 9x laptop available to you, install Linux on the laptop and configure it for multi-boot operation. Be sure to attempt to install and configure XFree86.

Windows NT

Configuring a multi-boot system that boots Windows NT and Linux is somewhat more difficult than configuring a multi-boot system that boots Windows 9x and Linux. Again, you'll find the task easier if you install Windows NT before installing Linux. However, the Linux installation program will not automatically configure the system to boot Windows NT as it will Windows 9x.

You can boot Linux using the Windows NT loader. The Windows NT loader configuration is stored in the hidden file c:\boot.ini. Here's a sample NT loader configuration file:

```
[boot loader]
timeout=60
default=multi(0)disk(0)rdisk(1)partition(1)\WINNT
```

```
[operating systems]
multi(0)disk(0)rdisk(1)partition(1)\WINNT="Windows NT
➥Workstation Version 4.00"
multi(0)disk(0)rdisk(1)partition(1)\WINNT="Windows NT
➥Workstation Version 4.00 [VGA mode]" /basevideo /sos
c:\="Microsoft Windows 95"
```

This configuration file contains two stanzas set off by titles enclosed in square brackets. The first stanza is titled [boot loader]. It contains two lines: one that specifies a timeout and one that specifies a default boot image. The timeout works much like LILO's timeout. NT automatically boots a default image if it finds no response to its prompt within the specified time period. The default boot image is specified by the number of its disk (rdisk) and partition (partition), both of which are numbered relative to 0. The default boot image in the sample configuration is located in the \WINNT directory of the file system on the specified partition.

The multi and disk parameters of the boot.ini file are used with SCSI disks. You shouldn't need to learn these NT-related details in order to prepare for the RHCE exam.

The second stanza is titled [operating systems]. Each line of the second stanza specifies a boot image and an associated label, which is enclosed in double quotes. Two forms of specification appear: One is used to specify an NT boot image, and the other is used to specify a non-NT boot image. In the sample configuration, the first two lines specify NT boot images, and the third line specifies a non-NT boot image.

To configure NT to boot Linux, install Linux using LILO as a secondary boot loader. Be sure to create a boot disk so that you can boot Linux before reconfiguring the NT loader.

Suppose the /dev/hda3 partition is the one Linux mounts as /boot. Boot Linux and issue the following command:

```
dd if=/dev/hda3 of=/boot/linux.ldr bs=512 count=1
```

This command copies the Linux boot sector from the /boot partition to the file /boot/linux.ldr.

Insert an MS-DOS formatted floppy disk into the floppy drive, and issue the commands

```
mount -t msdos /dev/fd0 /mnt/floppy
cp /boot/linux.ldr /mnt/floppy
umount /dev/fd0
```

Remove the floppy disk, and boot NT. Insert the floppy disk, and copy the file `linux.ldr` from the floppy disk to the `c:\` directory. Use a text editor to add the following line to the `boot.ini` file:

```
c:\linux.ldr="Linux"
```

When you boot NT, the NT loader displays a new line that's labeled `Linux`. Simply highlight the new line, and press Enter to boot Linux.

Note that if the Windows NT system uses a FAT rather than an NTFS file system, you can copy the `/boot/linux.ldr` file to the proper Windows NT file system without using a floppy disk. Just mount the file system, copy the file, then unmount the file system. Also note that, if you prefer, you can boot Windows NT by using LILO. Just add the Windows NT system to the LILO configuration file, specifying the `other` and `label` directives. Then, run `/sbin/lilo` to update the boot map and install the revised boot sector.

If you recompile your Linux kernel, you must run `/sbin/lilo`, and then repeat the boot sector installation procedure. Otherwise, the NT loader will be unable to find and load the new kernel.

See Exercise 8.4 to check whether you now understand how to configure a multi-boot system that boots both Linux and Windows NT.

EXERCISE 8.4

Configuring a System to Boot Linux and Windows NT

Configure a system for multi-boot operation using Windows NT and Linux.

Other Operating Systems

You can configure Linux to boot or be booted by other operating systems, including OS/2, FreeBSD, and NetBSD. The configuration procedure generally resembles that given for Windows NT or Windows 9*x*, depending on whether you prefer to use LILO as the primary boot loader or a secondary boot loader, respectively. Consult the operating system documentation to determine how to proceed. You'll probably find USENET newsgroups helpful in resolving any problems and questions you have.

Special Installations

This section explains how to perform several special types of installations:

PCMCIA Installations Installations for which you must access PCM-CIA hardware to perform the installation

Network Installations Installations that access distribution files supplied by a network server

Kickstart Installations Installations that proceed more or less automatically, under the control of a script

Performing PCMCIA Installations

If you require access to PCMCIA hardware during a Linux installation, you must use a special boot disk. The image for the special boot disk is located in the file pcmcia.img, in the images directory of the Red Hat Linux CD-ROM, the same location that holds the usual boot.img file.

Create a boot disk from this image file by using the procedure described in Chapter 6, "Installation Planning." To start the installation procedure, boot the system using this disk.

To install previous versions of Red Hat Linux, you used the standard boot disk and a supplementary PCMCIA disk. Some Red Hat documents have not yet been updated to reflect the new procedure.

Some Red Hat CD-ROMs contain bad installation images. If you encounter installation problems when using PCMCIA, check the Red Hat FTP server for updated images.

Now try Exercise 8.5 to perform a PCMCIA installation on your own.

EXERCISE 8.5

Performing a PCMCIA Installation

If you have a PCMCIA CD-ROM drive available to you, install Linux using it.

Performing Network Installations

A common method of installing Red Hat Linux is by means of a distribution CD-ROM. However, you can install Red Hat Linux from distribution media residing on an FTP, HTTP (Web), or NFS server. This is called a *network installation.*

At one time, Red Hat Linux supported network installation via Samba (SMB). This is no longer the case.

Prior to Red Hat Linux 6.2, the DNS server that resolved host names for the domain that includes the server had to be capable of providing a reverse name lookup for the server. The DNS server had to be able to map the IP number of the server to the server's host name. Under Red Hat Linux 6.2, this is no longer necessary.

If the server provides access to the distribution media by means of multiple services, it's useful to store the media only once. The following sequence of commands creates a copy of the distribution media, which is accessible to FTP and HTTP:

```
cp -a /mnt/cdrom/RedHat /home/ftp/pub
ln -s /home/ftp/pub/RedHat /home/httpd/html/RedHat
```

To provide access to the media via NFS, export the /home/ftp/pub/ RedHat directory by including the following line in the /etc/exports file:

```
/home/ftp/pub/RedHat (ro)
```

For more information on setting up FTP, HTTP, and NFS services, see Chapter 21, "Installing and Configuring Primary Network Services."

You can perform a graphical mode installation via NFS, but not via FTP or HTTP.

To install Red Hat Linux via a network server, create a boot disk from the image file bootnet.img, which resides in the images directory of the distribution CD-ROM. Then, start the installation procedure by booting from this disk. Note that network installations use text mode rather than graphical mode, so the installation menu does not give you the option to perform a graphical mode installation. After you select the language and keyboard, the Installation Method screen, shown in Figure 8.1, will appear. Select the service that will provide access to the installation media, and click OK.

FIGURE 8.1 The Installation Method screen

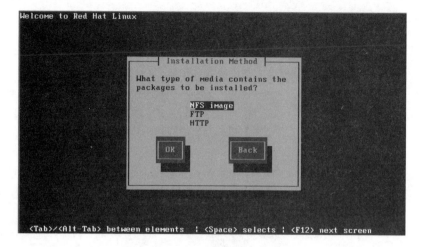

Recall that you don't use the mouse to click buttons when performing a text mode installation. Use navigation keys to select the button, and press Enter or the spacebar to click it.

If you select NFS, the NFS Setup screen, shown in Figure 8.2, will appear. Use this screen to specify the host name (or IP number) of the NFS server and the name of the exported directory that contains the RedHat subdirectory of the distribution CD-ROM.

FIGURE 8.2 The NFS Setup screen

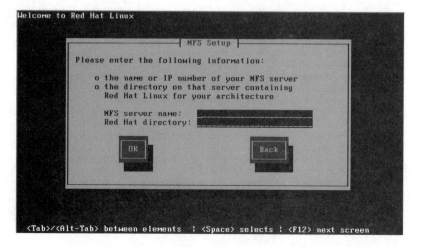

If you select FTP, the FTP Setup screen, shown in Figure 8.3, will appear. Use this screen to specify the host name (or IP number) of the FTP server and the name of the directory that contains the RedHat subdirectory of the distribution CD-ROM.

FIGURE 8.3 The FTP Setup screen

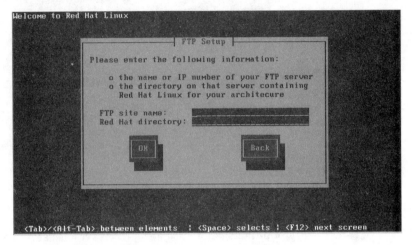

If you selected HTTP, the HTTP Setup screen, shown in Figure 8.4, will appear. Use this screen to specify the host name (or IP number) of the HTTP server and the name of the directory that contains the RedHat subdirectory of the distribution CD-ROM.

FIGURE 8.4 The HTTP Setup screen

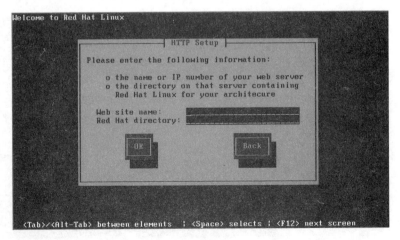

After you specify the host name (or IP number) of the server and the directory that contains the distribution media, the Configure TCP/IP screen, shown in Figure 8.5, will appear. If the client can obtain its network configuration via BOOTP or DHCP, select Use Dynamic IP Configuration and click OK. Otherwise, specify the IP number, netmask, gateway, and DNS server that the client should use, and click OK.

FIGURE 8.5   The Configure TCP/IP screen

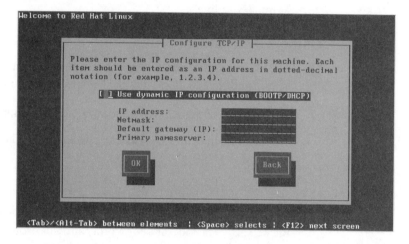

Once you've specified the TCP/IP information, the installation program accesses the distribution media via the server. Thereafter, the installation proceeds as usual.

Now try Exercise 8.6 to perform FTP, HTTP, and NFS network installations on your own.

EXERCISE 8.6

Performing Network Installations

If you have a network server available to you, perform the following installations.

1. Perform an FTP installation.

2. Perform an HTTP installation.

3. Perform an NFS installation.

Otherwise, after reading Chapter 21, configure a suitable server and perform the installations then.

Performing Kickstart Installations

A *kickstart installation* is a special type of installation in which responses to Installation dialog boxes are taken from a script rather than from user input. When the script is stored on a floppy disk, it has the name ks.cfg; when the script is accessed via NFS, you can specify its name. You can write your own kickstart script, but it's much easier to use the mkkickstart program to create a script patterned after a completed installation. You can then revise the script as you like.

Using *mkkickstart*

The mkkickstart program is not installed by default, so the usual first step is to install the mkkickstart package using the following command:

```
rpm -Uvh /mnt/cdrom/RedHat/RPMS/mkkickstart*.rpm
```

After installing the mkkickstart package, run the mkkickstart program as follows:

```
mkkickstart >ks.cfg
```

Notice how the output of the mkkickstart program is redirected to the file ks.cfg. The mkkickstart program will probably display a warning that reminds you to set the static IP address in the configuration file; this is normal.

Here's a sample ks.cfg file:

```
lang us
#network --static --ip 10.0.0.2 --netmask 255.255.255.0
➥--gateway 10.0.0.1 --nameserver 10.0.0.1
cdrom
device ethernet 3c90x
keyboard us
zerombr yes
clearpart --linux
part swap --size 526
part /space --size 10449
part /boot --size 40
part /usr --size 2001
part /home --size 4009
part /var --size 503
part / --size 1005
install
```

```
mouse genericps/2
timezone US/Pacific
xconfig --server "SVGA" --monitor "viewsonic17gs"
auth --useshadow --enablemd5
lilo --location mbr --linear
%packages
setup
filesystem
basesystem
...and so on...
%post
```

Editing the Configuration File

The configuration file requires some revision before it can be used. Notice that the network line is commented out. You should remove the comment character (#) and revise the IP number, netmask, and gateway. If you want the system to obtain its network configuration via BOOTP or DHCP, specify the following directive:

```
network --bootproto BOOTP
```

or

```
network --bootproto DHCP
```

Table 8.4 describes the other directives shown in the same configuration and a few additional directives you may find useful. Consult the kickstart documentation on the documentation CD-ROM, especially *The Official Red Hat Linux Reference Guide*, to learn more about these and other kickstart directives.

TABLE 8.4 Kickstart Directives

Directive	Meaning
auth --useshadow --enablemd5	Specifies that shadow passwords and MD5 encryption are to be used.
cdrom	Specifies that the installation media is on a local CD-ROM.
clearpart --all	Specifies that all existing partitions should be deleted.

TABLE 8.4 Kickstart Directives *(continued)*

Directive	Meaning
clearpart --linux	Specifies that all existing Linux partitions should be deleted.
device ethernet *device* [--opts "*options*"]	Specifies that the system has the indicated type of Ethernet adapter. The installer consults this directive when unable to successfully identify a network device by probing.
device scsi *device* [--opts "*options*"]	Specifies that the system has the indicated type of SCSI adapter. The installer consults this directive when unable to successfully identify a SCSI interface by probing.
install	Specifies that the installation type is Install rather than Upgrade.
keyboard us	Specifies that the keyboard is type US.
lang us	Specifies the language to be used in any dialog boxes used by the installer to request information.
lilo --append "*anything-needed*"	Specifies options to be appended to the LILO configuration file.
mouse genericps/2	Specifies that the mouse type is ps/2.
network --bootproto bootp	Specifies that the network configuration is to be obtained via BOOTP.
network --bootproto dhcp	Specifies that the network configuration is to be obtained via DHCP.
network --static--ip *ip* --netmask *mask* --gateway *gw*--nameserver *dns*	Specifies a static network configuration.
part /*mount* --size *size*	Specifies that a Linux partition of the specified size (in MB) should be created and mounted as the indicated directory.

TABLE 8.4 Kickstart Directives *(continued)*

Directive	Meaning
part swap --size *size*	Specifies that a swap partition of the indicated size (in MB) should be created.
rootpw --iscrypted *password*	Specifies the root password using encrypted text. This directive has a history of problems and is best avoided.
%packages	Specifies that the following lines name the packages to be installed.
%post	Specifies that the following lines are shell commands to be executed after installation.
timezone US/Pacific	Specifies that the time zone is US/Pacific.
upgrade	Specifies that the installation type is Upgrade rather than Install.
xconfig --server "*server*" --monitor "*monitor*"	Specifies that XFree86 should be configured using the specified X server and monitor.
zerombr yes	Specifies that any existing boot loader should be removed.

Setting Up the Servers

Rather than include the kickstart file on the boot media, you can use a DHCP server to provide it. To do so, specify

```
filename "/home/ftp/pub/ks.cfg";
```

in the /etc/dhcpd.conf file. You can store the kickstart file in a directory other than /home/ftp/pub, if you prefer; simply revise the filename directive accordingly.

If you prefer to have a separate kickstart file for each client system, specify the directive

```
filename "/home/ftp/pub/kickstart";
```

Then, in the directory /home/ftp/pub/kickstart, place the kickstart files, which must have names of the form *xxx.xxx.xxx.xxx*-kickstart, where *xxx.xxx.xxx.xxx* is the IP address of the client system.

When the installation program fetches the kickstart file via DHCP, it assumes that it should perform a network installation from an NFS server. By default, it tries to mount an NFS directory exported by the same host that answered the DHCP query. If you want to use a different host to service the NFS requests, include the following directive in the /etc/dhcpd.conf file:

```
next-server nfserver;
```

where *nfserver* is the host name or IP number of the desired NFS server on which the kickstart file resides. To give the location of installation media, you can specify a kickstart directive of the form

```
nfs --server server directory
```

where *server* specifies the NFS server and *directory* specifies the NFS-exported directory.

 For further information on setting up a DHCP server, see Chapter 23, "Understanding Secondary Network Services."

Performing the Kickstart Installation

To start the kickstart installation, specify the ks argument at the LILO prompt. Use the command

```
linux ks
```

if the kickstart file is to be obtained from a DHCP or NFS server. Use the command

```
linux ks=floppy
```

if the kickstart file resides on the root directory of the boot floppy disk.

If the kickstart installation needs information that it cannot find in a kickstart directive, it prompts for the information using the dialog box presented by a non-kickstart installation.

Now, test your understanding of kickstart installations by trying Exercise 8.7.

EXERCISE 8.7

Performing a Kickstart Installation

Perform a kickstart installation that replicates an existing Linux system on another computer.

Summary

In this chapter, you learned how to install Red Hat Linux in some unusual situations. The most important topics covered are:

Laptops   Installing Red Hat Linux on a laptop can present special compatibility issues.

Multi-Boot Installations   Using LILO—or another boot loader that offers similar capabilities—you can configure a system to boot multiple operating systems.

Special Installations: PCMCIA Hardware   You can install Red Hat Linux on systems that boot from PCMCIA hardware.

Special Installations: Network Installations   You can install Red Hat Linux from media that reside on an FTP, HTTP, or NFS server.

Special Installations: Kickstart Installations   You can install Red Hat Linux by using the `mkkickstart` program, which lets you automate the installation process.

Key Terms

Before going on to the next chapter, be sure you're familiar with the following terms:

boot arguments

boot loader

boot prompt

kickstart installation

multi-boot installation

network installation

primary boot loader

secondary boot loader

Additional Sources of Information

If you'd like further information about the topics presented in this chapter, you should consult the following sources:

- LILO's documentation files in `/usr/doc/lilo-*`

- *The Official Red Hat Linux Installation Guide*

- *The Official Red Hat Linux Reference Guide*

- *The Red Hat Linux Kickstart HOWTO*

- *The Win95 + WinNT + Linux Multiboot Using LILO Mini-HOWTO*

Review Questions

1. Which of the following statements are true of Linux laptop installations?

   A. Configuring sound is seldom a problem.

   B. Configuring video is seldom a problem.

   C. A given laptop may require a different hardware configuration than another laptop of the same model.

   D. Laptop installations are generally easier than desktop installations.

2. Which of the following statements are true of a multi-boot Linux installation?

   A. Linux can coexist with Windows 95 and Windows 98.

   B. Linux can coexist with Windows NT.

   C. Only one operating system runs at a time.

   D. You must install the Linux loader, LILO, on the MBR.

3. Which of the following statements are true of the Linux loader, LILO?

   A. When installed on the boot sector of a partition, LILO acts as a secondary boot loader.

   B. When installed on the boot sector of a partition, LILO acts as the primary boot loader.

   C. When installed on the MBR, LILO acts as a secondary boot loader.

   D. When installed on the MBR, LILO acts as the primary boot loader.

4. What must the LILO configuration for a non-Linux partition include?

   A. The `image` option

   B. The `label` option

   C. The `other` option

   D. The `root` option

5. What does a LILO prompt of L indicate?

   A. LILO's first stage loaded.

   B. LILO's second stage loaded.

   C. LILO's second stage started.

   D. LILO's third stage loaded.

6. Which of the following is the configuration file for the Windows NT boot loader?

   A. boot.ini

   B. boot.nt

   C. loader.ini

   D. loader.boot

7. You can perform a network installation using which of the following services?

   A. FTP

   B. HTTP

   C. NFS

   D. SMB

8. What must the server's DNS entries allow to perform a network installation?

   A. Mapping the host name to an IP number

   B. Mapping the host IP number to a host name

   C. Mapping the host IP address to a DHCP server

   D. Mapping the host name to a DHCP server

9. Which of the following statements are true of the mkkickstart program?

   A. The program generates a script that includes kickstart directives for the system on which it runs.

   B. The program is not installed by the default installation classes.

   C. The program writes the script to its standard output stream.

   D. The script it produces should be edited.

10. Where should you place the shell commands so that you can automatically execute shell commands as part of a kickstart installation?

    A. After the %packages directive

    B. After the %post directive

    C. As arguments of the shell directive

    D. In the file ks.com

11. What happens if you fail to specify information in a kickstart directive?

    A. The installation procedure prompts for the missing information.

    B. The installation procedure terminates abnormally.

    C. The installation procedure uses a default value.

    D. The installation fails.

12. What should you type at the LILO prompt to start a kickstart installation that fetches the kickstart file from a DHCP server?

    A. linux ks

    B. linux ks=dhcp

    C. linux ks=floppy

    D. linux ks=network

Answers to Review Questions

1. C. Laptop hardware varies; sound and video hardware are particularly problematical.

2. A, B, C. Linux can coexist with essentially any PC operating system, including those that require their own loader in the MBR.

3. A, D. The primary boot loader must be installed on the MBR.

4. C. Only the `image` option is required, but the `label` option is generally specified as well.

5. A. LILO has no third stage. The L prompt indicates a problem during loading of LILO's second stage.

6. A. None of the other files exist or are used by Windows NT.

7. A, B, C. Network installation via SMB is no longer supported.

8. A. Lookups must succeed; reverse lookups are no longer necessary. No DHCP server is required.

9. A, B, C, D. The program must generally be installed before use. It sends to its standard output stream a series of directives for the system on which it runs. You should edit the script to specify an appropriate network configuration.

10. B. Place the commands after the `%post` directive.

11. A. You needn't specify information you don't know when preparing the script, because the installation procedure will prompt you for missing information.

12. A. If you specify the `ks` argument, the installation procedure attempts to obtain the kickstart file via DHCP.

Configuration and Administration

Chapter

9

Configuring Install-Time Options after Installation

RHCE PREPARATION TOPICS COVERED IN THIS CHAPTER:

✓ **Understand and implement post-installation configuration of install-time options.**

- Be able to configure the keyboard.
- Be able to configure the mouse.
- Be able to set the system time.
- Be able to configure sound.
- Be able to configure the runlevel.
- Be able to configure authentication.
- Be able to configure basic networking.

he Red Hat Linux installation program presents a series of dialog boxes that make it easy to configure many devices and options. From time to time, you may, however, need to reconfigure a device or option. You could reinstall Red Hat Linux, but that's unnecessarily difficult and time-consuming. Instead, you can use the appropriate configuration program or tool, which enables you to reconfigure the device or option without otherwise disturbing the system configuration.

This chapter explains several configuration programs and tools that you can use to configure devices and options after the installation is complete. The focus in this chapter is on the most basic devices and options; subsequent chapters explain programs and tools suited for more sophisticated needs.

Configuring the Keyboard

To configure the system's keyboard, issue the command

```
kbdconfig
```

The Configure Keyboard screen, shown in Figure 9.1, will appear. To specify the keyboard type, highlight the keyboard in the list and click OK.

FIGURE 9.1 The Configure Keyboard screen

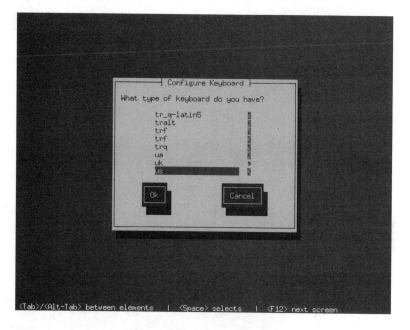

 You don't use the mouse to click buttons when using a text mode program. Use navigation keys to select the button, and press Enter or the spacebar to click it.

Configuring the Mouse

To configure the system's mouse, issue the command

`mouseconfig`

This command launches the Configure Mouse screen, shown in Figure 9.2.

FIGURE 9.2 The Configure Mouse screen

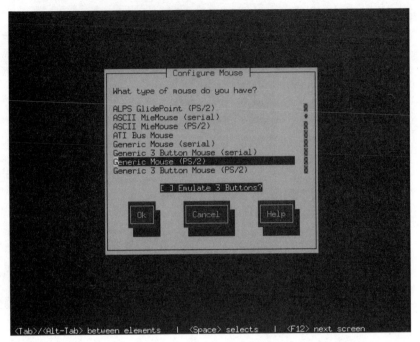

To specify the mouse type, highlight the mouse in the list. If you're not certain what type of mouse is connected to the system, select Generic Mouse (serial) or Generic Mouse (PS/2). If the mouse has two buttons, you should generally enable the Emulate 3 Buttons option. Click OK to accept your changes.

Setting the System Time Zone

To set the system time zone, issue the command

```
timeconfig
```

This command launches the Configure Timezones screen, shown in Figure 9.3. If the hardware clock is set to UTC/GMT, enable the Hardware Clock Set to GMT option. Select the time zone from the list and click OK to accept your changes.

FIGURE 9.3 The Configure Timezones screen

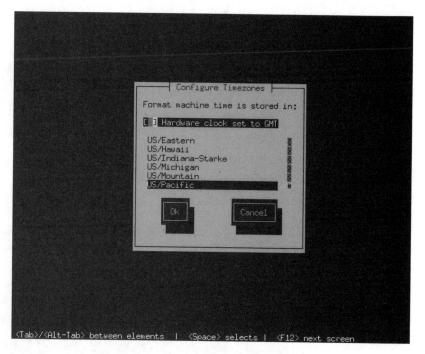

Configuring Sound

To configure the sound system, issue the command

```
sndconfig
```

This command launches a screen that explains that the command will probe for plug-and-play sound cards. Click OK. If the probe locates a card, the program displays information describing the card.

Otherwise, a message appears telling you that no card was found. Click OK to close the message box. The Card Type screen, shown in Figure 9.4. will then appear. Select the proper card type from the list, and click OK. The Card Settings screen appears, which lets you specify the I/O ports, IRQ, and DMAs used by that sound card. Specify the proper values, and click OK.

You may be informed that the file /etc/conf.modules will be overwritten; if so, click OK to let it proceed.

FIGURE 9.4 The Card Type screen

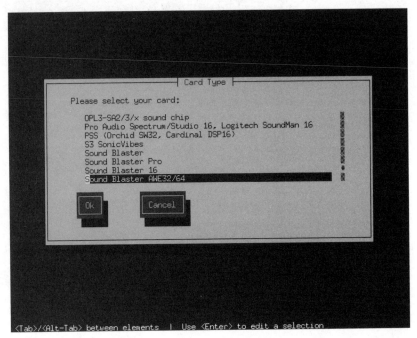

Finally, a sample sound is played. If you hear the sound, you know that the card has been properly configured. If the sound configuration program determines that your card supports MIDI (Musical Instrument Digital Interface), the program also plays a MIDI sample.

Using *linuxconf*

Red Hat Linux includes a general-purpose system administration tool, linuxconf, which you can use to perform a wide variety of tasks. The linuxconf tool can be run from a virtual console or within X. To launch linuxconf, issue the command

```
linuxconf
```

The linuxconf screen will appear. Figure 9.5 shows the graphical version of the linuxconf screen.

FIGURE 9.5 The linuxconf screen

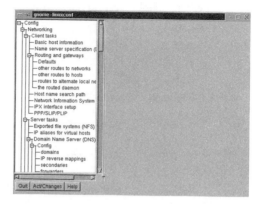

The left-hand side of the linuxconf screen contains a tree control that acts as a menu. Click a leaf item—an item at the end of a branch—to display the corresponding dialog box in the right-hand side of the screen. The text mode screen works similarly; however, text mode has lower resolution than graphical mode, so text mode cannot display the tree control and a dialog box at the same time. In text mode, you must exit the dialog box in order to view the tree control.

In either text or graphical mode, you can expand a branch of the tree by clicking the associated + icon, or you can collapse a branch of the tree by clicking the associated – icon. Buttons at the bottom of the screen let you quit the program, activate any changes you've specified, or access help.

The linuxconf help function is not fully complete; some topics lack help entries.

One somewhat confusing aspect of linuxconf is that it makes some configuration changes immediately after you accept them, but it makes other configuration changes only after you explicitly activate them. The subsection in this chapter titled "Activating Changes" explains why linuxconf does this and tells you how to activate pending changes. You should generally activate pending changes before exiting linuxconf.

The following subsections describe some common operations that you can perform using linuxconf. You can perform many more operations than described here; subsequent chapters will describe additional linuxconf features.

Configuring the Runlevel

To change the system runlevel, issue the command

init *n*

where *n* is the desired new runlevel. Table 9.1 summarizes the runlevels used by Red Hat Linux.

TABLE 9.1 Red Hat Linux Runlevels

Runlevel	Definition
0	Reserved: Setting this runlevel halts the system.
1	Reserved: Setting this runlevel sets single-user mode.
2	Multiuser mode without networking.
3	Multiuser mode with networking.
4	Not used: essentially identical to runlevel 3.
5	X-based log in.
6	Reserved: Setting this runlevel reboots the system.

You can use linuxconf to select the initial runlevel that the system assumes when booted. To do so, select Config ➢ Miscellaneous Services ➢ Initial System Services. The Init Default Runlevel screen will appear. Figure 9.6 shows the graphical version of this screen. Click the radio button corresponding to the desired default runlevel, and click Accept. The next time you boot the system, it should enter the specified runlevel.

FIGURE 9.6 The Init Default Runlevel screen

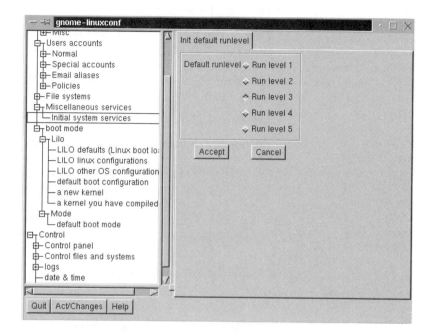

Configuring Authentication

The Red Hat Linux installation program lets you configure several authentication options. During installation you can implement the following options:

- Enable or disable shadow passwords
- Set a password for the root user
- Enable or disable creation of MD5 passwords

After installation, you can still easily enable or disable shadow passwords, set a new password for root, or enable or disable creation of MD5 passwords. The following sections show how this can be done.

Shadow Passwords

You can convert to and from shadow passwords after installation is completed. Recall that when shadow passwords are enabled, encrypted passwords are stored in a file (/etc/shadow) that is readable only by root. The

/etc/shadow file contains several fields in addition to the encrypted password, including the following:

- the date that the account was disabled, given as the number of elapsed days since January 1, 1970
- the date that the password was last changed, given as the number of elapsed days since January 1, 1970
- the number of days after which the password must be changed
- the number of days before the password may be changed
- the number of days before password expiration that the user is warned
- the number of days after password expiration that the account is disabled

Enabling shadow passwords improves system security. However, a handful of old UNIX programs may not function correctly if shadow passwords are enabled.

To enable shadow passwords, issue the command

pwconv

To disable shadow passwords, issue the command

pwunconv

Changing the *root* Password

You can easily change the root password using linuxconf. To do so, select Config ➤ Users Accounts ➤ Normal ➤ Change root Password. The Changing Password screen will appear. Figure 9.7 shows the graphical version of this screen.

FIGURE 9.7 The Changing Password screen

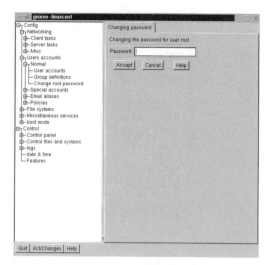

You must first enter the current root password and click Accept. If you enter the correct password, the program prompts for the new password. Type the new password, and click Accept. The program confirms your choice for the new password by asking you to enter the new password again. Do so, and click Accept to set the new password.

If you prefer using the command line, you can change the root password by issuing the passwd command, which will prompt you twice for the new password.

Configuring LILO

Rather than edit the /etc/lilo.conf file, you can use linuxconf to configure LILO. To edit LILO defaults, select Config ➢ Boot Mode ➢ LILO ➢ Configure LILO Defaults from linuxconf's menu tree. The LILO Defaults screen will appear; Figure 9.8 shows the graphical version of this screen.

FIGURE 9.8 The LILO Defaults screen

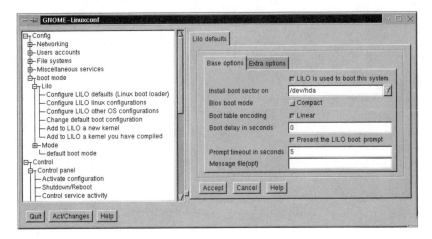

The LILO Defaults screen provides access to configuration options that correspond to LILO's global options, affecting every boot image. For example, you can use this screen to specify the location to which LILO is installed, the boot delay, and the prompt timeout. The screen does not include a control that lets you specify the default boot image. Another screen, described later in this subsection, provides access to this option.

Configuring Linux Boot Images

To add, change, or delete a Linux boot image, select Config ➢ Boot Mode ➢ LILO ➢ Configure LILO Linux Configurations from linuxconf's menu tree. The LILO Linux Configurations screen will appear; Figure 9.9 shows the graphical version of this screen.

FIGURE 9.9 The LILO Linux Configurations screen

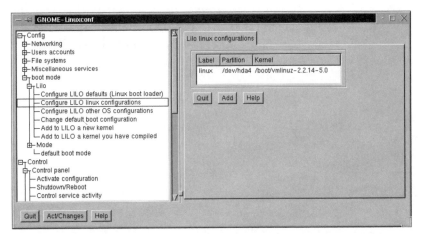

You can add a new Linux boot image by clicking Add. To edit or delete an existing Linux boot image, select the image and press Enter. The Linux Boot Configuration screen will appear. To delete the boot image, click the Delete button. To edit the boot image, make the desired changes and click Accept. The screen provides access to the LILO boot image options described in the previous chapter and several less commonly used options.

Configuring Non-Linux Boot Images

To add, change, or delete a non-Linux partition, select Config ➤ Boot Mode ➤ LILO ➤ Configure LILO Other OSs Configurations from linuxconf's menu tree. The LILO Other OS Configurations Screen will appear; Figure 9.10 shows the graphical version of this screen.

FIGURE 9.10   The LILO Other OSs Configurations screen

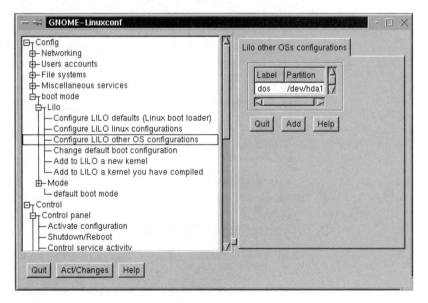

You can add a new non-Linux boot image by clicking Add. To edit or delete an existing non-Linux boot image, select the image and press Enter. The Other Operating System Setup screen will appear. To delete the boot image, click the Delete button. To edit the boot image, make the desired changes and click Accept. The Other Operating Systems Setup screen provides access to the label and other options described in the previous chapter. The text field labeled Partition to Boot corresponds to the other option.

Configuring the Default Boot Image

To specify the default boot image, select Config ➢ Boot Mode ➢ LILO ➢ Change Default Boot Configuration from linuxconf's menu tree. The Default Boot Configuration screen will appear; Figure 9.11 shows the graphical version of this screen.

FIGURE 9.11 The Default Boot Configuration screen

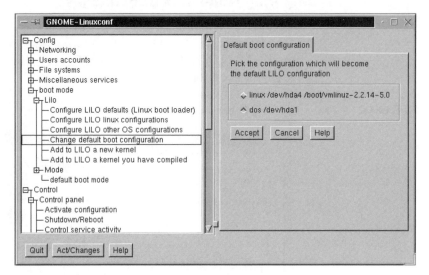

To specify a different default boot image, click the radio button corresponding to the desired default boot image, and click Accept.

Configuring Boot Options

You can use linuxconf to configure boot options. To do so, select Config ➢ Boot Mode ➢ Mode ➢ Default Boot Mode from linuxconf's menu tree. The Boot Mode Configuration screen will appear; Figure 9.12 shows the graphical version of this screen.

FIGURE 9.12 The Boot Mode Configuration screen

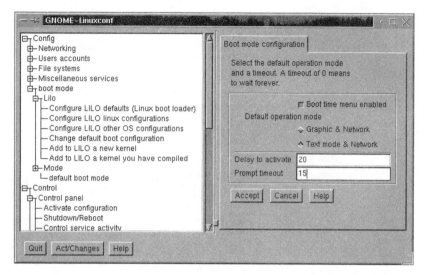

You can use this screen to enable or disable LILO's boot menu and to specify the boot delay and prompt timeout. The latter two options are also available on the LILO Defaults screen. You can also use the Boot Mode Configuration screen to specify whether the system starts in text mode (runlevel 3) or graphical mode (runlevel 5).

Configuring Networking

You can use linuxconf to configure basic and advanced networking options. This subsection explains how to configure basic options; subsequent chapters—especially Chapter 15, "Understanding Configuration Files and Scripts"—explain how to configure advanced options.

Configuring the Host Name

To configure the host name, select Config ➢ Networking ➢ Client Tasks ➢ Basic Host Information from linuxconf's menu tree. The This Host Basic Configuration screen will appear; Figure 9.13 shows the graphical version of this screen.

FIGURE 9.13 The This Host Basic Configuration screen

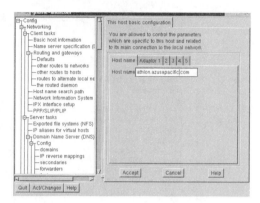

The graphical This Host Basic Configuration screen includes several tabs that let you select from among various windows. If the Host Name screen is not visible in the graphical screen, click the Host Name tab. To specify the host name, type it into the text box, and click Accept.

Configuring Network Adapters

To configure a network adapter, select Config ➢ Networking ➢ Client Tasks ➢ Basic Host Information from linuxconf's menu tree. The This Host Basic Configuration screen will appear. The graphical screen includes several tabs that let you select from among various windows. If the Adapter 1 screen is not visible in the graphical screen, click the Adapter 1 tab. The Adapter 1 screen will appear; Figure 9.14 shows the graphical version of this screen.

If you're using the text version of linuxconf, simply scroll to view the portion of the This Host Basic Configuration screen that pertains to Adapter 1. The linuxconf program provides access to configuration options for as many as 5 network adapters.

FIGURE 9.14   The Adapter 1 screen

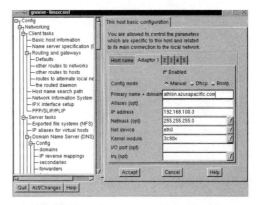

Using the Adapter 1 screen or one of the other adapter screens, you can enable or disable the adapter, and you can specify whether its configuration is static or obtained via DHCP or BOOTP. If the configuration is static, you can specify the fully qualified domain name (FQDN) using the text box labeled Primary Name + Domain. You can also specify the IP address, netmask, and several other options, including device options. Click Accept to save your changes.

Configuring Name Servers

To configure name servers, select Config ➢ Networking ➢ Client Tasks ➢ Name Server Specification from linuxconf's menu tree. The Resolver Configuration screen will appear; Figure 9.15 shows the graphical version of this screen.

FIGURE 9.15   The Resolver Configuration screen

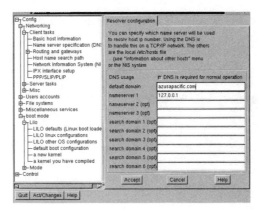

If DNS is not required for normal operation, disable DNS Is Required for Normal Operation. Otherwise, specify the default domain and the IP address (number) of the primary nameserver associated with the system. You can specify as many as two additional nameservers and as many as six additional search domains. Click Accept to save your changes.

Configuring the Default Gateway

To configure the default gateway, select Config ➢ Networking ➢ Client Tasks ➢ Routing and Gateways ➢ Set Defaults from `linuxconf`'s menu tree. The Defaults screen will appear; Figure 9.16 shows the graphical version of this screen.

FIGURE 9.16 The Defaults screen

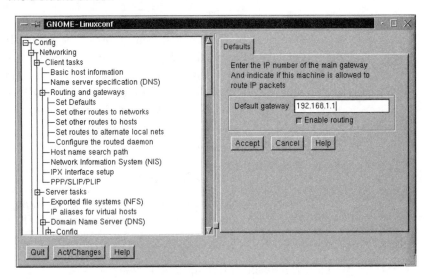

Specify the IP address of the default gateway. If you want this system to act as a router, turn on Enable Routing. For more information on configuring routing, see Chapter 29, "Configuring a Linux Router."

Activating Changes

As explained earlier, when you change a configuration option using `linuxconf`, the change may occur immediately, or it may remain pending until the change is activated. Although configuration files are updated immediately, most system services will not detect changes in their configuration until the services are restarted. When you instruct linuxconf to activate pending changes, it restarts those services whose configurations you've changed.

To activate pending changes, click Act/Changes. The Status of the System screen will appear; Figure 9.17 shows the graphical version of this screen.

FIGURE 9.17 The Status of the System screen

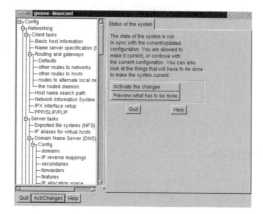

If you want to know what changes are pending, click Preview What Has to Be Done. The linuxconf program displays the pending changes. To activate pending changes, click Activate the Changes. To exit the Status of the System screen without activating any pending changes, click Quit.

You should generally activate pending changes before exiting linuxconf. If you neglect to do so, linuxconf will prompt you to confirm that you want to exit without activating the changes you specified.

Summary

In this chapter, you learned about configuring install-time options after installation has been completed. The most important topics covered are:

Keyboard   After installation, you can configure the keyboard by using the kbdconfig program.

Mouse   After installation, you can configure the mouse by using the mouseconfig program.

Time Zone   After installation, you can configure the time zone by using the timeconfig program.

Sound   After installation, you can configure sound by using the `sndconfig` program.

Default Run Level   After installation, you can configure the default run-level by using the `linuxconf` program.

Authentication   After installation, you can configure shadow passwords by using the `pwconv` or `pwunconv` program or change the `root` password by using the `linuxconf` program.

LILO Options   After installation, you can configure LILO options by using the `linuxconf` program.

Networking   After installation, you can configure networking by using the `linuxconf` program.

Key Terms

Before going on to the next chapter, be sure you're familiar with the following term:

Runlevel

Additional Sources of Information

If you'd like further information about the topics presented in this chapter, you should consult the following sources:

- *The Official Red Hat Linux Reference Guide*
- The man pages for the programs and tools described in the chapter

Review Questions

Please note that you may find several of these questions really easy, because they're purely recall questions. But, questions of this type sometimes show up on the written exam. They're trivial to answer from the keyboard but can be troublesome in a closed-book exam. I crammed them for the exam, and now I found myself looking back to check the answers! Even at the keyboard, you can waste precious minutes seeking the name of an important utility, so it's best to memorize the names of all programs you're likely to use on the performance-based exams. That way, you can direct your energies toward more significant issues.

1. Which of the following programs is used to configure the keyboard?

   A. kbconfig

   B. kbdconfig

   C. keyconfig

   D. keyboardconfig

2. Which of the following programs is used to configure the mouse?

   A. mousecfg

   B. mouseconfig

   C. mseconfig

   D. mousetest

3. Which of the following programs is used to configure sound?

   A. soundcfg

   B. sndconfig

   C. soundcfg

   D. soundconfig

4. Which runlevel causes an X-based login to appear when the system is booted?

   A. 2

   B. 3

   C. 4

   D. 5

5. Which of the following is true of `linuxconf`?

   A. It can be launched by issuing the `linuxconf` command.

   B. It operates in graphical mode.

   C. It operates in text mode.

   D. You must have a mouse to operate it.

6. When using `linuxconf`, when must you explicitly activate pending changes?

   A. If another user is running `linuxconf`

   B. If one or more system services must be restarted to effect the changes

   C. If the changes affect user accounts

   D. If the changes are complex

Answers to Review Questions

1. B. The `kbdconfig` program configures the keyboard.

2. B. The `mouseconfig` program configures the mouse.

3. B. The `sndconfig` program configures the sound system.

4. D . Runlevel 2 is multiuser mode without networking. Runlevel 3 is multiuser mode with networking. Runlevel 4 is essentially the same as runlevel 3.

5. A, B, and C. The `linuxconf` program operates in both text and graphical mode; it does not require a mouse.

6. B. The `linuxconf` program does not automatically restart services whose configurations you've changed until you instruct it to do so.

Chapter 10

Administering User Accounts and Groups

RHCE PREPARATION TOPICS COVERED IN THIS CHAPTER:

✓ Understand, and know how to create, different kinds of user accounts.

✓ Understand, and know how to configure, the user environment.

✓ Be familiar with system and user bash configuration files.

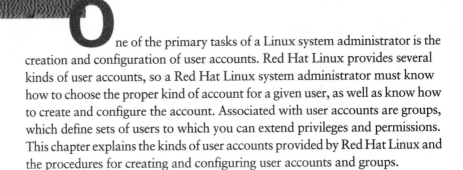

ne of the primary tasks of a Linux system administrator is the creation and configuration of user accounts. Red Hat Linux provides several kinds of user accounts, so a Red Hat Linux system administrator must know how to choose the proper kind of account for a given user, as well as know how to create and configure the account. Associated with user accounts are groups, which define sets of users to which you can extend privileges and permissions. This chapter explains the kinds of user accounts provided by Red Hat Linux and the procedures for creating and configuring user accounts and groups.

User Accounts

The /etc/passwd file defines Linux user accounts. Each line in the file describes a single user. Here is a typical /etc/passwd file:

```
root:x:0:0:root:/root:/bin/bash
bin:x:1:1:bin:/bin:
daemon:x:2:2:daemon:/sbin:
adm:x:3:4:adm:/var/adm:
lp:x:4:7:lp:/var/spool/lpd:
sync:x:5:0:sync:/sbin:/bin/sync
shutdown:x:6:0:shutdown:/sbin:/sbin/shutdown
halt:x:7:0:halt:/sbin:/sbin/halt
mail:x:8:12:mail:/var/spool/mail:
news:x:9:13:news:/var/spool/news:
uucp:x:10:14:uucp:/var/spool/uucp:
```

```
operator:x:11:0:operator:/root:
games:x:12:100:games:/usr/games:
gopher:x:13:30:gopher:/usr/lib/gopher-data:
ftp:x:14:50:FTP User:/home/ftp:
nobody:x:99:99:Nobody:/:
xfs:x:100:233:X Font Server:/etc/X11/fs:/bin/false
bill:x:500:500:Bill McCarty:/home/bill:/bin/bash
```

Each line contains several fields, delimited by colons. Following is a list of these fields and an explanation of each one.

User name   The login name associated with the user account.

Password   The login password associated with the user account (if shadow passwords are enabled, only the placeholder **x** appears).

User ID   A unique numerical ID associated with the user account.

Group ID   The numerical ID associated with the user's home group. Red Hat Linux defines a personal group for each user account.

Full name   The user's full name.

Home directory   The directory that is set at login as the current directory.

Shell   The command interpreter that is loaded when the user logs in via a command-line interface; the shell is not loaded when the user logs in via X.

Because all the lines of /etc/passwd have the same structure, you could say that Linux provides only a single kind of user account. However, Red Hat Linux recognizes the following kinds of user accounts:

- Ordinary user accounts, also known as shell accounts
- PPP accounts, for users who log in via PPP
- SLIP accounts, for users who log in via SLIP
- UUCP accounts, for users who log in via UUCP
- POP accounts, for users who access mail via POP, but don't actually log in
- Virtual POP accounts, for users who access mail via POP, on a server that provides virtual e-mail domains

Administering user accounts involves creating, configuring, and deleting user accounts. You can administer user accounts by using either the user-conf tool or the command line.

The next section explains how to administer user accounts via the userconf tool. The following section explains how to administer user accounts via the command line.

Administering User Accounts via the *userconf* Tool

The easiest way to administer user accounts is via the userconf tool, because it automatically performs several otherwise tedious operations. You can launch the userconf tool by issuing the command

    userconf

Figure 10.1 shows the userconf menu running from a console. If you prefer, you can run userconf from X, in which case the menu has a somewhat different appearance.

FIGURE 10.1 The userconf menu

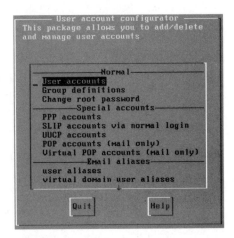

The linuxconf configuration program provides another way to access userconf. To access userconf via linuxconf, issue the command

    linuxconf

Then, navigate to the user account menu by choosing Config ➢ Users Accounts from the linuxconf menu. Figure 10.2 shows the linuxconf Users Accounts menu.

The instructions in this chapter assume you're using userconf; however, you can easily use linuxconf to perform any of the operations described.

FIGURE 10.2   The Linuxconf Users Accounts menu

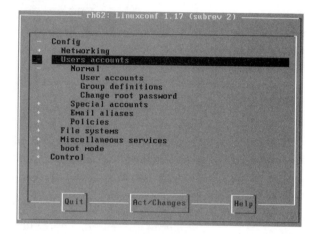

To administer a given kind of user account, highlight the kind you want to administer, and press Enter. If, however, you're using X, you can simply click the type of account you're interested in. The next several subsections explain how to administer the various kinds of accounts.

Creating Ordinary User Accounts

Ordinary user accounts—often called shell accounts—let the user log in and use the system. To create an ordinary user account follow these steps:

1. Launch userconf.

2. Choose Users Accounts, and press Enter. If you're using X, click Users Accounts. The Users Accounts screen, shown in Figure 10.3, will appear. If you're using X, this screen and subsequent screens will look somewhat different.

   Depending on the filter settings (in Control ➢ Features), you may see a Filter dialog box. Use the dialog box to limit the user accounts to those you want to see or press Accept to view all accounts.

FIGURE 10.3 The Users Accounts screen

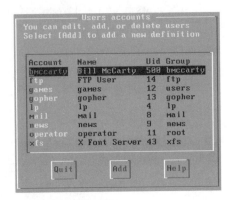

3. Click the Add button. The User Account Creation screen, shown in Figure 10.4, will appear.

4. Fill in the parameter fields. Unless you're using a very large window, some fields won't be visible; simply scroll the screen to view them. Refer to Tables 10.1 and 10.2 for information on each field. The privilege fields can have one of three values:

- Denied, which means the user lacks the privilege

- Granted, which means the user has the privilege, but must confirm authorization by entering the login password

- Granted/silent, which means the user has the privilege and need not confirm authorization by entering a password

FIGURE 10.4 The User Account Creation screen

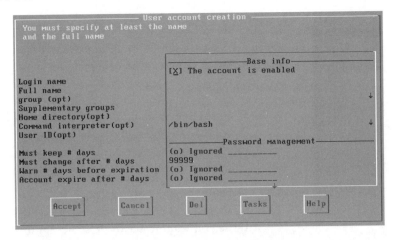

TABLE 10.1 User Account Parameters

Parameter	Description
The account is enabled	If checked, the user can log in.
Login name	The login name of the user account. The login name should not contain special characters other than dash (-) or underscore (_). The login name can be as many as 256 characters in length; however, most system administrators assign login names of not more than 8–10 characters in length.
Full name	The user's full name (optional).
Group	The numeric ID of user's home group (optional). By default, a personal group having the same name as the login is created.
Supplementary groups	Additional groups to which the user belongs (optional). By default, no additional groups are assigned.
Home directory	The user's home directory (optional). By default, the *directory /home/ login_name* is assigned, where *login_name* is the user's login name.
Command interpreter	The command interpreter (shell), /bin/bash by default (optional).
User ID	The numeric user ID (optional). By default, the next sequential numeric ID is assigned.
Must keep # days	Number of days the user must keep the password, or −1 if the password can be changed immediately.
Must change after # days	Number of days until the user must change the password, or 99999 if the password does not expire.
Warn # days before expiration	Number of days warning given before password expiration, or −1 if no warning is to be given.

TABLE 10.1 User Account Parameters *(continued)*

Parameter	Description
Account expire after # days	Number of days until the account expires, or –1 if the account never expires.
Expiration date	Expiration date of the account, or blank if the Account Expire After # Days parameter is specified.
Redirect messages to	User account to which e-mail for this account is redirected (optional).
Email alias	E-mail addresses (other than the login name) that should be directed to this account (optional).

TABLE 10.2 User Privilege Parameters

Privilege	Description
May use linuxconf	The user may access any linuxconf screen. However, unless the user is explicitly granted permission to activate configuration changes, the user may not do so.
May activate config changes	The user may activate linuxconf configuration changes.
May shutdown	The user may shut down the system. Even without this privilege, a user can use the console to shut down the system by pressing Ctrl+Alt+Del.
May switch network mode	The user may change system runlevels.
May view system logs	The user may view system logs.
SuperUser equivalence	The user may issue privileged commands.

TABLE 10.2 User Privilege Parameters *(continued)*

Privilege	Description
Apache administration	The user can configure the Apache Web server.
Mail to Fax manager	The user can configure the Mail to Fax service.
Samba administration	The user can configure Samba.
Message of the day	The user can modify the message of the day.
POP accounts manager	The user can administer POP accounts.
PPP accounts manager	The user can administer PPP accounts.
UUCP manager	The user can administer UUCP accounts.

5. Click the Accept button. The Changing Password dialog box, shown in Figure 10.5, will appear.

FIGURE 10.5 The Changing Password screen

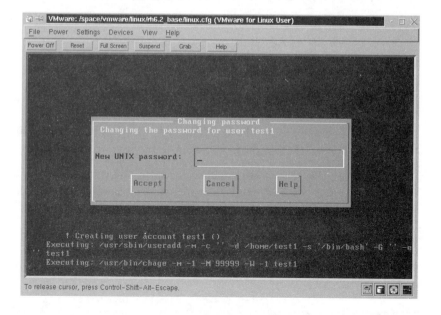

6. Type the desired password, and click the Accept button. The Changing Password dialog box will reappear.

7. Confirm the password you previously entered by retyping it. Click the Accept button. The Users Accounts screen will reappear.

8. When you're done administering user accounts, click the Quit button.

Now that you've seen how to use userconf to create an ordinary user account, you should complete Exercise 10.1.

EXERCISE 10.1

Creating an Ordinary User Account

System administrators must often create new user accounts. This exercise tests your ability to do so. If necessary, look back to the step-by-step procedure for using userconf. However, bear in mind that the RHCE exam is closed-book, so you won't be able to consult references when asked to perform this operation during the RHCE exam.

1. Use userconf to create an ordinary user account with a login of test101.

2. Verify that you can log in as test101 from the console.

Modifying Ordinary User Accounts

To modify an ordinary user account follow these steps:

1. Launch userconf.

2. Choose User Accounts and press Enter; or, if you're using X, click User Accounts. The Users Accounts screen appears.

    Depending on the filter settings (in Control ➤ Features), you may see a Filter dialog box. Use the dialog box to limit the user accounts to those you want to see, or press Accept to view all accounts.

3. Highlight the account you want to modify and press Enter; or, if you're using X, you can simply click the account.

4. Modify the fields as desired.

5. Click the Accept button.

Now that you've seen how to modify an ordinary user account, complete Exercise 10.2, so that you can be confident you're able to perform the operation yourself.

EXERCISE 10.2

Modifying an Ordinary User Account

The RHCE exam is likely to require you to modify a user account. This exercise tests your ability to do so. Look back to the step-by-step procedure if you need to. But, before moving on, be sure you can modify an ordinary user account without referring to the book: You won't be able to use the book during the RHCE exam.

1. Use userconf to modify the user test101 to have the full name "Test User."

2. Verify that your change is correct by logging in as test101 and issuing the finger command.

Creating and Modifying PPP User Accounts

PPP user accounts are used by users who log in via PPP from a remote location. The default command interpreter for PPP user accounts is usr/lib/linuxconf/lib/ppplogin. By default, PPP users are members of the pppusers group.

To create a PPP user account follow these steps:

1. Launch userconf.

2. Choose PPP Accounts and press Enter; or, if you're using X, click PPP Accounts and click the Special Accounts tab. The User Accounts screen appears.

   Depending on the filter settings (in Control ➤ Features), you may see a Filter dialog box. Use the dialog box to limit the user accounts to those you want to see, or press Accept to view all accounts.

3. Click the Add button. The User Account Creation screen, shown as Figure 10.6, will appear.

FIGURE 10.6 The User Account Creation screen

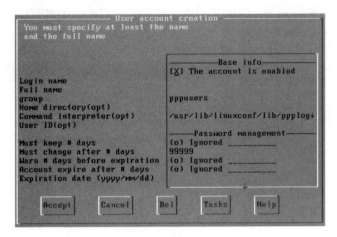

4. Fill in the parameter fields. Refer to Tables 10.1 and 10.2 for information on each field.

5. Click the Accept button. The Changing Password dialog box will appear.

6. Type the desired password, and click the Accept button. The Changing Password dialog box will reappear.

7. Confirm the password you previously entered by retyping it. Click the Accept button. The Users Accounts screen will reappear.

8. When you're done administering PPP user accounts, click the Quit button.

To modify a PPP user account follow these steps:

1. Launch userconf.

2. Choose PPP Accounts and press Enter; or, if you're using X, click PPP Accounts. The Users Accounts screen will appear.

   Depending on the filter settings (in Control ➤ Features), you may see a Filter dialog box. Use the dialog box to limit the user accounts to those you want to see, or press Accept to view all accounts.

3. Highlight the account you want to modify and press Enter; or, if you're using X, you can simply click the account.

4. Modify the fields as desired.

5. Click the Accept button.

Creating and Modifying SLIP User Accounts

SLIP user accounts are used by users who log in via SLIP from a remote location. The default command interpreter for SLIP user accounts is /sbin/diplogin. By default, SLIP users are members of the slipusers group.

To create a SLIP user account follow these steps:

1. Launch userconf.

2. Choose SLIP Accounts and press Enter; or, if you're using X, click SLIP Accounts. The Users Accounts screen will appear.

   Depending on the filter settings (in Control ➤ Features), you may see a Filter dialog box. Use the dialog box to limit the user accounts to those you want to see, or press Accept to view all accounts.

3. Click the Add button. The User Account Creation screen will appear.

4. Fill in the parameter fields. Refer to Tables 10.1 and 10.2 for information on each field.

5. Click the Accept button. The Changing Password dialog box will appear.

6. Type the desired password, and click the Accept button. The Changing Password dialog box will reappear.

7. Confirm the password you previously entered by retyping it. Click the Accept button. The Users Accounts screen will reappear.

8. When you're done administering SLIP user accounts, click the Quit button.

To modify a SLIP user account follow these steps:

1. Launch userconf.

2. Choose SLIP Accounts and press Enter; or, if you're using X, click SLIP Accounts. The Users Accounts screen will appear.

   Depending on the filter settings (in Control ➤ Features), you may see a Filter dialog box. Use the dialog box to limit the user accounts to those you want to see, or press Accept to view all accounts.

3. Highlight the account you want to modify and press Enter; or, if you're using X, you can simply click the account.

4. Modify the fields as desired.

5. Click the Accept button.

Creating and Modifying UUCP User Accounts

Before the advent of the Internet, UUCP was the main way in which Unix computers communicated; a few Linux sites use UUCP today. UUCP user accounts are used by processes that log in via UUCP from a remote location. The default command interpreter for UUCP user accounts is /usr/sbin/uucico. By default, UUCP users are members of the uucp group. The default home directory of a UUCP user is /var/spool/uucppublic.

To create a UUCP user account do the following:

1. Launch userconf.

2. Choose UUCP Accounts and press Enter; or, if you're using X, click UUCP Accounts.

3. The Users Accounts screen will appear.

   Depending on the filter settings (in Control ➢ Features), you may see a Filter dialog box. Use the dialog box to limit the user accounts to those you want to see, or press Accept to view all accounts.

4. Click the Add button. The User Account Creation screen will appear.

5. Fill in the parameter fields. Refer to Tables 10.1 and 10.2 for information on each field.

6. Click the Accept button. The Changing Password dialog box will appear.

7. Type the desired password, and click the Accept button. The Changing Password dialog box will reappear.

8. Confirm the password you previously entered by retyping it. Click the Accept button. The Users Accounts screen will reappear.

9. When you're done administering UUCP user accounts, click the Quit button.

To modify a UUCP user account do the following:

1. Launch userconf.

2. Choose UUCP Accounts and press Enter; or, if you're using X, click UUCP Accounts. The Users Accounts screen will appear.

   Depending on the filter settings (in Control ➢ Features), you may see a Filter dialog box. Use the dialog box to limit the user accounts to those you want to see, or press Accept to view all accounts.

3. Highlight the account you want to modify and press Enter; or, if you're using X, you can simply click the account.

4. Modify the fields as desired.

5. Click the Accept button.

Creating and Modifying POP User Accounts

POP user accounts are used by users who access mail via POP from a remote location. POP users don't actually log in to the system, so the POP User Accounts Creation screen doesn't include the Command Interpreter field. By default, POP users are members of the popusers group.

To create a POP user account do the following:

1. Launch userconf.

2. Choose POP Accounts and press Enter; or, if you're using X, click POP Accounts. The Users Accounts screen will appear.

   Depending on the filter settings (in Control ➤ Features), you may see a Filter dialog box. Use the dialog box to limit the user accounts to those you want to see, or press Accept to view all accounts.

3. Click the Add button. The User Account Creation screen will appear.

4. Fill in the parameter fields. Refer to Tables 10.1 and 10.2 for information on each field.

5. Click the Accept button. The Changing Password dialog box will appear.

6. Type the desired password, and click the Accept button. The Changing Password dialog box will reappear.

7. Confirm the password you previously entered by retyping it. Click the Accept button. The Users Accounts screen will reappear.

8. When you're done administering POP user accounts, click the Quit button.

To modify a POP user account follow theses steps:

1. Launch userconf.

2. Choose POP Accounts and press Enter; or, if you're using X, click POP Accounts. The Users Accounts screen will appear.

   Depending on the filter settings (in Control ➤ Features), you may see a Filter dialog box. Use the dialog box to limit the user accounts to those you want to see, or press Accept to view all accounts.

3. Highlight the account you want to modify and press Enter; or, if you're using X, you can simply click the account.

4. Modify the fields as desired.

5. Click the Accept button.

Enabling and Disabling User Accounts

If you want to lock out a user, you can disable the user's account. If a user's account is disabled, the user cannot log in or access the POP server. To disable a user account, perform the following steps:

1. Launch `userconf`.

2. Choose User Accounts and press Enter; or, if you're using X, click User Accounts. The Users Accounts screen will appear.

3. Select the user account you want to disable and press Enter; or, if you're using X, you can simply click the user account. The user information screen will appear.

4. Uncheck the box labeled The Account Is Enabled. Click the Accept button.

To enable a disabled user account, follow a similar procedure:

1. Launch `userconf`.

2. Choose User Accounts and press Enter; or, if you're using X, click User Accounts. The Users Accounts screen will appear.

3. Select the user account you want to disable and press Enter; or, if you're using X, you can simply click the user account. The User Information screen will appear.

4. Check the box labeled The Account Is Enabled. Click the Accept button.

Deleting User Accounts

If a user account is no longed needed, it's better to delete it than merely disable it. By deleting the account, you free the disk space occupied by the user's home directory and its contents.

To delete a user account, perform the following steps:

1. Launch `userconf`.

2. Choose User Accounts and press Enter; or, if you're using X, click User Accounts. The Users Accounts screen will appear.

3. Select the user account you want to delete and press Enter; or, if you're using X, you can simply click the user account. The User Information screen will appear.

4. To delete the account, click the Del button. The Deleting Account screen, shown as Figure 10.7, will appear.

FIGURE 10.7 The Deleting Account screen

5. Select one of the following desired options:

- Archive the Account's Data

- Delete the Account's Data

- Leave the Account's Data in Place

The default option, Archive the Account's Data, deletes the user from /etc/passwd and creates a gzip-compressed archive in the /home/ oldaccounts directory, which is automatically created if it does not exist. The file has the name

user-yyyy-mm-dd-xxx.tar.gz

where *user* is the userid, *yyyy-mm-dd* is the current date, and *xxx* is the process ID of the process that performed the deletion. The option Delete the Account's Data deletes the user's home directory and its contents.

6. Click the Accept button.

After studying the procedure for deleting a user account, complete Exercise 10.3, which tests your ability to perform that operation.

WARNING   A user may own files stored in directories other than the user's home directory. If you delete the user account, the files remain. Such files, called orphan files, are owned by the user ID of the deleted user account. If you create a new account that has the user ID of the deleted account, the new user account becomes the owner of the orphan files.

EXERCISE 10.3

Deleting a User Account

When a user account is no longer used, you should promptly remove it so that it cannot be used by a cracker intent on compromising security of your system. This exercise tests your ability to delete a user account. Look back to the procedure if you must, but be mindful that you won't have the luxury of doing so during the RHCE exam.

1. Use userconf to create an ordinary user account with a login of test101.

2. Delete the user account you created.

3. Inspect /etc/passwd to verify that the account was deleted.

Administering User Accounts via the Command Line

Some administrators prefer to use the command line to administer user accounts. Knowing the relevant commands is helpful, because you can use them to construct scripts that simplify common system administration tasks. The most important commands for administering users are the following:

- useradd, which creates a user account

- userdel, which deletes a user account

- usermod, which modifies a user account

- chfn, which changes the full name field associated with a user account

The full name field contains the so-called gecos information, including name, office location, phone number, and so on.

- **chsh**, which changes the command interpreter associated with a user account

Later in this chapter, you'll learn about additional commands that help administer passwords associated with user accounts.

The *useradd* Command

The useradd command, which is the same program as the adduser command, creates a new user account. The basic form of the command is:

```
useradd -d home -e expire -f inactive -g group -G groups
➥ -m -s shell -u uid username
```

Only the final argument (username), which specifies the login name, is required. The remaining arguments have these meanings:

-d *home*	Specifies the user's home directory.
-e *expire*	Specifies the expiration date of the account. Specified as *mm/dd/yy*.
-f *inactive*	Specifies the number of days after password expiration that the account is disabled. The default value, -1, prevents the account from being disabled.
-g *group*	Specifies the user's home group name or number. The default value is 100. Used with the –n flag.
-G *groups*	A comma-separated list of group names or numbers, specifying supplementary groups of which the user is to be made a member.
–m	Specifies that the user's home directory is to be automatically created.
–n	Specifies that no private user group should be created.
-s *shell*	Specifies the user's shell. If not specified, the system will launch the default shell when the user logs in.
-u *uid*	The numerical ID of the user. If not specified, the system chooses the next available user ID.

For more information on the useradd command, see its man page.

 When you create a user account, the account initially has no password. You should use the passwd command, described later in this chapter, to associate a password with the user account.

The *userdel* Command

The userdel command deletes a user account. The form of the command is

    userdel *user*

where *user* is the login name of the user to be deleted. If you want to delete the user's home directory and its contents, issue a command of the form:

    userdel -r *user*

For more information on the userdel command, see its man page.

 A user may own files stored in directories other than the user's home directory. If you delete the user account, the files remain. Such files, called orphan files, are owned by the user ID of the deleted user account. If you create a new account that has the user ID of the deleted account, the new user account becomes the owner of the orphan files.

The *usermod* Command

The usermod command lets you modify an existing user account. Its form resembles that of the useradd command

    usermod -d *home* -e *expire* -f *inactive* -g *group* -G *groups*
    ➡ -l *login* -s *shell* -u uid *username*

All arguments are optional, except the last; however, at least one additional argument must be specified. The argument -l login lets you change the login name associated with the account. The name of the user's home directory is not affected by this change.

For more information on the usermod command, see its man page.

The *chfn* Command

The chfn command lets you change the full name associated with a user account. The form of the command is

chfn *user*

where *user* is the login name of the account to be modified. The command will prompt for the following information, known as the gecos information:

- Name

- Office

- Office phone

- Home phone

If you don't wish to specify a value for a prompted field, simply press Enter.

You can also use the chfn command in non-interactive mode. See its man page for this and other information.

The *chsh* Command

The chsh command lets you change the command interpreter associated with a user account. The form of the command is

chsh −s shell *user*

where *shell* specifies the path of the desired command interpreter and *user* specifies the login name of the user account to be modified. Only approved command interpreters listed in /etc/shells can be specified.

For more information on the chsh command, see its man page.

You should now complete Exercise 10.4, which asks you to perform a variety of user administration tasks via the Linux command line.

EXERCISE 10.4

Administering User Accounts via the Command Line

Some Linux users know only a single way to perform a given task. When a system is broken or misconfigured, some ways of performing a task may not be available to you; for example, if X is not working, X-based tools will not be available. This exercise tests your ability to perform common user administration tasks by using the command line. At this point, you can look back to the relevant procedures, but you won't have the benefit of books or notes while taking the RHCE exam.

EXERCISE 10.4 *(continued)*

1. Use the command line to create an ordinary user account with a login of test101.

2. Use the command line to modify the account to have the associated full name goner.

3. Use the command line to delete the user account you created.

4. Inspect /etc/passwd to verify that the account was deleted.

Administering Groups via *userconf*

User groups—often simply called groups—let you associate a set of users, called members. You use the familiar Unix chmod command to specify permissions needed to access files and directories for the owner, members of the owning group, and others.

The /etc/group file defines Linux user groups. Each line in the file describes a single group. Here is a typical /etc/group file:

```
root::0:root
bin::1:root,bin,daemon
daemon::2:root,bin,daemon
sys::3:root,bin,adm
adm::4:root,adm,daemon
tty::5:
disk::6:root
lp::7:daemon,lp
mem::8:
kmem::9:
wheel::10:root
mail::12:mail
news::13:news
uucp::14:uucp
man::15:
games::20:
gopher::30:
dip::40:
ftp::50:
```

```
nobody::99:
users::100:
floppy:x:19:
console:x:101:
utmp:x:102:
pppusers:x:230:
popusers:x:231:
slipusers:x:232:
slocate:x:21:
xfs:x:233:
bill:x:500:
```

Each line contains the following fields, delimited by colons:

Group name   The name of the group defined by this line of the /etc/ group file.

Password   An encrypted password associated with the group. Under Linux, group passwords are not commonly used.

Group ID   The numerical ID associated with the group.

Members   The login names of the group members.

You can use linuxconf or userconf to create groups, change group membership, and delete groups. You can also accomplish these operations by using the command line. This section explains how to use userconf to administer groups; the following section explains how to use the command line to administer groups.

Creating a Group

To create a group by using userconf, follow this procedure:

1. Launch userconf.

2. Choose Group Definitions and press Enter; or, if you're using X, click Group Definitions.

   Depending on the filter settings (in Control ➤ Features), you may see a Filter dialog box. Use the dialog box to limit the user groups to those you want to see, or press Accept to view all groups. The Users Groups screen, shown in Figure 10.8, will appear.

FIGURE 10.8 The User Groups screen

3. Click the Add button. The Group Specification screen, shown in Figure 10.9, will appear.

FIGURE 10.9 The Group Specification screen

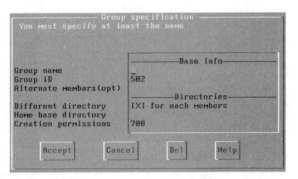

4. Fill in the parameter fields. Refer to Table 10.3 for information on each field.

5. Click the Accept button.

TABLE 10.3 Group Parameters

PARAMETER	DESCRIPTION
Group name	The name of the group.

TABLE 10.3 Group Parameters *(continued)*

PARAMETER	DESCRIPTION
Group ID	The numeric group ID.
Alternate members	User names of group members, separated by one or more spaces (optional).

Deleting a Group

To delete a group by using userconf, follow this procedure:

1. Launch userconf.

2. Choose Group Definitions and press Enter; or, if you're using X, click Group Definitions.

   Depending on the filter settings (in Control ➤ Features), you may see a Filter dialog box. Use the dialog box to limit the user groups to those you want to see, or press Accept to view all groups. The Users Groups screen will appear.

3. Select the group you want to delete and press Enter; or, if you're using X, click the group. The Group Specification screen will appear.

4. To delete the group, click the Del button. A dialog box will ask you to confirm the operation; click Yes to delete the group or No to abort the deletion.

Modifying Group Membership

You can modify group membership by modifying each affected user account or by modifying the group. Generally, it's more convenient to modify the group. To do so perform the following steps:

1. Launch userconf.

2. Choose Group Definitions and press Enter; or, if you're using X, click Group Definitions.

   Depending on the filter settings (in Control ➤ Features), you may see a Filter dialog box. Use the dialog box to limit the user groups to those you want to see, or press Accept to view all groups. The Users Groups screen will appear.

3. Select the group you want to modify and press Enter; or, if you're using X, click the group. The Group Specification screen will appear.

4. Modify the Alternate Members field as desired, and click the Accept button.

Before pressing on, complete Exercise 10.5, which tests your ability to perform common group administration tasks.

EXERCISE 10.5

Administering Groups

This exercise requires you to add and delete a user group. Look back to the step-by-step procedures if you must. But be ready to perform group administration operations without help before taking the RHCE exam.

1. Define new users with login names test01, test02, and test03.

2. Define a new group named testgroup.

3. Add each of the new users to the group.

4. Check your work by inspecting /etc/group.

5. Delete the test03 user from the group.

6. Check your work by inspecting /etc/group.

Administering Groups via the Command Line

You can use the command line to administer user groups. Commands let you create a group, delete a group, or modify group membership.

Creating a Group

To create a group via the command line, issue the groupadd command, which has the following form:

```
groupadd -g groupid group
```

You must specify the name of the group to be created, *group*. If you do not specify a group ID, the next group ID will be used. If you want to create a system group—one with a group ID less than 500—specify -r as an argument before the group name. See the man page for groupadd for additional information.

Deleting a Group

To delete a group via the command line, issue the groupdel command, which has the following form:

```
groupdel group
```

See the man page for groupdel for additional information.

Modifying Group Name

To modify the name of a group via the command line, issue the groupmod command, which has the following form:

```
groupmod -n newname group
```

See the man page for groupmod for additional information.

Modifying Group Membership

To modify membership of a group via the command line, you must manually edit /etc/group or issue the usermod command to adjust the group membership of each affected user. Generally, this means you must issue the command several times; thus, it's often more convenient to modify group membership via userconf than from the command line. The usermod command is described earlier in this chapter.

To check your understanding of group administration via the command line, complete Exercise 10.6.

EXERCISE 10.6

Administering Groups via the Command Line

This exercise tests your ability to use the command line to perform group administration tasks. You can look back to the explanation of the usermod command if you need help. But, before moving on, be sure you can complete the exercise without referring to the chapter. Otherwise, you won't be properly prepared for the RHCE exam.

Perform the operations given in Exercise 10.5, but use the command line rather than userconf.

Sharing Data

Often, users need to share data that they don't want others to be able to access or modify. A simple way of accomplishing this is to create a group for each set of users who want to share access to data, assign group ownership of the related files or directories to the new group, then assign access permissions that permit members of the group to perform authorized operations but exclude others from doing so.

For example, suppose tom, dick, and harry want to have access to the directory bigdeal, but want to prohibit access by others. You could create a group named tdandh (as a reminder of its members) and set the group ownership of the bigdeal directory to tdandh. Assign permissions of 770 to the directory, and you have the desired result.

Exercise 10.7 tests your ability to use access permissions to share data between two users.

EXERCISE 10.7

Sharing Data

This exercise requires you to create a user group and a directory and then set access permissions that give the group special access to a directory. If you need a review of the chmod command, look back to Chapter 3, "Unix Basics." Before moving on, be sure you can perform the exercise without assistance.

EXERCISE 10.7 *(continued)*

1. Create a directory named project.

2. Set up a group that includes the users ftp and lp.

3. Set permissions of the directory so that ftp and lp can read and write it, but others can only read it.

User Profile Customization

When a user logs in, the command interpreter executes several files that configure the user's environment. The files contain commands that set environment variables, adjust the path, create command aliases, and so on. By revising these files, you can configure a user's environment.

Systemwide User Profiles

The files executed when a user, whose shell is BASH, logs in include the following:

- /etc/bashrc, a file that establishes aliases and functions.

- /etc/profile, a file that sets environment variables and performs other operations, including executing files in the /etc/profile.d directory.

- /etc/profile.d, a directory that contains several small scripts. Those with filenames ending in .sh are executed by /etc/profile.

Here is a typical /etc/bashrc file:

```
# /etc/bashrc


# System wide functions and aliases
# Environment stuff goes in /etc/profile


# For some unknown reason bash refuses to inherit
# PS1 in some circumstances that I can't figure out.
# Putting PS1 here ensures that it gets loaded every time.
PS1="[\u@\h \W]\\$ "
```

Here is a typical /etc/profile file:

```
# /etc/profile

# System wide environment and startup programs
# Functions and aliases go in /etc/bashrc

PATH="$PATH:/usr/X11R6/bin"
PS1="[\u@\h \W]\\$ "

ulimit -c 1000000
if [ `id -gn` = `id -un` -a `id -u` -gt 14 ]; then
        umask 002
else
        umask 022
fi

USER=`id -un`
LOGNAME=$USER
MAIL="/var/spool/mail/$USER"

HOSTNAME=`/bin/hostname`
HISTSIZE=1000
HISTFILESIZE=1000

INPUTRC=/etc/inputrc
export PATH PS1 HOSTNAME HISTSIZE HISTFILESIZE USER
LOGNAME MAIL INPUTRC

for i in /etc/profile.d/*.sh ; do
        if [ -x $i ]; then
                . $i
        fi
done

unset i
export MPAGE="-2 -Plp"
```

The files in /etc/profile.d include the following:

- kde.csh, which sets up the KDE environment for C shell users

- kde.sh, which sets up the KDE environment for BASH shell users

- ang.sh, which sets up environment variables used by internationalization facilities

- mc.csh, which sets up the Midnight Commander environment for C shell users

- mc.sh, which sets up the Midnight Commander environment for BASH shell users

You can revise the contents of the /etc/profile.d directory, or add and delete files to customize the operations performed when a user logs in.

User Profiles

When you create a user account by using userconf or by using useradd with the −m argument, the contents of /etc/skel are copied to the user's home directory.

The files and directories in /etc/skel are generally hidden files and directories, having names with an initial dot (.). The default files include the following:

.Xdefaults   A file that establishes various X options.

.bash_logout   A file that clears the screen when the user exits the initial BASH shell.

.bash_profile   A file that invokes .bashrc and establishes the path and other environment variables.

.bashrc   A file that invokes /etc/bashrc.

.kde   A directory that contains a variety of subdirectories and files that are part of the KDE desktop environment and KDE applications, such as the KWM window manager.

.kderc   A file that specifies KDE options.

Desktop   A directory that contains files that configure the user's KDE desktop.

You can modify the contents of /etc/skel or add and remove files and directories. Doing so makes it possible to customize the user's environment.

Now, complete Exercise 10.8 to check your understanding of user profiles.

EXERCISE 10.8

Customizing User Profiles

The user profiles installed by default often fail to suit individual preferences. However, many users don't know how to customize their profiles.

Examine the contents of the user profile files in your home directory. Adjust one or more options to better suit your preferences. If you can't recall the names of the relevant files, look back to the explanation given in this subsection; however, before moving on to the next section, be sure you're able to identify the files without recourse to help.

Other User Administration Programs

To change the password associated with a user account, perform the following steps

1. Launch `userconf`.

2. Choose User Accounts and press Enter; or, if you're using X, click User Accounts. The Users Accounts screen will appear.

   Depending on the filter settings (in Control ➤ Features), you may see a Filter dialog box. Use the dialog box to limit the user accounts to those you want to see, or press Accept to view all accounts.

3. Highlight the account you want to modify and press Enter; or, if you're using X, you can simply click the account.

4. Click the Password button. The Changing Password dialog box will appear.

5. Type the desired password and click the Accept button. The Changing Password dialog box will reappear.

6. Confirm the password you previously entered by retyping it. Click the Accept button. The Users Accounts screen reappears.

You can also change the password associated with a user account by using the command line. Issue the passwd command, which has the following format:

passwd *user*

The program will prompt for the password twice in order to ensure that you typed it correctly.

The mkpasswd program is a helpful utility that generates random passwords or assign a random password to a user account. To generate a random password, issue the command

mkpasswd

The program will generate and display the password. To automatically assign a random password to a user account, issue the command

mkpasswd *user*

The command will assign and display the password.

Exercise 10.9 is the final exercise of this chapter. You should complete it in order to test your ability to administer passwords.

EXERCISE 10.9

Administering Passwords

Changing user passwords is one of the most frequent system administration tasks to be performed and, therefore, a task you should be able to perform fluently. Use the passwd command to change the password associated with your login account. If you can't recall how to do so, you can look back to the explanation given in this section. But bear in mind that you won't be able to refer to books or notes during the RHCE exam.

Summary

In this chapter, you learned about administering user accounts and groups. The most important topics covered are:

User Account Types   Red Hat Linux supports a variety of user account types, including ordinary user accounts, PPP user accounts, SLIP user accounts, UUCP user accounts, and POP user accounts.

Configuring User Accounts   You can configure user accounts by using the userconf program or the command line.

Disabling a User Account   Disabling a user account prevents it from being used; you can disable a user account by using the userconf program.

Deleting a User Account   Deleting a user account removes it from the system; you can delete a user account by using the userconf program. The program lets you delete or archive files in the account's home directory or leave the files in place.

User Groups   You can administer user groups by using the userconf command.

Sharing Data   You can use groups and the Linux file permission scheme to help you manage access to files and directories.

User Profiles   You can manage user profiles by modifying the scripts /etc/bashrc and /etc/profile and the scripts residing in /etc/profile.d and /etc/skel.

Other User Administration Programs   Other user administration programs include passwd, which lets you change the password associated with a user account, and mkpasswd, which generates and assigns a random password.

Key Terms

Before going on to the next chapter, be sure you're familiar with the following terms:

ordinary user

POP user

PPP user

SLIP user

user account

user group

UUCP user

Additional Sources of Information

If you'd like further information about the topics presented in this chapter, you should consult the following sources:

- *The Official Red Hat Linux Reference Guide*

- The man pages for commands described in this chapter

Review Questions

1. Which of the following are Red Hat Linux user account types?

   A. POP accounts

   B. PPP accounts

   C. SLIP accounts

   D. Usenet accounts

2. What is the relationship between `userconf` and `linuxconf`?

   A. You can use `linuxconf` to invoke `userconf`.

   B. You can use `userconf` to invoke `linuxconf`.

   C. You must invoke `linuxconf` before invoking `userconf`.

   D. You must invoke `userconf` before invoking `linuxconf`.

3. A user who has permission to use `linuxconf` may do which of the following tasks?

   A. May make configuration changes

   B. May activate configuration changes

   C. May give others permission to user `linuxconf`

   D. May give herself any desired permission

4. When you create a user account by using `useradd`, which of the following is true of the initial password?

   A. Locked

   B. Randomly chosen

   C. The same as the login name

   D. The same as your login name

5. The name of the default group assigned to a new user account is which of the following?

    A. Null

    B. The same as the login name

    C. The same as the name of the user who created the user account

    D. Users

6. What command generates random passwords?

    A. genpass

    B. mkpasswd

    C. newpass

    D. passwd

Answers to Review Questions

1. A, B, C. Although there is a UUCP account type, there is no Usenet account type.

2. A. You can invoke `userconf` from the command line or invoke it by means of `linuxconf`.

3. A, C. A user who has permission to use `linuxconf` may not activate configuration changes unless permission to do so has been explicitly given.

4. A. The password is initially locked; the user cannot log in until the account is unlocked by changing the password to a usable one.

5. B. Red Hat Linux assigns a new user to a personal group that has the same name as the user's login.

6. B. The `mkpasswd` command generates random passwords.

Chapter

11

Implementing User and Group Disk Space Quotas

RHCE PREPARATION TOPICS COVERED IN THIS CHAPTER:

✓ Understand quotas and be able to implement user and group quotas.

The administrator of a multiuser system is a bit like a playground supervisor: Both spend a great deal of time establishing and enforcing policies intended to promote sharing. Sharing is a simple matter when resources are plentiful, but sharing becomes complicated when users must contend for scarce resources. One of the scarcest of computer resources is disk space: A wag once commented that one can never be too rich, too thin, or have too much disk space.

Disk space quotas are a policy mechanism designed to facilitate sharing of disk space. An administrator can assign a user or group a fixed amount of disk space that the user cannot exceed. By limiting the amount of disk space that a user (or group) can consume, an administrator can prevent a greedy user from taking more than his or her share. This chapter explains disk space quotas and how to implement them.

Quota Concepts

Disk space quotas place limits on the amount of disk space a user or group can use. In the /etc/fstab file, you specify the partitions for which disk quotas are enabled. Only Linux ext2 partitions support disk quotas; you cannot enable quotas for other file system types.

The quota facility uses a pair of files stored in the root directory of a quota-enabled file system:

- quota.user, which stores quotas assigned to users

- quota.group, which stores quotas assigned to groups

For example, if a partition is mounted as /home, the files would be named /home/quota.user and /home/quota.group. The quotacheck command updates the contents of these files to reflect actual disk space usage. If the files do not exist, the command creates them.

The files contain binary information and cannot be edited directly. To establish a quota for a user or group, you use the edquota command. You can view the contents of the files by issuing the repquota command.

Quota tracking is initiated when the system boots. Commands in the /etc/rc.d/rc.sysinit script update usage data and turn on quota checking.

Quotas can be established for individual users or for groups. Two types of limits can be defined:

- Soft limits: Users or groups that exceed the soft limit are notified by e-mail when the warnquota program is run.

- Hard limits: Users or groups that exceed the hard limit are prevented from using additional disk space.

You can define a grace period that works with the soft limits. If the user continues to exceed the soft limit upon expiration of the grace period, the user is prevented from using additional space. You can specify limits on the number of disk blocks used, on the number of files (inodes) used, or both.

Consider the following example. Assume that user bob has the following limits:

- Soft disk space limit: 10000 blocks

- Hard disk space limit: 12000 blocks

- Soft inode limit: 100

- Hard inode limit: 120

Finally, suppose that a seven-day grace period is in effect and that bob currently has 5000 blocks of disk space and 50 inodes in use. If bob increases his disk usage to 11000 blocks, he'll receive an e-mail message something like this one:

```
Hi,


We noticed that you are in violation with the quotasystem
used on this system. We have found the following
violations:


      Block limits                    File limits
```

Filesystem	used	soft	hard	grace	used	soft	hard	grace
/dev/hdc	11000	10000	12000	7 days	50	100	120	7 days

We hope that you will cleanup before your grace period expires. Basically, this means that the system thinks you are using more disk space on the above partition(s) than you are allowed. If you do not delete files and get below your quota before the grace period expires, the system will prevent you from creating new files.

For additional assistance, please contact us at support@localhost or via phone at (xxx) xxx-xxxx or (xxx) xxx-xxxx.

If bob fails to reduce the number of blocks within seven days or if he increases his usage to 12000 blocks, he'll be prevented from using additional disk space until he reduces his usage below his soft quota.

Notice the blocked-out phone numbers in the quota violation e-mail. The contents of the e-mail are hard-coded in the source file warnquota.c. As a courtesy to users, you should install the source RPM, modify the message to better suit your local environment, and recompile and reinstall the package. However, you must have at least some skill in C programming in order to accomplish this.

Implementing Quotas

To implement quotas, follow these steps:

- Configure the kernel
- Install the quota package
- Revise /etc/fstab
- Establish the quota files
- Set quotas
- Turn on quota checking

The following subsections explain the steps.

Configuring the Kernel

In order to support quotas, a system's kernel must be properly configured. Specifically, the kernel must have been compiled with the CONFIG_QUOTA option enabled. Standard Red Hat Linux kernels include this option; however, if you compile your own kernel, you must enable it or you'll be unable to use quotas. See Chapter 18, "Configuring, Building, and Installing a Custom Kernel," for more information on compiling the Linux kernel.

Installing the *quota* Package

The `quota` package is part of the Red Hat Linux base component and is generally installed during installation. To check whether the package is installed, issue the command

```
rpm —qi quota
```

The command will print a short description of the package or a message stating that the package is not installed.

To install the `quota` package, move to the directory that contains it and issue the command

```
rpm —Uvh quota*.rpm
```

The `/etc/rc.d/rc.sysinit` file performs the following steps when the system is booted:

- runs `quotacheck` on the root file system
- runs `quotacheck` on all other local file systems
- turns on quota checking

Revising */etc/fstab*

To specify that a partition supports disk quotas, you must revise the partition's description in `/etc/fstab`. Here's a sample line file:

```
/dev/hda8      /              ext2     defaults         1 1
/dev/hda5      /boot          ext2     defaults         1 2
/dev/hda6      /home          ext2     defaults         1 2
/dev/hdc       /mnt/cdrom     iso9660  noauto,owner,ro  0 0
```

```
/dev/hda7      /usr           ext2     defaults        1 2
/dev/fd0       /mnt/floppy    ext2     noauto,owner    0 0
none           /proc          proc     defaults        0 0
none           /dev/pts       devpts   gid=5,mode=620  0 0
```

To specify that the /home partition supports user disk quotas, revise its line as follows:

```
/dev/hda6    /home    ext2 defaults,usrquota 1 2
```

To specify that the /home partition supports group disk quotas, you would revise its line as follows:

```
/dev/hda6    /home    ext2 defaults,grpquota 1 2
```

To specify that the /home partition supports both user and group disk quotas, you would revise its line as follows:

```
/dev/hda6    /home    ext2    defaults,usrquota,grpquota 1 2
```

Once you've revised the partition options, you must remount the partition. For example, to remount the /home partition, issue the command

```
mount -o remount /home
```

If you prefer, you can specify the usrquota or grpquota option by using linux-conf. Select Config ➤ File Systems ➤ Access Local Drive, select the desired partition, and specify the desired option or options on the Volume Specification screen.

Establishing the Quota Files

Once you've specified the partition or partitions that support disk quotas, you must establish the quota files quota.user and quota.group in each such partition. To do so, issue the quotacheck command:

```
quotacheck -avug
```

The command may require several minutes to complete its task of accumulating and storing a record of the disk space used by each user account and group.

To avoid a denial-of-service attack, you should verify that the created quota.user and quota.group files have read and write permissions only for their owner, which should be root.

> The files maintained by quotacheck must be kept in sync with the file systems. If the system is improperly shut down, the system will automatically run quotacheck when rebooted.

Setting Quotas

You're now ready to set quotas for users or groups. Bear in mind that you can set quotas for only those partitions that support them. Moreover, you can set only the type of quota for which the partition is configured. For example, if you configure the partition to support user quotas, you can set only user quotas, not group quotas.

Setting Default Quotas

Before setting quotas for particular users or groups, you may prefer to set default quotas. Default quotas apply to any user or group whose quota has not been set. To set default quotas, perform the following steps:

1. Launch linuxconf.

2. Select Config ➢ File Systems ➢ Set Quota Defaults. The Default Quota for Users and Groups screen, shown as Figure 11.1, will appear. If you're using X, the screen will look somewhat different.

FIGURE 11.1 The Default Quota for Users and Groups screen

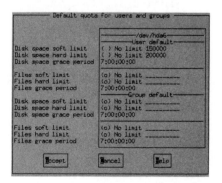

3. Specify the desired default limits and grace periods. A limit of zero (0) means there is no limit. Click the Accept button to save your changes.

Using linuxconf to set default quotas overwrites limits entered manually. It's best to set default quotas only once, before setting specific user quotas.

Setting a User Quota

To set a quota for a user, issue the command

```
edquota -u user
```

where *user* is the login name of the user. The **edquota** command launches the default editor (specified by the $EDITOR environment variable), which displays a series of lines resembling the following:

```
Quotas for user bill:
/dev/hda6: blocks in use: 1236, limits (soft = 0, hard = 0)
          inodes in use: 235, limits (soft = 0, hard = 0)
```

To specify a limit, change the appropriate number, save the file, and exit the editor. A limit of zero (0) means there is no limit. For example, you might revise the limits imposed on the user **bill** as follows:

```
Quotas for user bill:
/dev/hda6: blocks in use: 1236, limits (soft = 8000,
➥hard = 10000)
          inodes in use: 235, limits (soft = 0, hard = 0)
```

To verify that the quota has been set, issue the command

```
quota -u user
```

where *user* is the login name of the user. You should see the same information you entered by using the editor.

Setting a Group Quota

To specify a group quota, issue the command

```
edquota -g group
```

where *group* is the name of the group. The edquota command launches the default editor (specified by the $EDITOR environment variable), which displays a series of lines resembling the following:

```
Quotas for group users:
/dev/hda6: blocks in use: 12436, limits (soft = 0, hard = 0)
           inodes in use: 2135, limits (soft = 0, hard = 0)
```

To revise a limit, change the appropriate number, save the file, and exit the editor. A limit of zero (0) means there is no limit.

To verify that the quota has been set, issue the command

```
quota -g group
```

where *group* is the name of the group. You should see the same information you entered by using the editor.

Setting the Grace Period

To set the grace period, issue the command

```
edquota -t
```

The edquota command launches the default editor (specified by the $EDITOR environment variable), which displays a series of lines resembling the following:

```
Time units may be: days, hours, minutes, or seconds
Grace period before enforcing soft limits for users:
/dev/hda6: block grace period: 7 days, file grace period:
➥7 days
```

To revise a limit, change the appropriate number or time unit, save the file, and exit.

Setting Quotas for Multiple Users

You can use one user account as a template for setting quotas for other accounts. To do so, follow these steps:

1. Issue the command

   edquota −p *user*

   where *user* is the login name of the user account you want to use as a template. This establishes the specified user account as a template.

2. Issue the command

   edquota *user*

   where *user* is the login name of the user account you want to use as a template. The **edquota** command launches the default editor. Set the desired limits, save the file, and exit the editor. This establishes the desired quota for the template user account.

3. Issue the command

   edquota -p *user* *user1* *user2* ...

   where *user* is the login name of the user account you want to use as a template and the remaining arguments are login names of user accounts that you want to have the same quota as the template account.

Turning on Quota Checking

Finally, you're ready to actually turn on quota checking. Quota checking will be turned on when the system is booted. However, you can turn on quota checking without rebooting by issuing the command

   quotaon -av

This command turns on both user and group quotas. To turn on only user quotas, issue the command

   quotaon -avu

Similarly, to turn on only group quotas, issue the command

   quotaon -avg

To turn off quotas, issue the command

```
quotaoff -av
```

This command turns off both user and group quotas. To turn off only user quotas, issue the command

```
quotaoff -avu
```

Similarly, to turn off only group quotas, issue the command

```
quotaoff -avg
```

Administering Quotas

Once quotas are set up, you can use commands that report on the status of quotas. This first subsection of this section explains how. The second subsection explains how to set up quotas for partitions that are exported via NFS.

Quota Reports

To view the quota assigned to a user, issue the command

```
quota -u user
```

where *user* is the login name of the user. The resulting report will resemble the following:

```
Disk quotas for user test (uid 510):
     Filesystem  blocks    quota    limit    grace    files
     ➡quota   limit    grace
     /dev/hda6    804   150000   200000              152
     ➡0        0
```

A user can view his or her own quota by issuing the similar command

```
quota
```

However, only root can view the quotas of other users.

To view the quotas for multiple users, issue the command

```
repquota -a
```

The resulting report resembles the following:

```
Block limits                    File limits
User            used   soft   hard grace used soft hard grace
root       -- 1232356     0      0        7102    0    0
jczarnec --   11860 150000 200000         143    0    0
khahn      --     180 150000 200000        45    0    0
mhall      +-  192308 150000 200000 7days  247    0    0
plin       --   28672 150000 200000        216    0    0
mtuinstr --      184 150000 200000         46    0    0
dtc        --    3420 150000 200000        350    0    0
rlee       +-  173336 150000 200000 none   852    0    0
dchan      --     252 150000 200000         62    0    0
```

Note that users in violation of their quota—for instance, mhall—are flagged by a plus sign (+).

Quotas and NFS

If you export a directory via NFS, you can establish disk quotas that limit the disk space or inodes used by NFS users. Simply apply the desired limits to the local user account to which NFS maps the remote users. For example, if remote users are mapped to the local user nfsuser, set quotas on the nfsuser account. For more information on NFS, see Chapter 21, "Installing and Configuring Primary Network Services."

Now that you've learned about quotas and how to establish them, complete Exercise 11.1, which tests your ability to set up quotas.

EXERCISE 11.1

Setting Up Quotas

This exercise requires you to draw on your knowledge of disk quotas to set up quota checking. You can look back to explanations and procedures in this chapter. But, before moving on to the next chapter, be sure you can set up disk quotas without resorting to help, because you won't have access to help during the RHCE exam.

1. Establish user and group quotas on the /home or root partition of a system.

2. Establish default soft and hard limits for disk space usage.

3. Establish a grace period of five days.

EXERCISE 11.1 *(continued)*

4. Specify at least one user who has no disk space limit and another who has lesser limits than the default limits.

5. Turn on quota checking.

6. Verify your work by using the repquota command.

7. Verify your work by intentionally exceeding the soft limit on disk space. To exceed the quota in a controlled manner, issue a command of the form

   dd if=/dev/zero of=test count=*n*

where *n* is the number of blocks of data that will be written to the file named test.

Summary

In this chapter, you learned about disk space quotas. The most important topics covered are:

Disk Quotas   Disk quotas let you restrict the amount of disk space and the number of inodes allocated by a user. Disk quotas can be assigned to users or user groups.

Hard and Soft Limits   When a hard limit is exceeded, the user is prevented from allocating additional disk space or inodes. When a soft limit is exceeded, the user is notified.

Implementing Quotas   To implement quotas, you must install the quota package, which includes the quotacheck, edquota, quotaon, quotaoff, and quota commands.

The **quotacheck** Program   The quotacheck program establishes the quota control files, `quota.user` and `quota.group`.

The **edquota** Program   The edquota program lets you establish or revise the quota associated with a user or a user group.

The **quotaon** and **quotaoff** Programs   The quotaon and quotaoff programs let you turn quotas on and off, respectively.

The **quota** Program   The quota program lets you print reports that show the status of disk quotas.

Key Terms

Before going on to the next chapter, be sure you're familiar with the following terms:

grace period

group quota

hard limit

soft limit

user quota

Additional Sources of Information

If you'd like further information about the topics presented in this chapter, you should consult the following sources:

- *The Quota Mini-HOWTO*, by Albert M.C. Tam
- The man pages of commands mentioned in the chapter

Review Questions

1. You can associate quotas with which of the following?

   A. A directory

   B. A group

   C. A partition

   D. A user

2. Which of the following statements is correct if the disk space hard limit is zero?

   A. The user can create an unlimited number of files.

   B. The user can use an unlimited amount of disk space.

   C. The user cannot create disk files.

   D. The user is in violation of the disk space limit.

3. Suppose that a user owns 150 inodes and that the soft limit is 100 and the hard limit is 200. Which of the following is correct if the grace period has not expired?

   A. The user can create no more files.

   B. The user cannot append data to an existing file.

   C. The user cannot log off without deleting some files.

   D. The user will receive an e-mail notice of violation.

4. Suppose that a user owns 150 inodes and that the soft limit is 100 and the hard limit is 200. Which of the following is correct if the grace period has expired?

   A. The user can create no more files.

   B. The user cannot append data to an existing file.

   C. The user cannot log off without deleting some files.

   D. The user will receive an e-mail notice of violation when `warnquota` is run.

5. Which of the following commands lets you set a user's quota?

A. edquota

B. edquota *user*

C. edquota -p *user*

D. edquota -u *user*

6. What is the name of the file created when group quotas are used?

A. quota

B. quota.group

C. quota.user

D. quotas

Answers to Review Questions

1. B, C, D. Quotas established for users or groups are applied to a partition; you cannot establish a quota for a directory.

2. B. The disk space limit constrains the amount of disk space, not the number of files. A limit of zero means the user can use unlimited space.

3. D. Until the grace period expires, the user is free to exceed the soft limit.

4. A, D. Once the grace period has expired, the user must observe the soft limit; until the user frees some inodes, the user cannot create a new file.

5. D. The -u argument is required when setting a user's quota.

6. B. The `quotacheck` command creates the file `quota.group` when group quotas have been specified for the partition.

Chapter

12

Using RPM Packages

RHCE PREPARATION TOPICS COVERED IN THIS CHAPTER:

✓ Understand and be able to use the rpm command and its switches, particularly those related to the installation and querying of packages.

✓ Understand the basic elements of source (*.src.rpm) RPM packages.

One of the most significant contributions of Red Hat, Inc. to the Linux community has been Red Hat's support for development of the Red Hat Package Manager (RPM). Prior to RPM, installation of Linux software was largely a matter of hit and miss: Installation of one application often crippled another. Thanks to RPM, Linux system administrators can now install applications with confidence that the applications will operate correctly and will not conflict with other applications. This chapter explains the operation of the RPM facility and describes how to perform common RPM operations.

The Red Hat Package Manager (RPM)

Before RPM, Linux system administrators—like other Unix system administrators—installed programs by downloading TAR files, unpacking them, and compiling source files. Programs often conflicted in their use of common files, and software developers often made assumptions about the placement of files and the availability of commands and libraries. Consequently, system administrators regularly spent overtime hours coaxing programs to work.

RPM manages the software installation process by tracking information about installed software programs. Thus, system administrators rarely find that installing one program has broken another. RPM consists of three components, which manage system files as shown in Figure 12.1:

- Package files

- The RPM database

- The rpm command

FIGURE 12.1 The RPM facility

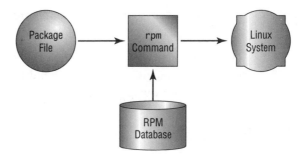

The following subsections explain these components.

Package Files

Package files replace the TAR files used before the advent of RPM. Like TAR files, package files contain the files that must be installed. Unlike TAR files, package files contain information describing the application or service contained in the *package*. For example, a package file identifies any capabilities, such as libraries or other packages, that must be installed in order for it to install and operate correctly. This information is called *dependency information*. Other information stored in packages includes:

- Name and version of the package
- Build date and build host
- Description of the package
- Size and MD5 checksum of each contained file
- Identity of the person or organization that built the package
- Package group to which the package belongs

The name of a package file has a specific structure that resembles the following:

package-version-buildarchitecture.rpm

where:

- *package* is the name of the package contained in the file. This lets you abbreviate the filename to accommodate restrictions imposed by DOS or other file systems that limit the number of characters in a filename.

- *version* is the version number of the package.

- *build* is the build number of the package.

- *architecture* is the computer architecture for which the package is designed.

For example, the package filename gnorpm-0.9-10.i386.rpm indicates that the file contains version 0.9, build 10, of a package named gnorpm that is intended for the i386 (Intel 386) architecture.

The RPM Database

Once a package is installed, information about the package is stored in the RPM database, which resides in /var/lib/rpm. When you issue an rpm command—for example, a command to install a package or a command to uninstall a package—the RPM facility inspects the package file and the RPM database. Thus, the RPM facility is able to determine whether execution of the command will leave the system in an inconsistent state. If so, the RPM facility suppresses the command and warns the user of the potential danger.

The *rpm* Command

The rpm command is the executable component of the RPM facility. Its host of switches and arguments enable you to perform operations such as:

- Installing packages

- Updating packages

- Removing packages

- Querying the RPM database

- Querying a package file

- Building a package file from source code

- Validating a package

- Validating a package file

When installing, updating, or removing packages, the rpm command performs several checks intended to ensure that the system is left in a consistent state. For example, when installing a package, rpm checks that:

- There is sufficient free disk space to accommodate the package

- Any capabilities required by the package (dependencies) are installed

- Installation of the package won't overwrite existing files

Special switches let you override these checks so that you can cope with unusual situations. The remaining sections of this chapter explain the operation of rpm within the context of common operations you'll need to know how to perform.

Adding Packages

To install a package, issue a command that has this form:

```
rpm -i package_file_name
```

where *package_file_name* specifies the name of the file that contains the package you want to install. If you like, you can list several package names or use shell meta-characters such as * to specify sets of files. For example, here's a typical command:

```
rpm -i gnorpm-0.9-10.i386.rpm
gnome-linuxconf-0.23-1.i386.rpm
```

The command installs the gnorpm package contained in the package file gnorpm-0.9-10.i386.rpm and the gnome-linuxconf package contained in the package file gnome-linuxconf-0.23-1.i386.rpm. First, of course, the command performs the checks described earlier; if any of the checks fail, the command fails without installing either specified package.

Many system administrators like to include the -v and -h flags, for example:

```
rpm -ivh gnorpm-0.9-10.i386.rpm
gnome-linuxconf-0.23-1.i386.rpm
```

The -v flag causes the command to print status information as it executes; it's especially helpful when you specify multiple files, because rpm prints a message as it begins installation of each file. The -h flag causes rpm to display 50 hash marks as it installs each package, helping you visualize the progress of each package installation. Here's a typical invocation of rpm that includes these flags:

```
# rpm -ivh gnorpm-0.9-10.i386.rpm
  ➥gnome-linuxconf-0.23-1.i386.rpm
gnorpm
#######################################
```

```
gnome-linuxconf
########################################
```

One of the advantages of the -vh is that it is very clear what packages have actually been installed. An annoying shortcoming of RPM is that it will exit with an error if a package is already installed. Without the -vh, it is sometimes difficult to tell which packages in a list of packages were installed before RPM aborted.

Another handy RPM feature is support for files stored on FTP servers. Rather than downloading the package file and installing the package, you can install directly from the FTP server by issuing a command that has this form:

```
ftp://server/path
```

where *server* is the host name or IP address of the anonymous FTP server and *path* specifies the path to the package file. For example, the following command installs a package that resides on Red Hat's anonymous FTP server:

```
rpm -ivh ftp://contrib.redhat.com/i386/RedHat/RPMS/
➡gnorpm-0.9-10.i386.rpm
```

If you need to access the FTP server by means of a particular account, issue a command that has the form

```
ftp://user:pass@server/path
```

where *user* and *pass* specify the user id and password and the remaining tokens have the meaning given previously. If the server listens on a nonstandard port, you can use this command form:

```
ftp://user:pass@server:port/path
```

where *port* is the number of the port on which the server listens.

The Red Hat Linux 6.2 and later versions of RPM support filename globbing, which lets you include wildcard characters. For example, the RPM command to install gnorpm could be written

```
rpm -ivh ftp://contrib.redhat.com/i386/RedHat/RPMS/
➡gnorpm*
```

One more handy RPM feature is that you don't need to specify the package files in any particular order, even if one or more of the specified packages depends on the capabilities of another. The rpm command detects any dependencies and installs the packages in an appropriate order.

If a package requires a *capability* that's provided neither by a package specified in the same command nor by an installed package, the rpm command prints an error message. For example:

```
# rpm -i gnorpm-0.9-10.i386.rpm
error: failed dependencies:
        usermode >= 1.13 is needed by gnorpm-0.9-10
        librpm.so.0 is needed by gnorpm-0.9-10
```

To resolve a *dependency*, you must install the appropriate package, providing the required capability, or upgrade an existing package to a later version. For instance, the error message states that a newer version of the usermode package is required and that the library named librpm.so.0 is required. Later in this chapter, you'll learn how to discover what capabilities a package provides so that you can determine, for example, what package will provide the librpm.so.0 library.

If you try to install a package that conflicts with an existing package or file, you'll see an error message that resembles this one:

```
# rpm -i gnorpm-0.9-10.i386.rpm
file /usr/bin/gnorpm from install of gnorpm-0.9-10
➥conflicts with file from package gnoway-0.8-5
file /usr/share/gnome/apps/System/gnorpm.desktop from
➥install of gnorpm-0.9-10 conflicts with file from
➥package gnoway-0.8-5
file /usr/share/gnome/help/gnorpm/C/gnorpm.html from
➥install of gnorpm-0.9-10 conflicts with file from
➥package gnoway-0.8-5
```

You'll see another sort of error message if you attempt to install a package for which there's insufficient disk space.

Suppose you install a software program distributed by means of a TAR file. Later, a newer version of the software is published, one that uses RPM for distribution. When you install the new package, RPM determines that it will overwrite existing files. Rather than overwrite files RPM recognizes as configuration files, it saves each existing configuration file by appending .rpmsave to its name.

To overcome errors and other exceptions, you may have occasional need for the following special rpm arguments:

- --force, which overwrites newer packages or existing files

- --nodeps, which skips dependency checking

- --replacefiles, which replaces files owned by another package

For example, to install the package gnorpm despite dependency problems, you might issue the command

```
rpm -i --nodeps gnorpm-0.9-10.i386.rpm
  ➥gnome-linuxconf-0.23-1.i386.rpm
```

The command will succeed regardless of dependency problems; however, the installed program will not function unless the required files are actually present.

Now that you know how to add a package by using the rpm command, complete Exercise 12.1, which tests your ability to use this command.

EXERCISE 12.1

Adding a Package

The RHCE exam will almost certainly require you to install one or more packages. To make sure you know how, use the rpm command to add a package to your system. Be sure to choose a package that's not already installed. Look back to the examples in this chapter if you must, but before taking the RHCE exam, be sure you know how to use the rpm command to add a package.

Removing Packages

To remove an installed package, issue a command of the form

```
rpm -e package_name
```

where *package_name* is the name of the installed package. You may find it easier to recall this command form if you think of erasing a package rather than removing it, because the *e* in *erase* corresponds to the -e flag. If you prefer, you can specify the --uninstall flag, which has the same meaning as the -e flag.

Users unfamiliar with the rpm command often specify a package name where a package filename is needed, and the reverse. Pay careful attention to which is required by each command form.

When the `rpm` command removes a package, it checks whether the package provides capabilities needed by other packages. If so, it suppresses execution and warns you. If necessary, you can override this check by specifying the `--nodeps` flag.

When the `rpm` command removes a package, it also saves any modified configuration files. Thus, when you need a little extra disk space to cope with some emergency, you can easily remove and later reinstall some packages.

Now, complete Exercise 12.2, which requires you to remove a package.

EXERCISE 12.2

Removing a Package

Often, a system administrator must free disk space on a system. One convenient way to do so is to delete a package, which can be reinstalled when more disk space is available. To verify your ability to remove a package, use the `rpm` command to remove the package you added in the previous exercise. As usual, you can consult this chapter for help; before taking the RHCE exam, though, be sure you can remove a package without the assistance of a book or notes.

Performing Updates and Fixes

From time to time, new versions of packages are published. Often, these contain bug fixes or new features that are important. RPM makes it easy to install new versions of packages. To do so, issue a command of the form

```
rpm -Uvh package_file_name
```

where *package_file_name* is the name of the file containing the new version of the package. You can omit the -v and -h flags, if you prefer. The -U flag causes the rpm command to remove the existing package (as though you'd performed an rpm -e) and then install the new package (as though you'd performed an rpm -i). When the rpm command removes the old package, it saves any modified configuration files, renaming them by appending .rpmsave to their names. If the package contained in the specified file is not currently installed, the rpm command installs it. Therefore, many system administrators use the -U flag in place of the -i flag; rpm -U will install the package if it is absent or update it if it is present.

A related flag, -F, lets you update a package only if it's present. For example, the command

```
rpm -Fvh gnorpm-0.9-10.i386.rpm
```

would update the gnorpm package only if the package is installed. The -F flag helps you keep your system current. Red Hat maintains a list of updated packages at www.redhat.com/support/errata. You should monitor the list and apply any fixes that you believe are important to the operation of your system by using the -F flag.

Now, complete Exercise 12.3, which requires you to update an RPM package.

EXERCISE 12.3

Updating a Package

As explained, a diligent system administrator monitors the Red Hat Errata page and timely applies useful fixes. To check your ability to do so, use the rpm command to update a package with a fix downloaded from the Red Hat Errata page. You can consult this chapter for help during the exercise, but bear in mind you won't have this opportunity during the RHCE exam.

Identifying Installed Packages

You can use RPM to learn the version and build numbers of an installed package. To do so, issue a command of the form

```
rpm -q package_name
```

where *package_name* is the name of the installed package. The output consists of a single line that gives the package name, version number, and build number—for example:

```
gnorpm-0.9-10
```

To learn the version and build number of each installed package, issue the command

```
rpm -qa
```

To verify your understanding of the `rpm` command's –q and –qa flags, complete Exercise 12.4.

EXERCISE 12.4

Identifying a Package

Often, it's handy to be able to determine what packages are installed on a system. To check your ability to perform this operation, use the `rpm` command to list the version and build numbers of the packages installed on your system. Look back to this chapter if you must, but be ready to perform this operation without help when taking the RHCE exam.

Determining File Ownership

You can use RPM to learn which package, if any, owns a particular file. To do so, issue a command of the form

```
rpm -qf filename
```

where *filename* is the name of the file, which must include the full path. For example, asking RPM to report the ownership of the file `/etc/inittab` yields output such as this:

```
# rpm -qf /etc/inittab
initscripts-4.16-1
```

Now, complete Exercise 12.5, which requires you to use the `rpm` command's –qf flag.

EXERCISE 12.5

Determining File Ownership

To check your understanding of the `rpm` command's –qf flag, use the `rpm` command to determine what package owns the file `/etc/inetd.conf`. You can refer to this chapter when doing this exercise, but be prepared to use the –qf flag without the help of books or notes during the RHCE exam.

Querying and Verifying Package Contents

The rpm command lets you query and verify package contents. For example, you can do the following:

- Print a description of a package

- List the files contained in a package

- Print scripts executed when installing or uninstalling a package

- Verify the integrity and authenticity of package contents

The next several subsections explain these operations.

Printing a Description of a Package

To print a description of an installed package, issue a command of the form

```
rpm -qi package_name
```

where *package_name* is the name of the installed package. For example, printing a description of the installed package gnorpm yields output resembling the following:

```
# rpm -qip gnorpm-0.9-10.i386.rpm
Name        : gnorpm              Relocations: (not
➥relocateable)
Version     : 0.9                 Vendor: Red Hat Software
Release     : 10                  Build Date: Sat Sep 25
➥13:51:53 1999
Install date: (not installed)     Build Host:
➥porky.devel.redhat.com
Group       : Applications/System Source RPM:
➥gnorpm-0.9-10.src.rpm
Size        : 434375              License: GPL
Packager    : Red Hat Software
➥<http://developer.redhat.com/bugzilla>
Summary     : A graphical front-end to RPM for GNOME.
Description :
GnoRPM is a graphical front-end to to the Red Hat Package
Manager (RPM). GnoRPM is similar to Glint, but is written
using the GTK+ widget set and the GNOME libraries.  GnoRPM
is currently in development, so some features are missing,
```

but you can currently query, install, upgrade, uninstall and verify packages using a GUI interface.

To print this information for a package file, issue a command of the form

```
rpm -qip package_file_name
```

where *package_file_name* is the name of the package file.

Listing Contained Files

To list the files contained in an installed package, issue a command of the form

```
rpm -ql package_name
```

where *package_name* is the name of the installed package. For example, listing the files of the gnorpm package produces output like this:

```
# rpm -ql gnorpm
/etc/pam.d/gnorpm-auth
/etc/security/console.apps/gnorpm-auth
/usr/bin/gnorpm
/usr/bin/gnorpm-auth
/usr/doc/gnorpm-0.9
/usr/doc/gnorpm-0.9/AUTHORS
/usr/doc/gnorpm-0.9/NEWS
/usr/doc/gnorpm-0.9/README
/usr/share/gnome/apps/System
/usr/share/gnome/apps/System/gnorpm.desktop
/usr/share/gnome/help/gnorpm/C/find-win.html
/usr/share/gnome/help/gnorpm/C/gnorpm.html
/usr/share/gnome/help/gnorpm/C/index.html
/usr/share/gnome/help/gnorpm/C/install-win.html
/usr/share/gnome/help/gnorpm/C/main-win.html
/usr/share/gnome/help/gnorpm/C/other-uses.html
/usr/share/gnome/help/gnorpm/C/preferences-win.html
/usr/share/gnome/help/gnorpm/C/query-win.html
etc.
```

To list the files contained in a package file, issue a similar command having the form

```
rpm -qlp package_file_name
```

Printing Scripts

To print the preinstallation and post-installation scripts associated with a package file, issue a command of the form

```
rpm -qp --scripts package_file_name
```

where *package_file_name* is the name of the file that contains the package. For example, listing the scripts of the at package produces output like this:

```
# rpm -qp --scripts at-3.1.7-11.i386.rpm
postinstall script (through /bin/sh):
touch /var/spool/at/.SEQ
chmod 600 /var/spool/at/.SEQ
chown daemon.daemon /var/spool/at/.SEQ
/sbin/chkconfig --add atd
preuninstall script (through /bin/sh):
if [ "$1" = 0 ] ; then
  /sbin/chkconfig --del atd
fi
```

Verifying Package Contents

RPM maintains a record on each file contained in an installed package. The record contains the file size, ownership, permissions, and MD5 checksum of each file and other information. If the file is a symbolic link, the record contains the path to which the link refers; if the file is a device file, the record contains the associated major and minor device numbers.

By means of these records, you can determine which files, if any, have been modified since installation of a package by issuing a command of the form

```
rpm -V package_name
```

where *package_name* is the name of the installed package. The output consists of one line for each file. Each line has three fields:

- Status, which indicates the status of the file. Table 12.1 describes the flags used to indicate status.

- Configuration, which contains a *c* if the file is a configuration file and a space otherwise.

- Filename, which gives the path and name of the file.

TABLE 12.1 Package Verification Flags

Code	Meaning
.	No change.
5	MD5 checksum has changed.
D	Device major or minor number has changed.
G	Owning group has changed.
L	Link path has changed.
M	File modes have changed.
S	File size has changed.
T	Modification time has changed.
U	Owning user has changed.

Here's an example that shows the status of the contents of the setup package:

```
# rpm -V setup
S.5....T c /etc/exports
S.5....T c /etc/hosts.allow
S.5....T c /etc/hosts.deny
S.5....T c /etc/printcap
S.5....T c /etc/profile
S.5....T c /etc/services
etc.
```

You can compare against package files rather than the database, if you prefer. This option is useful if you suspect the database may be corrupt. To do so, issue a command of the form

```
rpm -Vp package_file_name
```

where *package_file_name* is the name of the package file.

You can also verify the status of every installed package. To do so, issue the command

```
rpm --verify -a
```

Verifying Package Authenticity

GNU Privacy Guard (GPG) is an open source program similar to the more familiar Pretty Good Privacy (PGP) program, which lets you authenticate electronic documents. Authors of RPM packages can sign their work with a GPG key. If you've installed the GPG package, you can verify the authenticity of a signed package file. To do so, issue a command of the form

```
rpm -K package_file_name
```

where *package_file_name* is the name of the package file. You'll need to download and install Red Hat, Inc.'s GPG key; you can find the key on the Contacts page of their Web site, www.redhat.com.

Owing to US export restrictions, Red Hat Linux does not include PGP. You'll have to obtain it from another source, such as www.zedz.net.

Performing Advanced Queries

The rpm command includes an option that lets you query the RPM database for specific items of information, which you specify by means of the --queryformat flag. For example, the following command prints the name and size of every installed package, sorted by name:

```
# rpm -qa --queryformat "%-32{NAME}\t%10{SIZE}\n" | sort
AfterStep                             4248520
AfterStep-APPS                        1104878
AnotherLevel                           295682
ElectricFence                           45648
ImageMagick                           3098379
MAKEDEV                                 35719
MySQL                                16898048
MySQL-client                          7172590
MySQL-devel                           2188430
MySQL-shared                           569920
ORBit                                  892530
```

```
SysVinit                           172531
xVMware                          10788833
X11R6-contrib                      485824
XFree86                          14611173
XFree86-100dpi-fonts              1258246
etc.
```

The syntax of the `--queryformat` argument resembles that of the C `printf` library function. If you're unfamiliar with C, you'll find the syntax rather daunting, but you probably won't have to work with it on the RHCE exam. To learn the tags that correspond to RPM database items, issue the command:

```
rpm --querytags
```

A particularly useful query lists packages and the capabilities they provide. You can use such a query to learn, for example, what package provides the `librpm.so.0` library:

```
# rpm -qp --queryformat "%16{NAME}\t%10{PROVIDES}\n"
➡*.rpm | \grep librpm.so.0
rpm           librpm.so.0
```

The single line of output shows that the `rpm` package provides the `librpm.so.0` library, just as one might expect.

Red Hat Linux 6.2 and later include the `rpmdb-redhat` package that contains an alternate RPM database describing the contents of the release. If you install this package, you can use the `rpm` command's special `--redhatprovides` flag to determine what package owns a particular file. This capability is helpful in resolving dependencies. For example, suppose you try to install a package but receive an error message stating that a particular library is required—say, `libsample.so.1`. The following command identifies the package containing the missing library:

```
rpm -q --redhatprovides libsample.so.1
```

Working with Source RPM Packages

Ordinary RPM packages contain binary executable files. RPM also supports source RPM files, which contain source code and must, therefore, be compiled before installation. You'll find source RPMs on the auxiliary CD-ROM that's part of the Red Hat Linux distribution; you can also download them from ftp://contrib.redhat.com and other sites. Source RPMs have names of the form

package-version-build.src.rpm

As you can see, the name of a source RPM differs from that of a binary RPM in that it ends in .src.rpm rather than merely .rpm.

When you install a source RPM, its files are installed under the /usr/src/redhat directory tree, which contains these subdirectories:

BUILD   The source RPM is uncompressed, untarred, and patched here.

RPMS   When you compile a source RPM, the new binary RPM is saved here. The directory contains subdirectories for each supported architecture.

SOURCES   The source code—usually contained in a TAR file—and patches reside here.

SPECS   This directory contains SPEC files that list package sources, patches, compile-time options, post-install steps, and package information related to a source RPM.

SRPMS   When you create a new source RPM, it is saved here.

To build a binary RPM from a source RPM, move to the SPECS directory and issue a command of the form

rpm -bb *spec_file*

where *spec_file* is the name of the SPEC file associated with the source RPM. Table 12.2 describes other useful rpm command flags related to source RPMs.

TABLE 12.2   Source File Flags of the rpm Command

Flag	Meaning
-bp	%prep stage: unpack and patch source
-bl	%files stage: check that files exist

TABLE 12.2 Source File Flags of the rpm Command *(continued)*

Flag	Meaning
-bc	%build stage: make install
-bb	builds binary package
-ba	builds binary and source packages
--test	check syntax of SPEC file

If a SPEC file is contained within a TAR file, you need not unpack the TAR file. Instead, replace the -b flag with -t and specify the TAR file that contains the SPEC file. The rpm command supports both uncompressed and gzip-compressed TAR files.

You need not install a source RPM in order to compile it. Simply specify a command of the form

```
rpm --recompile source_package_file
```

where *source_package_file* is the name of the source RPM. To compile an uninstalled SRPM, build a corresponding binary RPM, and clean up the source files, issue a command of the form

```
rpm --rebuild source_package_file
```

where *source_package_file* is the name of the source RPM.

The current RHCE guidelines require only conceptual understanding of source RPMs and related rpm commands. You don't need to be an expert in working with source RPMs.

GnoRPM

Many desktop Linux users prefer a graphical user interface to a command line user interface. GnoRPM provides such users with an easy-to-use tool for manipulating RPM packages. Figure 12.2 shows the GnoRPM tool.

FIGURE 12.2 The GnoRPM tool

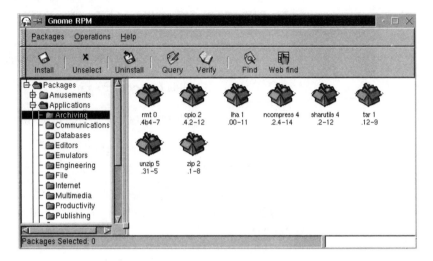

As a system administrator, you may need to perform package manipulations on systems that lack X, which GnoRPM requires. For example, suppose you want to install X on a system; you can't use GnoRPM, which requires X, to install X. Nevertheless, you should become familiar with GnoRPM in order to assist users who prefer using it to using the command line. GnoRPM lets you do the following:

- Install packages

- Upgrade packages

- Query packages

- Verify packages

- Uninstall packages

In addition, GnoRPM includes an interface to the rpmfind command, which helps you find packages stored on Internet FTP sites.

You'll find GnoRPM easy to use. If you need help understanding its more advanced features, consult its documentation files, which reside in /usr/doc/gnorpm*.

You should now complete Exercise 12.6, which requires you to use GnoRPM to remove a package.

EXERCISE 12.6

Removing a Package

Ordinary users often prefer GnoRPM to RPM, but even system administrators use GnoRPM to manipulate packages. This exercise tests your ability to use GnoRPM to remove a package. GnoRPM's point-and-click interface will probably be intuitive enough that you won't need to consult documentation. But if you find the GnoRPM puzzling, consult the documentation files identified in the chapter. Bear in mind that you may not have access to documentation during the RHCE exam.

1. Use the rpm command to install GnoRPM.

2. Use GnoRPM to inspect several installed packages and uninstalled package files.

Summary

In this chapter, you learned about packages and the Red Hat Package Manager (RPM). The most important topics covered are:

The Red Hat Package Manager (RPM)   RPM helps you install, uninstall, and manage software programs. The RPM facility consists of package files, the RPM database, and the rpm command.

Package Files   A package file may include programs, configuration files, and data files. A package file includes information about its contents, including version and dependency information.

Dependencies   When proper operation of a package requires an external resource, the package is said to have a dependent relationship with the external resource.

Capabilities   A package that provides a resource used by another package is said to provide a capability.

RPM Database   The RPM database, which resides in /var/lib/rpm, contains information describing each installed package.

The rpm Command The rpm command lets you perform a variety of operations, including installing a package, updating a package, removing a package, querying the RPM database, querying a package file, building a package file from source code, validating a package, and validating a package file.

Source RPM Packages Unlike ordinary RPM packages, which contain binary code, source RPM packages contain source code.

The GnoRPM Program GnoRPM provides an X-based graphical user interface to the rpm command.

Key Terms

Before going on to the next chapter, be sure you're familiar with the following terms:

build number

capability

dependency

dependency information

package

package files

version number

Additional Sources of Information

If you'd like further information about the topics presented in this chapter, you should consult the following sources:

- Edward C. Bailey's *Maximum RPM* (Red Hat Press, 1997)

- The man page for the rpm command

- *The Official Red Hat Linux Reference Guide*

- The *RPM HOWTO*, by Donnie Barnes (/usr/doc/HOWTO/RPM-HOWTO)

- The documentation for GnoRPM, /usr/doc/gnorpm*

Review Questions

1. Which of the following stores information about RPM packages?

   A. Package files

   B. The `install` command

   C. The `rpm` command

   D. The RPM database

2. Which of the following commands uninstalls the package xyz?

   A. `rpm -e xyz`

   B. `rpm -i xyz`

   C. `rpm -u xyz`

   D. `rpm --uninstall xyz`

3. To learn which package owns the file /etc/hosts, issue the command:

   A. `rpm -qf hosts`

   B. `rpm -qf /etc/hosts`

   C. `rpm -qF hosts`

   D. `rpm -qF /etc/hosts`

4. The -V flag causes RPM to report changed files. If the contents of a configuration file have been changed, which of the following flags will appear in the output?

   A. 5

   B. c

   C. S

   D. T

5. To list the name of each installed package, issue the command:

  A. rpm -q

  B. rpm -qa

  C. rpm -qi

  D. rpm -qp

6. The program that provides a graphical user interface to RPM is:

  A. GoRPM

  B. GnoRPM

  C. GnomeRPM

  D. GnomRPM

Answers to Review Questions

1. A, D. Both package files and the RPM database store information about RPM packages.

2. A, D. Both the -e and --uninstall flags uninstall the specified package.

3. B. The -qf flag causes RPM to report file ownership; the full path of the file must be specified.

4. A, B, D. The file size may not have changed, even though the contents of the file have changed.

5. B. The -qa flag causes RPM to list the name of each installed package.

6. B. GnoRPM is the tool that provides a graphical user interface to RPM.

Chapter 13

Understanding the Red Hat Linux File System Layout

RHCE PREPARATION TOPICS COVERED IN THIS CHAPTER:

✓ Know and understand the Red Hat Linux file system layout.

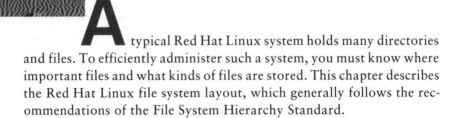

A typical Red Hat Linux system holds many directories and files. To efficiently administer such a system, you must know where important files and what kinds of files are stored. This chapter describes the Red Hat Linux file system layout, which generally follows the recommendations of the File System Hierarchy Standard.

Red Hat Linux File Systems

Like other Unix systems, Red Hat Linux has a hierarchical file system. The top-most directory—known as the root directory—of the file system contains several other directories, sometimes called subdirectories. These directories in turn generally contain subdirectories and files.

The directory structure is not arbitrary. For packages to work properly, the location of important files and directories must be standardized. The File System Hierarchy Standard codifies common practices and suggests improved practices for the structure of directories. The File System Hierarchy Standard is available via the Web, at `pathname.com/fhs`.

Though designed with Linux systems in mind, the standard is applicable to Unix systems generally. Distributors of Linux generally follow the recommendations of the File System Hierarchy Standard. However, the standard is somewhat loose and subject to interpretation. Consequently, two distributions that are held to follow the standard may nevertheless differ significantly in the structure of their file systems. Red Hat Linux follows the standard closely. The *Official Red Hat Linux Reference Guide* explains the standard and how Red Hat Linux implements the standard's recommendations.

The remaining sections of this chapter describe the standard directories of a Red Hat Linux system.

The Root Directory

The root directory (/) of a Linux system is the directory that contains all other directories and files. Other directories may be separately mounted and thus may or may not be present at system startup. Therefore, the file system that contains the root directory must contain all files necessary to operate the system in single-user mode. The root directory also contains all files needed to shut down and recover or repair the system.

The following directories are essential and must be part of the root file system:

- /bin, which contains binary files used by the system administrator and other users

- /dev, which contains device files

- /etc, which contains host-specific configuration data

- /lib, which contains system libraries

- /sbin, which contains binary files used by the system administrator

A boot or rescue floppy disk may contain only the essential directories on its root file system, which may be the only file system contained on the media. However, Linux systems typically include several other directories, which may be used as mounting points for non-root file systems or which may contain directories and files that reside on the root file system. Some commonly used directories include:

- /boot, which contains files needed by the boot loader when booting the system. These files could be placed in the root partition. However, Red Hat, Inc. recommends that they be placed in a separate partition to overcome common PC BIOS limitations on the location of boot data.

- /home, which contains users' home directories

- /lost+found, which contains files recovered during file system rebuilds

- /mnt, which contains mount points for temporarily mounted file systems

- /proc, which contains system information

- /root, which contains the home directory of the root user

- /tmp, which contains temporary files

- /usr, which contains shareable files not essential to basic system operation

- /var, which contains non-shareable files not essential to basic system operation

/bin: Essential Binary Files

The /bin directory contains binary files that are essential to system operation in single-user mode. These files are generally commands, which may be used by the system administrator and by users. Similar files not required for single-user mode are placed in /usr/bin. Table 13.1 lists files found in the /bin directory. Some of the files are symbolic links that provide alternate filenames. For example, /bin/csh is a symbolic link pointing to /bin/tcsh.

TABLE 13.1 Files in /bin

arch	df	igawk	netstat	sort
ash	dmesg	ipcalc	nice	stty
ash.static	dnsdomainname	kill	nisdomainname	su
awk	doexec	ksh	ping	sync
basename	domainname	linuxconf	ps	tar
bash	echo	ln	pwd	tcsh
bash2	ed	loadkeys	red	touch
bsh	egrep	login	remadmin	true
cat	ex	ls	rm	umount
chgrp	false	mail	rmdir	uname
chmod	fgrep	mkdir	rpm	userconf
chown	fsconf	mknod	rvi	usleep
consolechars	gawk	mktemp	rview	vi
cp	gawk-3.0.3	more	sed	view
cpio	grep	mount	setserial	ypdomainname

TABLE 13.1 Files in /bin *(continued)*

csh	gunzip	mt	sfxload	zcat
date	gzip	mv	sh	zsh
dd	hostname	netconf	sleep	

/boot: Boot Loader Files

As explained in Chapter 2, "Hardware Basics," many PCs contain BIOS code that cannot load a boot record unless the boot record is stored below a given cylinder (usually 1024) of a disk drive. Red Hat recommends that you avoid boot problems by placing boot loader files in a separate partition and placing the partition on a region of the disk that is accessible to the BIOS.

The /boot partition generally contains the first stage of the Linux loader (LILO) in its MBR, located on the first cylinder of the partition. It also contains files such as:

- LILO's second stage, which resides in the file boot.b

- the Linux kernel, generally named vmlinuz*

- module information that identifies system modules by name

- the system map file that records the location of kernel modules and symbols

- copies of disk areas overwritten by the loader during its installation

/dev: Device Files

The Linux /dev directory includes a variety of device files. Not every device file corresponds to an installed device; an installation script (/dev/MAKEDEV) creates a standard set of device files, whether the associated device is installed or not.

Table 13.2 summarizes some of the most important common device files. In addition, there are device files that correspond to:

- Various mice (for example, /dev/psaux)

- Memory and I/O ports (for example, /dev/mem)

- Various audio and multimedia devices (for example, /dev/audio)

- Specialized serial cards (for example, /dev/ttyC)
- Proprietary CD-ROM drives (for example, /dev/cdu31a)

TABLE 13.2 Important Device Files

Device File	Device
console	System console
cua*	Deprecated—originally referred to a serial port
fd*	Floppy drive
hd*	IDE hard disk or CD-ROM
lp*	Parallel port
md*	RAID array
null	Null output device
ramdisk	RAM disk
sd*	SCSI hard disk
sr*	SCSI CD-ROM
st*	SCSI tape
tpqic*, ntpqic*, rft*, nrft*	QIC tape
tty*	Terminal or pseudoterminal
ttyS*	Serial port
vc*	Contents of a tty device, such as a virtual console
zero	All binary 0s input device

/etc: Host-Specific Configuration Files

The /etc directory contains files and directories that are specific to the local host. Traditionally, some binary files resided in /etc; these are now found in /sbin and /usr/sbin. Some of the most important files and subdirectories are summarized in Tables 13.3 and 13.4, respectively.

TABLE 13.3 Important Files in /etc

File	Contents
adjtime	Time synchronization data
fdprm	Floppy disk parameters
fstab	File system table
gettydefs	Login terminal characteristics
group	User groups
inittab	System startup configuration
ld.so.conf	System library cache
lilo.conf	Linux loader configuration
motd	Message of the day
mtab	Mounted file system table
nsswitch.conf	List of sources for information on users, hosts, networks, and services.
mtools.conf	Configuration of mtools utilities
passwd	User accounts
profile	Shell initialization script
securetty	List of secure login terminals
shadow	User account encrypted passwords, if shadow passwords enabled

TABLE 13.3 Important Files in /etc *(continued)*

File	Contents
shells	List of approved shells
syslog.conf	System log configuration
exports	List of NSF exports
ftp*	FTP configuration files
host.conf	Host name resolution configuration (see also resolv.conf)
hosts	List of known hosts
hosts.allow	List of hosts allowed access to services
hosts.deny	List of hosts denied access to services
hosts.equiv	List of trusted hosts
inetd.conf	Configuration of Internet super-server, inetd
networks	List of known networks
printcap	Printer configuration
protocols	List of known protocols
resolv.conf	Hostname resolution configuration (see also host.conf)
rpc	List of RPC services
services	List of TCP/IP services

TABLE 13.4 Important Subdirectories of /etc

Subdirectory	Contents
cron*	Configuration of cron service
httpd	Configuration of http (Web) service

TABLE 13.4   Important Subdirectories of /etc *(continued)*

Subdirectory	Contents
pam.d	Configuration of PAM, Red Hat's security library
pcmcia	Configuration of PCMCIA slots and devices
ppp	Configuration of PPP services
rc.d	System initialization files
security	Security configuration
skel	User environment template files
sysconfig	System configuration
X11	X Window System configuration, including XF86Config file

/home: User Home Directories

The /home directory contains home directories of users other than root (whose home directory is /root). By default, a user's home directory is a subdirectory of /home having the same name as the user's login. However, particularly if a system has many user accounts, you may prefer to structure the /home directory differently. For example, a university might place students' home directories under /home/student and faculty members' home directories under /home/faculty, mounting disk volumes at these mount points.

/lib: Shared Libraries and Kernel Modules

The /lib directory contains libraries and modules needed to boot the system and run programs residing in the /sbin and /bin directories; other libraries reside in /usr/lib, /usr/X11R6/lib, and elsewhere. Modules reside in subdirectories of /lib/modules; each such subdirectory is named according to the version and build number of the kernel with which the modules are associated. For example, modules for build 15 of the Linux 2.2.9 kernel might be found in /lib/modules/2.2.9-15.

/lost+found: Recovered Files

When you recover a file system, files and file data may be partially recovered. For example, the recovery utility may recover a file's data but not the file's name. Such files are placed by the utility in the /lost+found subdirectory of the root directory of the file system.

/mnt: Mount Point for Temporarily Mounted File Systems

The /mnt directory exists as the standard parent directory of a set of directories for temporarily mounting file systems. Standard subdirectories include cdrom, a mount point for CD-ROM file systems, and floppy, a mount point for file systems residing on floppy disk.

/proc: System Information Virtual File System

The Linux /proc directory is a pseudo file system provided by the kernel that contains files and directories that let system administrators and programmers access system information. Some information in the /proc directory can be modified to configure system operation.

Some of the most important files and subdirectories in the /proc directory are summarized in Table 13.5. See the man page on proc for further information on the contents of the /proc directory.

TABLE 13.5 Important Files and Subdirectories of /proc

File or Subdirectory	Contnets
[*number*]	A directory that contains files and subdirectories that describe the process having the same ID as the directory name
cpuinfo	Various architecture-dependent information

TABLE 13.5   Important Files and Subdirectories of /proc *(continued)*

File or Subdirectory	Contnets
devices	Major device numbers and device groups
dma	Registered ISA DMA channels in use
filesystems	File system types supported by the kernel
interrupts	Information on interrupts and IRQs
ioports	Registered input/output ports
kcore	System physical memory contents
kmsg	Kernel message log
ksyms	Kernel exported symbols and definitions
loadavg	Average number of jobs in the run queue
meminfo	Memory allocation information
modules	List of loaded modules
net	Network status information
pci	Configuration of PCI devices
scsi	Status of SCSI input/output system
self	Information on the process for accessing the /proc file system
stat	Kernel and system statistics
sys	Kernel variables, some of which can be modified to configure kernel operation
uptime	The system up time and idle time
version	The version number of the running kernel

sbin: Essential System Binaries

The /sbin directory contains essential system binary files used by the system administrator; that is, files needed for system start-up, shut-down, and operation in single-user mode. Table 13.6 lists the most important files in /sbin.

TABLE 13.6 Files in /sbin

accton	getty	ksyms	netreport	rpcdebug
adjtimex	halt	ldconfig	nwmsg	rrestore
arp	hdparm	lilo	pam_filter	runlevel
askrunlevel	hwclock	loglevel	pcinitrd	sash
badblocks	ifconfig	losetup	pidof	scsi_info
cardctl	ifdown	lsmod	plipconfig	service
cardmgr	ifport	lspci	pnpdump	setpci
cfdisk	ifup	mailconf	portmap	setsysfont
chkconfig	ifuser	mgetty	poweroff	sfdisk
clock	init	mingetty	probe	shapecfg
ctrlaltdel	initlog	minilogd	pump	shutdown
debugfs	insmod	mkbootdisk	pwdb_chkpwd	slattach
depmod	insmod.static	mkdosfs	quotacheck	sln
dhcpcd	install-info	mke2fs	quotaoff	stinit
dnsconf	installkernel	mkfs	quotaon	sulogin
dump	ipchains	mkfs.ext2	raidhotadd	swapoff
dumpe2fs	ipchains-restore	mkfs.minix	raidhotremove	swapon
e2fsck	ipchains-save	mkfs.msdos	raidstart	telinit

TABLE 13.6 Files in /sbin *(continued)*

e2label	ipfwadm-wrapper	mkinitrd	raidstop	tune2fs
fdisk	ipmaddr	mkpv	rarp	update
fixperm	iptunnel	mkraid	rdump	uugetty
fsck	ipx_configure	mkswap	reboot	vgetty
fsck.ext2	ipx_internal_net	modinfo	restore	ypbind
fsck.minix	isapnp	modprobe	rmmod	
ftl_check	kbdrate	mount.ncp	rmmod.static	
ftl_format	kerneld	mount.ncpfs	rmt	
genksyms	killall5		route	

/tmp: Temporary Files

The /tmp directory contains temporary files and subdirectories that are automatically deleted by the tmpwatch utility when they've not been used for a specified period of time (by default, 10 days).

/usr: Shareable Files

The /usr file system may not be available, so it contains no files or directories that are essential for system operation. Normal operation of the system does not require modification of files in /usr, so its contents are shareable; often, for example, the /usr partition is an NFS-exported partition that resides on a remote system. Table 13.7 summarizes some important subdirectories of /usr.

TABLE 13.7 Important Subdirectories of /usr

Subdirectory	Contents
/usr/X11R6	X Window System binary files

TABLE 13.7 Important Subdirectories of /usr *(continued)*

Subdirectory	Contents
/usr/bin	Commands used by ordinary users
/usr/dict	Dictionary
/usr/doc	Documentation
/usr/games	Game-related binary files
/usr/include	Header files
/usr/info	Texinfo documentation files
/usr/lib	Programming libraries
/usr/local	Local files not part of the operating system
/usr/man	Man pages
/usr/sbin	System binaries not required to start, shut down, or run the system in single-user mode
/usr/share	Architecture-independent files
/usr/src	Source code

/var: Non-Shareable Files

Like the /usr file system, the /var file system may not be available, and so it contains no essential files or directories. Unlike /usr, however, /var contains files that are modified during system operation—for example, log files. Table 13.8 summarizes important subdirectories of /var.

TABLE 13.8 Important Subdirectories of /var

Subdirectory	Contents
/var/cache	Application cache files
/var/lock	Lock files
/var/log	Log and accounting files
/var/run	System information files
/var/spool	Spool files, including those for cron, lpd, and sendmail
/var/tmp	Temporary files
/var/yp	NIS files

Summary

In this chapter, you learned about the Red Hat Linux file system layout. The most important topics covered are:

The File System Hierarchy Standard   The File System Hierarchy Standard specifies the standard location and contents of important Linux directories.

The Root Directory (/)   The root directory contains all other directories.

The /bin Directory   The /bin directory contains essential binaries used by the system administrator and ordinary users.

The /boot Directory   The /boot directory contains files needed to boot Linux and files that can help debug the kernel. The associated file system is stored on a partition that generally contains LILO, which is used to boot Linux.

The /dev Directory   The /dev directory contains special files that correspond to hardware devices.

The /etc Directory The /etc directory contains files and directories whose contents are specific to the local host, particularly configuration information.

The /home Directory The /home directory generally contains users' home directories.

The /lib Directory The /lib directory contains libraries and loadable modules.

The /lost+found Directory The /lost+found directory contains files recovered—or partially recovered—by a file system utility.

The /mnt Directory The /mnt directory provides standard mount points for file systems.

The /proc Directory The /proc directory is the root directory of a pseudo file system that lets you view and modify system information.

The /sbin Directory The /sbin directory contains essential binaries used mainly by the system administrator.

The /tmp Directory The /tmp directory contains temporary files that are automatically deleted if they are not used for a specified period.

The /usr Directory The /usr directory contains a variety of nonessential directories.

The /var Directory The /var directory contains non-shareable files that are modified during system operation.

Key Terms

Before going on to the next chapter, be sure you're familiar with the following terms:

device file

temporary file

Additional Sources of Information

If you'd like further information about the topics presented in this chapter, you should consult the following sources:

- *The Official Red Hat Linux Reference Guide*
- *The File System Hierarchy Standard*, www.pathname.com/fhs
- The file /usr/doc/kernel-doc*/proc.txt, which explains the /proc file system

Review Questions

1. Which of the following are essential system directories?

   A. /bin

   B. /etc

   C. /usr/bin

   D. /var/log

2. What is the default directory that contains the Linux kernel?

   A. /

   B. /boot

   C. /dev

   D. /sbin

3. Which file contains the system startup information?

   A. /etc/inetd.conf

   B. /etc/inittab

   C. /usr/etc/inetd.conf

   D. /usr/etc/inittab

4. Which of the following directories might be the home directory of the user with login name red?

   A. /home/chicago/red

   B. /home/red

   C. /home/staff/red

   D. /home/swingshift/red

5. Which of the following files corresponds to the system console?

A. /dev/console

B. /dev/operator

C. /dev/ttyS1

D. /dev/vc1

6. Which of the following directories contains C header files needed to compile the Linux kernel?

A. /usr/c

B. /usr/header

C. /usr/include

D. /usr/src/header

Answers to Review Questions

1. A, B. The /usr and /var file systems are nonessential.

2. B. The Linux kernel resides in the /boot directory.

3. B. The system startup information resides in /etc/inittab.

4. A, B, C, D. A system administrator can structure the /home directory in almost any way.

5. A. The system console is known as /dev/console.

6. C. The /usr/include directory contains C header files.

Chapter

14

System Initialization

✓ Be familiar with and able to configure system
  initialization scripts.

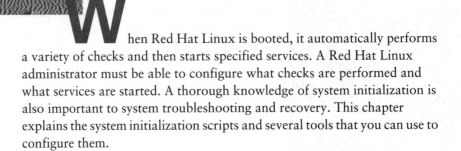

hen Red Hat Linux is booted, it automatically performs a variety of checks and then starts specified services. A Red Hat Linux administrator must be able to configure what checks are performed and what services are started. A thorough knowledge of system initialization is also important to system troubleshooting and recovery. This chapter explains the system initialization scripts and several tools that you can use to configure them.

System Initialization

Red Hat Linux generally follows the system initialization procedure inaugurated under AT&T SysV Unix. When a Red Hat Linux system boots, the system executes two main scripts:

- /etc/rc.d/rc.sysinit
- /etc/rc.d/rc

Essentially, the /etc/rc.d/rc.sysinit script initializes file systems and devices. It is a large script that invokes many commands. It also invokes the /etc/rc.d/rc.serial script, if one exists. The /etc/rc.d/rc.serial script initializes serial ports; it is used when special initialization must be performed—for example, when a multi-port serial card is installed.

Essentially, the /etc/rc.d/rc script initializes services. It is invoked at system start-up and whenever the system runlevel is changed. It invokes an appropriate set of runlevel scripts that start and stop facilities and services. On system start-up, it invokes the /etc/rc.d/rc.local script after all other runlevel scripts have executed. The contents of the /etc/rc.d/rc.local script are locally defined; you can use it to perform special initialization operations.

System initialization scripts may log error messages. If the system doesn't properly start up, you should examine /var/log/messages for relevant error messages.

The remaining sections of this chapter explain these scripts and their operation in more detail. They also explain how to configure what services are run at a given runlevel.

The */etc/rc.d/rc.sysinit* Script

As explained, the /etc/rc.d/rc.sysinit script initializes file systems and devices. It also performs several other operations. Here is a guide to the operations performed by the script; it can

- Checks for an /etc/sysconfig/network script, which sets environment variables describing the network configuration. If the /etc/sysconfig/network script exists, it executes it; otherwise, it sets environment variables that turn off networking and set the host name to localhost.

- Source the file /etc/rc.d/init.d/functions, which contains a group of shell functions. These functions are used by scripts in the /etc/rc.d/init.d directory. Included are functions that:

  - Start a program

  - Stop a program

  - Find the process ID of a program

  - Display the status of a program

  - Display success and failure messages that help track program start-up

  - Log start-ups, shutdowns, errors, and other messages

  - Request confirmation of sensitive actions

- Display a welcome banner that includes prompt for interactive start-up

- Set the logging level.

- Mount the /proc file system, configure kernel parameters by using sysctl, and set the system clock.

- Load the default keymap if /etc/sysconfig/console/default.kmap exists; otherwise loads the keymap specified in /etc/sysconfig/keyboard.

- Run the /sbin/setsysfont script, which sets the default system font.

- Activate the swap partitions specified in /etc/fstab.

- Set the host name and the NIS domain name, if applicable.

- Remount the root file system in read-only mode and checks its status if there is a problem with the root file system. If a serious error is found, the script starts a shell that enables you to attempt to repair the damaged file system.

- Set up configured ISA plug-and-play devices.

- Remount the root file system in read-write mode.

- Check disk quotas on the root file system.

- Set up /etc/mtab, which lists mounted file systems, and /etc/HOSTNAME, which identifies the host.

- Set up support for loadable kernel modules.

- Load the sound module, if a sound card is specified in /etc/conf.modules; load the MIDI module, if a MIDI interface is specified in /etc/conf.modules.

- Load the RAID devices specified in /etc/raidtab.

- Check the non-root file systems. If a serious error is found, the script starts a shell that enables you to attempt to repair the damaged file system. Otherwise, the script checks disk quotas on the non-root file systems and mounts those specified in /etc/fstab as automatically mountable. It then turns on disk quota checking, if the disk quota package is installed.

- Remove unneeded temporary files of various sorts, such as lock files.

- Initialize serial ports by running the script /etc/rc.d/rc.serial, if it exists. The /etc/rc.d/rc.serial script generally contains setserial commands that configure serial devices. It is not generally needed to configure standard PC serial ports and is included mainly for compatibility with older Linux releases.

- Load the SCSI tape module if a SCSI tape drive is present.

- Create the header file /boot/kernel.h, under some circumstances.

- Create symbolic links for /boot/System.map-*kernel_version*.

- Copy the boot messages to /var/log/dmesg, so that they can be read by the dmesg command.

During system start-up, the init process invokes /etc/rc.d/rc.sysinit and then invokes /etc/rc.d/rc. Chapter 15 describes this process in detail. In order to be prepared for the RHCE exam, you should generally be familiar with the steps performed by the /etc/rc.d/rc.sysinit script.

Now that you've had a tour of the /etc/rc.d/rc.sysinit script, complete Exercise 14.1, which requires you to study the script in more detail.

EXERCISE 14.1

The */etc/rc.d/rc.sysinit* Script

1. Understanding the /etc/rc.d/rc.sysinit script is helpful in resolving a variety of system start-up problems. To learn more about the script, examine it and find where it performs each of the operations identified in this section.

2. The script also performs several less significant operations. Find and identify these.

The */etc/rc.d/rc* Script

The /etc/rc.d/rc script sets a new runlevel and then runs a series of scripts associated with the specified runlevel. The scripts are contained in the directories

- /etc/rc.d/rc0.d
- /etc/rc.d/rc1.d
- /etc/rc.d/rc2.d
- /etc/rc.d/rc3.d
- /etc/rc.d/rc4.d
- /etc/rc.d/rc5.d
- /etc/rc.d/rc6.d

The name of each directory corresponds to that of the associated runlevel. Table 14.1 summarizes the runlevels used by Red Hat Linux.

TABLE 14.1 Summary of Runlevels

Runlevel	Description
0	System halt
1	Single-user mode
2	Multiuser mode, no NFS
3	Full multiuser mode
4	Unused
5	Full multiuser mode, with X-based login
6	System reboot

Runlevel Scripts

Each /etc/rc.d/rc?.d subdirectory contains a series of symbolic links that refer to scripts in the /etc/rc.d/init.d directory, called runlevel scripts. The most common runlevel scripts, which are used to start and stop system services, are summarized in Table 14.2. If you've installed optional packages, you may find other scripts in addition to those described in Table 14.2. The point of using symbolic links to refer to the scripts is that several symbolic links can refer to a single script file. If the script requires revision, only one file must be changed, which is a more convenient and less error-prone method than changing several files.

TABLE 14.2 Description of Common Runlevel Scripts

Script	Description
anacron	Runs commands at specified intervals; unlike crond, it does not assume that the system is continuously operational.
apmd	Advanced power management service, which monitors battery power levels.

TABLE 14.2 Description of Common Runlevel Scripts *(continued)*

Script	Description
`atd`	AT server, which processes commands specified via the at command.
`autofs`	Automatically mounts file systems.
`crond`	CRON server, which runs commands at user-specified intervals.
`gpm`	Mouse support for text mode programs.
`halt`	Reboots or halts the system.
`httpd`	Apache Web server.
`inet`	A variety of basic TCP/IP services; run under the control of inetd.
`keytable`	Loads the keyboard map.
`killall`	Kills running services.
`kudzu`	Checks at boot time for hardware changes.
`linuxconf`	A hook that allows linuxconf to perform specified actions on system start-up and shutdown.
`local`	The /etc/rc.d/rc.local script, which has locally specified contents.
`lpd`	LP service, which provides access to remote printers.
`named`	DNS server, which provides host name and IP address lookups.
`netfs`	Mounts network file systems.
`network`	Activates and deactivates network interfaces.
`nfs`	Network File System (NFS) server, which provides file sharing.
`pcmcia`	Activates and deactivates PCMCIA support.

TABLE 14.2 Description of Common Runlevel Scripts *(continued)*

Script	Description
portmap	Manages RPC connections used, for example, by NFS and NIS.
postgresql	Database management system.
random	Saves and restores the status of the random number generator to yield better-quality random numbers.
reboot	Symbolic link to halt script.
routed	RIP client and server, which automatically updates routes.
rstatd	RSTAT server, which provides performance metrics.
rusersd	RUSERS server, which helps locate users.
rwhod	RWHO server, which lists logged-in users.
sendmail	Mail server.
single	Puts the system in single-user mode.
smb	Samba (SMB) server, which provides authentication and file and printer sharing.
sound	Saves and restores sound card mixer settings.
sshd	SSH server, which provides secure logins and remote command execution.
syslog	Starts and stops system logging.
xfs	The X Window System font server.

Now that you've familiarized yourself with the most common runlevel scripts, complete Exercise 14.2 to learn more.

EXERCISE 14.2

Runlevel Scripts

Most Linux systems use additional scripts not listed in Table 14.2. To learn about the scripts installed on your system, examine the /etc/ rc.d/init.d directory and identify any scripts not found in Table 14.2. Inspect the contents of these scripts to learn what they do. Most scripts contain comments that explain their function.

Most of the scripts accept arguments that control their operation. The most common arguments are:

- start, which causes the script to start the associated service
- stop, which causes the script to stop the associated service
- restart, which causes the script to restart the associated service
- reload, which causes the script to re-read its configuration file
- status, which causes the script to report the status of the associated service

The linuxconf program uses these scripts to start and stop services. You can also manually invoke them to control services. For example, you could shut down the Web server (httpd service) by issuing the command

```
/etc/rc.d/init/d/httpd stop
```

Or, you could restart the server by issuing the command

```
/etc/rc.d/init/httpd restart
```

It's important to use the scripts in /etc/rc.d/init.d rather than controlling services some other way. For example, it's possible to start the Web server by issuing the command /usr/sbin/httpd. However, if you do so, Linux won't be able to clean up lock files and process identification files when you shut down the service. Worse, unless you use the runlevel scripts, you may unintentionally start multiple instances of a server.

The Symbolic Links in */etc/rc.d/rc?.d*

The symbolic links in /etc/rc.d/rc?.d have names such as K05keytable and S40atd. Links having names beginning with *K* are passed the stop argument when they are executed by /etc/rc.d/rc; links having names beginning with *S* are passed the start argument. Generally, the directory associated with a given runlevel will include either a *K* script or an *S* script for each installed service.

The two-digit number in the script names, called the *priority*, indicates the sequence in which scripts in a given directory are run; for example, the script K10xfs is run before the script K15gpm. Table 14.3 summarizes common runlevel scripts according to the runlevels at which they're executed.

TABLE 14.3 Summary of Common Runlevel Scripts by Runlevel

	Runlevel						
Script	0	1	2	3	4	5	6
K00linuxconf	X	X					X
K05keytable	X	X					X
K10xfs	X	X					X
K15gpm	X	X		X	X	X	X
K15httpd	X	X	X	X	X	X	X
K15sound	X	X	X				X
K20nfs	X	X	X				X
K20rstatd	X	X	X	X	X	X	X
K20rusersd	X	X	X	X	X	X	X
K20rwhod	X	X	X	X	X	X	X
K30sendmail	X	X		X	X	X	X
K35smb				X		X	
K45named	X	X	X				X
K45sshd	X	X	X				X

TABLE 14.3 Summary of Common Runlevel Scripts by Runlevel *(continued)*

	Runlevel						
Script	**0**	**1**	**2**	**3**	**4**	**5**	**6**
K50inet	X	X	X				X
K55routed	X	X	X	X	X	X	X
K60atd	X	X	X				X
K60crond	X	X					X
K60lpd	X	X					X
K80random	X						X
K85netfs	X	X	X				X
K89portmap	X	X	X				X
K90killall	X						X
K90mysql	X	X					X
K90network	X	X					X
K92apmd	X	X		X	X	X	X
K96pcmcia	X	X		X	X	X	X
K99syslog	X	X					X
S00halt	X						
S00single		X					
S00reboot							X
S05apmd			X				
S10network			X	X	X	X	
S11portmap				X	X	X	
S15netfs				X	X	X	

TABLE 14.3 Summary of Common Runlevel Scripts by Runlevel *(continued)*

	Runlevel						
Script	**0**	**1**	**2**	**3**	**4**	**5**	**6**
S20random		X	X	X	X	X	
S30syslog			X	X	X	X	
S40atd				X	X	X	
S40crond			X	X	X	X	
S45pcmcia			X				
S50inet				X	X	X	
S55named				X	X	X	
S55sshd				X	X	X	
S60lpd			X	X	X	X	
S60nfs				X	X	X	
S75keytable			X	X	X	X	
S85sound			X	X	X	X	
S85gpm			X				
S90mysql			X	X	X	X	
S90xfs			X		X	X	
S90xfs				X			
S99linuxconf			X	X	X	X	
S99local			X	X		X	

When a runlevel script terminates, it reports a completion status. The possible values of the completion status are:

- OK, which means that the script successfully started the associated service

- Passed, which means that the script encountered errors, but was able to recover and successfully start the associated service

- Failed, which means that the script was unable to start the associated service

The completion values appear on the console during system start-up.

Operation of the */etc/rc.d/rc* Script

As explained, the /etc/rc.d/rc script sets the specified runlevel and invokes the runlevel scripts appropriate to the specified new runlevel. Here is a detailed step-by-step guide to the operations it performs. It can

1. Source the file /etc/rc.d/init.d/functions, which contains a group of shell functions. These functions are used by scripts in the /etc/rc.d/init.d directory.

2. Determine the current and previous runlevels.

3. Check and note whether user confirmation mode is set.

4. Set the runlevel to the specified value.

5. Tell linuxconf the current runlevel.

6. Find the /rc/rc.d/rcn.d directory, where *n* is the new runlevel.

7. Run the kill script for each running service.

8. Run the start script for each service not already running.

During system start-up, the init process invokes /etc/rc.d/rc after completion of /etc/rc.d/rc.sysinit, based on the configuration of the /etc/inittab file. Chapter 15 describes this process in detail.

Associating Services with Runlevels

In principle, you could associate a service with its runlevels by creating and manipulating symbolic links in the /etc/rc.d/rc?.d directories. However, because such a process would be tedious and error-prone, several utilities are available to facilitate the task. These include:

- chkconfig, a command-line utility

- ksysv, a KDE-based utility

- ntsysv, a text-mode graphical utility

- tksysv, an X-based utility

The most important of these tools is chkconfig; other tools require support, such as X, which may not be available when configuring services. The chkconfig tool lets you:

- List installed services

- Add a service

- Delete a service

- Associate a service with a runlevel

Listing Services

To list the installed services and their associated runlevels, issue the command

```
chkconfig --list
```

The output will resemble the following:

```
httpd 0:off 1:off 2:off 3:off 4:off 5:off 6:off
apmd 0:off 1:off 2:on 3:off 4:off 5:off 6:off
atd 0:off 1:off 2:off 3:on 4:on 5:on 6:off
named 0:off 1:off 2:off 3:on 4:on 5:on 6:off
keytable 0:off 1:off 2:on 3:on 4:on 5:on 6:off
gpm 0:off 1:off 2:on 3:off 4:off 5:off 6:off
netfs 0:off 1:off 2:off 3:on 4:on 5:on 6:off
network 0:off 1:off 2:on 3:on 4:on 5:on 6:off
random 0:off 1:on 2:on 3:on 4:on 5:on 6:off
pcmcia 0:off 1:off 2:on 3:off 4:off 5:off 6:off
nfs 0:off 1:off 2:off 3:on 4:on 5:on 6:off
```

```
linuxconf 0:off 1:off 2:on 3:on 4:on 5:on 6:off
lpd 0:off 1:off 2:on 3:on 4:on 5:on 6:off
inet 0:off 1:off 2:off 3:on 4:on 5:on 6:off
portmap 0:off 1:off 2:off 3:on 4:on 5:on 6:off
sound 0:off 1:off 2:off 3:on 4:on 5:on 6:off
routed 0:off 1:off 2:off 3:off 4:off 5:off 6:off
rstatd 0:off 1:off 2:off 3:off 4:off 5:off 6:off
rusersd 0:off 1:off 2:off 3:off 4:off 5:off 6:off
rwhod 0:off 1:off 2:off 3:off 4:off 5:off 6:off
smb 0:off 1:off 2:off 3:off 4:off 5:off 6:off
sendmail 0:off 1:off 2:on 3:off 4:off 5:off 6:off
syslog 0:off 1:off 2:on 3:on 4:on 5:on 6:off
crond 0:off 1:off 2:on 3:on 4:on 5:on 6:off
xfs 0:off 1:off 2:on 3:on 4:on 5:on 6:off
ypbind 0:off 1:off 2:off 3:off 4:off 5:off 6:off
sshd 0:off 1:off 2:off 3:on 4:on 5:on 6:off
mysql 0:off 1:off 2:on 3:on 4:on 5:on 6:off
```

Each service is listed, followed by its status for each of the possible runlevels.

You may find it more convenient to issue this command, which sorts the output by the name of the service

```
chkconfig --list | sort
```

Adding a Service

To add a service, you must first ensure that the associated init.d script contains special comments. The first comment is a line that tells chkconfig the runlevels for which the service should be started and the start and stop priority numbers. The comment line contains the tokens # chkconfig: and then lists the runlevels. For example, the following comment specifies that a service runs at runlevels 2 and 5 and has start priority 20 and stop priority 80:

```
# chkconfig: 25 20 80
```

The second comment consists of one or more lines that describe the service. Each line other than the last must end with a backslash (\), which is the comment continuation character. For example, here's a typical comment, which describes the random service:

```
# description: Saves and restores system entropy pool for \
```

```
#               higher quality random number generation.
```

To add the service, issue the command

```
chkconfig --add name
```

where *name* is the name of the service. The chkconfig program creates the required symbolic links according to the comments in the init.d script.

Deleting a Service

To delete a service, issue the command

```
chkconfig --del name
```

where *name* is the name of the service. The chkconfig program deletes the associated symbolic links.

Associating a Service with Runlevels

To associate a service with one or more runlevels, issue the command

```
chkconfig name reset
```

where *name* is the name of the service. The chkconfig program creates the required symbolic links according to the comments in the init.d script. If you prefer, you can explicitly set a service to run or not run at specified levels regardless of the contents of the associated init.d script. To specify levels at which the service should run, issue the command

```
chkconfig --level levels name on
```

where *name* is the name of the service and *levels* is a series of digits that specify the runlevels. For example, the command

```
chkconfig --level 35 lunch on
```

specifies that the lunch service will run at levels 3 and 5.

To specify levels at which the service should not run, issue the command

```
chkconfig --level levels name off
```

where *name* is the name of the service and *levels* is a series of digits that specify the runlevels. For example, the command

```
chkconfig --level 24 lunch off
```

specifies that the lunch service will not run at levels 2 and 4.

Now, try your hand at Exercise 14.3, which requires you to use chkconfig.

EXERCISE 14.3

Associating Services with Runlevels

The RHCE exam is likely to require you to configure services to run at specified levels. Perform the following operations to verify your ability to do so:

1. Use chkconfig to determine what services run at what runlevels.

2. Using a system that has Apache installed, configure the httpd service to run only at runlevel 5.

3. Use the init command to change the current runlevel so that you can verify that your change succeeded.

Look back to the chapter if you must, but be prepared to use chkconfig without helps during the RHCE exam.

The */etc/rc.d/rc.local* Script

The /etc/rc.d/rc.local script is a special script run by symbolic links in the directories associated with runlevels 2, 3, and 5. Its start priority is 99, which means it runs after all other runlevel scripts. By default, it creates

- The /etc/issue file

- The /etc/issue.net file

The /etc/issue file is listed when a user logs in by using a local console. By default, the file reports the release of Red Hat Linux and the kernel version:

```
Red Hat Linux release 6.0 (Hedwig)
Kernel 2.2.5-15 on an i686
```

The /etc/issue.net file is listed when a user logs in by using a remote console—for example, by initiating a Telnet session. By default, the file reports the release of Red Hat Linux and the kernel version:

```
Red Hat Linux release 6.0 (Hedwig)
Kernel 2.2.5-15 on an i686
```

It's considered good practice to change the contents of /etc/issue.net so that would-be hackers gain less information about your system. You may also want to display a banner stating any restrictions on system use.

You can easily modify the /etc/rc.d/rc.local script to put a different message in /etc/issue.net or to perform other host-specific initialization. Since the script is executed last, all other system services associated with the current runlevel should be operational when the script executes.

To learn more about the rc.local script, complete Exercise 14.4.

EXERCISE 14.4

The */etc/rc.d/rc.local* Script

System administrators often modify the rc.local script to customize system start-up. To learn more about system start-up, inspect the /etc/rc.d/rc.local script of a configured Red Hat Linux system to see what modifications, if any, the system administrator has made to the script.

Summary

In this chapter, you learned about system initialization. The most important topics covered are:

System Initialization   When a system is booted, it runs the script /etc/rc.d/rc.sysinit, which initializes file systems and devices, and then the script d/etc/rc.d/rc, which initializes services.

The /etc/rc.d/rc.sysinit Script   The /etc/rc.d/rc.sysinit script performs about two dozen operations, ranging from setting up networking to saving the boot log.

The /etc/rc.d/rc Script   The /etc/rc.d/rc script runs a series of scripts associated with the default runlevel. The scripts are pointed to by symbolic links that reside in the directory named /etc/rc.d/rc?.d, where *?* is the default runlevel.

Runlevels   Red Hat Linux defines seven runlevels, numbered 0 to 6. System operation generally proceeds under runlevel 3 or 5. Other levels are useful for troubleshooting and repair.

Runlevel Scripts   The runlevel scripts reside in /etc/rc.d/init.d. They generally accept the arguments start, stop, restart, and status.

Symbolic Links to Runlevel Scripts   The symbolic link to a runlevel script has a name of the form *XNNService*, where *X* has the value K or S, *NN* determines the order in which the script is run, and *Service* specifies the associated service. A K script is used to stop a service, and an S script is used to start a service.

Functions   The script `/etc/rc.d/init.d/functions` contains several useful functions. This file is sourced by other runlevel scripts.

Configuring Services   You can associate a service with a runlevel by using any of several utilities, including `chkconfig`, `ksysv`, `ntsysv`, and `tksysv`.

The `/etc/rc.d/rc.local` Script   The `/etc/rc.d/rc.local` script is used to perform locally specified initialization operations.

Key Terms

Before going on to the next chapter, be sure you're familiar with the following terms:

Priority

Runlevel

Runlevel script

Additional Sources of Information

If you'd like further information about the topics presented in this chapter, you should consult *The Official Red Hat Linux Reference Guide*.

Review Questions

1. Which of the following file systems is mounted first?

    A. The non-root file systems, in read-only mode

    B. The non-root file systems, in read-write mode

    C. The root file system, in read-only mode

    D. The root file system, in read-write mode

2. What script invokes the runlevel scripts?

    A. `/etc/rc.d/rc`

    B. `/etc/rc.d/rc.local`

    C. `/etc/rc.d/rc.serial`

    D. `/etc/rc.d/rc.sysinit`

3. Which of the following scripts would be executed first if all were part of the same directory?

    A. `K05alpha`

    B. `K10beta`

    C. `S01delta`

    D. `S05gamma`

4. To see the runlevels associated with the service `grub`, which command must be issued?

    A. `chkconfig`

    B. `chkconfig grub`

    C. `chkconfig --grub`

    D. `chkconfig --list`

5. Which of the following tools can be used only under X?

   A. chkconfig

   B. ksysv

   C. ntsysv

   D. tksysv

6. To change the information placed in /etc/issue.net, which file should you modify?

   A. /etc/rc.d/rc

   B. /etc/rc.d/rc.local

   C. /etc/rc.d/rc.serial

   D. /etc/rc.d/rc.sysinit

Answers to Review Questions

1. C. The system first mounts the root file system in read mode; later, it mounts all file systems in read-write mode.

2. A. The rc script invokes the scripts in the /etc/rc.d/r?.d directories.

3. A. The kill scripts are executed before start scripts; within a type, scripts are executed by priority.

4. D. The --list command causes chkconfig to list services and their associated runlevels.

5. B, D. The ksysv program requires X. The tksysv program uses the TK widget set and operates only under X.

6. B. The file rc.local builds the /etc/issue.net file.

Chapter

15

Understanding Configuration Files and Scripts

RHCE PREPARATION TOPICS COVERED IN THIS CHAPTER:

✓ Understand the role of the scripts and configuration files under /etc/sysconfig.

✓ Understand the role of the scripts and configuration files under /etc/sysconfig/network-scripts.

✓ Understand how Plug-and-Play cards, including sound cards, are configured.

✓ Understand the role and contents of /etc/inittab.

✓ Understand the role and contents of /etc/fstab.

In addition to the AT&T SysV Unix-style start-up scripts, Red Hat Linux uses several other sets of scripts during system initialization. This chapter describes these scripts and explains how to use them to configure system start-up.

The */etc/sysconfig* Network Files and Scripts

When the `/etc/rc.d/init.d/network` network start-up script runs, it brings up the configured network interface devices. It does so by invoking a set of scripts stored in the `/etc/sysconfig/network-scripts` directory. Table 15.1 summarizes these scripts, which can perform a variety of operations beside bringing up network interfaces.

TABLE 15.1 Scripts in /etc/sysconfig/network-scripts

Script	Description
chat-*	Chat scripts for PPP and SLIP connections
ifcfg-*	Stores the configuration of the associated interface; for example, ifcfg-eth0 stores the configuration of the first Ethernet card, and ifcfg-lo stores the configuration of the TCP/IP dummy loopback device
ifdhcp-done	Configures /etc/resolv.conf if DHCP is used

TABLE 15.1   Scripts in /etc/sysconfig/network-scripts *(continued)*

Script	Description
ifdown-*	Brings down the associated protocol; for example, ifdown-ppp brings down PPP
ifdown-post	Brings down a specified device
ifup-*	Brings up the associated protocol; for example, ifup-ppp brings up PPP
ifup-aliases	Adds IP aliases for a specified device
ifup-post	Brings up a specified device, adding static routes and aliases and setting the host name
ifup-routes	Adds static routes for a specified device

The *ifcfg-* * Scripts

Each ifcfg-* script stores the configuration for a network interface. The scripts /sbin/ifup and /sbin/ifdown use these configuration scripts to bring up or bring down, respectively, an interface. For example, a system that has an Ethernet network interface will store the interface configuration in /etc/sysconfig/network-scripts/ifcfg-eth0; if the system has a second Ethernet network interface, the interface configuration will be stored in /etc/sysconfig/network-scripts/ifcfg-eth1, and so on. To bring up the first Ethernet card, you can issue the command

```
/sbin/ifup ifcfg-eth0
```

or simply

```
/sbin/ifup eth0
```

The command supplies the ifcfg- prefix if you omit it.

The `ifup` and `ifdown` scripts use the `ifconfig` command (described in a subsection below), which is a privileged command. Therefore, ordinary users cannot execute the `ifup` and `ifdown` scripts, unless you specify that the associated interface is user controllable. However, non-privileged users may require a simpler user interface than that provided by the `ifup` and `ifdown` scripts. Such users may prefer to use the `usernet` and `usernetctl` commands, which are available to them if the interface is user controllable. See the `usernet` and `usernetctl` man pages for details.

The `ifcfg-*` scripts contain commands that set the values of environment variables that specify the network configuration. For example, here's a typical `ifcfg-eth0` script:

```
DEVICE="eth0"
IPADDR="192.168.1.3"
NETMASK="255.255.255.0"
ONBOOT="yes"
BOOTPROTO="none"
```

If you used `linuxconf` to establish the network configuration, the file will likely contain statements that set a variety of IPX-related environment variables, even if your system is not configured for IPX. The example configuration corresponds to a static Ethernet configuration. It includes

- The device name, `DEVICE=eth0`

- The IP address, `IPADDR=192.168.1.3`

- The network subnet mask, `NETMASK=255.255.255.0`

- A parameter indicating that the device should be started when the system boots, `ONBOOT=yes`

- A parameter indicating that the configuration is static, `BOOTPROTO=none`

A static Ethernet configuration may also include

- A network address, NETWORK=192.168.1.0

- A network broadcast address, BROADCAST=192.168.1.255

If you configure an interface to obtain its configuration via DHCP, the contents of the file are somewhat different. It includes the following:

- The device name, DEVICE=eth0

- The boot protocol, BOOTPROTO=dhcp

- A parameter indicating that the device should be started when the system boots, ONBOOT=yes

You can revise the network configuration via linuxconf or netcfg, or you can modify the files by using a text editor.

The */etc/sysconfig/network* Script

Global network configuration information affecting each interface is stored in /etc/sysconfig/network. Here's a typical /etc/sysconfig/network file.

```
NETWORKING=yes
FORWARD_IPV4="yes"
HOSTNAME="athlon.azusapacific.com"
GATEWAY="192.168.1.1"
GATEWAYDEV="eth1"
```

The file indicates that networking is active and that the system will route packets. The host name of the system is athlon.azusapacific.com; its default gateway is 192.168.1.1, which is accessible via the Ethernet interface known as eth1. If the system used NIS, the file would also indicate the NIS domain with which it's associated.

Now, complete Exercise 15.1, which asks you to study the networking configuration files.

EXERCISE 15.1

Network Configuration Scripts

For the RHCE exam, it's important to know how to configure networking with and without the use of configuration utilities. To configure networking without using configuration utilities, you must know the name and function of each network configuration file. To learn more about these files, inspect the network configuration files of a working Linux server. Verify that you understand the role and contents of each file. For now, you can freely refer to this book and other documentation. But before taking the RHCE exam, be sure that you can find each file and explain its function without consulting any documentation.

Network Administration Commands

Several commands help you administer networking. Among the most important are the following:

- ifconfig
- netstat
- arp

This section explains the operation of these commands.

The *ifconfig* Command

The ifconfig command reports the status of a network interface and lets you add or remove an interface. It's run by the /etc/sysconfig/network-scripts ifup and ifdown scripts.

Reporting Network Interface Status

To obtain a report on the status of network interfaces, issue the command

```
ifconfig
```

The output of the command will resemble the following:

```
eth0 Link encap:Ethernet  HWaddr 00:40:05:68:02:30
     inet addr:192.168.100.2  Bcast:192.168.100.255
     ➡ Mask:255.255.255.0
     UP BROADCAST RUNNING MULTICAST  MTU:1500  Metric:1
     RX packets:1601111 errors:0 dropped:0 overruns:0
     ➡ frame:0
     TX packets:1549740 errors:49 dropped:0 overruns:0
     ➡ carrier:98
     collisions:952 txqueuelen:100
     Interrupt:10 Base address:0x6100

eth1 Link encap:Ethernet  HWaddr 00:A0:CC:25:8A:EC
     inet addr:192.168.1.1  Bcast:192.168.1.255
     ➡ Mask:255.255.255.0
     UP BROADCAST RUNNING MULTICAST  MTU:1500  Metric:1
     RX packets:2063495 errors:0 dropped:0 overruns:0
     ➡ frame:0
```

```
          TX packets:2181226 errors:0 dropped:0 overruns:0
          ➡ carrier:0
          collisions:37470 txqueuelen:100
          Interrupt:11 Base address:0x6000

lo    Link encap:Local Loopback
          inet addr:127.0.0.1  Mask:255.0.0.0
          UP LOOPBACK RUNNING  MTU:3924  Metric:1
          RX packets:75545 errors:0 dropped:0 overruns:0
      ➡frame:0
          TX packets:75545 errors:0 dropped:0 overruns:0
          ➡ carrier:0
          collisions:0 txqueuelen:0
```

The example output shows two Ethernet cards, eth0 and eth1, plus the TCP/IP dummy loopback device, lo. Table 15.2 describes the fields included in the report.

TABLE 15.2   Fields in ifconfig Output

Field	Description
Link encap	The type of interface
Hwaddr	The hardware address (MAC) of the interface
inet addr	The IP address of the interface
Bcast	The broadcast address for the network
Mask	The netmask for the subnet
Status	The interface status (for example, UP BROADCAST RUNNING MULTICAST)
MTU	The maximum transfer unit size (bytes)
Metric	The interface metric, which is used by some routing protocols
RX packets	The number of packets received and the number of errors, dropped packets, overruns, and bad frames that have occurred

TABLE 15.2 Fields in `ifconfig` Output *(continued)*

Field	Description
TX packets	The number of packets transmitted and the number of errors, dropped packets, overruns, and dropped carriers that have occurred
collisions	The number of Ethernet collisions
txqueuelen	The transmit queue length
Interrupt	The IRQ of the interface
Base address	The I/O port address of the interface

If you want a report on the status of a particular network interface, issue a command of the form

    ifconfig *if*

where *if* is the name of the interface. For example, the command

    ifconfig eth0

reports the status of the eth0 interface.

Now, complete Exercise 15.2, which familiarizes you with the output of the `ifconfig` command.

EXERCISE 15.2

Viewing Network Status

The `ifconfig` command is one of the most basic and important networking commands. To learn more about it, use the `ifconfig` command to view the status of a working Linux server. Be sure you can explain the meaning of each output field. When doing this exercise, refer back to Table 15.2 as necessary, but be thoroughly familiar with the output format before taking the RHCE exam.

Adding and Dropping Network Interfaces

To add an interface, specify a command of the form

    ifconfig *device* *ipaddr*

where *device* is the name of the device and *ipaddr* is the IP address of the interface. For example, the command

    ifconfig eth0 192.168.1.1

establishes an Ethernet interface with IP address 192.168.1.1. You can specify several additional options. For instance, the command

    ifconfig eth0 192.168.1.1 netmask 255.255.255.0 broadcast
    ➥ 192.168.1.255

establishes an Ethernet interface with IP address 192.168.1.1, network subnet mask 255.255.255.0, and network broadcast address 192.168.1.255. See the ifconfig man page for additional options.

To drop an interface, specify a command of the form

    ifconfig *device* down

where *device* is the name of the device. For example, the command

    ifconfig eth0 down

drops the eth0 interface.

WARNING   When you reconfigure an interface by using ifconfig, your changes are lost when the system is rebooted, because the system initialization scripts issue the ifconfig command with parameter values specified in the network configuration files. You should understand the ifconfig command so that you understand the operation of these scripts. You'll issue the ifconfig command primarily for troubleshooting network problems and making other temporary network reconfigurations. To change the network configuration permanently, you should use a configuration utility or edit the network configuration files.

The *netstat* Command

The `netstat` command reports a variety of network-related information. For example, the command

```
netstat -r -n
```

reports the kernel's routing table. The output of the `netstat` command resembles the following:

```
Kernel IP routing table
Destination     Gateway Genmask           Flags MSS Window irtt
Iface
192.168.1.3     *       255.255.255.255 UH      0 0        0 eth1
192.168.100.3 *         255.255.255.255 UH      0 0        0 eth0
192.168.100.0 *         255.255.255.0   U       0 0        0 eth0
192.168.1.0     *       255.255.255.0   U       0 0        0 eth1
127.0.0.0       *       255.0.0.0       U       0 0        0 lo
default     192.168.1.1 0.0.0.0         UG      0 0        0 eth1
```

The output shows several destinations accessible via network interfaces. In the example, the first two lines describe interfaces installed in the system. The following two lines describe networks available via these interfaces; the Genmask column gives the network mask associated with each network. The next-to-last line describes the loopback network, which is associated with the dummy loopback device. The last line shows the default route, which is used for network addresses that do not match a defined destination address. Table 15.3 describes the flags that appear in the fourth column of the output.

TABLE 15.3 Flags Reported by `netstat`

Flag	Description
G	The route establishes a gateway.
U	The associated interface is up.
H	The route specifies a route to a single host, not a network.
D	The entry was created in response to an ICMP message.
M	The entry was modified in response to an ICMP message.

Another useful form of the `netstat` command reports connections to hosts outside a masqueraded network. To view this report, issue the command

```
netstat -M
```

The output resembles the following:

```
IP masquerading entries
prot   expire source                         destination    ports
tcp  14:53.71 bigtop.azusapacific.com home.apu.edu   1047
➥-> ssh (63685)
```

The output shows the protocol (TCP), the expiration time of the masqueraded connection (14:53.71), the local host (`bigtop.azusapacific.com`), destination (`home.apu.edu`), port (1047), and service (`ssh`).

Now, complete Exercise 15.3 to gain some experience in using the `netstat` command.

EXERCISE 15.3

Viewing Network Status

The `netstat` command conveniently provides useful information about network status. To gain experience using the `netstat` command, use the `netstat -n -r` command to view the network status of a working Linux server. Explain each field of the output, referring to this chapter and other documentation as needed. However, before taking the RHCE exam, be sure you can interpret the output of the `netstat` command without recourse to help.

The *arp* Command

The `arp` command lets you view or modify the kernel's *Address Resolution Protocol (ARP)* table, which maps IP addresses to hardware addresses (*MAC addresses*) of interfaces. The `arp` command is especially helpful in detecting and dealing with duplicate IP addresses. However, hosts appear in the ARP table only after they've been sent Ethernet packets.

To view the ARP table, issue the command

```
arp -a
```

Output of the command resembles the following:

```
bigtop.azusapacific.com (192.168.1.90) at
➥00:E0:98:77:08:40
   [ether] on eth1
```

The report indicates the host name, IP address, Ethernet address, and interface associated with systems on a locally accessible network.

To delete the ARP entry for a host, issue a command of the form

```
arp -d host
```

where *host* is the host name of the system you want to delete from the table. To specify an ARP entry for a host, issue a command of the form

```
arp -s host mac_addr
```

where *host* is the host name of the system you want to delete from the table and *mac_addr* is the hardware (MAC) address you want to associate with the host. For example, to specify an ARP entry for the host happy, with MAC address 00:E0:98:77:08:41, issue the command

```
arp -s happy 00:E0:98:77:08:41
```

Other */etc/sysconfig* Files

In addition to the network script and the network-scripts subdirectory, the /etc/sysconfig directory contains scripts that contain configurations for a variety of system facilities. Table 15.4 summarizes these.

TABLE 15.4 Files and Directories in /etc/sysconfig

File/ Directory	Description
apmd	Contains Advanced Power Management configuration
clock	Contains clock configuration, indicating whether the clock is set to Universal Coordinated Time (UTC)
console	Contains console configuration, including key maps (directory)

TABLE 15.4   Files and Directories in /etc/sysconfig *(continued)*

File/ Directory	Description
init	Contains system start-up configuration, including how service start-up status should be reported
keyboard	Contains keyboard configuration, including the identity of the default key map
mouse	Contains mouse configuration, including the type of mouse and whether three-button emulation is required
network	Contains network configuration, including the host name and gateway
network- scripts	Contains network configuration scripts (directory)
pcmcia	Contains PCMCIA configuration, including whether PCMCIA should be loaded on boot-up
sendmail	Contains sendmail configuration, including whether sendmail runs as a daemon
soundcard	Contains sound configuration, including the sound card type
static-routes	Contains static routes, including the associated device, network address, and gateway

The linuxconf program lets you configure most of these facilities. If you prefer, most of the files can be safely revised by using a text editor. However, the sound configuration is an exception. You should use the sndconfig utility to configure sound; you should not manually edit the /etc/sysconfig/soundcard file.

The following subsections provide additional information on Advanced Power Management, PCMCIA, plug-and-play devices, and sound.

Advanced Power Management (APM) Configuration

Advanced Power Management (APM) helps conserve electrical power. It is especially useful for battery-operated computers, such as laptops; however, many modern desktop computers support APM, which you can use to shut down peripherals that aren't being used. When APM is used with a laptop and it detects low battery conditions, it dims the display, slows the CPU clock, and turns off peripherals to save power. The file `/etc/sysconfig/apmd` contains the APM configuration, which is referenced by the script `/etc/rc.d/init.d/apmd`. See *The Battery-Powered Linux Mini-HOWTO* for more information on configuring and using APM.

PCMCIA Configuration

The PCMCIA service manages PCMCIA cards. The file `/etc/sysconfig/pcmcia` contains PCMCIA service configuration information, which is referenced by the script `/etc/rc.d/init.d/pcmcia`. Configuration information for PCMCIA devices resides in `/etc/pcmcia`. If you recompile the Linux kernel of a system that uses PCMCIA, you must also recompile and install the PCMCIA package. For more information on PCMCIA, see the Linux PCMCIA Web site, `pcmcia.sourceforge.org`.

Plug-and-Play Configuration

As described in Chapter 2, plug-and-play devices are designed to be automatically configured by cooperation between the BIOS and operating system. Linux, however, does not fully support plug-and-play for ISA interface cards.

When using Linux with a BIOS that supports plug-and-play, set the BIOS to indicate that the operating system does not support plug-and-play. You can then configure ISA plug-and-play cards by following this procedure:

1. Issue the command

   ```
   pnpdump >/etc/isapnp.conf
   ```

   This command dumps the configuration of each installed plug-and-play card in the specified file, `/etc/isapnp.conf`.

2. Using a text editor, revise the `/etc/isapnp.conf` file. The file contains commented lines for each possible configuration of each plug-and-play device. You must uncomment the desired configuration for each device. You must also uncomment the line at the end of the device configuration, which specifies that the device is active.

3. Issue the command

```
isapnp /etc/isapnp.conf
```

This command configures installed plug-and-play cards according to the configuration given in /etc/isapnp.conf. The Linux boot sequence issues this command to configure plug-and-play devices during system start-up.

For more information on Linux support for plug-and-play, see www.roe-stock.demon.co.uk/isapnptools.

Sound Configuration

The sndconfig command detects and configures most plug-and-play sound cards. The command places sound configuration information in /etc/conf.modules and /etc/isapnp.conf, as well as /etc/sysconfig/soundcard.

If you're using the GNOME desktop manager under X, the GNOME sound manager, esd, will manage your sound card and allow multiple applications to access it simultaneously. However, if you execute an application that is not aware of esd, it may conflict with other applications. To avoid this, invoke the application by using the esddsp wrapper. Start the application by issuing the command

```
esddsp application
```

where *application* is the name or path of the application. The KDE application kaudioserver performs a function similar to that of esd.

The *etc/fstab* File

The /etc/fstab file describes the file systems associated with a Linux system. Here are the contents of a typical /etc/fstab file:

```
/dev/hda1     /dos          msdos     defaults   0 2
/dev/hda5     /boot         ext2      defaults   1 2
/dev/hda6     /usr          ext2      defaults   1 2
/dev/hda7     /home         ext2      defaults   1 2
/dev/hda8     /var          ext2      defaults   1 2
/dev/hda9     /             ext2      defaults   1 1
/dev/hda10    swap          swap      defaults   0 0
/dev/hda11    /space        ext2      defaults   1 2
/dev/fd0      /mnt/floppy   ext2      noauto     0 0
```

```
/dev/cdrom   /cdrom1      iso9660   noauto,ro   0 0
/dev/hdd     /cdrom2      iso9660   noauto,ro   0 0
none         /proc        proc      defaults    0 0
none         /dev/pts     devpts    mode=0622   0 0
```

Each line in the file describes a file system. The fields are as follows:

- The device file.

- The mount point.

- The file system type. Table 15.5 summarizes the file system types supported by Linux.

- The mount options. Table 15.6 summarizes the available options.

- The dump flag. The value 1 indicates a file system that should be automatically included in a system dump; the value 0 indicates a file system that should not be included.

- The file system check sequence. The value 1 indicates the root file system; the value 2 indicates a non-root file system that should be automatically checked; the value 0 indicates a file system that should not be automatically checked.

TABLE 15.5 Linux File System Types

File System Type	Description
adfs	Acorn RiscOS file system
affs	AmigaOS file system
coda	Coda, an advanced network file system similar to NFS
devpts	A virtual file system for pseudo terminals
ext2	The standard Linux file system
hfs	Apple Macintosh file system
hpfs	IBM OS/2 file system
iso9660	The standard CD-ROM file system
minix	Tannenbaum's MINIX file system

TABLE 15.5 Linux File System Types *(continued)*

File System Type	Description
msdos	Uncompressed MS-DOS file systems
ncpfs	Novell NetWare file system
nfs	Unix network file system
ntfs	Microsoft Windows NT file system
proc	The /proc virtual file system
qnx4fs	QNX file system
romfs	Read-only file system for RAM disks
smbfs	Microsoft SMB (LAN Manager) file system
sysv	SCO, Xenix, and Coherent file system
ufs	BSD, SunOS, FreeBSD, NetBSD, OpenBSD, and NeXTstep file system
umsdos	Linux file system running on top of MS-DOS file system
vfat	Microsoft Windows 9x file system

TABLE 15.6 Mount Options

Option	Description
async	Perform all input and output asynchronously.
atime	Update inode access times on the file system.
auto	Automatically mount the file system in response to mount -a.
defaults	Enable the options rw, suid, dev, exec, auto, nouser, and async.

TABLE 15.6 Mount Options *(continued)*

Option	Description
dev	Interpret character or block special devices on the file system.
exec	Permit execution of binary files on the file system.
noatime	Do not update inode access times on the file system.
noauto	Do not automatically mount the file system in response to mount -a.
nodev	Do not interpret character or block special devices on the file system.
noexec	Do not permit execution of binary files on the file system.
nosuid	setuid and setgid permissions of files in the file system are not effective.
nouser	An ordinary user may not mount the file system (default).
remount	Remount a mounted file system to enable a different set of options. Often used to remount a read-only file system in read-write mode.
ro	Mount the file system in read-only mode.
rw	Mount the file system in read-write mode.
suid	setuid and setgid permissions of files in the file system are effective.

TABLE 15.6 Mount Options *(continued)*

Option	Description
sync	Perform all input and output synchronously.
user	Permit an ordinary user to mount the file system. Implies the options noexec, nosuid, and nodev.

You can modify the contents of the /etc/fstab file by using linuxconf, or, if you prefer, you can use a text editor. Now try your hand at configuring file systems by completing Exercise 15.4.

EXERCISE 15.4

Configuring File Systems

Configuring file systems is an important and common system administration task that is likely to appear on the RHCE exam. To hone your skills in preparation for the exam, modify the /etc/fstab file to specify that a non-root partition will be mounted in read-only mode. Boot the system and verify that your change was correct. Restore the original configuration and reboot the system.

If necessary, you can refer to this book while doing the exercise. But before taking the RHCE exam, be prepared to perform operations such as this without the assistance of books or documentation.

The *init* Process and the */etc/inittab* File

The init process is responsible for spawning log-in processes and managing the system *runlevel*. Its configuration file, /etc/inittab, determines the services that should be active at each defined runlevel.

Managing Runlevels

You can determine the current runlevel by issuing the command

```
runlevel
```

Its output consists of the previous runlevel, followed by the current runlevel. For example, the output

```
5 3
```

indicates that the previous runlevel was 5 and the current runlevel is 3.

To change the runlevel, issue the command

```
init n
```

where *n* is the desired runlevel. The command form

```
telinit n
```

has the same effect. The distinguishing feature of `telinit` is its ability to specify that the change of runlevel should occur after a specified interval. For example, the command

```
telinit -t 60 3
```

specifies that the runlevel should be set to 3 after a delay of 60 seconds.

You can switch to runlevel 6, which causes the system to reboot, through any of the following ways:

- Issue the command `telinit 6` or `init 6`
- Issue the command `shutdown -r now`
- Issue the command `reboot`
- Press Ctrl+Alt+Del

The `shutdown` command provides several useful options. In place of `now`, you can include an argument of the form +*min*, where *min* specifies the number of minutes until the reboot takes place. You can also include an argument of the form `-t` *sec*; this option causes the command to warn users of the impending shutdown *sec* seconds before it takes place.

You can switch to runlevel 0, which causes the system to halt, through any of the following ways:

- Issue the command `telinit 0` or `init 0`
- Issue the command `shutdown -h now`
- Issue the command `halt`

The options *+min* and -t *sec* can be used with the -h argument of the shutdown command.

The */etc/inittab* File

The /etc/inittab file determines the processes that should be active at each runlevel. Lines in the file have the form

id:runlevels:action:process

The fields are as follows:

- id, a 1-4 character unique identification. For login processes, id should be the tty suffix of the corresponding tty.

- runlevels, a list of runlevels for which the action should be taken. If omitted, the action is taken for each runlevel.

- action, which specifies the action to be taken. Table 15.7 summarizes the available actions.

- process, which specifies the program to be executed.

Lines beginning with a hash mark (#) are ignored.

TABLE 15.7 Actions Specifiable in /etc/inittab

Action	Description
boot	The specified process is executed during system boot. The runlevels field is ignored.
bootwait	The process is executed during system boot; init waits for its termination. The runlevels field is ignored.
ctrlaltdel	The process is executed when init receives the SIGINT signal, meaning that someone on the system console has pressed the Ctrl+Alt+Del key combination.
initdefault	Specifies the initial runlevel, which is entered after system boot. The process field is ignored.
kbrequest	The process is executed when init receives a signal from the keyboard handler that a special key combination was pressed on the console keyboard.
off	No action taken.

TABLE 15.7 Actions Specifiable in /etc/inittab *(continued)*

Action	Description
once	The process is executed once when the specified runlevel is entered.
ondemand	The process is executed whenever the specified runlevel (a, b, or c) is called. However, no runlevel change will occur.
powerfail	The process is executed when the power goes down. The init process will not wait for the process to finish.
powerfail now	This process is executed when init is told that the battery of the external Uninterrupted Power Supply (UPS) is almost exhausted.
powerokwait	This process is executed when init is informed that the power has been restored.
powerwait	The process is executed when the power goes down. The init process will wait for the process to finish.
respawn	The process is restarted whenever it terminates.
sysinit	The process is executed during system boot, before any boot or bootwait entries. The runlevels field is ignored.
wait	The process is executed once when the specified runlevel is entered; init will wait for its termination.

Here are the contents of a typical /etc/inittab file:

```
id:3:initdefault:

si::sysinit:/etc/rc.d/rc.sysinit

l0:0:wait:/etc/rc.d/rc 0
l1:1:wait:/etc/rc.d/rc 1
l2:2:wait:/etc/rc.d/rc 2
l3:3:wait:/etc/rc.d/rc 3
l4:4:wait:/etc/rc.d/rc 4
l5:5:wait:/etc/rc.d/rc 5
l6:6:wait:/etc/rc.d/rc 6
```

```
ud::once:/sbin/update

ca::ctrlaltdel:/sbin/shutdown -t3 -r now

pf::powerfail:/sbin/shutdown -f -h +2 "Power Failure;
➥System Shutting Down"

pr:12345:powerokwait:/sbin/shutdown -c "Power Restored;
➥Shutdown Cancelled"

1:2345:respawn:/sbin/mingetty tty1
2:2345:respawn:/sbin/mingetty tty2
3:2345:respawn:/sbin/mingetty tty3
4:2345:respawn:/sbin/mingetty tty4
5:2345:respawn:/sbin/mingetty tty5
6:2345:respawn:/sbin/mingetty tty6

x:5:respawn:/etc/X11/prefdm -nodaemon
```

If you change the contents of /etc/inittab, you must instruct the init
process to reread the file. To do so, issue the command

```
init q
```

Summary

In this chapter, you learned about configuration files and scripts. The
most important topics covered are:

The /etc/sysconfig Directory   The /etc/sysconfig directory contains a variety of files that hold configuration information, including configuration information for Advanced Power Management (APM),
PCMCIA cards, plug-and-play cards, and sound. The network-scripts
subdirectory contains scripts used to start up, shut down, and configure
networking.

The ifcfg-* Scripts   The ifcfg-* scripts store network interface configuration information.

The **/etc/sysconfig/network** Script   The /etc/sysconfig/
network script stores global network configuration information—that is,
configuration information that applies to each network interface.

Network Administration Commands   Among the most important network administration commands are ifconfig, which lets you configure
a network interface; netstat, which lets you view network status information; and arp, which lets you view and modify the system Address Resolution Protocol (ARP) table.

The **/etc/fstab** File   The /etc/fstab file contains file system configuration options.

The **/etc/inittab** File   The /etc/inittab file contains configuration
options for init, the daemon responsible for login processes and runlevel
management.

Key Terms

Before going on to the next chapter, be sure you're familiar with the following terms:

Address Resolution Protocol (ARP)

Advanced Power Management (APM)

MAC addresses

runlevel

Additional Sources of Information

If you'd like further information about the topics presented in this chapter,
you should consult the following sources:

- *The Official Red Hat Linux Reference Guide*

- *The Battery-Powered Linux Mini-HOWTO*

- The Linux PCMCIA Web page, pcmcia.sourceforge.org

- The Linux ISA plug-and-play Web page, www.roestock
  .demon.co.uk/isapnptools

- The initialization scripts documentation files, /usr/doc/
  initscripts*/*

Review Questions

1. To add Ethernet device `eth1` with IP address 192.168.1.1, which of the following commands should be issued?

A. `ifconfig -ip 192.168.1.1 eth1`

B. `ifconfig 192.168.1.1 eth1`

C. `ifconfig eth1 192.168.1.1`

D. `ifconfig eth1 -ip 192.168.1.1`

2. To bring down the device `eth1`, which of the following commands should be issued?

A. `ifconfig eth1 down`

B. `ifconfig ifcfg-eth1 down`

C. `/sbin/ifdown eth1`

D. `/sbin/ifdown ifcfg-eth1`

3. To view the kernel's routing table, which of the following commands should be issued?

A. `netstat -i`

B. `netstat -m`

C. `netstat -M`

D. `netstat -r`

4. Which of the following commands brings up the device `eth2`?

A. `ifup eth2`

B. `ifup ifcfg-eth2`

C. `ifup /etc/sysconfig/eth2`

D. `ifup /etc/sysconfig/network-scripts/eth2`

5. Which of the following commands properly mounts a Windows 95 file system?

   A. `mount -t fat32 /dev/hda1 /dos -o ro`

   B. `mount -t msdos /dev/hda1 /dos -o ro`

   C. `mount -t vfat /dev/hda1 /dos -o ro`

   D. `mount -t win95 /dev/hda1 /dos -o ro`

6. Which of the following commands will reboot the system?

   A. `init 6`

   B. `reboot`

   C. `shutdown -r now`

   D. `telinit 6`

Answers to Review Questions

1. C. To add the device, specify the device name and the IP address.

2. A, C, D. You can bring down the device by using /sbin/ifdown or ifconfig; however, ifconfig does not accept the script name ifcfg-eth1 as an argument.

3. D. The -r flag causes the netstat command to report the routing table.

4. A, B. The command requires a device name; you must not specify a path.

5. C. The Windows 95 file system has type vfat. It's possible to mount a Windows 95 file system as an msdos file system, but doing so may disrupt the long filenames of files that you manipulate.

6. A, B, C, D. Any of the alternatives will work; in addition, pressing Ctrl+Alt+Del will reboot the system.

Using the *cron* System

RHCE PREPARATION TOPICS COVERED IN THIS CHAPTER:

✓ Understand the cron system and be capable of scheduling jobs using cron and anacron.

The *cron* system lets the system administrator and ordinary users schedule jobs for automatic execution at specified intervals and times. By default, a Red Hat Linux system runs several cron jobs that facilitate system administration. As a Red Hat Linux system administrator, you need to know how to manage the cron system. You also need to understand the jobs that cron is automatically configured to run on your behalf. This chapter describes the cron system and the default jobs it runs.

The *cron* System

The cron system lets users schedule jobs for automatic execution at specified times and intervals. The jobs run using the owning user's login; by default, the results of jobs are sent to the owning user via e-mail. A utility program lets a user run a text editor to specify what jobs to run and when to run them.

The cron system consists of the following components:

- /usr/sbin/crond, the cron service, which runs continuously
- /etc/crontab, the system cron table, which specifies default jobs defined by Red Hat
- /usr/bin/crontab, the program that lets users create and manage cron table entries
- /var/spool/cron, the directory that holds cron files created by users

- /etc/cron.d, the directory that holds cron files created by package installation scripts

- /etc/cron.allow and /etc/cron.deny, files that let you restrict access to the cron system

The next section explains user cron tables and how to use them. The following section explains the system cron table; remaining sections of the chapter explain the default jobs included in the system cron table.

User *crontab*s

When a user accesses the cron system, the system creates the file /var/spool/cron/*user*, where *user* is the login name of the user. This file—called the *cron* file, *cron* table, or *crontab*–contains entries that specify what jobs to run and when to run them.

By default, ordinary users are allowed to access the cron system. However, the system administrator can restrict this privilege. If the file /etc/cron.allow exists, only users listed in the file can access the cron system. Similarly, if the file /etc/cron.deny exists, no user listed in the file can access the cron system.

A user who is allowed to access the cron system can perform these operations:

- Revise the entries in the crontab.

- List the existing cron jobs.

- Delete the crontab.

The following subsections explain these operations.

Editing the User *crontab*

A user can edit the user's crontab entries by issuing the command

    crontab -e

Similarly, the root user can edit a user's crontab entries by issuing a command of the form

    crontab -u *user* -e

where *user* is the login name of the user whose crontab is to be edited.

In response to the `crontab -e` command, the `cron` system will launch the default system editor. If you prefer to use a different editor, you can set the environment variable EDITOR before issuing the `crontab` command. For example,

```
export EDITOR=/usr/bin/pico
crontab -e
```

lets the user edit the `crontab` by using the `pico` editor.

A user can remove the user's `crontab` entirely, by issuing the command

```
crontab -r
```

The `root` user can remove a user's `crontab` by issuing a command of the form

```
crontab -u user -r
```

where *user* is the login name of the user whose `crontab` is to be removed.

The `crontab` entries are specified as specially formatted lines; the next subsection explains the format in which they must appear.

Format of the *crontab* File

The *crontab* file may contain these sorts of lines:

- Comment lines
- Environment settings
- `cron` commands

Within a line, leading spaces and tabs are ignored. Blank lines and lines beginning with a hash mark (#) are considered comment lines and are ignored by the `cron` system.

Specifying Environment Settings

Environment setting lines have the form

```
name = value
```

Such lines specify environment variable names and associated values. A `cron` job can access these environment variables. The following environment variables are available without explicit definition:

- SHELL is bound to /bin/sh
- LOGNAME is bound to the user's login name

- HOME is bound to the user's home directory, as specified in /etc/passwd

You can specify new values for the SHELL or HOME environment variables. However, you cannot specify a new value for the LOGNAME environment variable.

By default, the output of a `cron` job is sent via e-mail to the owning user. However, you can override this action by specifying a value for the MAILTO environment variable. By defining the variable this way:

```
MAILTO=""
```

no output will be sent. If you bind the MAILTO environment variable to an e-mail address, the output will be sent to the specified address. For example, if you specify

```
MAILTO="admin@bigtop.azusapacific.com"
```

the output of `cron` jobs will be mailed to admin@bigtop.azusapacific.com.

Specifying *cron* Commands

The command lines in the `crontab` have the following form:

```
minute hour day_of_month month day_of_week command
```

The lines contain six fields, each separated by one or more spaces from adjacent fields. Table 16.1 describes the first five fields, which specify the interval or time of execution of the specified command.

The `cron` system checks its `crontab` files every minute and executes entries with time specifications that match the current date and time. A field that contains an asterisk (*) matches any value. Note that additional options will be covered later in this chapter.

TABLE 16.1 Date Fields in the crontab File

Field	Description
minute	A value from 0 to 59, or *
hour	A value from 0 to 23, or *
day_of_month	A value from 1 to 31, or *
month	A value from 1 to 12, where 1 denotes January, or *
day_of_week	A value from 0 to 7, where either 0 or 7 denotes Sunday, or *

A `crontab` entry is considered to match the current time when the minute and hour fields match the current time and the month field matches the current month. An entry is considered to match the current date when the day of month field matches the current day of the month or the day of week field matches the current day of the week: it is not necessary that both the day of the month and day of the week match. If both the time and date match the current time and date, the specified command is executed. Table 16.2 describes some example `crontab` entries.

TABLE 16.2 Example Time Specifications in the `crontab` File

Time Specification	Meaning
5 12 * * *	Run at 5 minutes after noon, every day.
5 * * * *	Run at 5 minutes after each hour.
15 17 1 * *	Run at 5:15 P.M. on the first of each month.
45 16 * * 5	Run at 4:45 P.M. on each Friday.
00 15 * 12 5	Run at 3:00 P.M. on each Friday in December.

You can also specify ranges and lists of numbers. For example, 8–10 in the hour field would match 8:00, 9:00, and 10:00 A.M. Similarly, 8–10,13 in the hour field would match 8:00, 9:00, and 10:00 A.M. and 1:00 P.M.

You can specify step values, which are used with ranges. For example, 0–10/2 in the hour field refers to midnight, 2:00, 4:00, 6:00, 8:00 and 10:00 A.M. The specification */2 means that the specified command should be executed every two hours.

If you prefer, you can use names in the month and day of week fields. To do so, use the first three letters of the month or day, in either uppercase or lowercase. For example,

```
0 19 * dec fri
```

specifies execution at 7:00 P.M. on each Friday in December. You cannot use ranges or lists of month or day names; if you want to specify a range or list, you must use numbers.

The final field of each `crontab` line specifies the command. If you include a percent sign (%) in the command, only the portion of the field before the percent sign is executed. Any remaining characters in the command are sent as standard input to the command; subsequent percent signs in the command are replaced by newline characters. To embed a percent sign in a command, precede it with a backslash (\), which allows it to escape the special meaning of the percent sign.

For example, the following command, taken from the man page for `crontab`, sends mail to a user:

```
mail -s "It's 10pm" joe%Joe,%%Where are your kids?%
```

The percent signs are sent as newlines, which serve as responses to the prompts of the `mail` command.

To learn more about working with `cron`, complete Exercise 16.1.

EXERCISE 16.1

Editing Your *cron* Table

Here's a simple exercise that will give you practice in defining a cron job. Log in as an ordinary user and use the `crontab` command to create a cron job that runs the w command every night at 12:05 A.M. Check the next morning to verify that the output is in your e-mail inbox.

You can look back to the material in this chapter to help you complete the exercise. But, before taking the RHCE exam, be sure you can perform operations such as this without the help of books or notes.

Listing the User *crontab*

A user can list the contents of the user's `crontab` by issuing the command

```
crontab -l
```

The output is listed in the format of the `crontab`, which is explained in the preceding subsection. For example, here's typical output you might see:

```
crontab -l
# DO NOT EDIT THIS FILE - edit the master and reinstall.
```

```
# (/tmp/crontab.4014 installed on Tue Apr 18 09:40:56 2000)
# (Cron version -- $Id: crontab.c,v 2.13 1994/01/17 03:20:37
#    vixie Exp $)
5 0 * * * w
```

The output gives the creation date of the crontab, which resides in /var/spool/cron; the file /tmp/crontab.4014 mentioned in the sample output is merely a temporary copy of the crontab. Note that the output includes a caution against directly editing the crontab; to edit the crontab, you must follow the procedure given in the preceding subsection.

The root user can list the contents of a user's crontab by issuing a command of the form

```
crontab -u user -l
```

where *user* is the login name of the user whose crontab is to be listed.

Now, complete Exercise 16.2, which tests your ability to list a cron table.

EXERCISE 16.2

Listing Your *cron* Table

Working with cron is fairly straightforward, but practice will help you determine the extent of your skill. To gauge your understanding of cron, log in as an ordinary user and use the crontab command to view your cron table. Unless you've previously established one, you should see a message indicating that no cron entries exist.

You can look back to the material in this chapter to help you complete the exercise. But, before taking the RHCE exam, be sure you can list your cron table without the help of books or notes.

The System *crontab*

In addition to the user crontab files stored in /var/spool/cron, the cron system has a system cron file, stored in /etc/crontab. Here are the contents of a typical /etc/crontab file:

```
SHELL=/bin/bash
PATH=/sbin:/bin:/usr/sbin:/usr/bin
MAILTO=root
HOME=/
```

```
# run-parts
01 * * * * root run-parts /etc/cron.hourly
02 4 * * * root run-parts /etc/cron.daily
22 4 * * 0 root run-parts /etc/cron.weekly
42 4 1 * * root run-parts /etc/cron.monthly
```

The format of the /etc/crontab file differs slightly from that of the user crontab files. It includes a user id field, which specifies the user id under which the associated command is run. The user id field is the sixth field of each line, placed just before the command field.

The default Red Hat Linux /etc/crontab file contains four command lines, each of which specifies the run-parts script as the command to be run. The run-parts script takes a single argument, which is a directory. The script executes the files contained in the specified directory. The /etc/crontab file uses run-parts to execute hourly, daily, weekly, and monthly jobs. Thus, it's not necessary to edit the /etc/crontab file; you merely place the script you want to execute—or a symbolic link to the script—in one of the /etc/cron.* directories. As root, however, you can edit the file by using a text editor; you don't need to use the crontab command.

If you change the /etc/crontab file, the cron system will detect the changed modification date of the file. You do not need to restart or signal the cron daemon.

Red Hat Linux also has a set of system crontab files stored in /etc/cron.d; these files are created by package installation scripts. They have the same format as /etc/crontab. The modutils package, for example, installs the file /etc/crond.d/kmod. Here are the contents of a typical /etc/cron.d/kmod file:

```
# rmmod -a is a two-hand sweep module cleaner
*/10 * * * *    root    /sbin/rmmod -as
```

This file runs the rmmod command every 10 minutes, unloading unused modules.

The next several sections describe the standard hourly, daily, weekly, and monthly jobs executed by the Red Hat Linux cron system.

Hourly *cron* Jobs

The `/etc/crontab` file designates the `/etc/cron.hourly` directory as the location for scripts that will be executed hourly. By default, that directory is empty. However, you can add your own hourly scripts to the directory.

Daily *cron* Jobs

By default, Red Hat Linux runs the following daily `cron` jobs:

- `logrotate`
- `makewhatis`
- `locate`
- `tmpwatch`

A detailed understanding of these jobs is not required for the RHCE exam. The following subsections briefly describe them.

The *logrotate* Job

The daily `logrotate` job is a simple script that invokes the `logrotate` command:

```
#!/bin/sh
/usr/sbin/logrotate /etc/logrotate.conf
```

The `logrotate` command allows automatic rotation, compression, removal, and mailing of log files. You can consult its man page for details, in particular the format of its configuration file.

The *makewhatis* Job

The `whatis` command provides access to a database of key words found in the man pages. For example, if you issue the command

```
whatis rm
```

the command responds with

```
rm (1)                  - remove files or directories
```

The same database supports the `apropos` command, which lists man pages related to a specified topic. For example, if you issue the command

```
apropos cron
```

the command responds with

```
cron(8)    - daemon to execute scheduled commands
crontab(1) - maintain crontab files for individual users
crontab(5) - tables for driving cron
```

You can also invoke the apropos command by using the command form

```
man -k topic
```

where *topic* specifies the subject in which you're interested.

In order to maintain the database used by whatis and apropos, the makewhatis command must be run periodically. In order to do so, the default Red Hat Linux cron system runs the /etc/cron.daily/ makewhatis.cron script daily:

```
#!/bin/bash
LOCKFILE=/var/lock/makewhatis.lock

# the lockfile is not meant to be perfect, it's just in case
# the two makewhatis cron scripts get run close to each
# other to keep them from stepping on each other's toes.
# The worst that will happen is that they will temporarily
# corrupt the database...
[ -f $LOCKFILE ] && exit 0
touch $LOCKFILE
makewhatis -u -w
rm -f $LOCKFILE
exit 0
```

The -u option causes makewhatis to add information on new man pages to the database. You can consult the makewhatis man page for details.

The *locate* Program

The locate command makes it possible to find the directory in which a file resides, given the name of the file or a pattern that matches the name. For example, to find directories that contain files with names that include the characters *linux.words*, issue the command

```
locate linux.words
```

Output of the command resembles the following:

```
/usr/dict/linux.words
/usr/doc/words-2/README.linux.words
/usr/doc/words-2/README2.linux.words
```

Unlike the find command, which provides a similar capability, the locate command uses a database. The database speeds execution of the locate command relative to that of the find command. However, the database must be regularly updated in order to be useful and will not reflect files added since the most recent update.

The default Red Hat Linux cron system runs the script /etc/cron.daily/ slocate.cron daily:

```
#!/bin/sh
NETMOUNTS=`mount -t nfs,smbfs,ncpfs | cut -d ' ' -f 3`
NETPATHS=`echo $NETMOUNTS | sed -e 's| |,|g'`

if [ -n "$NETPATHS" ]; then
  /usr/bin/slocate -u -e
➥"$NETPATHS,/tmp,/var/tmp,/usr/tmp,/afs,/net,/proc"
else
  /usr/bin/slocate -u -e "/tmp,/var/tmp,/usr/tmp,/afs,/net,
    ➥/proc"
fi
```

The symbolic link /usr/bin/slocate refers to /usr/bin/updatedb, the utility program that rebuilds the database used by the locate command. You can consult the man pages of locate and updatedb for details; however, you do not need detailed knowledge of these commands in order to be prepared for the RHCE exam.

The *tmpwatch* Job

Another daily task shouldered by the cron system is the deletion of stale temporary files. The script /etc/cron.daily/tmpwatch, executed daily, invokes the following command:

```
/usr/sbin/tmpwatch 240 /tmp /var/tmp /var/catman/cat?
```

The tmpwatch command deletes files that have not been accessed in 10 days (240 hours) and that reside in the /tmp /var/tmp, and /var/catman/cat?

directories. You can consult the man pages of tmpwatch for details; however, you do not need detailed knowledge of these commands in order to be prepared for the RHCE exam.

Weekly *cron* Jobs

The Red Hat Linux cron system executes one weekly job by default, /etc/cron.weekly/makewhatis.cron. Here are the contents of a typical /etc/cron.weekly/makewhatis.cron file

```
#!/bin/bash
LOCKFILE=/var/lock/makewhatis.lock

# the lockfile is not meant to be perfect, it's just in case
# the two makewhatis cron scripts get run close to each
# other to keep them from stepping on each other's toes.
# The worst that will happen is that they will temporarily
# corrupt the database...
[ -f $LOCKFILE ] && exit 0
touch $LOCKFILE
makewhatis -w
rm -f $LOCKFILE
exit 0
```

This script resembles the similar daily script, that runs the makewhatis command with the -u option. The absence of the -u option causes the makewhatis command to update the database with respect to every man page, not merely those that are new. Thus, the weekly job is somewhat more time consuming than the daily job. You can consult the makewhatis man page for details; however, you do not need detailed knowledge of the makewhatis command in order to be prepared for the RHCE exam.

Monthly *cron* Jobs

The /etc/crontab file designates the /etc/cron.monthly directory as the location for scripts that will be executed monthly. By default, that directory is empty. However, you can add your own monthly scripts to the directory.

A Desktop Job Scheduler: *anacron*

The cron utility assumes that a system is continuously powered on. If you install cron on a desktop system that's powered on intermittently, you may find that cron jobs are seldom executed. For instance, a cron job scheduled to run at 2:00 A.M. will run only if the system is powered on at that time. However, when you power on a system that has *anacron* installed, anacron will execute any jobs skipped during the time the system was powered off.

The anacron utility is not as flexible as cron. It cannot schedule jobs at intervals smaller than one day nor guarantee the time at which a job is run. Moreover, it does not run continuously as a daemon; it must be executed in a startup script, initiated manually, or defined as a cron job.

To start anacron, issue the command

```
anacron -s
```

The –s flag, which specifies serial execution, causes anacron to start jobs one at a time. This avoids clogging the system with a backlog of jobs. When you install the anacron package, a System V init script named anacron is placed in the /etc/rc.d/init.d directory. You can use linuxconf or another configuration utility to configure anacron to start when the system boots.

The anacron utility's configuration file, /etc/anacrontab, is generally edited by hand. Its format is simpler than that of the crontab file, as shown by the following typical *anacrontab* file:

```
SHELL=/bin/sh
PATH=/usr/local/sbin:/usr/local/bin:/sbin:/bin:/
➥usr/sbin:/usr/bin

# These entries are useful for a Red Hat Linux system.
1     5      cron.daily     run-parts /etc/cron.daily
7     10     cron.weekly    run-parts /etc/cron.weekly
30    15     cron.monthly   run-parts /etc/cron.monthly
```

The file can contain lines that assign values to environment variables; the first two lines of the example set the value of the SHELL and PATH environment variables. The lines that specify anacron jobs have four fields:

- period, which specifies the execution interval in days
- delay, which specifies a delay in minutes before the job is started

- job identifier, a string that uniquely identifies the anacron job

- command, which specifies the command to be executed and any command arguments

For more information on anacron, see the man pages for anacron and anacrontab.

Summary

In this chapter, you learned about the cron system. The most important topics covered are:

The cron System   The cron system lets you schedule tasks for subsequent execution at specified times or intervals.

The System cron Table   The system cron table resides in /etc/crontab. It specifies the regular execution of scripts in the directories /etc/cron.hourly, /etc/cron.daily, /etc/cron.weekly, and /etc/cron.monthly.

User cron Tables   User cron tables reside in /var/spool/cron.

Package-Related cron Tables   Package-related cron tables reside in /etc/cron.d.

Restricting Access to cron   You can restrict access to cron by means of its configuration files, /etc/cron.allow and /etc/cron.deny.

Format of a cron Table Line   The fields with a cron table line are given in the following order: minute, hour, day of month, month, day of week.

Important Tasks Controlled by cron   Important tasks controlled by cron include logrotate, makewhatis, locate, and tmpwatch.

Key Terms

Before going on to the next chapter, be sure you're familiar with the following terms:

anacron

anacrontab file

cron

crontab file

Additional Sources of Information

If you'd like further information about the topics presented in this chapter, you should consult the man pages for crond, crontab(1), and crontab(5).

Review Questions

1. Which of the following time specifications defines a cron job that executes at 4:15 P.M. every Sunday?

   A. 15 16 * * 0

   B. 15 16 * * 7

   C. 15 16 * * sun

   D. 15 16 * * SUN

2. Which of the following time specifications defines a cron job that executes at 8:00 P.M. on the 1st and 15th of the month, and every Friday?

   A. 0 20 *   * *

   B. 0 20 *   * 5

   C. 0 20 1,15 * *

   D. 0 20 1,15 * 5

3. Which of the following environment variables can be set in a crontab file?

   A. EDITOR

   B. HOME

   C. LOGNAME

   D. SHELL

4. To embed a newline character in a cron command, which of the following must be specified?

   A. A caret (^)

   B. A hash mark (#)

   C. A newline escape sequence (\n)

   D. A percent sign (%)

5. If a package requires cron services, where does its crontab reside?

   A. /etc/cron.d

   B. /etc/cron.hourly or the daily, weekly, or monthly cron directory

   C. /etc/crontab

   D. /var/spool/cron

6. To specify a new system crontab entry, what do you do?

   A. You edit the /etc/crontab file

   B. You issue the command crontab -e

   C. You issue the command crontab -e as root

   D. You place a script or symbolic link in an /etc/cron.* directory

Answers to Review Questions

1. A, B, C, D. The day the of week can be specified as a number or name, which can be uppercase or lowercase. The values 0 and 7 both denote Sunday.

2. D. A command executes when either the day of the month or day of week matches.

3. A, B, D. HOME, LOGNAME, and SHELL have default values. The value of LOGNAME cannot be changed. You are free to define additional environment variables, such as EDITOR.

4. D. A percent sign in a cron command is replaced by a new line.

5. A. Packages install personal crontab files in /etc/cron.d.

6. A, D. The system administrator does not use crontab to revise the system crontab file.

Chapter

17

Understanding the Kernel

RHCE PREPARATION TOPICS COVERED IN THIS CHAPTER:

- ✓ Understand essential kernel concepts, such as monolithic versus modular kernels.

- ✓ Be able to install kernel sources and development tools needed to rebuild the Linux kernel.

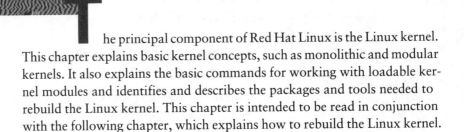

he principal component of Red Hat Linux is the Linux kernel. This chapter explains basic kernel concepts, such as monolithic and modular kernels. It also explains the basic commands for working with loadable kernel modules and identifies and describes the packages and tools needed to rebuild the Linux kernel. This chapter is intended to be read in conjunction with the following chapter, which explains how to rebuild the Linux kernel.

Kernel Basics

The Linux operating system takes its name from its kernel, the Linux kernel. The kernel is the most basic component of an operating system. Much of a typical kernel is resident in memory at all times, whereas other operating system components are loaded when needed and then discarded. The kernel manages system resources such as the processor, memory, and devices and provides services used by other components of the operating system.

Unlike the kernels of most commercial operating systems, the Linux kernel is distributed in source form. This lets system administrators compile custom kernels that closely match the unique requirements of host systems. Being able to build a custom kernel offers the promise of improved system efficiency and performance, but the system administrator must understand the Linux kernel if these advantages are to be realized.

This section explains fundamental kernel concepts, including:

- Kernel versions and version numbers

- Kernel types (monolithic and modular)

- Kernel-related files

- The kernel source tree and its structure

- How to obtain and install a non–Red Hat kernel from the Linux Kernel Archives

The following section explains Linux kernel modules.

Kernel Versions

Releases of the Linux kernel are designated by three numbers—for example, Linux 2.4.3. These numbers are called:

- The major version (2)

- The minor version (4)

- The patch level (3)

New *major versions* are released every several years and provide significant improvements in kernel capability and performance. However, because the kernel architecture may change with the release of a new major version, non-kernel software designed to work with a previous major release may need to be reconfigured or even modified.

Minor versions are released more frequently than major versions. Software doesn't generally need to be reconfigured or modified to work with a new minor version of the kernel.

At any time, two releases of Linux are undergoing development. The release with an even minor number is called the *stable release*—for example, Linux 2.4.3. Development of the stable kernel focuses more on fixing defects than on adding new features. The release with an odd minor number is called the *developmental release*—for example, Linux 2.5.10. Development of this release focuses on new—and sometimes experimental—features. Therefore, as the release names suggest, the developmental release tends to be less stable than the stable release. System administrators generally do not install a developmental release except on computers that provide non-critical functions.

The third number making up the kernel version number is the *patch level*. Patch releases occur even more frequently than minor releases, particularly patch releases of the developmental release. Sometimes several patches are released in a single week.

Linux kernels are released via the Linux Kernel Archive Web site, `www.kernel.org`. Red Hat, Inc. downloads released kernels and repackages them as RPMs for easy distribution and installation. Red Hat, Inc. also specially configures the kernel and applies patches that modify and extend functionality.

In addition to the major-minor-patch versioning of Linux kernels, Red Hat, Inc. encourages use of what they call the *extraversion code*, which distinguishes differently configured versions of the same kernel release. As explained in the next chapter, you can specify an extraversion code when you build a Red Hat Linux kernel. The extraversion code takes the form of a sequential number and a short descriptive name. For example, build #20 of a Linux 2.4.6 kernel supporting SMP might be named `2.4.6-20smp`. Using the extraversion code facilitates having several Linux kernels on a single system. When you build a new kernel you can keep a copy of the old kernel on the system. That way, if the new kernel fails to operate properly, you can simply reboot the system by using the old kernel, rather than perform some more elaborate recovery operation.

Many Red Hat Linux users and system administrators never compile a Linux kernel. Instead, they download and install kernel updates in package form. However, you may want to build a custom kernel for reasons such as these:

- You want to configure an especially secure system and therefore want to disable unneeded capabilities that might present security risks. For example, you plan to use a Linux system as a router and therefore don't need or want some of the capabilities included in the standard Red Hat Linux kernel.

- You want to enable capabilities not available in the standard Red Hat Linux kernel, such as advanced routing options.

- You want to alter operating parameters not configurable during operation. For example, you want to use more than 1GB of RAM and therefore need to reconfigure the balance between user-space and kernel-space memory.

- You're curious to learn more about the Linux kernel. Building a custom kernel is a good way to do so.

Kernel Types

Originally, the Linux kernel was a *monolithic* kernel, a kernel that resides in a single file. You can still build a monolithic kernel if you choose, but most Linux kernels are now *modular* kernels that reside in a set of files, called *modules*. A modular Linux kernel can load modules when they're needed and unload them when they're no longer needed. Typically, any modules not needed during boot are compiled as modules rather than being incorporated into the kernel. Such modules include peripheral device drivers, supplementary file systems, and so on.

Table 17.1 summarizes characteristics of monolithic and modular Linux kernels. The greater flexibility of the modular kernel generally outweighs the slightly faster execution and slightly greater security of the monolithic kernel.

TABLE 17.1 Monolithic and Modular Kernels

Monolithic Kernel	Modular Kernel
Slightly faster execution	Slightly faster boot
Slightly more secure	Less RAM required
	More flexible
	Less frequent kernel rebuilds

If you choose to build and use a monolithic kernel, you should remove all device probes from /etc/rc.d/rc.sysinit and remove the module sweeper script, /etc/cron.d/kmod.

Kernel-Related Files

Even a monolithic Linux kernel requires several support files. This subsection describes the principal files associated with the Linux kernel. These include:

- Boot files needed for booting the system
- RPM package files needed to install or build a kernel
- RPM package files containing utilities needed to build a kernel

Boot Files

The Linux boot files reside in the /boot file system so that they can be accessed by PC BIOS code that's incapable of accessing every sector on a large hard disk. The principal Linux boot files are:

- vmlinu*: The Linux kernel, which can have an arbitrary name. Generally, the name includes *vmlinux* or *vmlinuz*. If LILO is used to boot the system, the kernel filename will be referenced in the /etc/ lilo.conf file.

- boot.b: LILO's second stage.

- initrd: A file containing a RAM disk that contains drivers (modules) available to the kernel at boot time. It is often needed to boot from a SCSI hard drive; otherwise it is not generally needed for normal system operation.

- boot.*nnnn*: A backup copy of the original master boot record, before the installation of LILO. The file is not needed for normal system operation. The *nnnn* part of the name is the hexadecimal device number of the hard drive—for example, boot.0300 or boot.0305.

- System.map: A file needed by utilities that read the /proc file system and used to debug the kernel.

To reinforce your understanding of the /boot directory, complete Exercise 17.1.

EXERCISE 17.1

Inspecting the */boot* Directory

A good way to learn about the /boot directory is to study it. Inspect the /boot directory of your system, and locate each of the files mentioned in this subsection.

Kernel RPMs

As explained, Red Hat, Inc. publishes RPMs that contain the Linux kernel. A standard installation of Red Hat Linux includes the kernel package, which contains a precompiled modular kernel and associated modules. On the Intel 386 platform, the standard installation also includes the kernel-pcmcia-cs package, which contains the daemon and drivers needed to support PCMCIA cards.

To build a custom kernel, you must install two packages containing the kernel source:

- `kernel-source`

- `kernel-headers`

To install the packages, move to the directory that contains them and issue the command

```
rpm -Uvh kernel-source-*.i386.rpm kernel-headers-*.i386.rpm
```

When installed, the files of these packages reside in `/usr/src/linux-`*version*, where *version* is the version of the Linux kernel contained in the package. If you want to view kernel documentation without installing the kernel source and headers, which are relatively large, you can install the `kernel-doc` package. That package contains the kernel files that otherwise reside in `/usr/src/linux/Documentation`, but it places them in `/usr/doc`.

If you prefer to work from a source RPM, you can install the package `kernel-source-`*version*`.src.rpm`, where *version* is the version number of the Linux kernel contained in the package. This package contains the source files as released on `www.kernel.org`, plus patches applied by Red Hat, Inc. The package installs the source files in the `/usr/src/redhat` directory.

To learn more about the kernel sources, complete Exercise 17.2.

EXERCISE 17.2

Installing the Kernel Sources

To learn more about the Linux kernel sources, you should install and study them.

1. If you have not previously installed the Linux kernel sources, install the `kernel-source`, `kernel-headers`, and `kernel-doc` packages.

2. Inspect the `/usr/src/linux` directory and its subdirectories.

Utilities

To build the Linux kernel, you must have available the C compiler, certain software development utilities, and certain libraries. The required packages are:

- `egcs-`*version*`.i386.rpm`: the GNU C compiler

- `cpp-`*version*`.i386.rpm`: the GNU C preprocessor

- `dev86-`*version*`.i386.rpm`: an 80x86 assembler and linker

- make-*version*.i386.rpm: the GNU make utility

- glibc-devel-*version*.i386.rpm: header files and libraries for the standard C library

- ncurses-*version*.i386.rpm: the ncurses library, which provides a terminal-independent application programming interface for character-mode video displays

- ncurses-devel-*version*.i386.rpm: header files and libraries for development using ncurses (needed only when building the kernel by using the menuconfig utility)

In each case, *version* stands for the version number of the package.

To install these packages, move to the directory containing them and issue the command

```
rpm -Uvh egcs-*.i386.rpm \
  cpp-*.i386.rpm \
  dev86-*.i386.rpm \
  make-*.i386.rpm  \
  glibc-devel-*.i386.rpm \
  ncurses-*.i386.rpm \
  ncurses-devel-*.i386.rpm
```

Now, get ready to build a kernel by completing Exercise 17.3.

EXERCISE 17.3

Installing the Tools Needed to Build the Kernel

In the remainder of this chapter, you'll learn how to build a new kernel. To be ready to build a kernel, you should install the necessary tools.

1. Determine which of the tools needed to build the kernel already reside on your system.

2. Install any of the tools not already installed.

For now, you can look back to the rpm command that identifies the packages and shows how to install them. But before taking the RHCE exam, be able to install these tools without recourse to a book or crib sheet.

The Kernel Source Tree

As explained, the RPM packages that contain the Linux kernel source install their files in the /usr/src directory. The binary RPMs place their files in the linux-*version* subdirectory—for example, linux-2.4.2—and the (optional) source RPM places its files in the redhat subdirectory. As a convenience, the installation script of the kernel package creates the symbolic link /usr/src/linux, which refers to the /usr/src/linux-*version* directory. The directory contains about two dozen files and directories; Table 17.2 describes several of the most important ones.

TABLE 17.2   Important Files and Directories in /usr/src/linux

File or Directory	Description
arch/i386/config.in	Current kernel configuration options, as written by the kernel configuration program or script
arch/i386/boot/bzImage	Compiled kernel image
Documentation	Directory containing a variety of useful documentation
README	README file for the Linux kernel

Now take a few minutes to complete Exercise 17.4, which guides you in exploring the Linux source tree.

EXERCISE 17.4

Exploring the Linux Source Tree

Knowing how to find important files will save you significant time during the RHCE exam. Follow these steps to become more familiar with the Linux source tree:

1. If you have not previously installed the Linux kernel sources, install the kernel-source, kernel-headers, and kernel-doc packages.

2. Inspect the /usr/src/linux directory and its subdirectories. Find each of the files and directories listed in Table 17.2.

Installing a Kernel *tar* File

If you want to build a kernel from sources that have not been packaged by Red Hat, Inc. as an RPM, you can download a `tar` file from the Linux Kernel Archives Web site, `www.kernel.org`. Download the file into the `/usr/src` directory, and then install it by issuing the following commands:

```
cd /usr/src
mkdir linux-version
rm linux
ln -s linux-version linux
tar zxvf linux-version.tar.gz
```

where *version* is the version of the Linux kernel contained in the `tar` file. Once the file is installed, you can build the kernel by following the procedure given in the next chapter.

Some kernel archives store kernels compressed using the BZIP utility, which yields smaller archive files. For instructions on using the BZIP utility, see its man page.

Kernel Modules

Kernel modules are files that contain dynamically loadable kernel components, such as device drivers. Linux 2.0 required external assistance to load and unload modules; however, Linux 2.2 introduced the `kmod` thread that automatically loads modules when needed.

This section describes the location at which kernel modules reside, the kernel module configuration file `/etc/conf.modules`, and the principal commands for managing kernel modules:

- `depmod`, which creates a database that describes module dependencies
- `lsmod`, which lists loaded modules
- `modprobe`, which loads kernel modules
- `rmmod`, which unloads kernel modules

Module Location

The standard location for kernel modules is the directory /lib/modules/ *version*, where *version* is the version number of the associated Linux kernel. The Red Hat extraversion code ensures that the modules of differently configured kernels of the same release do not conflict.

To view the version and extraversion code of the running kernel, issue the command

uname -r

The output of the command consists of simply the kernel version and extraversion code. For example:

2.4.5-15

The modules associated with the example kernel reside in /lib/modules/ 2.4.5-15.

The kernel modules directory contains several subdirectories. These typically include:

- block, which contains modules related to block devices

- cdrom, which contains modules related to CD-ROM devices

- fs, which contains modules related to file systems

- ipv4, which contains modules related to TCP/IP networking

- misc, which contains a variety of module types

- net, which contains modules related to networking

- pcmcia, which contains modules related to PCMCIA support

- scsi, which contains modules related to SCSI devices

- video, which contains modules related to video and video devices

A kernel module subdirectory may itself contain one or more subdirectories.

Listing Loaded Modules: *lsmod*

To see what modules are currently loaded, issue the lsmod command, which lists resident modules. Following is typical output of the lsmod command:

```
#lsmod
Module                 Size  Used by
vmnet                 14856  3
vmppuser               5156  0  (unused)
```

parport_pc	5012	0	[vmppuser]
parport	7092	0	[vmppuser parport_pc]
vmmon	16180	0	
nfsd	150936	8	(autoclean)
lockd	30856	1	(autoclean) [nfsd]
sunrpc	52356	1	(autoclean) [nfsd lockd]
3c90x	21596	2	(autoclean)
nls_cp437	3548	1	(autoclean)
msdos	8220	1	(autoclean)
fat	25664	1	(autoclean) [msdos]
emu10k1	59492	0	
soundcore	2372	4	[emu10k1]

The output of the command reports

- The name of each module

- The size of each module

- A count of the number of uses of the module

- The names of other modules referring to the module

Now that you've met the lsmod command, complete Exercise 17.5.

EXERCISE 17.5

Viewing Loaded Modules

The lsmod command is simple to use, and very helpful in managing modules. To become better acquainted with the command, use it to identify modules resident in your system.

Unloading Idle Modules: *rmmod*

When a module has been idle for not more than 10 minutes, the /etc/cron.d/kmod cron jobs will unload it, unless you've disabled the job. However, you can unload an idle module at any time by issuing the command

rmmod *module*

where *module* is the name of the idle module you want to unload. You can specify several modules, separating each module name from adjacent module names by one or more spaces. The order in which multiple modules are specified is irrelevant; the `rmmod` command removes the modules simultaneously. If a module is in use or referred to by a loaded module, it cannot be removed.

To remove all idle modules, issue the command

```
rmmod -a
```

To gain practical experience working with modules, complete Exercise 17.6.

EXERCISE 17.6

Unloading Sound Drivers

It's not often necessary to unload a module, but for the RHCE exam, it's important that you know how. If your system includes a configured sound card, you can perform the following steps to learn more about modules:

1. Make sure no applications are using the sound adapter.

2. Use `lsmod` to identify the resident modules. Look at the module names and decide which modules are likely to be sound modules.

3. Use `rmmod` to unload the sound modules. Because some modules are used by other modules, you'll probably find that you cannot unload modules in an arbitrary order. If a module can't be unloaded, try another. Keep trying until you've deleted all the sound modules.

Loading Modules: *modprobe* and *insmod*

To load a module, issue a command of the form

```
modprobe module.o
```

or, more simply:

```
modprobe module
```

where *module.o* is the name of the object file that contains the compiled module. If the module accepts or requires parameters, include them on the command line—for example:

```
modprobe fancycard.o irq=11 align=no
```

If the specified module requires other modules, modprobe will automatically find and load them by searching the database built by the depmod command, described in a subsequent subsection.

The modprobe command has two main modes of operation. In one, it can probe using a single module name or a series of candidate module names. When you specify a series and modprobe successfully loads a candidate module, it ceases probing. To initiate probing, issue a command of the form

```
modprobe -t dir pattern
```

where *dir* specifies a subdirectory of /lib/modules/*version* and pattern is a regular expression that specifies the names of the candidate module files. For example, to load a module from the /lib/modules/2.4.5-15/net directory, where the currently running kernel is version 2.4.5-15, issue the command

```
modprobe -t net '*'
```

In its other main operating mode, the modprobe command attempts to load every candidate module contained in a particular directory. For instance, to attempt to load every module in the /lib/modules/2.4.5-15/ misc directory, issue the command

```
modprobe -a -t misc '*'
```

Of course, it's unlikely that you'd ever want to attempt to load every module. Instead, you'd specify a pattern that identifies only the relevant module files.

Like the modprobe command, the insmod command loads a kernel module. However, the insmod command does not attempt to load dependent modules. Therefore, the modprobe command is more commonly used, except in scripts that handle module dependencies in their own fashion rather than rely on modprobe, such as scripts that execute during system start-up when the module dependency database may not have been updated.

If your Linux system includes a sound adapter, complete Exercise 17.7 to gain practical experience in loading drivers.

EXERCISE 17.7

Loading a Driver

To configure a Linux system to use a new hardware device, often you must load a module that functions as a driver for the device. Sometimes it's necessary to load a module that provides a special function, such as IP masquerading of FTP transfers. If your system has a sound adapter, you can perform this exercise, which lets you practice working with modules.

EXERCISE 17.7 *(continued)*

1. Make sure no applications are using the sound adapter.

2. If necessary, unload the sound driver by using rmmod.

3. Use modprobe to load the proper driver for the card.

You can look back to the chapter and to the results of Exercise 17.6 to help you. But before taking the RHCE exam, be sure you know how to load a module without assistance from a book or notes.

Updating the Module Dependency Database: *depmod*

The ability of the modprobe command to correctly identify modules that depend on other modules and load them as a group is quite convenient. However, proper operation depends on having an up-to-date list of modules that identifies the other modules each module requires. The depmod command constructs a database that contains this information. The /etc/rc.d/rc.sysinit script invokes the depmod command to establish such a database whenever the system is booted. The form of command issued is

```
depmod -a
```

which completely rebuilds the module database.

Configuring Modules: The */etc/conf.modules* File

The /etc/conf.modules file lets you specify a variety of parameters that control the operation of depmod and modprobe. For example, you can specify:

- Aliases that let you refer to modules by more convenient names

- Default parameters to be passed to a module when it is loaded

- Shell commands to be executed when a module is loaded or unloaded

Here is a typical /etc/conf.modules file:

```
alias sound emu10k1
alias parport_lowlevel parport_pc
alias eth0 3c90x
alias eth1 3c90x
options opl3 io=0x388
pre-install emu10k1 insmod soundcore
post-remove emu10k1 rmmod soundcore
```

This file defines four aliases. For instance, it allows the emu10k1 module to be referred to as sound. It defines an option passed to the op13 module when the module is loaded; this option specifies that the input/output port is 0x388. Finally, it specifies commands executed when the emu10k1 module is loaded (pre-install) and unloaded (post-install).

The /etc/conf.modules file can contain these types of lines:

- Parameter definition lines of the form

parameter = value

A parameter definition line defines a parameter and binds it to the specified value. The following types of parameter definitions are allowed:

- depfile=*directory*, which specifies the location of the module dependency database generated by depmod.

- path=*directory*, which specifies a directory to be searched for modules.

- path[*type*]=*directory*, which specifies a directory containing modules of the specified type. The value of *type* can be used with the -t argument of the modprobe command.

By default, the module configuration includes the paths and options shown in the following list.

Default Module Configuration Options

```
depfile=/lib/modules/\

    `uname -r`/modules.dep

path[boot]=/lib/modules

path[fs]=/lib/modules/`uname -r`

path[misc]=/lib/modules/`uname -r`

path[net]=/lib/modules/`uname -r`

path[scsi]=/lib/modules/`uname -r`

path[cdrom]=/lib/modules/`uname -r`

path[ipv4]=/lib/modules/`uname -r`

path[ipv6]=/lib/modules/`uname -r`

path[sound]=/lib/modules/`uname -r`

path[fs]=/lib/modules/default

path[misc]=/lib/modules/default
```

```
path[net]=/lib/modules/default
path[scsi]=/lib/modules/default
path[cdrom]=/lib/modules/default
path[ipv4]=/lib/modules/default
path[ipv6]=/lib/modules/default
path[sound]=/lib/modules/default
path[fs]=/lib/modules
path[misc]=/lib/modules
path[net]=/lib/modules
path[scsi]=/lib/modules
path[cdrom]=/lib/modules
path[ipv4]=/lib/modules
path[ipv6]=/lib/modules
path[sound]=/lib/modules
```

- Option lines of the form

  `options module symbol=value`

  where *module* specifies the name of a module, *symbol* specifies an argument known to the module, and *value* specifies the value of the argument. Option lines specify arguments to be sent to modules. Multiple pairs of symbols and values can be specified; separate each pair from adjacent pairs by one or more spaces.

- Alias lines of the form

  `alias alias_name actual_name`

  An alias line establishes an alias, or alternative name, for a module.

- Pre-install lines of the form

  `pre-install module command`

  A pre-install line specifies a command to be executed before the specified module is installed.

- Install lines of the form

  `install module command`

An install line specifies a command to be executed to install the specified module.

- Post-install lines of the form

  `post-install` *module* *command*

  A post-install line specifies a command to be executed after the specified module is installed.

- Pre-remove lines of the form

  `pre-remove` *module* *command*

  A pre-remove line specifies a command to be executed before the specified module is removed.

- Remove lines of the form

  `remove` *module* *command*

  A remove line specifies a command to be executed to remove the specified module.

- Post-remove lines of the form

  `post-remove` *module* *command*

  A post-remove line specifies a command to be executed after the specified module is removed.

- A keep line of the form

  `keep`

  A keep line indicates that any paths specified by parameter lines are to be used in addition to, rather than as replacements for, the default module path.

The `/etc/conf.modules` file can also contain comments. Empty lines and all text following a hash mark (#) are ignored.

Now, complete Exercise 17.8, which looks at the /etc/conf.modules file.

EXERCISE 17.8

Inspecting the */etc/conf.modules* File

Inspect the /etc/conf.modules file on your system. Be sure you understand, and can explain, its contents. Refer to the chapter and other information, such as kernel documentation, as needed. Be sure you generally understand the function and structure of the /etc/conf.modules file before taking the RHCE exam.

Summary

In this chapter, you learned about the Red Hat Linux kernel. The most important topics covered are:

Linux Kernel Numbering   Linux kernels have an associated number of the form $x.y.z$, where x is the major version number, y is the minor version number, and z is the patch level.

Kernel Types   A kernel with an even minor number is a stable kernel. A kernel with an odd minor number is a developmental kernel.

Extraversion Code   Red Hat, Inc. recommends using a kernel number of the form $x.y.z-c$, where x is the major version number, y is the minor version number, z is the patch level, and c is the extraversion code. The extraversion code lets you distinguish kernels having the same major, minor, and patch numbers, but built with different options.

Kernel Types   A monolithic kernel consists of a single load module. A modular kernel, such as the Linux kernel, includes modules that can be loaded when needed. A modular kernel is more compact and flexible than a monolithic kernel.

Kernel-Related Files, Directories, and Packages   The bootable Linux kernel and its associated files generally reside in /boot. The source code for the Linux kernel resides in /usr/src/linux. The kernel configuration options are stored in the file /usr/src/linux/arch/i386/config.in, and the compiled kernel is written to /usr/src/linux/arch/i386/boot/bzImage.

To compile a Linux kernel, you should install several packages, including `kernel-source`, `kernel-headers`, `egcs`, `cpp`, `dev86`, `make`, `glibc-devel`, `ncurses`, `ncurses-devel`.

Kernel Modules   The kernel module configuration file is `/etc/conf.modules`. Important commands for working with kernel modules include `depmod`, `lsmod`, `modprobe`, `rmmod`, and `uname`.

Key Terms

Before going on to the next chapter, be sure you're familiar with the following terms:

> developmental release
>
> extraversion code
>
> major versions
>
> minor versions
>
> modular
>
> modules
>
> monolithic
>
> patch level
>
> stable release

Additional Sources of Information

If you'd like further information about the topics presented in this chapter, you should consult the following sources:

- The Linux kernel documentation in `/usr/src/linux/Documentation`

- The man pages for the commands that manipulate modules: `lsmod`, `rmmod`, `modprobe`, `depmod`

Review Questions

1. Which of the following is generally true of monolithic Linux kernels in comparison to modular Linux kernels?

   A. They boot faster.

   B. They execute faster.

   C. They occupy less RAM.

   D. They're more flexible.

2. What is the minor version number of Linux 2.4.5-6?

   A. 2

   B. 4

   C. 5

   D. 6

3. Which of the following kernels is part of the stable release development tree?

   A. 2.4.5-test

   B. 2.4.6-stable

   C. 2.5.5-test

   D. 2.5.6-stable

4. What command displays the version number of the running Linux kernel?

   A. dmesg

   B. motd

   C. uname

   D. w

5. Which of the following commands loads the module known as heavy?

   A. depmod heavy

   B. insmod heavy

   C. load heavy

   D. modprobe heavy

6. Which of the following correctly specifies the common name of the Linux kernel?

   A. /boot/bzImage

   B. /boot/kernel

   C. /boot/vmlinuz

   D. /boot/vmlinux

7. Which of the following /etc/conf.modules lines specifies a command to be used when loading a module?

   A. path=

   B. pre-install

   C. install

   D. post-install

Answers to Review Questions

1. B. Monolithic kernels do not use loadable modules to communicate with devices, so they execute somewhat faster than modular kernels. But they're larger and therefore slower to boot. They're also much less flexible.

2. B. The major version number is 2. The minor version number is 4. The patch level is 5. The extraversion code is 6.

3. A, B. The minor version of a stable kernel is even.

4. C. The `uname -r` command displays the kernel version information.

5. B, D. Either the `insmod` or `modprobe` command can be used to load a module. The `insmod` command, however, does not automatically load other modules needed by the specified module.

6. C. The common name of the Linux kernel is `/boot/vmlinuz`; however, the filename is arbitrary.

7. C. The `install` line specifies the command to be used to load a module.

Chapter

18

Configuring, Building, and Installing a Custom Kernel

RHCE PREPARATION TOPICS COVERED IN THIS CHAPTER:

✓ Be able to configure, build, and install the Linux kernel and modules from source.

✓ Be familiar with kernel configuration issues associated with using Red Hat Linux as a router.

At one time, building a custom `kernel` was a rite of passage for Unix system administrators. Today, building a Linux kernel is relatively simple. This chapter explains the procedure for configuring, building, and installing a custom Linux kernel.

Configuring the Kernel

This section and the following sections explain the procedure for configuring, building, and installing the Linux kernel. To help you keep your place, procedurally important subsections are titled with a step number that indicates their place in the following overall process:

1. Change to the kernel source directory.

2. Recover the default configuration (optional).

3. Define the extraversion code.

4. Specify the kernel configuration options.

5. Build the kernel and modules.

6. Install the kernel and modules.

7. Create the boot driver ramdisk.

8. Revise the LILO configuration.

9. Create a new boot disk.

Step #1: Changing to the Kernel Source Directory

Configuring the kernel, like building and installing the kernel, is done from the root directory of the kernel source tree, /usr/src/linux. To begin configuring the kernel, you should change to that directory:

```
cd /usr/src/linux
```

Step #2: Recovering the Default Configuration

If you have already built a kernel on the local host, you may want to simply tweak the kernel configuration. However, if you've not previously built a kernel, you should recover the default Red Hat Linux kernel configuration. To do so, issue the commands

```
cp configs/kernel arch/i386/defconfig
make mrproper
make oldconfig
```

where *kernel* is the name of the file in the configs directory that corresponds to the standard kernel on which you want to base your new kernel. The make mrproper command removes old configuration files and the results of previous builds. The make oldconfig command sources the config.in file, referring to the defconfig file to determine default values for parameters.

Step #3: Defining the Extraversion Code

As explained in the previous chapter, Red Hat, Inc. recommends that you define an extraversion code that distinguishes differently configured kernels of the same version. To do so, edit the file /usr/src/linux/Makefile. The first few lines of the file should resemble the following:

```
VERSION = 2
PATCHLEVEL = 2
SUBLEVEL = 12
EXTRAVERSION = -20
```

Add some descriptive text following the -20 in the fourth line, which specifies the Red Hat build number. For example, if the new kernel supports Wireless Access Protocol (WAP), you might revise the line to read

```
EXTRAVERSION = -20WAP
```

The extraversion code is reported by uname and determines the subdirectory of /lib/modules into which kernel modules are installed, preventing conflicts between modules of similar kernels.

Step #4: Specifying the Kernel Configuration Options

The kernel configuration options reside in the file /usr/src/linux/.config. In principle, you could modify this file by using a text editor. However, Linux provides three utilities that make kernel configuration much simpler:

- config

- menuconfig

- xconfig

To use one of these utilities, issue a command of the form

    make *utility*

where *utility* is the name of one of the three utilities.

The config utility is the oldest of the three utilities. It is a text-based, question-and-response utility that is available as a part of many Linux distributions. However, most users find it clumsy to use. A significant drawback is that config provides no way to modify a response once entered. So, if you discover you've responded incorrectly, you must exit the procedure (by typing Ctrl+C) and start over. The dialog provided by config resembles the following:

```
# make config
rm -f include/asm
( cd include ; ln -sf asm-i386 asm)
/bin/sh scripts/Configure arch/i386/config.in
#
# Using defaults found in .config
#
*
* Code maturity level options
*
Prompt for development and/or incomplete code/drivers
(CONFIG_EXPERIMENTAL) [Y/n/?]
*
* Processor type and features
*
Processor family (386, 486/Cx486, 586/K5/5x86/6x86,
```

➥Pentium/K6/TSC, PPro/6x86MX) [386]
 defined CONFIG_M386
Maximum Physical Memory (1GB, 2GB) [1GB]
 defined CONFIG_1GB
Math emulation (CONFIG_MATH_EMULATION) [Y/n/?] n
MTRR (Memory Type Range Register) support (CONFIG_MTRR)
➥[Y/n/?]
Symmetric multi-processing support (CONFIG_SMP) [N/y/?]
*
* Loadable module support
*
Enable loadable module support (CONFIG_MODULES) [Y/n/?]
Set version information on all symbols for modules
➥(CONFIG_MODVERSIONS) [Y/n/?]
Kernel module loader (CONFIG_KMOD) [Y/n/?]
*
* General setup
*
Networking support (CONFIG_NET) [Y/n/?]
PCI support (CONFIG_PCI) [Y/n/?]
PCI access mode (BIOS, Direct, Any) [Any]
 defined CONFIG_PCI_GOANY
 PCI quirks (CONFIG_PCI_QUIRKS) [Y/n/?]
 PCI bridge optimization (experimental)
 ➥(CONFIG_PCI_OPTIMIZE) [N/y/?]
 Backward-compatible /proc/pci (CONFIG_PCI_OLD_PROC)
 ➥[Y/n/?]
MCA support (CONFIG_MCA) [N/y/?]
SGI Visual Workstation support (CONFIG_VISWS) [N/y/?]
System V IPC (CONFIG_SYSVIPC) [Y/n/?]
BSD Process Accounting (CONFIG_BSD_PROCESS_ACCT) [Y/n/?]
Sysctl support (CONFIG_SYSCTL) [Y/n/?]
Kernel support for a.out binaries (CONFIG_BINFMT_AOUT)
➥[M/n/y/?]
Kernel support for ELF binaries (CONFIG_BINFMT_ELF)
➥[Y/m/n/?]
Kernel support for MISC binaries (CONFIG_BINFMT_MISC)
➥[M/n/y/?]
Kernel support for JAVA binaries (obsolete)

➡(CONFIG_BINFMT_JAVA) [M/n/y/?]
Parallel port support (CONFIG_PARPORT) [M/n/y/?]

Of course, this is only a small part of the actual dialog.

The menuconfig utility is a favorite among system administrators. Like config, it has a text-based interface and can therefore be used remotely—for example, over a telnet or ssh connection. However, menuconfig—as its name suggests—provides a menu-based interface that lets you cycle through configuration options until you arrive at a configuration you approve. Thus, it's much less clumsy to use than the config utility. It also includes a useful help facility that explains the selected configuration option. Figure 18.1 shows the main screen of the menuconfig utility.

FIGURE 18.1 The main menu of menuconfig

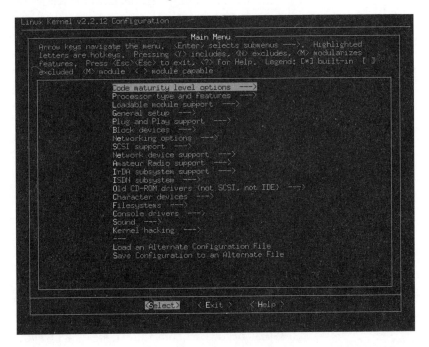

If the host system supports X, you can use the xconfig utility. The xconfig utility has an attractive and easy-to-use interface that fully supports a mouse or other X-supported pointing device. Like menuconfig, it provides a help facility. Figure 18.2 shows the main screen of the xconfig utility.

FIGURE 18.2 The xconfig screen

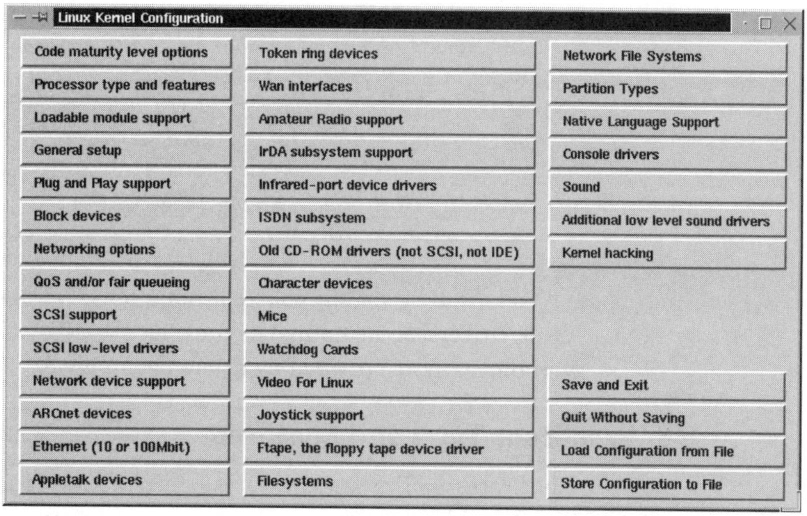

The remaining subsections of this section briefly explain the configuration options provided by the Linux kernel. Relatively more attention is given to configuration options you're more likely to work with, especially those that you may need to use in the RHCE exam exercises.

Many configuration options provide three alternatives:

- Yes, which inserts support for the option into the kernel

- No, which omits support for the option

- Module, which compiles a loadable module that provides support for the option

The responses are typically abbreviated by *y* for yes, *n* for no, and *m* for module. In general, you should respond *y* to options needed at boot time, *m* to options needed during operation or likely to be needed in the future, and *n* to other options. An option is considered enabled if you respond *y* or *m*.

Code Maturity Level

Figure 18.3 shows the Code Maturity Level Options screen of `xconfig`. If you're using `config` or `menuconfig`, you have access to the same options.

FIGURE 18.3 Code Maturity Level Options

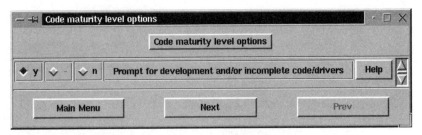

You should generally enable Prompt for Development and/or Incomplete Code/Drivers. Some Linux facilities, such as NFS, may not operate correctly without support provided by development code.

Processor Type and Features

The Processor Type and Features screen of xconfig is shown in Figure 18.4. You should generally:

- Select the highest processor family that includes the CPU of your system.

- Turn math emulation off, unless your CPU is a 386 or 486SX.

- Turn Symmetric Multiprocessing Support (SMP) off, unless your system's motherboard has multiple CPUs installed.

If you unnecessarily enable math emulation or SMP, your kernel may require somewhat more memory or your system may operate somewhat more slowly.

FIGURE 18.4 Processor Type and Features

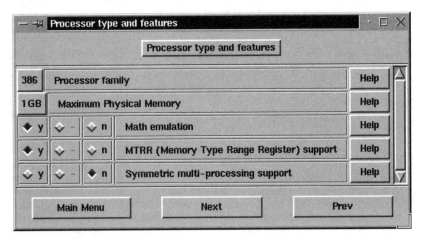

Loadable Module Support

Figure 18.5 shows the Loadable Module Support screen of xconfig. You should generally use it to enable Loadable Module Support.

FIGURE 18.5 Loadable Module Support

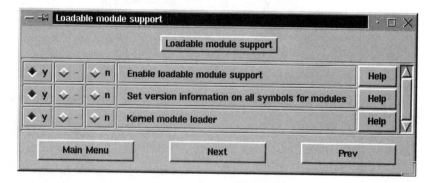

General Setup

Figure 18.6 shows the General Setup screen of xconfig. If your system has one or more network interfaces, you should generally enable the Networking option. If your system's motherboard supports PCI, you should generally enable PCI support.

FIGURE 18.6 General Setup

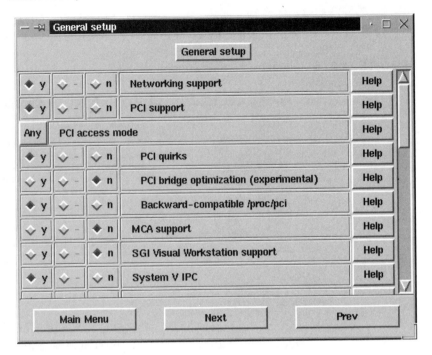

Plug-and-Play Support

Figure 18.7 shows the plug-and-play support screen of xconfig. You should generally enable plug-and-play support if your system includes plug-and-play cards or a parallel port. Enable support for parallel port devices, if any are present or likely to be present.

FIGURE 18.7 Plug-and-Play Support

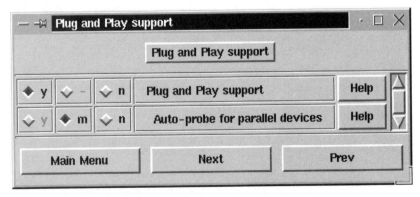

Block Devices

Figure 18.8 shows the Block Devices screen of xconfig. Use it to enable support for block devices (hard disks, CD-ROM drives, and so on) installed or likely to be installed.

FIGURE 18.8 Block Devices

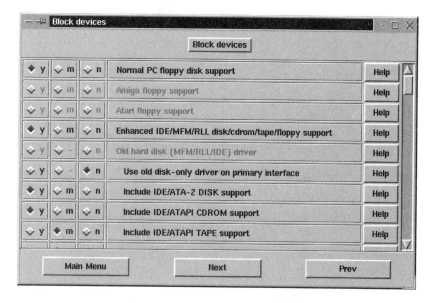

Networking Options

Figure 18.9 shows the Networking Options screen of xconfig. Use it to enable support for network facilities and protocols your system must support. The principal IP-related options are:

- Packet socket

- Kernel/User netlink socket

- Routing messages

- Netlink device emulation

- Network firewalls

- Socket filtering

- Unix domain sockets

- TCP/IP networking

- IP: multicasting
- IP: advanced router
- IP: kernel level autoconfiguration
- IP: firewalling
- IP: firewall packet netlink device
- IP: transparent proxy support
- IP: masquerading
- IP: ICMP masquerading
- IP: masquerading special modules support
- IP: ipautofw masq support (EXPERIMENTAL)
- IP: ipportfw masq support (EXPERIMENTAL)
- IP: ip fwmark masq-forwarding support (EXPERIMENTAL)
- IP: masquerading virtual server support (EXPERIMENTAL)
- IP masquerading VS table size (the Nth power of 2)

You can use the help facility of `menuconfig` or `xconfig` to learn more about these options. If you plan to use the host as a router rather than as a desktop or server system, you should enable the IP: `Advanced Router` option; otherwise, you should disable the option.

FIGURE 18.9 Networking Options

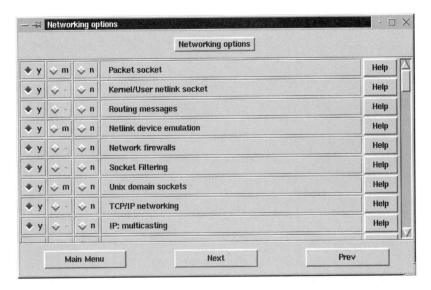

QoS and/or Fair Queueing

This option is presented by menuconfig near the end of the networking options, whereas xconfig presents it as a separate screen. This option, which lets you install a non-standard IP packet scheduler, is recommended "only for experts."

SCSI Support

Figure 18.10 shows the SCSI Support screen of xconfig. If the system includes SCSI devices, you should enable appropriate options.

FIGURE 18.10   SCSI Support

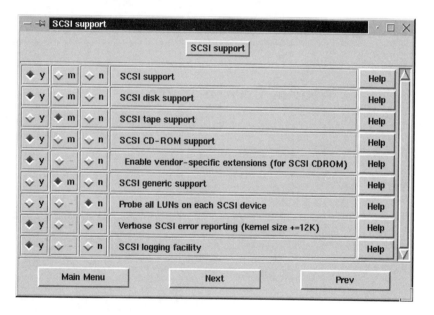

SCSI Low-Level Drivers

Figure 18.11 shows the SCSI Low-Level Drivers screen of xconfig. These options are included by menuconfig as part of its SCSI Support screen. If the system includes one or more SCSI interfaces, you should enable the appropriate support. If the system must boot from a SCSI device, you may prefer to include the support in the kernel rather than as a module; otherwise, you must use mkinitrd to prepare an appropriate ramdisk, as described later in this chapter.

FIGURE 18.11 SCSI Low-Level Drivers

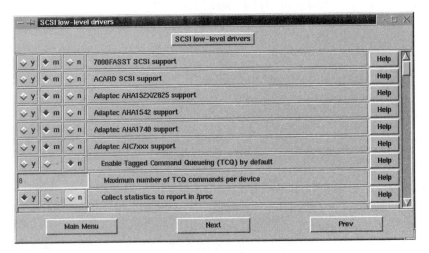

Network Device Support

Figure 18.12 shows the Network Device Support screen of xconfig. If the system includes one or more network interfaces, you should enable the appropriate support.

FIGURE 18.12 Network Device Support

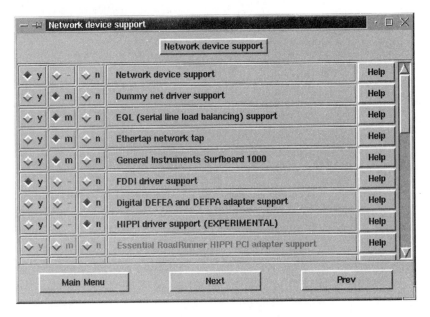

Amateur Radio Support

The Amateur Radio Support screen lets you configure support for packet radio. These options are not generally required.

IrDA Subsystem Support

The IrDA Subsystem Support screen of xconfig, shown in Figure 18.13, lets you configure support for devices that communicate with the system via infrared. These options are not generally required.

FIGURE 18.13 IrDA Subsystem Support

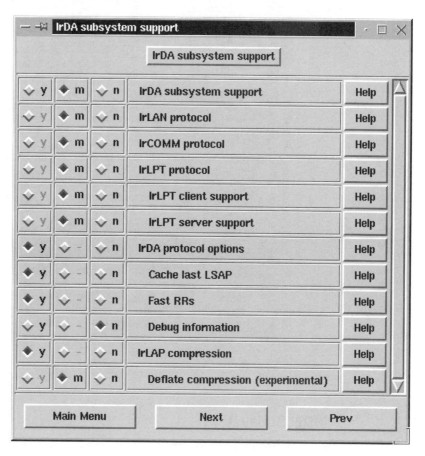

Infrared-Port Device Drivers

The Infrared-Port Device Drivers screen of xconfig, shown in Figure 18.14, lets you configure drivers for devices that communicate with the system via infrared. These options are included by menuconfig as part of its IrDA Subsystem Support screen and are not generally required.

FIGURE 18.14 Infrared-Port Device Drivers

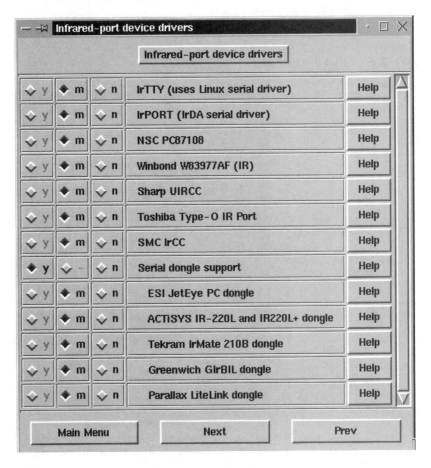

ISDN Subsystem

Figure 18.15 shows the ISDN Subsystem screen of xconfig. Unless the system is attached to an ISDN device, you should disable this option. Many modern ISDN modems attach to a system via Ethernet; such modems do not require ISDN support.

FIGURE 18.15 ISDN Subsystem

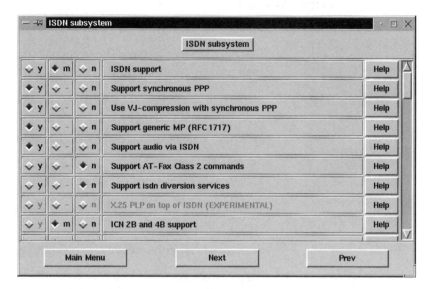

Old CD-ROM Drivers

Figure 18.16 shows the Old CD-ROM Drivers screen of xconfig. Unless the system includes one or more old CD-ROM drivers that use a proprietary interface (that is, neither IDE nor SCSI), you should disable this option.

FIGURE 18.16 Old CD-ROM Drivers

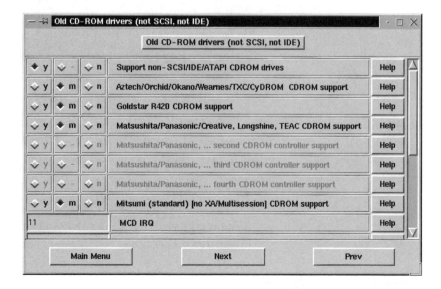

Other Options

Several other configuration option screens are available. These include:

- Character Device Options. The menuconfig utility presents these as a single screen; xconfig presents them as a series of screens:

  - Character Devices, which lets you configure options related to virtual terminals, multi-port serial cards, and other character-mode devices.

  - Mice, which lets you configure mouse options.

  - Watchdog Cards, which lets you configure options for special watchdog timer cards.

  - Video for Linux, which lets you configure options for radio and TV cards.

  - Joystick Support, which lets you configure joystick options.

- Floppy Tape Support, which lets you configure support for tape drives that use a floppy disk interface. The menuconfig utility presents these options as part of the Block Devices screen.

- File System and Partition Options. The menuconfig utility presents these as a single screen; xconfig presents them as a series of screens:

  - File Systems, which lets you configure support for file systems.

  - Network File Systems, which lets you configure support for network file systems.

  - Partition Types, which lets you configure support for non-Linux (that is, non-MS-DOS) partition tables.

  - Native Language Support, which lets you configure support for native language extension.

- Console Drivers, which lets you configure options related to the console and frame buffer devices.

- Sound, which lets you configure support for sound. The menuconfig utility presents these as a single screen; xconfig presents them as a series of two screens:

  - Sound, which lets you configure support for sound.

  - Additional Low-Level Sound Drivers, which lets you configure drivers for sound cards.

- Kernel hacking, which lets you configure support for kernel testing. Enabling this option impairs security, so you should generally not enable it.

Step #5: Building the Kernel and Modules

To build the kernel and modules, issue the following sequence of commands:

```
make bzImage
make modules
```

The commands perform the following operations:

- `make bzImage` compiles the kernel

- `make modules` compiles loadable modules

The commands generally take some time to execute. You may prefer, then, to execute them as a single command so that you need not monitor the system to see when it's time to enter the next command. Here's how to do so:

```
make bzImage modules
```

After building a kernel for the first time, you can use an alternative set of commands. First, create your kernel configuration in the usual way by using `make config`, `make menuconfig`, `make xconfig`, or `make oldconfig`. Then, issue the commands

```
make dep
make clean
make bzImage
make modules
```

or issue the single command

```
make dep clean bzImage modules
```

The `make dep` command propagates your configuration choices through the source tree and the `make clean` command removes the results of previous builds. The order in which these two commands are given does not matter. The remaining two commands have their usual effect.

Step #6: Installing the Kernel and Modules

When the build is complete, install the kernel and modules by issuing commands of the following form:

```
cp /usr/src/linux/arch/i386/boot/bzImage
➥/boot/vmlinuz-version
make modules_install
cp /usr/src/linux/System.map /boot/System.map-version
cp /usr/src/linux/.config /boot/config-version
```

where *version* is the version and extraversion code associated with the new kernel. The last command is not absolutely necessary. However, it's handy to have a copy of a kernel's configuration stored with the kernel.

Step #7: Creating the Boot Driver Ramdisk File

If the system uses SCSI or RAID devices during boot, you should create a ramdisk file containing appropriate drivers. The kernel loads the ramdisk file and accesses drivers as needed during boot-up.

To create the ramdisk file, issue a command of the form

```
mkinitrd /boot/initrd-version.img version
```

where *version* is the version and extraversion code associated with the new kernel. The `mkinitrd` command examines the modules library `lib`, automatically selects the proper modules, creates the ramdisk file, and packs the modules into the ramdisk file.

Step #8: Revising the LILO Configuration

To boot the new kernel, you generally must revise the LILO configuration. Using a text editor, add lines of the following form to `/etc/lilo.conf`:

```
image=/boot/vmlinuz-version
  label= vmlinuz-version
  root=/dev/xxx
  initrd=/boot/initrd-version.img
  read-only
```

where *version* is the version and extraversion code associated with the new kernel and *xxx* is the root partition of the Linux system. If you prefer some other label text, specify a different value for `label`.

After saving the modified file, run the LILO boot map installer:

```
/sbin/lilo -v
```

Step #9: Creating a New Boot Disk

Whenever you install a new kernel, you should create a new boot disk that contains it. To do so, issue a command of the form

```
mkbootdisk -device /dev/fd0 -verbose version
```

where *version* is the version and extraversion code associated with the new kernel. If you want to write the kernel to a floppy drive other than /dev/fd0, specify the device file of the desired floppy drive; for example, /dev/fd1.

After creating the boot disk, boot the system by using LILO and check that it operates properly. If you can't boot the system using the new kernel, boot the system using the old kernel by specifying the label of the old kernel in response to the LILO prompt.

Now you're ready to make a custom kernel by following the steps of Exercise 18.1.

EXERCISE 18.1

Making a Custom Linux Kernel

Creating a custom kernel was once a Linux rite of passage. But after studying this chapter, you should be able to compile a custom kernel without loss of sanity. Here's the process you should follow:

1. Create a Linux boot disk and test it to be sure it successfully boots your system.

2. Configure a Linux kernel with any options you like, so long as they're not incompatible with the hardware of your system.

3. Build and install the kernel, creating a ramdisk and boot disk for the new kernel.

4. Install the new kernel in the LILO configuration, leaving the new kernel in place.

EXERCISE 18.1 *(continued)*

5. Check the new kernel to see that you can boot it and that your system operates correctly.

6. Check that you can use LILO to boot the old kernel.

Look back to the chapter and other documentation, particularly the descriptions of kernel options, as needed. If the new kernel doesn't work, recover your system by using LILO or the boot disk containing the original kernel.

Before taking the RHCE exam, you should be able to build a custom kernel without needing to access this book or other help.

Summary

In this chapter, you learned about building a custom kernal. The most important topics covered are:

Compiling and Installing a Kernel   The steps involved in compiling and installing a kernel are:

1. Change to the kernel source directory.

2. Recover the default configuration (optional).

3. Define the extraversion code.

4. Specify the kernel configuration options.

5. Build the kernel and modules.

6. Install the kernel and modules.

7. Create the boot driver ramdisk.

8. Revise the LILO configuration.

9. Create a new boot disk.

Kernel Configuration Options   The main categories of kernel configuration options are:

- Code Maturity Level

- Processor Type and Features

- Loadable Module Support

- General Setup
- Plug-and-Play Support
- Block Devices
- Networking Options
- QoS and/or Fair Queueing
- SCSI Support
- SCSI Low-Level Drivers
- Network Device Support
- Amateur Radio Support
- IrDA Subsystem Support
- Infrared-Port Device Drivers
- ISDN Subsystem
- Old CD-ROM Drivers
- Other Options

Key Terms

Before going on to the next chapter, be sure you're familiar with the following terms:

kernel

extraversion code

Additional Sources of Information

If you'd like further information about the topics presented in this chapter, you should consult the following sources:

- *The Official Red Hat Linux Reference Guide*
- The Linux kernel archives, www.kernel.org.
- The documentation files in the kernel source tree, particularly those in /usr/src/linux/Documentation
- *The Linux Kernel HOWTO*, by Brian Ward, /usr/doc/HOWTO/ Kernel-HOWTO (somewhat out of date, but still valuable)

Review Questions

1. The kernel configuration resides in which of the following files?

   A. `/usr/src/linux/.config`

   B. `/usr/src/linux/config.in`

   C. `/usr/src/linux/config`

   D. `/usr/src/linux/linux.cfg`

2. Which of the following is a kernel configuration tool that can be used over a telnet connection?

   A. `make config`

   B. `make linux`

   C. `make menuconfig`

   D. `make xconfig`

3. If you respond *m* to the prompt for a device driver, what is the result?

   A. The driver is compiled as a loadable module.

   B. The driver is compiled as part of the kernel.

   C. The driver is not compiled.

   D. You cannot respond *m* to the prompt for a device driver.

4. To optimize the kernel to operate as a router rather than as a host, which option should you enable?

   A. `IP: Advanced Router`

   B. `IP: Host off`

   C. `IP: Optimize as Router, Not Host`

   D. `IP: Router Only`

5. The file that defines the value of the extraversion code is which of the following?

A. /usr/src/linux/make

B. /usr/src/linux/Make

C. /usr/src/linux/makefile

D. /usr/src/linux/Makefile

6. Which of the following typical commands that are used to install a new kernel is necessary?

A. cp /usr/src/linux/.config \
/boot/config-2.4.5-1r1

B. cp /usr/src/linux/arch/i386/boot/bzImage \
/boot/vmlinuz-2.4.5-1r1

C. cp /usr/src/linux/System.map \
/boot/System.map-2.4.5-1r1

D. make modules_install

7. To create a new boot disk, which of the following commands should you issue?

A. mkbootdisk -device /dev/fd0 -verbose 2.4.5

B. mkbootdisk -device /dev/fd0 -verbose 2.4.5-10

C. mkbootdisk /dev/fd0 -verbose 2.4.5

D. mkbootdisk /dev/fd0 -verbose 2.4.5-10

Answers to Review Questions

1. A. The kernel configuration resides in the hidden file .config. The file config.in is provided as an argument to scripts/Configure. If the file .config does not exist, the file arch/i386/defconfig provides the defaults. The default configurations for Red Hat Linux kernels reside in configs.

2. A, C. Both config and menuconfig have text-based user interfaces.

3. A. The response *m* compiles support for a driver or other facility as a loadable kernel module.

4. C. To configure the kernel to operate as a router rather than as a host, you should enable the IP: Optimize as Router, not Host option. This suppresses default support typically needed by hosts but not routers.

5. D. The value of the extraversion code is defined in /usr/src/linux /Makefile.

6. B, C, D. You must install the kernel, system map, and modules, but you need not install the system map and configuration.

7. B. You must include the argument -device. The version argument should include the extraversion code so that the command can locate the proper kernel image.

Chapter

19

Managing Shared Libraries

RHCE PREPARATION TOPICS COVERED IN THIS CHAPTER:

✓ Understand and be able to revise the loader configuration file, `/etc/ld.so.conf`.

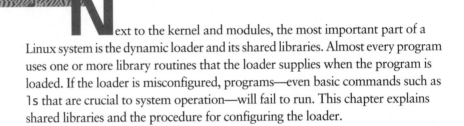

ext to the kernel and modules, the most important part of a Linux system is the dynamic loader and its shared libraries. Almost every program uses one or more library routines that the loader supplies when the program is loaded. If the loader is misconfigured, programs—even basic commands such as ls that are crucial to system operation—will fail to run. This chapter explains shared libraries and the procedure for configuring the loader.

Shared Library Concepts

The programming language C is the most popular language for writing Linux programs. However, C programs as written by a programmer are not immediately ready for execution, because computers do not process C programs. Instead, a computer requires programs to be expressed in a form known as *machine language*. The machine language accepted by one computer model is closely related to the computer's internal architecture and thus not generally compatible with machine languages accepted by other computers. Therefore, a computer program must undergo a transformation—generally, a series of transformations—before it can be executed. Figure 19.1 illustrates this process.

Programs written in a scripting language such as Perl, Python, or the bash shell can be executed immediately. That's the primary distinction between a scripting language and ordinary programming languages.

FIGURE 19.1 Creating and running a program

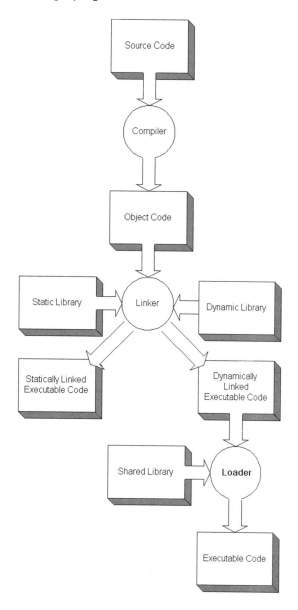

The form of program written by a programmer is called *source code*. A special program called a *compiler* transforms source code into a form known as *object code*. Object code closely resembles machine language, but, like source code, it is not executable. A programmer doesn't generally write code to handle common operations, such as counting the number of characters in a text string; otherwise, the programmer would be writing the same code again and again.

Instead, common operations are written once and organized as a *library*. When a programmer needs to perform one of these operations, the programmer simply writes a reference to the library routine. This speeds the programming process and reduces programming errors.

A special program called a *linker* combines object code with the necessary library routines to create a *statically linked* executable program. A statically linked executable is ready to run.

Statically linked programs suffer several disadvantages. For example, every executable program that uses the library routine to count the number of characters in a text string must contain the machine language instructions to perform this operation. If a system contains thousands of programs that use dozens or hundreds of library routines, considerable disk space is wasted in redundantly storing the routines. Moreover, suppose an error is found in a library routine: every program that uses the routine contains the erroneous code. Fixing the defect requires linking every program that uses the erroneous routine to a corrected library.

Generally, a better approach is to *dynamically link* programs. A dynamically linked program does not contain the library routines it references. Instead, it contains special *stubs* that specify the library routines the program needs. When a dynamically linked program is loaded, a special *dynamic loader* resolves the program's library references. The system keeps one copy of a dynamically loaded routine in its virtual memory; all programs that use the routine share access to the same copy.

Dynamically linked programs save disk space, because programs do not contain redundant copies of library routines. Moreover, fixing a defective library routine is as simple as replacing the containing library: every subsequent reference to the routine will resolve to the corrected copy. Dynamically linked programs do execute slightly more slowly, but the difference is seldom significant.

X programs that use the Motif library are often distributed in statically linked form, but the aversion to dynamic linking has nothing to do with performance. The software license of the Motif library restricts its distribution. Statically linked executables do not run afoul of the license.

Linux Shared Libraries

Linux executable program files generally use a structure known as *ELF* (executable and linking format). However, older executable files sometimes use a format known as a.out. One complication of this inconsistency is that several system libraries exist separately in both ELF and a.out formats. Eventually, support for a.out will likely disappear.

The Linux linker is known as /usr/bin/ld. At one time, Linux had separate dynamic loaders for a.out files (/lib/ld.so) and ELF files (/lib/ld-linux.so-1). However, Linux now uses a single dynamic loader, /lib/ld-*version*.so, to support both file formats. For compatibility, Red Hat Linux includes both the old and new versions of the Linux dynamic loader.

Library Locations and Filenames

Linux shared libraries are stored in several directories, such as:

- /lib, the main shared libraries

- /usr/lib, supplementary shared libraries

- /usr/i486-linux-libc5/lib, shared libraries for use with the old version of the C standard library, libc5

- /usr/X11R6/lib, shared libraries related to XFree86

- /usr/i486-linuxaout/lib, a.out shared libraries

Static library files have names of the form *libname*.a, where *libname* is the name of the library. Dynamic library files are specially named in a manner designed to achieve upward compatibility with new releases of shared libraries. The name of a shared library generally has the form *libname-major.minor.patch*.so, where:

- *libname* is the name of the library

- *major* is the major release number of the library

- *minor* is the minor release number of the library

- *patch* is the patch level of the library

- so indicates that the file is a shared library

For example, the standard C library might reside in a file named libc-2.1.1.so. If a library has been freshly released, the patch level or minor release level may be omitted and the filename will have the form *libname-major.minor.so* or *libname-major.so*.

In addition to the library file, there are two symbolic links, which point to the library file:

- *libname.so*

- *libname.so.major*

Programs are linked against one or the other of the symbolic links rather than against the library file. Thus, the loader is able to locate the required library even if the patch level or minor release numbers change.

Viewing Library References

To determine the dynamic libraries needed by a program, issue a command of the form

```
ldd programfile
```

where *programfile* is the name of the program. For example, to determine the dynamic libraries required by the rm command, issue the command

```
# ldd /bin/rm
    libc.so.6 => /lib/libc.so.6 (0x40019000)
    /lib/ld-linux.so.2 => /lib/ld-linux.so.2 (0x40000000)
```

The example output shows that the rm command requires version 6 of libc and that the loader resolved this reference to /lib/libc.so.6. The output also shows that the current version of the Linux dynamic loader is version 2. The rm command requires relatively little library support in comparison to, for example, the linuxconf command, which references six libraries:

```
# ldd /bin/linuxconf
    libm.so.6 => /lib/libm.so.6 (0x40019000)
    libncurses.so.4 => /usr/lib/libncurses.so.4 (0x40035000)
    libdl.so.2 => /lib/libdl.so.2 (0x40072000)
    libcrypt.so.1 => /lib/libcrypt.so.1 (0x40075000)
    libgd.so.1 => /usr/lib/libgd.so.1 (0x400a3000)
    libc.so.6 => /lib/libc.so.6 (0x400d9000)
    /lib/ld-linux.so.2 => /lib/ld-linux.so.2 (0x40000000)
```

Now complete Exercise 19.1, which gives you experience in using the ldd command.

Viewing Library References

Here's a simple puzzle that will give you an opportunity to use the ldd command. Use the ldd command to view library references associated with arbitrary executables in the /bin directory and /usr/bin directory. Can you see a pattern that distinguishes the source of the executables?

Specifying Library Paths

If the loader is unable to locate a library required by a program, it prints an error message and halts the loading process. If the library resides on the system, you can inform the loader of its location by setting the environment variable LD_LIBRARY_PATH. For example, to specify that the loader should search the directories /usr/local/lib and /usr/local/otherlib for required libraries, issue the command

```
export LD_LIBRARY_PATH=/usr/local/lib:/usr/local/otherlib
```

The specified directory or directories are searched in addition to the default directories, which therefore need not be explicitly specified.

Installing Shared Libraries

When you install an RPM package that includes a shared library, the installation script should automatically update the shared library configuration. However, if you install a non-RPM package you may need to revise the shared library configuration manually.

The shared library configuration resides in the file /etc/ld.so.conf, which contains a list of directories that contain shared libraries, one directory on each line. Here are the contents of a typical ld.so.conf file:

```
/usr/lib
/usr/i486-linux-libc5/lib
/usr/X11R6/lib
/usr/i486-linuxaout/lib
```

Notice that the main library shared directory, /lib, is not listed; if it could not be found, essentially no commands, including those needed to update the shared library configuration, would work. Therefore, the location of this library is built into the loader and need not be specified in the configuration file.

To add a directory to the shared library configuration, use a text editor to add a line specifying the directory name to /etc/ld.so.conf. Then, issue the command

```
ldconfig -v
```

The command is necessary, because the loader keeps a cache of directory and library names in the file /etc/ld.so.cache. The cache improves performance but must be rebuilt by the ldconfig command so that the loader will begin searching the newly specified directory.

Finding the Package Containing a Shared Library

When installing an RPM package, you may encounter an error message telling you that a required library is not available. Unfortunately, the name of the package that contains the required library may not be obvious. The following rather cryptic command may be helpful in such situations:

```
rpm -qp --filebypkg *.rpm \
   |grep '\.so' |sort > /tmp/liblist
```

The command places in the file /tmp/liblist a list of shared library files contained in package files residing in the current directory.

The Shared Library File Ownership Table, which you'll find on the companion CD, summarizes the output of this command when run against the contents of the RPMS directory of the Red Hat Linux distribution CD-ROM disk. You don't need to be familiar with the contents of this table to be prepared for the RHCE exam, but it will expedite installation of packages that require library support.

Under Red Hat Linux 6.2, you can access shared library file ownership information even more simply by installing the rpmdb-redhat package. You can then query the alternate RPM database for this information by issuing the command

```
rpm -q --redhatprovides <library pathname>
```

Summary

In this chapter, you learned about shared libraries. The most important topics covered are:

Program Forms   Programmers write source code, which a compiler translates into object code. Object code can be stored in a library for reuse.

Program Linking   A linker combines object code modules to create an executable program. A statically linked program does not refer to external libraries. A dynamically linked program refers to external libraries, which must be present when the program is run.

Linux Executables   Most Linux executables are organized using the structure called ELF (executable and linking format). Older executables may use the obsolete `a.out` structure.

Shared Libraries   The most important shared libraries are:

`/lib`   The main shared libraries

`/usr/lib`   Supplementary shared libraries

`/usr/i486-linux-libc5/lib`   Shared libraries for use with the old version of the C standard library, libc5

`/usr/X11R6/lib`   Shared libraries related to XFree86

`/usr/i486-linuxaout/lib`   The `a.out` shared libraries

The `ldd` Command   The `ldd` command lets you determine which shared libraries a program references.

The Library Path   The environment variable `LD_LIBRARY_PATH` specifies the library search path.

The Shared Library Configuration   The file `/etc/ld.so.conf` contains the shared library configuration, which consists of a list of installed libraries. You may need to revise the file if you install a non-RPM package or unpackaged software.

Querying RPM Package Files   You can query RPM packages files to determine which file, if any, contains a particular shared library.

Key Terms

Before going on to the next chapter, be sure you're familiar with the following terms:

a.out

compiler

dynamic loader

dynamically linked

ELF

library

linker

machine language

object code

source code

statically linked

stubs

Additional Sources of Information

If you'd like further information about the topics presented in this chapter, you should consult the following sources:

- *The ELF-HOWTO*, by Daniel Barlow, /usr/doc/HOWTO/ELF-HOWTO

- The man pages for ldd and ldconfig

Review Questions

1. Which of the following is an advantage of static linking in comparison to dynamic linking?

   A. Errors in library routines are easier to correct.

   B. Executables occupy less disk space.

   C. License restrictions of libraries may not apply.

   D. Programs run faster.

2. The predominant form of Linux executables is which of the following?

   A. `a.out`

   B. COFF

   C. ELF

   D. iBCS

3. Which of the following names has the proper form for a standard symbolic link to a shared library?

   A. `library.so`

   B. `library.so.3`

   C. `library.so.3.2`

   D. `library.so.3.2.1`

4. Which of the following names has the proper form for a shared library name?

   A. `library.so.1`

   B. `library.so.1.2`

   C. `library-1.2.so`

   D. `library-1.2.3.so`

5. To determine which shared libraries are accessed by a program, what is the command that must be issued?

    A. ld

    B. ld.so

    C. ldconfig

    D. ldd

6. The environment variable that establishes a supplementary set of library paths is which of the following?

    A. LD_LIBRARY_PATH

    B. LD_SO_PATH

    C. LIBRARY_PATH

    D. SO_PATH

7. Which of the following is not a directory that appears in the shared library configuration file?

    A. /lib

    B. /lib/i486-linux-libc5/lib

    C. /usr/lib

    D. /usr/lib/X11R6/lib

Answers to Review Questions

1. C, D. Statically linked programs may not be subject to the license restrictions that affect the related library. They run slightly faster than dynamically linked programs, but the difference is seldom significant.

2. C. The predominant form of Linux executables is ELF; some older executables use the `a.out` format.

3. A, B. The symbolic link includes the library name or the library name and major version; it does not include the minor version or patch level.

4. C, D. The name of a shared library must end with `.so` and can omit reference to the minor version or minor version and patch level.

5. D. The `ldd` command prints the shared libraries to which an executable is bound.

6. A. The environment variable that sets up a supplementary shared library search path is `LD_LIBRARY_PATH`.

7. A. The `/lib` directory is essential and therefore is not explicit in the shared library configuration file.

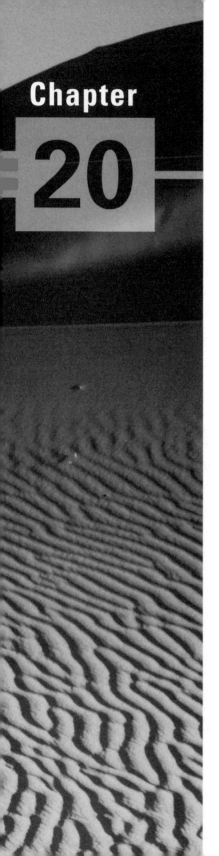

Chapter

20

Working in Single-User and Rescue Mode

RHCE PREPARATION TOPICS COVERED IN THIS CHAPTER:

✓ Be able to use single-user and rescue modes for system recovery.

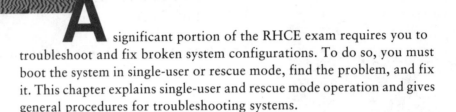

A significant portion of the RHCE exam requires you to troubleshoot and fix broken system configurations. To do so, you must boot the system in single-user or rescue mode, find the problem, and fix it. This chapter explains single-user and rescue mode operation and gives general procedures for troubleshooting systems.

System Recovery

From time to time, you may attempt to boot a Linux system only to find that the system won't boot. You may see error messages pointing to problems such as:

- Missing or corrupt LILO installation
- Kernel panic
- Missing or corrupt kernel
- Damaged file system
- Inability to enter runlevel 2, 3, or 5
- Unknown root password

To fix the system, you must boot it. Unless the system is suffering from a hardware problem, you'll probably be able to boot it using either single-user mode or rescue mode. Once you succeed in booting the system, you can study its configuration files and logs to determine the cause of the problem, fix the problem, and reboot the system. The next section explains single-user mode and single-user mode recovery procedures. The following section explains rescue mode and rescue mode recovery procedures.

Single-User Mode

Single-user mode provides a simple way to recover from problems that do not affect LILO, the kernel, or the root file system. Problems with non–root file systems, runlevels, and failing services can often be repaired in single-user mode.

Entering Single-User Mode

To enter single-user mode, respond *linux* **single** or *linux* **emergency** at the boot prompt, where *linux* is the label associated with your kernel in the LILO configuration file. If you prefer a shorter response, you can type *linux* **s**, which is equivalent to *linux* **single**.

The boot parameter—**s**, **single**, or **emergency**–is passed to the **init** process, which places the system in single-user mode when system startup is complete. If you specify the **emergency** parameter, **init** also omits loading of initial processes; this option is helpful if your `/etc/inittab` file is incorrect.

The system does not prompt for a password, but places you in a shell with **root** privileges.

Because anyone with access to the system console can boot a system in single-user mode and obtain privileged access, you should maintain good physical security of computer systems. Alternatively, you can configure the system BIOS to boot only from the hard drive, restrict access to the system BIOS, lock the system case, and configure LILO to restrict access to single-user mode.

The Single-User Mode Environment

When you enter single-user mode as explained in the preceding subsection, only the root file system is mounted, and the PATH environment variable may not be set to its usual value. Therefore, you may need to type the full path name of commands you want to execute. You won't initially have access to commands stored in `/usr/bin` and `/usr/sbin`, for example; only commands residing in `/bin` and `/sbin` are available.

Configuration Files to Examine

Generally, when a system fails to properly boot, it has been wrongly configured. You have—or another system administrator has—made an error in revising a configuration file or using `linuxconf` or another configuration utility. Here are some configuration files that you should examine in your search for the problem:

- `/etc/conf.modules`
- `/etc/fstab`
- `/etc/inittab`
- `/etc/lilo.conf`
- `/etc/rc.d/*`
- `/etc/yp.conf`, if the system uses Network Information Service (NIS)

Pay particular attention to `/etc/fstab` and `/etc/lilo.conf`, which—when wrongly configured—are common causes of system startup problems.

General Single-User Mode Procedure

Here's a general troubleshooting procedure for single-user mode:

1. Boot in single-user mode by responding *linux* **s** to the boot prompt image label where *linux* denotes the label associated with the kernel image to be loaded.

2. When the system is booted, you'll have access to a `bash` shell session that has only the root partition mounted.

3. Identify the available partitions: `fdisk -l`.

4. Check the non–root file systems: `e2fsck -y /dev/xxx`, where *xxx* is the partition on which the root file system resides.

5. If LILO is damaged or missing, mount the /**boot** partition: `mount /dev/xxx /boot`, where *xxx* is the partition on which the root file system resides.

6. Find and fix any wrongly configured facilities. Be sure to check `/etc/lilo.conf` and `/etc/fstab`.

7. If `/etc/lilo.conf` or the kernel has changed, run the `lilo` map installer: `/sbin/lilo`.

8. Reboot the computer: `shutdown -r now`.

Now practice working in single-user mode, by completing Exercise 20.1.

EXERCISE 20.1

Using Single-User Mode

It's important that you be skilled in using single-user mode, which you'll probably find useful in the troubleshooting portion of the RHCE exam. To gain experience in using single-user mode, perform these steps:

1. Boot a system in single-user mode.

2. Identify the available disk partitions.

3. Check the integrity of the non–root file systems.

4. Mount the /boot partition and run the LILO map installer.

5. Reboot the system.

If you need to look back to the chapter or access other documentation, feel free to do so. But, before taking the RHCE exam, be sure you can perform operations such as these without resorting to help.

Rescue Mode

Rescue mode is useful when you cannot boot a system, even in single-user mode. Rescue mode supplies a root file system taken from a ramdisk image, so you have access to common shell commands even if no partitions on the system's hard disk can be mounted. With skill and insight, you can use these commands to find and fix the problem.

Preparing Rescue Mode Media

Prior to Red Hat Linux 6.1, the distribution media contained the file rescue.img, which held a ramdisk image suitable for mounting as a root file system. To enter rescue mode, you had to create a floppy disk containing the ramdisk image. The floppy was loaded as the root file system in response to a special boot prompt reply.

However, in Red Hat Linux 6.1 and later, the standard installation media provide for rescue mode, so no special floppy disk is required. Nevertheless, many Red Hat Linux users prefer the Red Hat Linux 6.0 approach to rescue mode. If you have a Red Hat Linux 6.0 distribution CD-ROM, you can follow the procedure in the next subsection to use the Red Hat Linux 6.0 rescue facility.

To use the Red Hat Linux 6.1 rescue facility, boot the system by using the installation floppy disk or the installation CD-ROM. In response to the boot prompt, reply `linux rescue`.

The rescue facility will ask you to choose your language and keyboard style. It will then attempt to locate the RPMS and `base` directories of the Red Hat Linux distribution media. If the system's CD-ROM drive contains a distribution CD-ROM, the system will enter rescue mode. Otherwise, the rescue facility will prompt you for the location of these directories, which may be a CD-ROM drive or local hard drive. Generally, you should insert an installation CD-ROM in the CD-ROM drive and direct the rescue mode facility to that device. However, if the system contains a readable file system holding the RPMS and `base` directories, you can direct the rescue facility to the partition on which the file system resides.

You can use a bootnet.img floppy as a rescue disk, obtaining the rescue environment from a suitably configured NFS server.

Using the Red Hat Linux 6.0 Rescue Facility

The Red Hat Linux 6.0 rescue facility is not supported by Red Hat Linux 6.2 and later. Therefore, use of the Red Hat Linux 6.0 rescue facility is no longer allowed during the RHCE exam. However, if you're responsible for administering Red Hat Linux 6.0 systems, you need to know how to use this facility.

To use the Red Hat Linux 6.0 rescue facility, you must create a boot disk and rescue disk from images on the Red Hat Linux distribution CD-ROM. Alternatively, you can use your system's boot disk and create only the rescue disk.

Creating the Boot Disk

To create a boot disk from the image on the Red Hat Linux distribution CD-ROM, insert the media, mount the CD-ROM as /mnt/cdrom, and issue the following command:

```
dd if=/mnt/cdrom/images/boot.img of=/dev/fd0
```

The boot disk contains the kernel and all modules necessary to boot the system. If you prefer, you can use a boot disk created from your system by issuing the mkbootdisk command.

Creating the Rescue Disk

To create the rescue disk from the image on the Red Hat Linux distribution CD-ROM, insert the media, mount the CD-ROM as /mnt/cdrom, and issue the following command:

```
dd if=/mnt/cdrom/images/rescue.img of=/dev/fd0
```

The ramdisk image includes a root file system that supports important recovery commands.

Booting in Rescue Mode

To boot a system using Red Hat Linux 6.0, insert the boot disk in the floppy drive and start the system. In response to the boot prompt, type **linux rescue**. When prompted, replace the boot disk with the rescue disk. When booting completes, you'll find yourself in a single-user shell that resembles that provided by the current Red Hat Linux rescue mode.

The Rescue Mode Environment

The commands available in rescue mode are a small subset of those generally available under Red Hat Linux. They include:

anaconda	gzip	mkfs.ext2	ps
badblocks	head	mknod	python
bash	hwclock	mkraid	python1.5
cat	ifconfig	mkswap	raidstart
chatter	init	mlabel	raidstop
chmod	insmod	mmd	rcp
chroot	less	mmount	rlogin
clock	ln	mmove	rm
collage	loader	modprobe	rmmod
cp	ls	mount	route
cpio	lsattr	mpartition	rpm

dd	lsmod	mrd	rsh
ddcprobe	mattrib	mread	sed
depmode	mbadblocks	mren	sh
df	mcd	mshowfat	sync
e2fsck	mcopy	mt	tac
fdisk	mdel	mtools	tail
fsck	mdeltree	mtype	tar
fsck.ext2	mdir	mv	touch
ftp	mdu	mzip	traceroute
genhdlist	mformat	open	unmount
gnome-pty-helper	minfo	pico	uncpio
grep	mkdir	ping	uniq
gunzip	mke2fs	probe	zcat

This subsection highlights several especially useful commands, explaining how they're useful in troubleshooting and recovery.

The *fdisk* Command

The fdisk command will tell you what partitions exist on local hard drives. You need to know this information in order to know what partitions to check and then mount. To report the existing partitions on local hard drives, issue the command

```
fdisk -l
```

The partition type will help you determine the partitions of interest. Here's typical output of fdisk:

```
Disk /dev/hda: 255 heads, 63 sectors, 2489 cylinders
Units = cylinders of 16065 * 512 bytes

   Device Boot    Start      End      Blocks   Id  System
/dev/hda1   *         1      127     1020096    6  FAT16
/dev/hda2           128     2489    18972765    5  Extended
/dev/hda5           128      132       40131   83  Linux
/dev/hda6           133      387     2048256   83  Linux
/dev/hda7          1091     1157      538146   82 Linux swap
```

In the example, partitions `hda5` and `hda6` are Linux partitions that you'd want to check and possibly mount.

The *e2fsck* Command

The `e2fsck` command checks a Linux file system for damage and, optionally, repairs simple damage. To check a file system, issue a command of the form

```
e2fsck -y /dev/xxx
```

where *xxx* is the partition that contains the file system. The `-y` flag instructs `e2fsck` to automatically attempt to repair damage, rather than prompt you for each error found; without the flag, the command can become tiresome when a file system contains numerous errors.

Linux stores information about file systems in special areas called *superblocks*. If a file system is corrupt, you can sometimes recover it by instructing Linux to use an alternate superblock. To do so, you must know the location of the alternate superblock; usually they are written at intervals of 8192 blocks, so the first alternate superblock is likely to be located in block 8193. To instruct `e2fsck` to attempt to recover a file system by using superblock 8193, issue a command of the form

```
e2fsck -b 8193 -y /dev/xxx
```

where *xxx* is the partition that contains the file system.

When a large file system is created, sparse superblocks may be used. Sparse superblocks are written at intervals of 32768 blocks. Therefore, the first alternate sparse superblock resides in block 32769.

You can use the `dumpe2fs` command to learn the location of alternate superblocks of an undamaged file system. If you're concerned about the possibility of file system damage, you should run the command on each of your file systems and retain the output so that it's available during recovery procedures. Here's typical output of the `dumpe2fs` command:

```
dumpe2fs 1.14, 9-Jan-1999 for EXT2 FS 0.5b, 95/08/09
Filesystem volume name:    boot
Last mounted on:           <not available>
Filesystem UUID:           c10e5c68-d5a7-11d3-93c2-
8a83fd607d
Filesystem magic number:   0xEF53
Filesystem revision #:     0 (original)
Filesystem features:       (none)
```

```
Filesystem state:          not clean
Errors behavior:           Continue
Filesystem OS type:        Linux
Inode count:               10040
Block count:               40131
Reserved block count:      2006
Free blocks:               36575
Free inodes:               10016
First block:               1
Block size:                1024
Fragment size:             1024
Blocks per group:          8192
Fragments per group:       8192
Inodes per group:          2008
Inode blocks per group:    251
Last mount time:           Fri Mar  3 11:54:29 2000
Last write time:           Wed Apr 19 14:21:06 2000
Mount count:               1
Maximum mount count:       20
Last checked:              Fri Mar  3 11:45:58 2000
Check interval:            15552000 (6 months)
Next check after:          Wed Aug 30 12:45:58 2000
Reserved blocks uid:       0 (user root)
Reserved blocks gid:       0 (group root)

Group 0: (Blocks 1 -- 8192)
  Block bitmap at 3 (+2), Inode bitmap at 4 (+3)
  Inode table at 5 (+4)
  5657 free blocks, 1984 free inodes, 2 directories
  Free blocks: 2521-2536, 2552-8192
  Free inodes: 25-2008
Group 1: (Blocks 8193 -- 16384)
  Block bitmap at 8195 (+2), Inode bitmap at 8196 (+3)
  Inode table at 8197 (+4)
  7937 free blocks, 2008 free inodes, 0 directories
  Free blocks: 8448-16384
  Free inodes: 2009-4016
Group 2: (Blocks 16385 -- 24576)
  Block bitmap at 16387 (+2), Inode bitmap at 16388 (+3)
```

```
    Inode table at 16389 (+4)
    7937 free blocks, 2008 free inodes, 0 directories
Free blocks: 16640-24576
    Free inodes: 4017-6024
  Group 3: (Blocks 24577 -- 32768)
    Block bitmap at 24579 (+2), Inode bitmap at 24580 (+3)
    Inode table at 24581 (+4)
    7937 free blocks, 2008 free inodes, 0 directories
    Free blocks: 24832-32768
    Free inodes: 6025-8032
  Group 4: (Blocks 32769 -- 40130)
    Block bitmap at 32771 (+2), Inode bitmap at 32772 (+3)
    Inode table at 32773 (+4)
    7107 free blocks, 2008 free inodes, 0 directories
    Free blocks: 33024-40130
    Free inodes: 8033-10040
```

The first block of each group is a superblock. Therefore, the file system shown in the example output has superblocks at blocks 1, 8193, 16385, 24577, and 32769. If the primary superblock at block 1 is damaged, one of the alternate superblocks may be intact.

The *lilo* Command

The lilo command installs the LILO boot loader and updates the boot map. Normally, you perform these operations by issuing the command

```
/sbin/lilo
```

However, when operating in rescue mode, the root file system of the local hard disk is not mounted as the root directory. Running lilo in the usual way would not properly update the /**boot** directory of the local hard drive. Instead, you should issue a command of the form

```
/sbin/lilo -r path
```

where *path* is the current mount point of the root file system of the local hard drive. For example, if the root file system of the local hard drive is mounted as /mnt/hd, issue the command

```
/sbin/lilo -r /mnt/hd
```

Alternatively, you can issue the `chroot` command to establish a changed-root environment and then issue the `lilo` command in the ordinary manner:

```
chroot /mnt/hd
/sbin/lilo
```

The *sync* Command

When operating in rescue mode, you generally cannot shut down the system in the usual, orderly way by using the `shutdown` command. However, if you abruptly power off or reset the system, you may corrupt one or more file systems. So, a modified shutdown procedure must be used.

When you're ready to restart the system, issue a sequence of commands of the following form:

```
sync
sync
sync
cd /
umount fs1 fs2 ...
```

where *fs1*, *fs2*, ... represent mounted file systems of the local hard drive. When the umount command completes, you can power off or reset the system.

WARNING   The /dev directory in the rescue mode environment may not include device files for devices you want to access. The rescue-mode mount command can sometimes create the proper device file automatically; but, if you're having trouble accessing a device, you may need to issue the mknod command to create the proper device file.

Configuration Files to Examine

The files suggested for examination in single-user mode are relevant for examination in rescue mode:

- /etc/conf.modules
- /etc/fstab
- /etc/inittab

- `/etc/lilo.conf`
- `/etc/rc.d/*`
- `/etc/yp.conf`, if the system uses NIS

As in single-user mode, pay particular attention to `/etc/fstab` and `/etc/lilo.conf`, which—when wrongly configured—are common causes of system startup problems.

General Rescue Mode Recovery Procedure

Here's a general troubleshooting procedure for rescue mode:

1. Boot from a system boot disk or the installation CD-ROM. Respond **linux rescue** to the prompt for the boot image label. When the system is booted, you'll have access to a `bash` shell session that has no mounted local file systems—that is, no file systems from the hard drive.

2. Create a mount point for the local file systems: `mkdir /mnt/hd`.

3. Identify the available partitions: `fdisk -l`.

4. Check the root file system: `e2fsck -y /dev/xxx`, where *xxx* is the partition on which the root file system resides. You may need to first create the device file by issuing the command `mknod /dev/xxx`.

5. Mount the root file system: `mount /dev/xxx /mnt/hd`, where *xxx* is the partition on which the root file system resides.

6. Establish a changed-root environment, making your work more convenient: `chroot /mnt/hd`.

7. If LILO is damaged or missing, mount the `/boot` partition: `mount /dev/xxx /boot`, where *xxx* is the partition on which the root file system resides.

8. Fix any wrongly configured facilities by using the `pico` editor. Be sure to check `/etc/lilo.conf` and `/etc/fstab`.

9. If `/etc/lilo.conf` or the kernel has changed, run the `lilo` map installer: `/sbin/lilo`.

10. Commit the changes: `sync; sync; sync`.

11. Unmount any mounted file systems: `cd /; umount /boot`.

12. Reset the computer.

Now complete Exercise 20.2 to gain experience working in rescue mode.

EXERCISE 20.2

Using Rescue Mode

Properly configured Linux systems seldom fail. But when they do, skill in using rescue mode is important to troubleshoot and fix the problem. To gain experience working in rescue mode, perform the following steps:

1. Boot a system in rescue mode.

2. Identify the available disk partitions.

3. Check the integrity of the root file system and then mount it.

4. Check the integrity of the non–root file systems.

5. Mount the /boot partition, and run the LILO map installer.

6. Commit your changes, and reboot the system.

You can use this book and other help to complete the exercise. But, before taking the RHCE exam, be sure that you can perform operations such as these without resorting to books or notes.

Summary

In this chapter, you learned about working in single-user and rescue modes. The most important topics covered are:

Single-User Mode You can boot Linux in single-user mode by typing *linux* **s**, *linux* **single**, or *linux* **emergency** in response to the LILO prompt. Single-user mode is used to troubleshoot or repair a system. The root file system must be intact for a system to successfully boot in single-user mode.

Rescue Mode You can boot Linux in rescue mode by booting from installation media and typing **rescue** in response to the boot prompt. Previous to Red Hat Linux 6.1, you had to boot by using a special rescue disk. Rescue mode provides only a limited set of available programs.

Important Files   When a system does not boot properly, you can boot it in single-user mode and check the following configuration files as possible causes of the problem:

- `/etc/conf.modules`
- `/etc/fstab`
- `/etc/inittab`
- `/etc/lilo.conf`
- `/etc/rc.d/*`
- `/etc/yp.conf`, if the system uses NIS

Checking File Systems   To check a Linux native file system for errors, or to repair errors, use the `e2fsck` utility. When invoked with appropriate options, the `fsck` utility invokes `e2fsck`.

Leaving Rescue Mode   The usual shutdown commands are not available in rescue mode. You must issue the `sync` and `umount` commands before shutting down a system operating in rescue mode.

Key Terms

Before going on to the next chapter, be sure you're familiar with the following terms:

rescue mode

single-user mode

superblocks

Additional Sources of Information

If you'd like further information about the topics presented in this chapter, you should consult *The Official Red Hat Linux Reference Guide.*

Review Questions

1. Which of the following files is a likely source of configuration errors that could prevent a system from properly starting up?

   A. /etc/fstab

   B. /etc/hosts

   C. /etc/inittab

   D. /etc/lilo.conf

2. To shut down a system operating in single-user mode, what should be done?

   A. Issue the shutdown command

   B. Issue the sync and umount commands

   C. Press the system reset button

   D. Turn off the power

3. To update the LILO boot map in rescue mode, which of the following commands should be issued?

   A. /sbin/lilo

   B. /sbin/lilo -v

   C. /sbin/lilo -r /mnt/boot

   D. /sbin/lilo /etc/lilo.conf

4. To list the existing partitions of the local hard drives, which of the following should be issued?

   A. fdisk -l

   B. fdisk -p

   C. fdisk -lp

   D. fdisk -r

5. To check the Linux partition /dev/hdb2 for errors, which of the following commands should be issued?

A. e2fsck /dev/hdb2

B. e2fsck -y /dev/hdb2

C. e2fsck -y -b /dev/hdb2

D. e2fsck -y -b 8193 /dev/hdb2

6. When recovering a system by using rescue mode, when should you mount the /boot partition?

A. Always

B. Only if it resides on the first hard drive

C. Only if you need to check its file system

D. Only if you need to run the LILO boot map installer

7. Unless sparse superblocks are used, the Linux file system generally stores a backup superblock in which block?

A. 1

B. 4097

C. 8193

D. 16385

Answers to Review Questions

1. A, C, D. The /etc/hosts file is unlikely to prevent a system from properly starting up, though it may prevent proper operation.

2. A. The sync and umount commands are used to shut down a system operating in rescue mode. You should not shut down a Linux system by turning off power or resetting the system.

3. C. You must use the -r flag to tell lilo that the root directory of the local hard drive is not mounted as the current root directory.

4. A. The -l parameter directs fdisk to report on local hard drives.

5. A, B, D. The -b flag requires an argument specifying an alternate superblock. It instructs e2fsck to attempt recovery using the alternate superblock.

6. D. You don't need to mount a file system in order to check it; mount the /boot file system only if you need to update the boot map.

7. C. Superblocks are generally stored every 8192 blocks; the primary superblock is in block 1. With sparse superblocks, superblocks appear every 32K, so the backup superblock is found at 32769.

Network Services Administration

## PART IV

Chapter

21

Installing and Configuring Primary Network Services

RHCE PREPARATION TOPICS COVERED IN THIS CHAPTER:

✓ Understand and be capable of installing and configuring: Apache, BIND (DNS), FTP, Mail (sendmail and pop/imap), NFS, and Samba.

✓ Be sufficiently familiar with the function, configuration, and logging of primary network services as to be capable of basic troubleshooting.

his chapter is one of the most important chapters of this book—perhaps the most important chapter—from the standpoint of your preparation for the RHCE exam. One of the three RHCE exam components requires you to install and configure a specified set of network services. Your ability to excel in that component of the exam depends upon your grasp of the material in this chapter, which explains primary network services and how to install, configure, and troubleshoot them.

The key to this chapter and the related component of the RHCE exam is the chapter exercises. You should resolve to complete every step of every exercise in this chapter. Sometimes an exercise will lead you into study of man pages or other documentation. This is an essential part of the exercises. The ability to access and interpret system documentation distinguishes the experienced system administrator from the inexperienced system administrator. Your skill in using documentation will help you cope with unexpected problems that arise during the RHCE exam.

This first section of the chapter provides basic information about TCP/IP services. Subsequent sections explain the primary Linux TCP/IP services.

TCP/IP Services

All primary Linux network services are TCP/IP services—that is, services based on the TCP/IP family of protocols. A TCP/IP service has an associated number known as a *port*; ports are numbered from 0 to 65535. The ports of common TCP/IP services are termed *well-known ports*; the file /etc /services contains a list of these ports, which is given in Table 21.1.

TABLE 21.1 Well-Known Services and Their Ports

Service	Port/Type	Comment
tcpmux	1/tcp	TCP port service multiplexer
rtmp	1/ddp	Routing Table Maintenance Protocol
nbp	2/ddp	Name Binding Protocol
echo	4/ddp	AppleTalk Echo Protocol
zip	6/ddp	Zone Information Protocol
echo	7/tcp	
echo	7/udp	
discard	9/tcp	sink null
discard	9/udp	sink null
systat	11/tcp	users
daytime	13/tcp	
daytime	13/udp	
netstat	15/tcp	
qotd	17/tcp	quote
msp	18/tcp	message send protocol
msp	18/udp	message send protocol
chargen	19/tcp	ttytst source
chargen	19/udp	ttytst source
ftp-data	20/tcp	
ftp	21/tcp	

TABLE 21.1 Well-Known Services and Their Ports *(continued)*

Service	Port/Type	Comment
fsp	21/udp	fspd
ssh	22/tcp	SSH Remote Login Protocol
ssh	22/udp	SSH Remote Login Protocol
telnet	23/tcp	
smtp	25/tcp	mail
time	37/tcp	timeserver
time	37/udp	timeserver
rlp	39/udp	resource location
nameserver	42/tcp	name (IEN 116)
whois	43/tcp	nicname
re-mail-ck	50/tcp	Remote Mail Checking Protocol
re-mail-ck	50/udp	Remote Mail Checking Protocol
domain	53/tcp	nameserver
domain	53/udp	nameserver
mtp	57/tcp	deprecated
bootps	67/tcp	BOOTP server
bootps	67/udp	
bootpc	68/tcp	BOOTP client
bootpc	68/udp	
tftp	69/udp	

TABLE 21.1 Well-Known Services and Their Ports *(continued)*

Service	Port/Type	Comment
gopher	70/tcp	Internet Gopher
gopher	70/udp	
rje	77/tcp	netrjs
finger	79/tcp	
www	80/tcp	http
www	80/udp	HyperText Transfer Protocol
link	87/tcp	ttylink
kerberos	88/tcp	kerberos5 krb5
kerberos	88/udp	kerberos5 krb5
supdup	95/tcp	
linuxconf	98/tcp	
hostnames	101/tcp	hostname
iso-tsap	102/tcp	tsap
csnet-ns	105/tcp	cso-ns
csnet-ns	105/udp	cso-ns
poppassd	106/tcp	Eudora
poppassd	106/udp	Eudora
rtelnet	107/tcp	Remote Telnet
rtelnet	107/udp	
pop-2	109/tcp	postoffice

TABLE 21.1 Well-Known Services and Their Ports *(continued)*

Service	Port/Type	Comment
pop-2	109/udp	
pop-3	110/tcp	POP version 3
pop-3	110/udp	
sunrpc	111/tcp	portmapper
sunrpc	111/udp	portmapper
auth	113/tcp	authentication tap ident
sftp	115/tcp	
uucp-path	117/tcp	
nntp	119/tcp	readnews untp
ntp	123/tcp	
ntp	123/udp	Network Time Protocol
netbios-ns	137/tcp	NETBIOS Name Service
netbios-ns	137/udp	
netbios-dgm	138/tcp	NETBIOS Datagram Service
netbios-dgm	138/udp	
netbios-ssn	139/tcp	NETBIOS Session Service
netbios-ssn	139/udp	
imap2	143/tcp	imap
imap2	143/udp	imap
snmp	161/udp	Simple Net Mgmt Protocol

TABLE 21.1 Well-Known Services and Their Ports *(continued)*

Service	Port/Type	Comment
snmp-trap	162/udp	snmptrap
cmip-man	163/tcp	ISO management over IP (CMOT)
cmip-man	163/udp	
cmip-agent	164/tcp	
cmip-agent	164/udp	
mailq	174/tcp	Mailer transport queue for Zmailer
mailq	174/tcp	Mailer transport queue for Zmailer
xdmcp	177/tcp	X Display Manager Control Protocol
xdmcp	177/udp	
nextstep	178/tcp	NeXTStep NextStep
nextstep	178/udp	NeXTStep NextStep
bgp	179/tcp	Border Gateway Protocol
bgp	179/udp	
prospero	191/tcp	Cliff Neuman's Prospero
prospero	191/udp	
irc	194/tcp	Internet Relay Chat
irc	194/udp	
smux	199/tcp	SNMP Unix Multiplexer
smux	199/udp	
at-rtmp	201/tcp	AppleTalk routing
at-rtmp	201/udp	
at-nbp	202/tcp	AppleTalk name binding

TABLE 21.1   Well-Known Services and Their Ports *(continued)*

Service	Port/Type	Comment
at-nbp	202/udp	
at-echo	204/tcp	AppleTalk echo
at-echo	204/udp	
at-zis	206/tcp	AppleTalk zone information
at-zis	206/udp	
qmtp	209/tcp	The Quick Mail Transfer Protocol
qmtp	209/udp	The Quick Mail Transfer Protocol
z3950	210/tcp	wais # NISO Z39.50 database
z3950	210/udp	wais
ipx	213/tcp	IPX
ipx	213/udp	
imap3	220/tcp	Interactive Mail Access
imap3	220/udp	Protocol v3
rpc2portmap	369/tcp	
rpc2portmap	369/udp	Coda portmapper
codaauth2	370/tcp	
codaauth2	370/udp	Coda authentication server
ulistserv	372/tcp	Unix Listserv
ulistserv	372/udp	
https	443/tcp	MCom
https	443/udp	MCom
snpp	444/tcp	Simple Network Paging Protocol

TABLE 21.1 Well-Known Services and Their Ports *(continued)*

Service	Port/Type	Comment
snpp	444/udp	Simple Network Paging Protocol
ssmtp	465/tcp	SMTP over SSL
saft	487/tcp	Simple Asynchronous File Transfer
saft	487/udp	Simple Asynchronous File Transfer
exec	512/tcp	
biff	512/udp	comsat
login	513/tcp	
who	513/udp	whod
shell	514/tcp	cmd
syslog	514/udp	
printer	515/tcp	spooler
talk	517/udp	
ntalk	518/udp	
route	520/udp	router routed
timed	525/udp	timeserver
tempo	526/tcp	newdate
courier	530/tcp	rpc
conference	531/tcp	chat
netnews	532/tcp	readnews
netwall	533/udp	for emergency broadcasts
gdomap	538/tcp	GNUstep distributed objects
gdomap	538/udp	GNUstep distributed objects

TABLE 21.1   Well-Known Services and Their Ports *(continued)*

Service	Port/Type	Comment
uucp	540/tcp	uucpd
afpovertcp	548/tcp	AFP over TCP
afpovertcp	548/udp	AFP over TCP
remotefs	556/tcp	rfs_server rfs
klogin	543/tcp	Kerberized rlogin
kshell	544/tcp	krcmd
snews	563/tcp	NNTP over SSL
npmp-local	610/tcp	dqs313_qmaster
npmp-local	610/udp	dqs313_qmaster
npmp-gui	611/tcp	dqs313_execd
npmp-gui	611/udp	dqs313_execd
hmmp-ind	612/tcp	dqs313_intercell
hmmp-ind	612/udp	dqs313_intercell
ssl-ldap	636/tcp	LDAP over SSL
kerberos-adm	749/tcp	Kerberos kadmin
kerberos4	750/udp	kerberos-iv kdc
kerberos4	750/tcp	kerberos-iv kdc
kerberos_master	751/udp	Kerberos authentication
kerberos_master	751/tcp	Kerberos authentication
passwd_server	752/udp	Kerberos passwd server
krb_prop	754/tcp	Kerberos slave propagation
krbupdate	760/tcp	kreg

TABLE 21.1   Well-Known Services and Their Ports *(continued)*

Service	Port/Type	Comment
kpasswd	761/tcp	kpwd
webster	765/tcp	Network dictionary
webster	765/udp	
omirr	808/tcp	omirrd
omirr	808/udp	omirrd
supfilesrv	871/tcp	SUP server
rsync	873/tcp	rsync
rsync	873/udp	rsync
simap	993/tcp	IMAP over SSL
spop3	995/tcp	POP-3 over SSL
socks	1080/tcp	socks proxy server
socks	1080/udp	socks proxy server
kpop	1109/tcp	Pop with Kerberos
supfiledbg	1127/tcp	SUP debugging
rmtcfg	1236/tcp	Gracilis Packeten remote config server
xtel	1313/tcp	french minitel
ingreslock	1524/tcp	
ingreslock	1524/udp	
prospero-np	1525/tcp	Prospero non-privileged
prospero-np	1525/udp	
support	1529/tcp	GNATS

TABLE 21.1 Well-Known Services and Their Ports *(continued)*

Service	Port/Type	Comment
datametrics	1645/tcp	old-radius
datametrics	1645/udp	old-radius
sa-msg-port	1646/tcp	old-radacct
sa-msg-port	1646/udp	old-radacct
radius	1812/tcp	Radius
radius	1812/udp	Radius
radacct	1813/tcp	Radius Accounting
radacct	1813/udp	Radius Accounting
cfinger	2003/tcp	GNU Finger
knetd	2053/tcp	Kerberos de-multiplexor
zephyr-srv	2102/udp	Zephyr server
zephyr-clt	2103/udp	Zephyr serv-hm connection
zephyr-hm	2104/udp	Zephyr hostmanager
eklogin	2105/tcp	Kerberos encrypted rlogin
ninstall	2150/tcp	ninstall
ninstall	2150/udp	ninstall
cvspserver	2401/tcp	CVS client/server operations
cvspserver	2401/udp	CVS client/server operations
venus	2430/tcp	codacon port
venus	2430/udp	Venus callback/wbc interface
venus-se	2431/tcp	tcp side effects
venus-se	2431/udp	udp sftp side effect

TABLE 21.1 Well-Known Services and Their Ports *(continued)*

Service	Port/Type	Comment
codasrv	2432/tcp	not used
codasrv	2432/udp	server port
codasrv-se	2433/tcp	tcp side effects
codasrv-se	2433/udp	udp sftp side effect
afbackup	2988/tcp	Afbackup system
afbackup	2988/udp	Afbackup system
icp	3130/tcp	Internet Cache Protocol (Squid)
icp	3130/udp	Internet Cache Protocol (Squid)
mysql	3306/tcp	MySQL
mysql	3306/udp	MySQL
fax	4557/tcp	FAX transmission service (old)
hylafax	4559/tcp	HylaFAX client-server protocol (new)
rfe	5002/tcp	Radio Free Ethernet
rfe	5002/udp	Actually uses UDP only
cfengine	5308/tcp	CFengine
cfengine	5308/udp	CFengine
noclog	5354/tcp	noclogd with TCP
noclog	5354/udp	noclogd with UDP
hostmon	5355/tcp	hostmon uses TCP
hostmon	5355/udp	hostmon uses TCP
postgres	5432/tcp	POSTGRES

TABLE 21.1 Well-Known Services and Their Ports *(continued)*

Service	Port/Type	Comment
postgres	5432/udp	POSTGRES
ircd	6667/tcp	Internet Relay Chat
ircd	6667/udp	Internet Relay Chat
bbs	7000/tcp	BBS service
webcache	8080/tcp	WWW caching service
webcache	8080/udp	WWW caching service
tproxy	8081/tcp	Transparent Proxy
tproxy	8081/udp	Transparent Proxy
mandelspawn	9359/udp	mandelbrot
amanda	10080/udp	amanda backup services
kamanda	10081/tcp	amanda backup services (Kerberos)
kamanda	10081/udp	amanda backup services (Kerberos)
amandaidx	10082/tcp	amanda backup services
amidxtape	10083/tcp	amanda backup services
isdnlog	20011/tcp	isdn logging system
isdnlog	20011/udp	isdn logging system
vboxd	20012/tcp	voice box system
vboxd	20012/udp	voice box system
binkp	24554/tcp	Binkley
binkp	24554/udp	Binkley
asp	27374/tcp	Address Search Protocol

TABLE 21.1 Well-Known Services and Their Ports *(continued)*

Service	Port/Type	Comment
asp	27374/udp	Address Search Protocol
tfido	60177/tcp	Ifmail
tfido	60177/udp	Ifmail
fido	60179/tcp	Ifmail
fido	60179/udp	Ifmail

Under Linux, only privileged users can access ports 0 to 1023, which are therefore known as *privileged ports*. This restriction improves system security by preventing a non-privileged user from substituting a phony service in place of a real one. When a client accesses a service bound to a privileged port, the client has some confidence that the service has not been compromised.

To understand how port numbers are used, consider how you address mail to someone living in an apartment: you write the street address and an apartment number. An IP number resembles the street address in this analogy: many services may be available on the host bound to the IP number. A port number identifies a particular service in much the same way that an apartment number identifies a particular unit within an apartment complex.

When a client accesses a service, the client uses a port on the client host. To pass information to the client, the server uses the client host's IP address and the client's port number. Thus, four elements are involved in communication between a client and server:

- The server host IP address

- The server port

- The client host IP address

- The client port

Collectively, these elements are referred to as a *socket*.

Accessing a service involves a standard process, called the *bind-listen-connect-accept* process:

1. The server process binds itself to a port on the server host and begins listening for client requests.

2. A client process requests an available port on the client host and uses it to connect to the server process via the server process's port.

3. The server process accepts the connection by requesting an available port on the server host and informing the client to communicate using that port.

Figure 21.1 shows the bind-listen-connect-accept process.

FIGURE 21.1 The bind-listen-connect-accept process

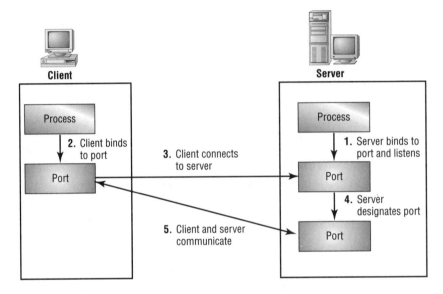

A TCP/IP service can operate either of two ways:

- stand-alone

- inetd

A stand-alone service runs continuously as a daemon process. An inetd service runs under the control of the inetd process and is started only when a client request arrives. The service runs only as long as necessary to satisfy the request and then terminates. If a service is heavily used or requires a relatively long time to start, it's best run as a stand-alone service. However, services that are seldom used and quick to start can be run more efficiently as inetd services, because they consume resources such as memory only when running.

To specify that a service runs as an inetd service, specify the service in inetd's configuration file, /etc/inetd.conf. The inetd service binds itself to the service's designated port and listens for client requests. When one is received, the inetd service starts the proper server and hands off the request.

The remaining sections of this chapter explain the primary Linux network services:

- The Apache Web server
- The Berkeley Internet Name Daemon (BIND) server
- The File Transfer Protocol (FTP) server
- The mail servers (`sendmail`, POP, and IMAP)
- The Network File System (NFS) server

The Apache Web Server

Apache is an HTTP 1.1–compliant, open-source Web server that is widely used. The March 2000 Netcraft survey (`www.netcraft.com`) showed that over 7.8 million Web sites, about 61 percent of Web sites surveyed, were running Apache; in contrast, only about 21 percent of Web sites were running Microsoft's Internet Information Server.

Apache is fast and reliable. Moreover, many third-party modules that extend its function are available. You can obtain information about these modules from the Apache Modules Registry Web site, `modules.apache.org`. Among the most popular Apache modules are:

- `mod_auth` and related modules, which perform user authentication
- `mod_frontpage`, which provides server-side support for Microsoft's Front Page extensions
- `mod_include`, which provides server-side includes
- `mod_info`, which lets you view the server configuration via a Web browser
- `mod_perl`, which incorporates Perl functionality into the server
- `mod_php3`, which incorporates PHP functionality into the server
- `mod_rewrite`, which lets you manipulate URLs
- `mod_speling`, which incorporates a spelling checker into the server

U.S. export laws restrict the import and export of software that employs encryption. To avoid restrictions on the distribution of Apache, Apache does not include support for Secure Socket Layer (SSL), an important Web technology that enables secure transactions. However, you can obtain Apache-SSL, a version of Apache that includes support for SSL from the Apache-SSL project

Web site, www.apache-ssl.org, or from ftp.zedz.net. Alternatively, you can use the Apache SSL module, mod_ssl or purchase a commercial version of Apache that provides SSL support, such as that sold by Red Hat.

Installation

To install the standard version of Apache, move to the directory containing the RPM packages and issue the following command:

```
rpm -Uvh apache-[^d]*.rpm
```

If you need to be able to compile Apache modules, you should also install the apache-devel package:

```
rpm -Uvh apache-devel*.rpm
```

The [^d] in the command to install the apache package prevents simulation installation of the apache-devel package.

If you prefer to access Apache documentation from your local hard drive rather than via the Web, you can install the apache-manual package, which places important Apache documents in /home/httpd/html/manual/.

Basic Configuration

The configuration files for Apache reside in /etc/httpd/conf. They are:

- access.conf
- httpd.conf
- srm.conf

At one time, each file contained directives of a particular sort. More recent versions of Apache have relaxed restrictions on file content, so the presence of three files can be viewed as a mere historical artifact.

The current version of Red Hat Linux places all of the configuration information in the file httpd.conf; the other two files contain only comment lines, which have a hash mark (#) as the first non-blank character. The httpd.conf file has three main sections, which are marked off by comments:

- Section 1, the global environment

- Section 2, the main server configuration

- Section 3, virtual host configurations

The directives included in Section 1 affect the operation of the server as a whole, including the main configuration and all virtual host configurations. Directives in Section 2 affect only the main server configuration. Directives in Section 3, if present, affect only the virtual host configuration to which they pertain. The next several subsections examine the `httpd.conf` file and its directives more closely.

Section 1: The Global Environment

The directive in Section 1 lets you specify configuration options that affect all server configurations, such as:

- The type of configuration: stand-alone or `inetd` (generally stand-alone)

- The names and locations of available Apache modules

- The number of server processes to start and the minimum and maximum number to maintain

Unless you want to operate the server in `inetd` mode, install custom modules, or modify the number of server processes, you may not need to modify the directives in Section 1. You can consult the Apache online documentation at `www.apache.org` for help in understanding unclear directives.

Section 2: The Main Configuration

Section 2 of the `httpd.conf` file contains directives that affect the operation of only the main configuration of the server; the directives do not affect the operation of virtual hosts, if any are configured. Primary configuration items include:

- The host name of the server

- The port number on which the server listens (generally port 80)

- The user and group IDs under which the daemon runs (generally `nobody`)

- The type of logging desired: logging by IP address or host name (generally logging by IP address, which is more efficient)

- The location of the root directory (generally `/home/httpd/html`)

- The name of users' HTML subdirectory (generally `~/public_html` or `~/www`)

- The path where CGI scripts reside

- The location of icons used when formatting directory indexes

- Configuration options for special content handlers

Generally, you should revise the `ServerName` directive, which specifies the name of the host with which the server is associated, and the `ServerAdmin` directive, which specifies the e-mail address of the server administrator. You may need to change other directives, depending on your requirements.

Section 3: The Virtual Host Configuration

Virtual hosting, also known as multi-homing, is an important Apache feature that lets a single Web server respond to several IP addresses or host names. For example, a single instance of Apache could be configured to respond to queries directed to `www.able.com` and `www.baker.com`. Virtual hosting lets two or more organizations share a single Web server. If you want to configure Apache to support virtual hosts, you must revise the directives in Section 3 of the `httpd.conf` file. You should specify:

- The IP address or addresses of the virtual hosts

- The e-mail address of the administrator of each virtual host

- The host name of each virtual host

- The names of the log files associated with each virtual host

- The location of the document root and CGI directory for each virtual host

Here is a typical virtual host configuration for two hosts— `www.firsthost.com` and `www.secondhost.com`—both of which are assigned IP address 192.169.100.1:

```
NameVirtualHost 192.169.100.1

<VirtualHost firsthost.com>
ServerAdmin webmaster@firsthost.com
DocumentRoot /home/httpd/html/firsthost/
ServerName www.firsthost.com
ErrorLog logs/firsthost-error-log
TransferLg logs/firsthost-access-log
ScriptAlias /cgi-bin/ /home/httpd/cgi-bin/firsthost/
</VirtualHost>

<VirtualHost secondhost.com>
ServerAdmin webmaster@secondhost.com
```

```
DocumentRoot /home/httpd/html/secondhost/
ServerName www.secondhost.com
ErrorLog logs/secondhost-error-log
TransferLg logs/secondhost-access-log
other options here, e.g., <Directory>
ScriptAlias /cgi-bin/ /home/httpd/cgi-bin/secondhost/
</VirtualHost>
```

If the IP address in NameVirtualHost is the only IP address for the host, you should include a VirtualHost entry describing the main configuration.

Administration

The server administration script for Apache is /etc/rc.d/init.d/httpd. By invoking this script with the proper argument, you can control the operation of the server.

Starting and Restarting the Service

To start the Apache Web server, issue the command

/etc/rc.d/init.d/httpd start

To restart the Apache Web server, issue the command

/etc/rc.d/init.d/httpd restart

If the server is configured for inetd operation, you don't need to—and should not—start or restart it.

Stopping the Service

To stop the Apache Web server, issue the command

/etc/rc.d/init.d/httpd stop

If the server is configured for inetd operation, you can't stop it by using the httpd script; you must reconfigure inetd.

Reloading the Configuration File

To cause Apache to reload its configuration file, issue the command

```
/etc/rc.d/init.d/httpd reload
```

You should instruct Apache to reload its configuration file after saving a revised version of the file. When possible, it's better to reload the configuration file rather than stop and restart the service.

Checking Service Status

To check the status of the Apache Web server, issue the command

```
/etc/rc.d/init.d/httpd status
```

If the server is configured for inetd operation, you can't check its status by using the httpd script.

Troubleshooting the Service

To troubleshoot Apache, check the system log (/var/log/messages) and the Apache log files (/var/log/httpd/*) for relevant error messages. To check the virtual host configuration, issue the command

```
/usr/sbin/httpd -S
```

The server should report the virtual host name and port number of the main server and each configured virtual host.

For further information on Apache, see the online documentation available on the Apache Web site, www.apache.org/docs. If you installed the apache-manual package, you can access local documentation stored in HTML format in the /home/httpd/html/manual directory.

Now take time to complete Exercise 21.1, which involves installation and configuration of Apache.

EXERCISE 21.1

Installing and Configuring Apache

To gain experience with Apache, install the apache and apache-manual packages. Configure two virtual hosts that share a single IP address. Using a browser, verify that you can access each virtual host. Be sure that each host is accessing its own root document by modifying the root documents so that their contents are distinct.

You'll likely need to consult this chapter and the Apache documentation to complete this exercise. But, before taking the RHCE exam, be sure you can perform these and similar operations without using external documentation.

The BIND Name Server

The Berkeley Internet Name Daemon (BIND) resolves IP addresses to host names and host names to IP addresses. This service is often called Domain Name Service (DNS). The overwhelming majority of DNS servers on the Internet run the same server that is distributed as part of Red Hat Linux. Many servers have names that resemble the name of the associated program; however, BIND's associated program, /usr/sbin/named, is oddly named.

Red Hat Linux helps you configure either of two sorts of DNS:

- A caching-only DNS server

- A regular DNS server

A caching-only DNS server may improve DNS performance of a host that has a slow-speed connection to the Internet. A caching-only name server contacts a regular name server to resolve IP addresses and host names. But once an IP address or host name has been resolved, the caching-only name server stores the result so that future references to the IP address or host name can be resolved without querying a name server.

Installation

Red Hat Linux includes these BIND-related packages:

- `bind`, which provides a regular DNS server

- `bind-utils`, a set of useful utilities for administering BIND

- `caching-nameserver`, which configures BIND to provide a caching-only name server

In addition, it includes the `bind-devel` package, which is needed only when doing software development of programs that invoke the BIND application programming interface.

To install BIND, move to the directory that contains the packages and issue the following command

```
rpm -Uvh bind-*.rpm
```

If you want to configure a caching-only name server, also issue the following command

```
rpm -Uvh caching-nameserver-*.rpm
```

Basic BIND Configuration

To establish Domain Name Service (DNS), you must configure the main DNS configuration file, `/etc/named.conf`. Generally, you must also configure a set of files known as *zone files*, which generally reside in `/var/named`. A zone file is either:

- A *forward zone file*, used to map host names to IP addresses

- A *reverse zone file*, used to map IP addresses to host names

- A hint file, which identifies the root name servers responsible for answering DNS queries for all registered domains

If you require a caching-only name server, installation of the caching-nameserver package correctly configures BIND. However, you can improve the efficiency of name lookup by modifying the default caching-nameserver configuration to include a forwarders statement in /etc/named.conf. The forwarders statement has the form forwarders {*IP_address*}, where *IP_address* specifies the IP address of a DNS service that will respond to queries not resolvable from the cache. If you like, you can specify the IP addresses of multiple servers; just separate each from the next by a semicolon.

The /etc/named.conf file identifies each zone file. If the zone file is a forward zone file, /etc/named.conf identifies the domain to which the zone file applies; if the zone file is a reverse zone file, /etc/named.conf identifies the network to which the zone file applies. The /etc/named.conf file also indicates whether the local DNS is a master DNS or slave DNS for the zone. A master DNS is the primary name server for its zone, called the *start of authority* for the zone. A slave DNS obtains information from a master DNS, which it regularly contacts in order to keep its information up to date.

Here is a typical /etc/named.conf file, the format of which is described by the named man page:

```
options {
        directory "/var/named";
};
zone "." {
        type hint;
        file "named.ca";
};
zone "azusapacific.com."{
        type master;
        file "named.azusapacific.com";
};
zone "0.0.127.in-addr.arpa"{
        type master;
        file "named.local";
};
zone "1.168.192.in-addr.arpa"{
        type master;
        file "named.reverse";
};
```

The contents of a correct `named.ca` hint file can be obtained via FTP from `ftp://ftp.rs.internic.net/domain/named.root`. The remaining files must be coded by hand. A forward zone file typically specifies:

- The host that is the start of authority (SOA) for the zone

- The e-mail address of the administrator responsible for the zone

- Mappings from host names to IP addresses for hosts in the zone

In addition, the zone file may specify secondary name servers, mail exchange records, and host aliases (called *canonical names* or CNAMEs). Here is a typical forward zone file:

```
@                     IN     SOA    azusapacific.com.
                      root.azusapacific.com. (
                            200002051 ; serial time
                            43200     ; refresh time
                            3600      ; retry time
                            3600000   ; expire time
                            2419200   ; default_ttl
                      )
@                     IN     NS     azusapacific.com.
@                     IN     MX     10        azusapacific.com.
localhost             IN     A      127.0.0.1
azusapacific.com.     IN     A      192.168.1.1
bill                  IN     A      192.168.1.2
toshiba               IN     A      192.168.1.99
router                IN     CNAME  azusapacific.com.
www                   IN     CNAME  azusapacific.com.
ftp                   IN     CNAME  azusapacific.com.
mail                  IN     CNAME  azusapacific.com.
```

Note the unusual use of a period in the e-mail address of the zone administrator (`root.azusapacific.com`) and following the domain name (`azusapacific.com.`). The underlying concept is that all host names, fully qualified or not, end with a dot when specified in the zone file and other DNS configuration files. The format of the file is more fully described in the `named` man page.

The series of numbers in the SOA record specify:

- A serial number used by slaves to determine when information has changed

- The refresh interval at which slaves should check the serial number, specified in seconds

- The interval at which a slave should retry after a failed refresh, specified in seconds

- The interval at which to discard cached information in refreshes that have failed, specified in seconds

- The default interval during which negative responses should be cached, specified in seconds

Here is a typical reverse zone file:

```
@                IN     SOA     azusapacific.com.
root.azusapacific.com. (
                        2000032502 ; serial
                        43200 ; refresh
                        3600 ; retry
                        3600000 ; expire
                        2419200 ; default_ttl
                        )
@                IN     NS      azusapacific.com.
1                IN     PTR     wall.azusapacific.com.
2                IN     PTR     p3.azusapacific.com.
3                IN     PTR     p2.azusapacific.con
99               IN     PTR     laptop.azusapacific.com.
```

Administration

The server administration script for named is /etc/rc.d/init.d/named. By invoking this script with the proper argument, you can control the operation of the server.

Starting and Restarting the Service

To start BIND, issue the command

```
/etc/rc.d/init.d/named start
```

To restart BIND, issue the command

```
/etc/rc.d/init.d/named restart
```

Stopping the Service

To stop BIND, issue the command

```
/etc/rc.d/init.d/named stop
```

Checking Service Status

To check the status of BIND, issue the command

```
/etc/rc.d/init.d/named status
```

Forcing a Database Reload

You should instruct BIND to reload its database whenever you change a BIND configuration file. To instruct BIND to reload its database, issue the command

```
/etc/rc.d/init.d/named reload
```

Logs

By default, BIND logs messages to the system log, /var/log/messages. If BIND is not functioning properly, check the log for error messages that point to the problem.

Further Information

Extensive documentation on BIND is available in /usr/doc/bind-*. You can also find information on the Web, at the Internet Software Consortium's Web site, www.isc.org.

Now take the time to complete Exercise 21.2, which gives you practical experience in configuring BIND.

EXERCISE 21.2

Installing and Configuring BIND

Next to SENDMAIL, BIND is perhaps the most difficult of Unix services to configure. However, you need not be a BIND expert in order to pass the RHCE exam. Perform the following steps to gain experience working with BIND:

1. Install BIND.

2. Create a set of zone files for a hypothetical domain. Use IP addresses from a reserved block, such as 192.168.1.0-192.168.1.255.

3. Configure /etc/named.conf to refer to your zone files.

4. Start BIND and verify that it can resolve forward and reverse refer-ences. You can verify BIND's operation by using the `ping` command to `ping` by host name or IP address. Note that, in Red Hat 6.2, spec-ifying an IP address as the target of the `ping` command causes the command to perform a reverse lookup of the specified IP address. If you don't desire this behavior, you can specify the –n flag.

You'll probably need some help in performing this exercise, so feel free to look back to this chapter and to consult other documentation. However, before taking the RHCE exam, be sure you can perform operations such as these without needing to consult books, notes, or other help.

FTP

The Washington University (St. Louis) FTP server is the most widely used FTP server on the Internet. It lets users upload and download files and directories. The FTP daemon is named `/usr/sbin/in.ftpd`; however, its man page is named `ftpd`.

Three levels of FTP access are provided:

- User access, access by users who have a login account on the server host. This level of access accords users the usual access privileges defined by their user ID.

- Guest access, access by users who have a special guest account that provides only FTP access. This level of access accords users specially defined access privileges.

- Anonymous access, access by users who have no defined account on the server host. This level of access accords users access to only a specified directory and its subdirectories (usually, `/home/ftp`). This restriction is enforced by means of a `chroot`ed environment.

The Washington University FTP server can log all accesses. It also provides capabilities that let clients transfer compressed files or transfer entire directories with a single command.

Installation

The Washington University FTP server is distributed as two packages:

- wu-ftpd, which contains the FTP server
- anonftp, which contains the anonymous FTP server

If you require anonymous FTP service, you should install both packages. However, if you don't require anonymous FTP service, you should install only the wu-ftpd package. Unnecessarily installing anonymous FTP may make your system somewhat more vulnerable to attack by crackers.

Basic Configuration

The FTP service has three basic configuration files:

- /etc/ftpaccess, which specifies global options and user permissions
- /etc/ftphosts, which specifies client hosts that may or may not access the FTP service
- /etc/ftpusers, which specifies users who *may not* access the FTP service. Typically, the file includes entries for root, bin, daemon, adm, lp, sync, shutdown, halt, mail, news, uucp, operator, games, and nobody

Here are the contents of a typical ftpaccess file:

```
class   all    real,guest,anonymous   *

email root@localhost

loginfails 5

readme   README*      login
readme   README*      cwd=*

message /welcome.msg           login
message .message               cwd=*

compress        yes            all
tar             yes            all
chmod           no             guest,anonymous
delete          no             guest,anonymous
overwrite       no             guest,anonymous
rename          no             guest,anonymous

log transfers anonymous,real inbound,outbound
```

```
shutdown /etc/shutmsg

passwd-check rfc822 warn
```

Check the man pages `ftpaccess` and `ftphosts` for information on the format of the configuration directives.

Administration

By default, the FTP service is run as an `inetd` service. Thus, it is not necessary to start, restart, or stop the service.

The FTP service places log entries in the system log, `/var/log/messages`. If the FTP service is not operating properly, check the contents of the system log for log entries that point to the problem.

A common requirement is for a set of directories to be accessible via anonymous FTP, HTTP, and NFS. The FTP server does not follow symbolic links, so the directories must be subdirectories of the directory designated as the home directory of the `ftp` user, generally `/home/ftp` directory. To provide access via HTTP, establish symbolic links pointing to the directories. To provide access via NFS, simply export the directories.

Further Information

You can find further information on FTP in the man page for `ftp` and `ftpd`, the man pages for `ftpaccess` and `ftphosts`, and on the Web at www.wu-ftpd.org.

To try your hand at installing and configuring FTP, complete Exercise 21.3.

EXERCISE 21.3

Installing FTP

FTP is a popular service, so you should be certain you're familiar with its installation, configuration, and operation. To gain first-hand experience, perform these steps:

1. Install the wu-ftpd and anonftp packages.

2. Verify that you can log in and perform transfers using a defined user account.

3. Verify that you can log in and perform transfers anonymously.

You can consult this book and other helps while completing the exercise. However, before taking the RHCE exam, be sure you can install, configure, and use FTP without help.

Mail

Mail involves two facilities: mail transfer and mail access. The Red Hat Linux mail transfer agent (MTA) is `sendmail`, which is the most popular MTA on the Internet. Red Hat Linux provides access to mail via the Post Office Protocol (POP) or the Interim Mail Access Protocol (IMAP).

The `sendmail` program is extremely flexible, but is relatively large and complex. Its features include:

- The ability to decode and handle a wide range of destination address formats

- Support for virtual mail domains and user aliases

- Extensive security and anti-spam facilities

How Mail Works

A user typically composes mail by means of a mail client application. Popular clients include Linux and non-Linux programs such as:

- Eudora

- Mutt

- Netscape Communicator

- Microsoft Outlook

- Pegasus

- Pine

After composing a mail message, the user sends the message, which is transmitted by a Simple Mail Transfer Protocol (SMTP) server. This can be accomplished in a variety of ways. Some mail clients, including most Linux clients, spawn a `sendmail` process to transmit a message; others depend on the availability of a remote SMTP server.

If sendmail is used, the sendmail process—which is bound to port 25—uses DNS to obtain the Mail Exchange (MX) information that pertains to the destination host, which specifies the mail gateway host through which mail messages for the destination host should be sent. The sendmail process then uses SMTP to transfer the message to the mail gateway host. The gateway host, in turn, transfers the message to the destination host. The SMTP server of the destination host accepts or refuses the message, based on the server configuration. For example, the server may refuse messages from unresolvable domain names, which may indicate that the message has been sent by a *spammer*, an unauthorized user who subverts an insecure mail server in order to transmit large volumes of junk mail. Figure 21.2 illustrates the mail transfer process.

FIGURE 21.2 The mail transfer process

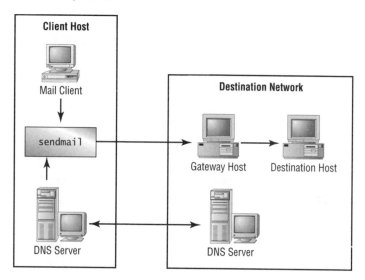

Once a message has been delivered, the recipient can access it while logged in to the destination host. Alternatively, the user can access the message from a remote host, which contacts a POP or IMAP server on the destination host. The IMAP protocol is newer and generally superior to the POP protocol. For example, POP always sends passwords across the Internet as clear text; IMAP can encrypt them.

Installation

The sendmail program is contained in several packages:

- sendmail, which contains the program itself

- `sendmail-cf`, which contains files needed to revise the `sendmail` configuration

- `sendmail-doc`, which contains the `sendmail` documentation

The optional packages `sendmail-cf` and `sendmail-doc` together require only about 2MB of disk space. So, it's usually reasonable to install all three packages. To install `sendmail`, move to the directory containing the packages and issue the command

```
rpm -Uvh sendmail-*.rpm
```

The POP3 and IMAP server both reside in the package `imap`. To install them, move to the directory containing the package and issue the command

```
rpm -Uvh imap-*.rpm
```

sendmail Configuration

The `sendmail` program has several main configuration files:

- `/etc/sendmail.cf`, which contains the mail configuration directives

- `/etc/sendmail.cw`, which specifies the hosts on behalf of which the server will accept mail

- `/etc/aliases`, which specifies user mail aliases

You can revise the `sendmail` configuration in any of several ways:

- By using the `linuxconf` utility's `mailconf` subsystem. This is generally the simplest and best approach.

- By using the `m4` macro processor to generate a revised configuration. The file `/usr/doc/sendmail/README.cf` explains the procedure.

- By manually editing the `/etc/sendmail.cf` file, a method recommended only for `sendmail` gurus.

imap Configuration

You generally do not need to configure IMAP or POP. However, both services are run via `inetd`, the default configuration of which is not appropriate for running these services. The `/etc/inetd.conf` file contains lines that reference the POP and IMAP services, but these lines are commented out in the distributed configuration:

```
#pop-2    stream   tcp   nowait   root   /usr/sbin/tcpd ipop2d
#pop-3    stream   tcp   nowait   root   /usr/sbin/tcpd ipop3d
```

```
#imap    stream  tcp   nowait  root   /usr/sbin/tcpd imapd
```

To properly configure inetd, simply locate each of these lines, remove the hash mark (#) at the beginning of the line, and save the revised file. Then restart inetd by issuing the command

```
killall -HUP inetd
```

Administration of *sendmail*

The server administration script for sendmail is /etc/rc.d/init.d/ sendmail. By invoking this script with the proper argument, you can control the operation of the server.

Starting and Restarting the Service

To start sendmail, issue the command

```
/etc/rc.d/init.d/sendmail start
```

To restart sendmail, issue the command

```
/etc/rc.d/init.d/sendmail restart
```

Stopping the Service

To stop sendmail, issue the command

```
/etc/rc.d/init.d/sendmail stop
```

Checking Service Status

To check the status of sendmail, issue the command

```
/etc/rc.d/init.d/sendmail status
```

Logs

In addition to log entries posted to the system log (/var/log/messages), sendmail keeps its own log file, /var/log/maillog. If mail service is not operating properly, check both log files for clues to the source of the problem.

Further Information

For further information on sendmail, see the sendmail Web site, www.sendmail.org, the contents of the sendmail-doc package, which reside in /usr/doc/sendmail, and the following man pages:

- aliases
- mailstats
- makemap
- newaliases
- praliases
- rmail
- sendmail

For further information on IMAP and POP, see the documentation files in /usr/doc/imap-* and the man pages imapd and popd.

Now complete Exercise 21.4 to acquire practical experience with Linux mail services.

EXERCISE 21.4

Installing and Configuring Mail Services

Mail service is ubiquitous, so every system administrator must be familiar with the installation and configuration of mail. Perform these steps to gain first-hand experience with mail:

1. Install all three sendmail packages and the IMAP/POP package.

2. Use mailconf to specify the systems for which mail will be accepted.

3. Use mailconf to specify several user mail aliases.

4. Use a mail client, such as pine, to verify that your mail configuration operates properly.

You can refer back to this book for help in configuring mail. However, before taking the RHCE exam, be sure you can perform simple mail configuration operations such as these without the aid of books or notes.

NFS

The Network File System (NFS) provides shared access to files and directories. In operation, an NFS server designates one or more directories as available to clients. The designated directories are referred to as *shares*, which are said to have been *exported* by the server. Once exported by an NFS server, an NFS share can be mounted by a client system in much the same way that a local file system is mounted. The Linux NFS implementation is functionally similar to NFS implementations available on other Unix systems, and its client is largely compatible with NFS version 3.0.

An NFS server runs three NFS-related daemons:

- portmap, which forwards client requests to the correct NFS process

- rpc.nfsd, which translates remote file access requests to local file access requests

- rpc.mountd, which mounts and unmounts file systems

A host may be both NFS server and client, in which case it runs all three daemons.

Installation

Under Red Hat Linux 6.2, much of the NFS code has been incorporated in the Linux kernel. To use NFS, you'll require only these packages:

- nfs-utils, which contains utilities needed for using NFS

- portmap, which contains files related to portmap and is used by NFS servers

To install NFS, move to the directory containing the packages and issue the command

```
rpm -Uvh nfs-utils-*.rpm portmap-*.rpm
```

Server Configuration

The NFS server configuration file is /etc/exports, each line of which is a directive that specifies a share (that is, an exported directory) and the associated access permissions. Here is a line from a typical /etc/exports file:

```
/exports/database fred.azusapacific.com bob.azusapacific.com
```

The general form of the directive is:

```
path host_list
```

where *path* is the absolute path of the shared directory and *host_list* is a list of one or more hosts that can access the share. Each host should be separated from adjacent hosts by one or more spaces.

A host may be specified in any of several ways:

- By using a host name, if the host is part of the local domain
- By using a fully qualified domain name
- By using a host name containing a wild card (*)
- By using an IP address
- By using a network address, such as 192.168.1.0/255.255.255.0

A wildcard character matches at most a single component of the host name. For example, the host name specifier `*.azusapacific.com` matches `www.azusapacific.com` but not `www.science.azusapacific.com`. A wildcard can match part of a component of a host name. For example, the host specifier `dtc*.azusapacific.com` matches `dtc01.azusapacific.com`, `dtc02.azusapacific.com`, and so on.

By default, clients are permitted read-only access to a share, notwithstanding information to the contrary in the `exports` man page. To allow read-write access, follow the host specifier with (`rw`). For example, here's a typical read-write share:

```
/exports/database fred.azusapacific.com(ro)
➥bob.azusapacific.com(rw)
```

The host `fred` is permitted read-only access whereas the host `bob` is permitted read-write access. Be careful not to insert a space between the host specifier and the permission.

By default, if a client is logged in as `root`, the client is not given `root` access to shared files; instead, such requests are mapped to user id 65535. If you want to permit `root` access, specify the `no_root_squash` option. For example:

```
/exports/database bob.azusapacific.com(rw,no_root_squash)
```

The `/etc/exports` file is easily edited by hand. However, if you prefer, `linuxconf` provides a facility for administering NFS shares.

Client Configuration

As explained, a client can treat an exported directory much like a local file system. To mount a shared directory, a special form of the `mount` command is used. For example:

```
mount -t nfs server:/exports/databases /mnt/database
```

This command mounts the directory /exports/databases that is exported by the host named server as the local directory /mnt/database. The special syntax *server:* is used to specify the NFS server that provides the share, and the file system type is specified as nfs.

The script /etc/rc.d/init.d/netfs runs at boot time, automatically mounting the NFS directories specified in /etc/fstab. If you want an NFS share to be automatically mounted at boot time, simply include it in the /etc/fstab file. For example:

```
server:/exports/database /mnt/database  nfs  defaults  0  2
```

Several mount options let you control the operation of an NFS share:

- hard,intr lets you kill or interrupt requests blocked by an unavailable server.

- nolock disables file locking so that the NFS client can access an NFS server that lacks locking capability.

- rsize=8192 and wsize=8192 allocates read and write (respectively) buffers larger than the default size and significantly improve NFS throughput.

You can use linuxconf to mount NFS shares or specify NFS shares to be included in /etc/fstab. Start linuxconf, and choose Access NFS Volume ➢ Add from the menu.

The nfslock service provides file locking services for NFS clients. If your NFS client needs to lock files, be sure to enable the nfslock service.

Red Hat Linux also provides the autofs service, which you can configure to mount NFS shares on demand. The autofs service is contained in the optional package of the same name. See the man pages auto.master, autofs(5), autofs(8), and automount for more information.

NFS Administration

The main server administration scripts for NFS are /etc/rd.d/init.d/portmap and /etc/rd.d/init.d/nfs. By invoking these scripts with the proper argument, you can control the operation of the NFS server.

Starting and Restarting NFS

To start the NFS server, issue the commands

```
/etc/rc.d/init.d/portmap start
/etc/rc.d/init.d/nfs start
```

To restart the NFS server, issue the commands

```
/etc/rc.d/init.d/portmap restart
/etc/rc.d/init.d/nfs restart
```

Stopping the NFS Server

To stop the NFS server, issue the commands

```
/etc/rc.d/init.d/nfs stop
/etc/rc.d/init.d/portmap stop
```

Controlling NFS Server Operation

The `exportfs` command lets you control operation of the NFS server on the local host:

- `exportfs -v` lists shared directories and the associated options
- `exportfs -a` *share* exports the specified share
- `exportfs -a` exports all shares listed in `/etc/exports`
- `exportfs -u` *share* unexports the specified share
- `exportfs -ua` unexports all shares
- `exportfs -r` refreshes the share list

In particular, you should issue the command

```
exportfs -r
```

after any modification of the `/etc/exports` file.

Checking Service Status

To check the status of the NFS server while logged in to the server host, issue the following commands

```
/etc/rc.d/init.d/nfs status
/etc/rc.d/init.d/portmap status
```

To check the status of a remote NFS server, issue the command

```
rpcinfo -p server
```

where *server* is the host name of the NFS server.

To list the shares exported by a server, issue the command

```
showmount -e server
```

where *server* is the host name of the NFS server.

Logging

The NFS facility logs messages to the system log file, /var/log/messages. If NFS is not operating properly, check the system log for messages that point to the source of the problem.

Now take time to complete Exercise 21.5, which gives you experience in working with NFS.

EXERCISE 21.5

Installing and Configuring NFS

NFS is an important network service, especially where Unix systems are popular. To gain experience working with NFS, perform these steps:

1. Install the NFS server packages on one host and the NFS client packages on another.

2. Export the /tmp directory of the NFS server, using default permissions.

3. Access the shared directory from the client host and attempt to read a file. The operation should complete successfully.

4. Access the shared directory from the client host and attempt to write a file. The operation should fail.

5. Revise the share permissions to allow read-write access.

6. Access the shared directory from the client host and attempt to write a file. The operation should complete successfully.

You can access this book and the NFS documentation while performing this exercise. But, before taking the RHCE exam, be sure you can perform such operations as these without using books or other external documentation.

Samba

Samba is an open-source implementation of the System Message Block (SMB) service used by Microsoft Windows 9*x* and NT, which is sometimes known as Common Internet File System (CIFS). Samba is widely used throughout the Unix and Linux communities. Samba originated in the work of Andrew Tridgell, who reverse engineered the SMB protocol. Subsequently, a worldwide team formed to maintain and enhance Samba.

Samba enables Windows clients to access Linux file systems and printers by using the Network Neighborhood facility of the Windows file manager. Unix and Linux clients can also access shared file systems and printers. Samba is popular even in computing environments that lack Windows clients, because its authentication mechanisms are superior to those of NFS.

SMB is a high-level protocol built on Microsoft's NetBIOS protocol, which can be run over a TCP/IP network. NetBIOS duplicates several TCP/IP functions. For example, it has its own host name resolution service, Windows Internet Naming Service (WINS).

Samba actually has two associated services:

- **smbd**, which authenticates clients, authorizes client access to shares, and provides shared access to files and printers.

- **nmbd**, which provides a browsing facility that lets clients discover servers and their shares. It also acts as a WINS server, resolving NetBIOS host names to IP addresses.

At any time, one SMB server acts as the *browse master* for a network served by SMB. The browse master (or master browser, as it's sometimes called) maintains information on available servers and shares and responds to client inquiries attempting to discover servers and shares. Eligible SMB servers compete in an *election* that determines which becomes the browse master. A Samba server can be configured to participate in such an election or to override the election, becoming the browse master despite the presence of other candidate servers.

Linux clients can access SMB shares in either of two ways. The smbclient program provides FTP-like access to shared files and printers, and the smbmount command lets you mount a shared file system much as you would a local file system. The standard printtool utility lets you configure access to Samba printers.

Installation

Samba is contained in three packages:

- `samba-common`, which contains files needed by Samba clients and servers

- `samba`, which contains the Samba server

- `samba-client`, which contains the Samba `smbclient`, `smbmount`, and `smbprint` programs and associated files and documentation

Samba is frequently updated; you should consider downloading the latest packages from the Samba Web site, `www.samba.org`, rather than installing packages contained on Red Hat Linux distribution media.

To install a Samba server, move to the directory containing the packages and issue the command

```
rpm -Uvh samba-*.rpm
```

This command installs both the Samba server and the Samba client, which is helpful in troubleshooting the server. To install only the Samba client, move to the directory containing the packages and issue the command

```
rpm -Uvh samba-common-*.rpm samba-client-*.rpm
```

Basic Server Configuration

The main Samba configuration file is `/etc/smb.conf`, which is described in the man page `smb.conf`, in the documentation files residing in `/usr/doc/samba*` and on the Samba Web site, `www.samba.org/docs`. The configuration file contains two types of directives:

- Global directives, which configure the server

- Service directives, which configure shared files and printers

This section explains the contents of the Samba configuration file. You can use a text editor to configure Samba by revising the contents of the file. If you prefer using a graphical tool to configure Samba, you can use `linuxconf`. Also, the `swat` package provides a Web-based interface for configuring Samba.

Samba Global Directives

Here are the global directives contained in a simple Samba configuration:

```
# specify the name of the workgroup
workgroup = MYGROUP
```

```
# specify the descriptive text associated with the server
# and shown by the network neighborhood and net view
# facilities
comment = Router

# specify the hosts that can access the server
hosts allow = 192.168. 127. 10.0.0.

# specify that security is imposed at the user level
security = user

# Automatically share all printers defined in the
# printcap file
load printers = yes

# map users with invalid passwords to the guest user id
map to guest = Bad User

# specify the log file name -- use a separate log for each
# client host
log file = /var/log/samba/samba-log.%m

# specify the maximum log file in kbytes
max log size = 50

# set socket options to tailor performance
socket options = TCP_NODELAY

# specify the name of the printcap file
printcap name = /etc/printcap

# specify a batch file downloaded and run when a user
# logs in
logon script = %u.bat

# act as a logon server for Windows 9x clients
domain logons = Yes

# set the level for browse elections to ensure that
```

```
# Samba wins
os level = 69

# force an election to determine the master browser
preferred master = Yes

# nmbd should collect a browse list
domain master = Yes

# specify that nmbd will act as a WINS server
wins support = Yes

# specify how printer status information is to be determined
printing = bsd

# check every access for a lock
strict locking = Yes
```

You should tailor the following directives—and other directives as needed—to your local requirements:

- workgroup

- comment

- hosts allow

The hosts allow directive identifies the client hosts permitted to access the server. The local host address, 127.0.0.1, should generally be included in the list of hosts. Several formats are allowed:

- IP address—for example, 192.168.1.0

- IP address and subnet mask—for example, 192.168.1.0/255.255.255.0

- Partial IP address—for example, 192.168. (note the trailing dot)

- host name—for example, client.azusapacific.com

- domain or subdomain name—for example, .azusapacific.com (note the lack of a wildcard and the leading dot)

For Windows 9x and NT clients, you should generally specify user as the value of the security parameter. However, if you prefer authorization to be handled on a per-share basis, specify the value share. Or, if you prefer authorization to be handled by another server—for example, a Windows NT Primary Domain Controller (PDC)—specify the value server. If the client participates in an NT domain, specify the value domain.

Samba Service Directives

Here is a typical set of service directives that set up a shared directory:

```
[cdrom]
comment = CDROM mounted in /mnt/cdrom
path = /mnt/cdrom
read only = Yes
browseable = Yes
valid users = fred, bob
```

The directives establish a share known as cdrom, which provides read-only access to the /mnt/cdrom directory of the Samba server. Only the users fred and bob can access the share. If you want to create a publicly available share, omit the valid users directive and specify public = yes. If you want to grant access to all members of a group, specify @*group*, where *group* is the name of the group.

If you want users to be able to write to the share, omit the read only directive and specify writable = yes. If you don't want the share to be visible in a browse list, such as the Windows Network Neighborhood, specify browseable = No.

Here is a sample printer share:

```
[printers]
comment = All Printers
path = /var/spool/samba
public = yes
guest ok = yes
admin users = bob
create mask = 0700
print ok = Yes
browseable = Yes
printable = yes
```

Samba lets you conveniently establish a home directory for a user. To do so, use the homes section of the smb.conf file. For example:

```
[homes]
comment = Home Directories
read only = No
create mask = 0750
browseable = No
```

If you want Samba to function as a logon server, you should define a netlogon share. For example:

```
[netlogon]
comment = Samba Network Logon Service
```

```
path = /home/netlogon
guest ok = Yes
browseable = No
locking = No
```

Client Configuration and Use

If a Samba server has been correctly configured, you should be able to view browseable shares in the Network Neighborhood of a Windows 9*x* client, map them to drive letters, and drag and drop files in the usual manner.

To access a Samba share or a Windows 9*x*/NT share from a Linux host, issue a command of the form

```
smbmount //server/share /mount_point
```

where *server* is the host name of the server, *share* is the name of the share, and *mount_point* is the local directory that should become the mount point. The share is mounted with the permissions associated with the user executing the smbmount command. To allow non-privileged users to mount shares, you can modify the permissions of smbmnt and smbumount to include setuid (mode 4755). However, you may prefer to install smbclient and instruct users in its use; this is a less convenient but more secure approach. To access a share by using smbclient, issue a command of the form

```
smbclient //server/share
```

where *server* is the host name of the server and *share* is the name of the share.

Advanced Server Configuration

SMB clients on computers running Windows 95 OSR2, Windows 98, and Windows NT with Service Pack 3 and greater use encrypted passwords, which are not compatible with the default configuration of Samba. You can accommodate such clients by any of several means:

- Configure the client host to use plain-text passwords. However, doing so may compromise security.

- Use a Windows NT Primary Domain Controller (PDC) for authentication and authorization and configure Samba to use encrypted passwords.

- Configure Samba to use encrypted passwords and maintain a file containing the encrypted passwords.

For information on configuring Samba to use encrypted passwords, see the file ENCRYPTION.txt that resides under /usr/doc/samba*/docs.

Administration

The main server administration script for Samba is `/etc/rc.d/init.d/smb`. By invoking this script with the proper argument, you can control the operation of the Samba server.

Starting and Restarting Samba

To start the Samba server, issue the command

```
/etc/rc.d/init.d/smb start
```

To restart the Samba server, issue the command

```
/etc/rc.d/init.d/smb restart
```

Stopping Samba

To stop the Samba server, issue the command

```
/etc/rc.d/init.d/smb stop
```

Checking Samba Status

To check the status of the Samba server, issue the command

```
/etc/rc.d/init.d/smb status
```

Logs

Samba startups and shutdowns are logged in the system log file, `/var/log/messages`. In addition, Samba logs messages to its own log files. The location and names of Samba's log files are configured in the `/etc/smb.conf` file. However, they generally reside in `/var/log/samba`. If Samba is not operating properly, check these log files for clues to the problem.

Troubleshooting the Service

Samba includes several tools for diagnosing and troubleshooting. After revising the Samba configuration file, you should issue the command

```
testparm
```

This command checks the Samba configuration files for errors. To help ensure reliable operation, you should correct the errors before starting Samba.

To list the available shares on a server, issue a command of the form

```
smbclient -L server -N
```

where *server* is the host name of the server. For example, to list the available shares on the local host, issue the command

```
smbclient -L localhost -N
```

If no shares are visible, the WINS server may not be responding. To investigate, issue a command of the form

```
nmblookup -B server _ _SAMBA_ _
```

where *server* is the host name of the server. The command should display the IP address of the specified host. You should also check that SMB clients are properly configured to use WINS. To do so, issue the command

```
nmblookup -d 2 '*'
```

Client hosts on the local network should respond with their IP addresses.

For further information on troubleshooting Samba, see the file DIAGNOSIS.txt that resides under /usr/doc/samba*/docs.

Now complete Exercise 21.6, which gives you hands-on experience with Samba.

EXERCISE 21.6

Installing and Configuring Samba

Samba is more secure than NFS and has considerable and growing popularity in the Unix community. To gain experience with Samba, perform these steps:

1. Install the Samba server packages.

2. Configure Samba to provide:

   - A read-only file share

   - A read-write file share

   - A printer share

3. Test the shares by accessing them using a Windows 95 OSR1 client.

You can access any available documentation while working on this exercise. However, before taking the RHCE exam, be prepared to perform these operations without the assistance of external documentation.

Summary

In this chapter, you learned about installing and configuring primary network services. The most important topics covered are:

Network Services   Network services and their associated port are listed in /etc/services.

Ports   Ports 0-1023 are privileged ports and can be accessed only by processes running with a user ID of 0, the user ID of the root user.

The Bind-Listen-Connect-Accept Process   The bind-listen-connect-accept process is the process whereby TCP clients and servers communicate.

Configuring the Apache Web Server   The Apache Web sever has three configuration files:

- /etc/httpd/conf/access.conf

- /etc/httpd/conf/httpd.conf

- /etc/httpd/conf/srm.conf

Red Hat Linux places all Apache directives in the file /etc/httpd/conf/httpd.conf, which has three sections:

Section 1   The global environment

Section 2   The main server configuration

Section 3   Virtual host configurations

Configuring Apache for Virtual Hosts   To configure Apache for virtual hosts, you must specify:

- The IP address or addresses of the virtual hosts

- The e-mail address of the administrator of each virtual host

- The host name of each virtual host

- The names of the log files associated with each virtual host

- The location of the document root and CGI directory for each virtual host

The Berkely Internet Name Daemon (BIND)   BIND provides Domain Name Services (DNS). The corresponding daemon is /usr/sbin/named.

File Transfer Protocol (FTP)   FTP makes possible the transfer of files from system to system. FTP defines three user classes:

- Ordinary users
- Guest users
- Anonymous users

Mail   The mail system includes mail transfer agents (MTA), which deliver mail to a mailbox, and mail access clients, which access mailboxes and send mail, usually by means of a separate MTA. The standard Red Hat Linux MTA is `sendmail`; Red Hat Linux provides a variety of mail clients, supporting access to both the Post Office Protocol (POP) and Interim Mail Access Protocol (IMAP) mailboxes.

Network File System (NFS)   NFS is a Unix facility that supports sharing of files and directories. Red Hat Linux provides an implementation of NFS that is largely compatible with Sun's NFS 3.0.

Samba   Samba is an open source implementation of a server largely compatible with Microsoft's file and printer sharing facility, variously known as LAN Manager or Common Internet File System (CIFS), based on the System Message Block (SMB) protocol. Samba can provide file and printer sharing between Microsoft and Unix/Linux servers and clients. Samba can also perform many of the functions of a Microsoft Windows NT primary domain controller (PDC), including user authentication.

Key Terms

Before going on to the next chapter, be sure you're familiar with the following terms:

bind-listen-connect-accept process

browse master

canonical names

election

forward zone file

port

privileged ports

reverse zone file

shares

socket

spammer

start of authority

well-known ports

zone files

Additional Sources of Information

If you'd like further information about the topics presented in this chapter, you should consult the following sources:

- For further information on NFS, see the man pages

  - exportfs

  - exports

  - mount

  - nfsstat

  - portmap

  - rquotad

  - showmount

- Also see the *NFS HOWTO*, by Nicolai Langfeldt, /usr/doc/HOWTO /NFS-HOWTO.

- The *Official Guide to Red Hat Linux* also provides information on configuring and using NFS.

- For further information on Samba, see the man pages

  - lmhosts

  - make_smbcodepage

  - nmbd

  - nmblookup

  - samba

- smb.conf
- smbclient
- smbd
- smbmnt
- smbmount
- smbpasswd
- smbrun
- smbspool
- smbstatus
- smbtar
- swat
- testparm
- testprns

- Also see the documentation files residing in /usr/doc/samba* and on the Samba Web site, www.samba.org/docs.

- *Linux Apache Web Server Administration*, by Charles Aulds, (Sybex, 2000)

- *Linux DNS Server Administration*, by Craig Hunt, (Sybex, 2000)

- *Linux Samba Server Administration*, by Roderick W. Smith, (Sybex, 2000)

Review Questions

1. Which of the following is the number of a privileged port?

    A. 1

    B. 100

    C. 10000

    D. 100000

2. The Apache directive that specifies the IP address of a virtual host is which of the following?

    A. AddressVirtualHost

    B. NameVirtualHost

    C. ServerName

    D. ServerIP

3. What does a reverse zone file do?

    A. It maps IP addresses to host names.

    B. It maps IP addresses to NetBIOS host names.

    C. It maps host names to IP addresses.

    D. It maps NetBIOS host names to IP addresses.

4. Which of the following packages must be installed to host an NFS server?

    A. knfsd

    B. knfsd-clients

    C. netfs

    D. portmap

5. What files can an anonymous FTP user access?

    A. Files and directories in the home directory of the user `ftp`

    B. Files in any world-readable directory

    C. Files in the `/tmp` directory

    D. Files readable via the user's account

6. Which of the following could specify a host in the `hosts allow` directive of the Samba configuration file?

    A. `*.example.com`

    B. `.example.com`

    C. `www`

    D. `www.example.com`

7. To list the available Samba shares, which of the following commands could you issue?

    A. `nmblookup -B server`

    B. `nmblookup -d server`

    C. `smbclient -L server -N`

    D. `testparm`

Answers to Review Questions

1. A, B. Privileged ports are numbered 0–1023.

2. B. The NameVirtualHost directive specifies the IP address of a virtual host; the ServerName directive specifies the host name of a virtual host.

3. A. The reverse zone file maps IP addresses to host names; the forward zone file maps host names to IP addresses.

4. C, D. The knfsd, knfsd-clients and portmap packages are required. Alternatively, you can install the nfs-utils package, which supplies all needed functions.

5. A. An anonymous FTP user can access only files and directories in the home directory of the ftp user. Symbolic links are not followed. An anonymous FTP user need not have a user account.

6. B, C, D. Wildcards are not used in the host specifier of the hosts allow directive.

7. C. The smbclient command can list available shares.

Chapter

22

Restricting Access to Primary Network Services

RHCE PREPARATION TOPICS COVERED IN THIS CHAPTER:

✓ Be familiar with and capable of implementing access restrictions for primary network services.

✓ Understand basic NIS concepts and the components associated with NIS and LDAP.

✓ Understand the purpose of the PAM subsystem and be capable of implementing basic PAM configuration changes.

In general, a host that is part of a network is subject to more frequent and greater security threats than a stand-alone host. And, in general, larger networks are subject to greater security risks than smaller networks. An Internet host, for example, faces a variety of threats. However, by controlling access to a network host, you can reduce its exposure to security threats.

Red Hat Linux provides three principal mechanisms for controlling access to a host:

TCP Wrappers   By configuring TCP wrappers, you can restrict the hosts allowed to access a host's services.

Pluggable Authentication Module (PAM) Facility   By configuring the Pluggable Authentication Module (*PAM*) facility, you can restrict the users allowed to log in to a host.

ipchains Firewall   You can restrict access to the ports used by services by configuring an ipchains firewall.

This chapter explains the first two mechanisms: TCP wrappers and the PAM facility, which is usually known simply as PAM. In addition, it explains the Network Information Service (NIS) and the Lightweight Directory Access Protocol (LDAP), two mechanisms that allow you to centrally control user accounts and other system information. Chapter 30, "Configuring a Firewall Using ipchains," explains the third mechanism.

The *inetd* Service

The TCP wrappers facility operates in conjunction with the inetd service. This section explains the inetd service; the following section explains how to configure TCP wrappers, which work with the inetd service.

As explained in the previous chapter, services can run standalone or under the control of inetd, which is sometimes known as the Super Server. Services running under the control of inetd do not consume memory or processor resources while they are idle; therefore, running services under the control of inetd can increase system efficiency. Services that are lightly used and start quickly are good candidates for running under control of inetd. Services that are heavily used operate more efficiently without the overhead imposed by inetd, and services that are slow to start run poorly under control of inetd.

In operation, the inetd daemon monitors the ports of services running under its control. When a client request is received, inetd launches the service, which satisfies the client request.

The inetd configuration file is /etc/inetd.conf. An easy way to improve system security is to disable unnecessary services. For services that run under control of inetd, disabling a service is as simple as commenting out the related line or lines in /etc/inetd.conf.

Here are the contents of a typical inetd.conf file:

```
#echo    stream  tcp     nowait  root    internal
#echo    dgram   udp     wait    root    internal
#discard         stream  tcp     nowait  root    internal
#discard         dgram   udp     wait    root    internal
#daytime         stream  tcp     nowait  root    internal
#daytime         dgram   udp     wait    root    internal
#chargen         stream  tcp     nowait  root    internal
#chargen         dgram   udp     wait    root    internal
#time    stream  tcp     nowait  root    internal
#time    dgram   udp     wait    root    internal
#
# These are standard services.
#
ftp      stream  tcp     nowait  root    /usr/sbin/tcpd
  ➥in.ftpd -l -a
telnet   stream  tcp     nowait  root    /usr/sbin/tcpd
  ➥in.telnetd
#
# Shell, login, exec, comsat and talk are BSD protocols.
#
shell    stream  tcp     nowait  root    /usr/sbin/tcpd
  ➥in.rshd
login    stream  tcp     nowait  root    /usr/sbin/tcpd
  ➥in.rlogind
```

```
#exec    stream  tcp      nowait  root    /usr/sbin/tcpd
  ➥in.rexecd
#comsat dgram    udp      wait    root    /usr/sbin/tcpd
  ➥in.comsat
talk     dgram   udp      wait    root    /usr/sbin/tcpd
  ➥in.talkd
ntalk    dgram   udp      wait    root    /usr/sbin/tcpd
  ➥in.ntalkd
#dtalk   stream  tcp      waut    nobody /usr/sbin/tcpd
  ➥in.dtalkd
#
# Pop and imap mail services et al
#
#pop-2   stream  tcp      nowait  root    /usr/sbin/tcpd
  ➥ipopd
#pop-3   stream  tcp      nowait  root    /usr/sbin/tcpd
  ➥ipop3d
#imap    stream  tcp      nowait  root    /usr/sbin/tcpd
  ➥imapd
#
# The Internet UUCP service.
#
#uucp    stream  tcp      nowait  uucp    /usr/sbin/tcpd
#  /usr/lib/uucp/uucico    -l
#
# Tftp service is provided primarily for booting.  Most
# sites run this only on machines acting as "boot servers.
# " Do not uncomment this unless you *need* it.
#
#tftp    dgram   udp      wait    root    /usr/sbin/tcpd
  ➥in.tftpd
#bootps dgram    udp      wait    root    /usr/sbin/tcpd
  ➥bootpd
#
# Finger, systat and netstat give out user information
# which may be valuable to potential "system crackers."
# Many sites choose to disable some or all of these
# services to improve security.
#
```

```
finger  stream  tcp      nowait  root    /usr/sbin/tcpd
    ➥in.fingerd
#cfinger stream tcp      nowait  root    /usr/sbin/tcpd
    ➥in.cfingerd
#systat stream  tcp      nowait  guest   /usr/sbin/tcpd
    ➥/bin/ps -auwwx
#netstat         stream tcp      nowait guest
 ➥/usr/sbin/tcpd  /bin/netstat    -f inet
#
# Authentication
#
auth   stream  tcp     nowait    nobody   /usr/sbin/
    ➥in.identd   in.identd -l -e -o
```

Notice that many of the lines begin with a hash mark (#). These are comment lines, which are ignored by the inetd server. The general format of the remaining lines is

service socket_type protocol wait_option userid
    ➥*program_path arguments*

where

- *service* is a service listed in /etc/services

- *socket_type* has the value stream for TCP services and dgram for UDP services (see the man page inetd.conf for other values that are sometimes used)

- *protocol* is tcp or udp

- *wait_option* is wait for UDP services and nowait otherwise (see the man page inetd.conf for other values that are sometimes used)

- *userid* specifies the user id under which the service runs (the user id is usually root)

- *program_path* specifies the path of the executable file. (When TCP wrappers are used, *program_path* specifies the path of the tcpd program, as explained in the next section.) Note that the program names of many TCP services begin with in.

- *arguments* are arguments used by the program

The example file enables only the following services:

- telnet
- ftp
- talk
- ntalk
- shell
- login
- finger
- auth

All of these services, with the exception of auth, run using TCP wrappers, as explained in the next section.

When you revise the inetd.conf file, you must prompt inetd to reread the file. To do so, issue the command:

```
killall -HUP inetd
```

For more information on inetd, see *NET-3-HOWTO*, by Terry Dawson and Alessandro Rubini, /usr/doc/HOWTO/NET-3-HOWTO.

To see firsthand how inetd works, complete Exercise 22.1.

EXERCISE 22.1

Configuring *inetd*

The inetd facility is used by many—perhaps most—Linux systems that offer network services. So, it's important for you to be familiar with inetd. To observe the effect of inetd configuration changes, perform the following steps:

1. Comment out the inetd.conf line that refers to telnet.

2. Prompt inetd to reload its configuration.

3. Attempt to telnet to the local host. The client request will not be accepted.

4. Identify each service that is enabled in inetd.conf. Disable any services that are not actually needed.

For now, you can look back to the chapter and other sources to help you perform these operations. But, before taking the RHCE exam, be sure you can work with inetd without referring to materials that won't be available during the exam.

TCP Wrappers

The tcpd program can control access to services that run under inetd. To use tcpd to control access to a particular service, specify tcpd as the program that should run when a client request for that service is received. The name of the program that provides the service—and any run-time arguments you want to pass to the program—is specified as arguments of the tcpd command. A service that runs this way is said to run with a TCP wrapper. In the example inetd.conf file given earlier, telnet and most other services ran with a TCP wrapper.

The tcpd program uses two configuration files: /etc/hosts.allow and /etc/hosts.deny. The /etc/hosts.allow file contains directives that specify services and the hosts allowed to use them; the /etc/hosts.deny file contains similar directives that specify services and the hosts forbidden to use them. When a host attempts to access a service that has a TCP wrapper, the authorization process works like this:

1. If the /etc/hosts.allow file contains a line specifying that the host is allowed to access the service, tcpd authorizes the access.

2. If the /etc/hosts.deny file contains a line specifying that the host is forbidden to access the service, tcpd denies the access.

3. In all other cases, tcpd authorizes the access.

The */etc/hosts.allow* File

As explained earlier, if the /etc/hosts.allow file contains a line specifying that a host is allowed to access a service, tcpd authorizes the access. The lines in the file have the general form

service: host_list

where *service* identifies a service that goes by the same name used in the /etc/inetd.conf and /etc/services files, and *host_list* specifies one or more hosts that are allowed to access the service. Each host is separated from the following host by a comma.

Hosts can be specified in any of the following several ways:

- By an IP address, such as 192.168.1.1

- As a network address/netmask pair, such as 192.168.1.0/ 255.255.255.0

You can also specify a range of addresses by specifying an incomplete IP address followed by a dot. For example, 192.168.1. refers to the same range of IP addresses as 192.168.1.0/255.255.255.0.

- By a host name, such as www.azusapacific.com

- By a domain or subdomain name, such as .azusapacific.com (note the leading dot)

- By the keyword LOCAL, which denotes the local host

Owing to a quirk in implementation, the keyword LOCAL matches any host name that has no dots. For example, LOCAL will match a host name entered in /etc/hosts without a dot. If you use the keyword LOCAL, be sure that you don't unintentionally give non-local hosts special privileges.

- By the keyword ALL, which denotes all hosts

You can also use the keyword EXCEPT to specify exceptions to a general rule. For example, the directive

    in.ftpd: ALL EXCEPT 192.168.1.0/192.168.1.255

specifies that all hosts except those in the range 192.168.1.0 to 192.168.1.255 may access the FTP service.

You can use the keywords ALL and EXCEPT to specify services, as well as hosts. For example, the directive

    ALL EXCEPT in.telnetd: www.azusapacific.com

specifies that the host www.azusapacific.com may access all services except telnet.

The portmap service is configured to use TCP wrappers, even though its is not mentioned in the inetd.conf file. However, you must not use a host or domain name to specify access to the portmap service; use only IP addresses or the keywords ALL and EXCEPT.

The */etc/hosts.deny* File

As explained earlier, if the /etc/hosts.deny file contains a line specifying that a host is forbidden to access a service, tcpd refuses the access unless the access is authorized by a line in the /etc/hosts.allow file. The lines in the /etc/hosts.deny file have the same form as those in the /etc/hosts.allow file. If an access is not explicitly authorized by the /etc/hosts.allow file or forbidden by the /etc/hosts.deny file, the access is authorized.

The portmap service is configured to use TCP wrappers, even though it is not mentioned in the inetd.conf file. However, you must not use a host or domain name to specify access to the portmap service; use only IP addresses or the keywords ALL and EXCEPT. Note that denying access to all services via the ALL keyword can implicitly deny access to portmap, which will break the Network File System (NFS) and other services that rely on portmap.

Checking TCP Wrappers

The positive/negative logic behind TCP wrappers can easily become confusing. The tcpdchk command can help you determine that you've properly configured TCP wrappers. Issue the command

```
tcpdchk -v
```

The command will respond by listing the rules you specified, like this:

```
Using network configuration file: /etc/inetd.conf

>>> Rule /etc/hosts.allow line 6:
daemons:  ALL
clients:  .apu.edu 216.126.187.244 127.0.0.
access:   granted
```

You can inspect the output to determine whether tcpd understands your specifications the same way you do.

Another useful command is tcpdmatch. Issue a command in the form

```
tcpdmatch service host
```

where *service* specifies a service configured to use TCP wrappers, and *host* specifies a real or hypothetical host. The command determines whether your configuration permits the specified host to access the specified service and reports the result. The following is an example of such a result.

```
tcpdmatch in.ftpd www.example.net
client:  address  192.168.1.1
server:  process  in.ftpd
access:  granted
```

Substituting Services by Using *twist*

The twist directive can be used in the /etc/hosts.allow and /etc/hosts.deny files to substitute an alternative service for the requested service. For example, the /etc/hosts.allow line

```
in.telnetd: .example.net : twist /usr/local/sbin/telnetd
```

substitutes the program /usr/local/sbin/telnetd in place of the usual telnet service for client hosts in the example.net domain.

You can also use a twist directive in the /etc/hosts.deny file. For example, the directive

```
in.telnetd: .example.net : twist /bin/echo Hosts from
    ↪example.net not welcome
```

displays a customized unwelcome message for client hosts in the example.net domain.

Further Information

For further information on TCP wrappers, see the man pages hosts_access (5) and hosts_options (5). Now, see how TCP wrappers work by completing Exercise 22.2.

EXERCISE 22.2

Specifying TCP Wrappers

TCP wrappers are an important element of a network security policy and generally should be implemented for hosts attached to a non-local network. To see how TCP wrappers work, perform the following steps:

1. Specify a TCP wrapper that denies telnet access to the local host. Verify that the access from the local host is blocked, but that it is not blocked elsewhere.

2. Specify a TCP wrapper that denies telnet access to hosts other than the local host. Verify that the access from the local host is not blocked, but that it is blocked elsewhere.

In performing the required operations, you can consult the chapter and other sources. However, before taking the RHCE exam, be sure you're able to implement TCP wrappers without needing such help.

Network Information Service (NIS)

Red Hat Linux includes an implementation of version 2 of Sun Microsystem's (Sun) Network Information Service (NIS), formerly known as Yellow Pages (YP). NIS facilitates management of a local area network by letting you centralize information on user accounts, mail aliases, hosts, networks, and so on. A network managed by NIS is called an NIS domain and must include a master server; it can also include slave servers. The databases that contain network information are referred to as *maps*. An element of information contained in a map, such as the name and IP address of a network, is called a *key*.

NIS is not highly secure; for example, a user with access to an NIS server can obtain the complete contents of the server's NIS maps. Sun's newer NIS+ facility is more secure. However, Red Hat Linux supports only NIS+ clients; NIS+ servers are not supported.

The Red Hat Package Manager (RPM) packages related to NIS are:

- ypbind, the NIS client

- ypserv, the NIS server

- yp-tools, useful NIS tools and utilities

In addition, NIS requires the portmap service.

The file /etc/nsswitch.conf specifies the NIS configuration. An NIS server stores information about the domain in /var/yp/domain; NIS clients store cached information in /var/yp/binding.

You can easily determine whether a host is managed by NIS. Issue the command

```
domainname
```

If the host is part of an NIS domain, the command will report the name of the domain.

NIS Commands

Among the most important commands and programs used by an NIS client are:

ypbind   Finds NIS information and stores it in /var/yp/binding

ypwhich   Returns the name of the NIS server

ypcat   Prints keys in the specified map

yppoll   Prints the version number of the specified map, and identifies the server on which the map resides

ypmatch   Prints selected keys of the specified map

yppasswd   Changes NIS passwords

Among the most important commands and programs used by an NIS server are:

ypserv   The executable name of the NIS daemon

makedbm   Makes a map database from a text file

yppush   Notifies slave servers of map updates

yppasswdd   The daemon that handles NIS password changes

For more information on these commands, see the associated man pages.

NIS Configuration

The main NIS configuration file is /etc/nsswitch.conf. Here are the contents of that file as it's distributed with Red Hat Linux:

```
# /etc/nsswitch.conf
#
# An example Name Service Switch config file. This file
# should be sorted with the most-used services at the
# beginning.
#
# The entry '[NOTFOUND=return]' means that the search for an
# entry should stop if the search in the previous entry
# turned up nothing. Note that if the search failed due to
# some other reason (like no NIS server responding) then
# the search continues with the next entry.
#
# Legal entries are:
#
#       nisplus or nis+         Use NIS+ (NIS version 3)
#       nis or yp               Use NIS (NIS version 2),
#                                   also called YP
#       dns                     Use DNS (Domain Name
#                                   Service)
#       files                   Use the local files
#       db                      Use the local database
#                                   (.db) files
#       compat                  Use NIS on compat mode
#       [NOTFOUND=return]       Stop searching if not found
#                                   so far
#
#

# To use db, put the "db" in front of "files" for entries
# you want to be looked up first in the databases
#
# Example:
#passwd:     db files nisplus nis
#shadow:     db files nisplus nis
#group:      db files nisplus nis
```

```
passwd:     files nisplus nis
shadow:     files nisplus nis
group:      files nisplus nis

#hosts:     db files nisplus nis dns
hosts:      files nisplus nis dns

services:   nisplus [NOTFOUND=return] files
networks:   nisplus [NOTFOUND=return] files
protocols:  nisplus [NOTFOUND=return] files
rpc:        nisplus [NOTFOUND=return] files
ethers:     nisplus [NOTFOUND=return] files
netmasks:   nisplus [NOTFOUND=return] files
bootparams: nisplus [NOTFOUND=return] files

netgroup:   nisplus

publickey:  nisplus

automount:  files nisplus
aliases:    files nisplus
```

The second important NIS configuration file is /etc/yp.conf. Here are the contents of the /etc/yp.conf file as it's distributed with Red Hat Linux.

```
# /etc/yp.conf - ypbind configuration file
# Valid entries are
#
#domain NISDOMAIN server HOSTNAME
#       Use server HOSTNAME for the domain NISDOMAIN.
#
#domain NISDOMAIN broadcast
#       Use broadcast  on  the local net for domain
#         NISDOMAIN
#
#ypserver HOSTNAME
#       Use server HOSTNAME for the  local  domain.  The
#       IP-address of server must be listed in /etc/hosts.
#
```

Each line, other than comment lines, names an NIS map and specifies the sources used to obtain its keys in the order in which they should be searched. Table 22.1 summarizes NIS maps, and Table 22.2 summarizes the keywords used to specify the sources.

TABLE 22.1   NIS Maps

NIS Map	Shared by Default	Description
aliases	no	Mail aliases
ethers	no	Ethernet addresses
group	yes	User groups
hosts	yes	Host names and IP numbers
netgroup	yes	List of hosts and users
networks	yes	Network names and IP numbers
passwd	yes	User account information
protocols	yes	Network protocols
publickey	no	Keys used by secure_rpc
rpc	yes	RPC call names
services	yes	Network services
shadow	no	Shadow passwords

TABLE 22.2   Sources of NIS Maps

Source	Description
compat	NIS (in a mode compatible with old versions of the standard C library)
db	Local database

TABLE 22.2 Sources of NIS Maps *(continued)*

Source	Description
dns	DNS
files	Local files
nis	NIS
nisplus	NIS+

For more information on NIS, see *NIS HOWTO,* by Thorsten Kukuk, /usr/doc/HOWTO/NIS-HOWTO.

Lightweight Directory Access Protocol (LDAP)

The Lightweight Directory Access Protocol (LDAP) provides databases that can store arbitrary information. Consequently, LDAP can serve a variety of uses. Among them, LDAP can provide a more secure alternative to NIS when combined with Secure Socket Layer (SSL). For example, LDAP with SSL features encrypted data transfer and Access Control Lists (ACLs) to specify which users can access information stored in an LDAP database. Unlike NIS, which relies on refresh intervals to inform slave hosts of changes to stored maps, LDAP can push database updates to clients.

LDAP is contained in the package openldap, which provides

slapd   The LDAP daemon that runs on port 389

slurpd   An LDAP daemon that replicates an LDAP database

The main LDAP configuration file is /etc/openldap/slapd.conf. For more information on LDAP, see the files in /usr/doc/openldap-* and the documentation available on the LDAP Web site, www.openldap.org. Also see the following man pages pertaining to LDAP:

- centipede
- chlog2replog
- edb2ldif

- fax500
- go500
- go500gw
- in.xfingerd
- ldap.conf
- ldapadd
- ldapd
- ldapdelete
- ldapfilter.conf
- ldapfriendly
- ldapmodify
- ldapmodrdn
- ldappasswd
- ldapsearch
- ldapsearchprefs.conf
- ldaptemplates.conf
- ldbmcat
- ldif
- ldif2id2children
- ldif2id2entry
- ldif2index
- ldif2ldbm
- mail500
- rcpt500
- slapd
- slapd.conf
- slapd.replog
- slurpd
- ud
- ud.conf

Pluggable Authentication Module (PAM) Facility

The Red Hat Linux Pluggable Authentication Module (PAM) facility is more commonly known simply as PAM. PAM lets you configure security policies for a variety of programs. Each PAM-aware program has a configuration file that resides in /etc/pam.d. The contents of the file associated with a program determine how the program authorizes access to its functions. By using PAM, you can configure authorization policies without modifying and recompiling programs.

PAM consists of a series of library modules that are dynamically loaded. The configuration file of a PAM-aware program determines the modules, and hence the actions, that are used to verify authorizations. Following is a list of some of the most important PAM modules:

pam_access.so   This module restricts the hosts from which a service can be accessed.

pam_console.so   This module confers special privileges to users logged on via the console by making them members of the special, dynamic group console. By this means, console users are able to access the floppy drive, sound subsystem, and joystick and can perform privileged operations such as rebooting and shutting down the system.

pam_listfile.so   This module consults a specified file to determine authorizations. The FTP service uses this module to deny FTP access to users listed in /etc/ftpusers.

pam_nologin.so   This modules prevents users other than root from logging in while the /etc/nologin file exists.

pam_securetty.so   This module prohibits logging in as root from a tty device other than those listed in /etc/securetty.

pam_time.so   This module restricts the times at which a user can access a service by day or time of day.

PAM-Aware Programs

Among the programs that are PAM-aware are:

chfn

chsh

ftp

gnorpm-auth

halt

imap

kde

linuxconf

linuxconf-pair

login

passwd

pop

poweroff

ppp

reboot

rexec

rlogin

rsh

samba

shutdown

ssh

su

sudo

xdm

xscreensaver

xserver

PAM Configuration Files

A PAM configuration file specifies a series of modules that should be loaded and executed to authorize access to the related facility. A module generally returns a pass/fail value. The values returned by the series of modules are used to determine whether to grant or deny access.

The directives contained in a PAM configuration file have the following general format:

```
module_type control_flag module_path arguments
```

The *module_type* field indicates the type of authorization performed. The types of authorization that can be performed are:

account   Indicates that access is restricted by the age of the password, the time of day, the available resources, or the location of the user.

auth   Indicates that the user is to be authenticated, for example, by prompting for a password.

password   Indicates that the user's authentication information may be updated if appropriate, such as when a user changes his or her password.

session   Indicates the tasks that should be performed before or after the user is granted access.

The *control_flag* field indicates how a module's return value affects the overall result. The control flag value can be any of the following:

- optional
- required
- requisite
- sufficient

All modules with the control flag values required and requisite must return a pass; otherwise, authorization is denied. Normally, all modules are executed; however, if a module that has the control flag value requisite fails, access is immediately denied. Similarly, if a module that has the control flag value sufficient succeeds, access is immediately granted. A module that has the control flag value optional does not affect the overall result.

The *module_path* field specifies the location of the module to be executed. See the documentation files in /usr/doc/pam-* for a complete list of available modules and a description of their function and operation.

The *arguments* field specifies one of these values:

debug   Indicates that debugging information should be sent to the system log.

no_warn   Indicates that the module should not issue warning messages.

use_first_pass   Indicates that the module should use a previously entered password rather than prompt for one.

try_first_pass   Indicates that the module should use a previously entered password rather than prompt for one. However, if the previously entered password fails, the module will prompt for a new one.

use_mapped_pass   Indicates that the module should use a previously entered response to generate an encrypted or decrypted key used to store or retrieve a password.

Now, complete Exercise 22.3 to gain practical experience working with PAM.

EXERCISE 22.3

Configuring PAM

Every Red Hat Linux system is preconfigured to use PAM. Unless you're content with the default configuration, you'll need to have some skill in working with PAM in order to establish an improved configuration. Perform these steps to gain experience working with PAM:

1. Revise the PAM configuration file for FTP to allow the root user to access the FTP service. Verify that it's possible for root to do so.

2. Revise the appropriate PAM configuration file to permit remote logins by the root user. Verify that it's possible for root to log in remotely.

3. Restore the original PAM configurations to avoid a possible security breach.

You can refer to the chapter and to the PAM documentation in completing this exercise. However, before taking the RHCE exam, be sure you're sufficiently skilled in using PAM to be able to perform operations such as these without referring to books, notes, or other help.

Summary

In this chapter, you learned about restricting access to network services. The most important topics covered are:

The inetd Service   The inetd service mediates requests for TCP services, launching the appropriate server when a client request is received. The service's configuration file is /etc/inetd.conf.

TCP Wrappers   The tcpd daemon can restrict access to services controlled by inetd. The /etc/hosts.allow and /etc/hosts.deny configuration files identify the hosts that are permitted or forbidden access to services. The associated twist program can be used to respond to client requests by substituting a specified program for the service that would otherwise be launched.

Network Information Service (NIS)   NIS provides a set of centralized databases—called maps–that help manage user accounts, mail aliases, hosts, networks, and other information across a network. NIS contains several security flaws and is not widely used.

Lightweight Directory Access Protocol (LDAP)   LDAP provides databases that can be used to store arbitrary information, including information on user accounts and other information of the sort maintained by NIS. LDAP is generally considered more secure than NIS.

Pluggable Authentication Module (PAM) Facility   The PAM facility is a Red Hat Linux facility that lets you configure security-related options of PAM-aware programs. For example, you can use the PAM facility to tailor the policies that restrict the form of valid passwords. PAM configurations for PAM-aware programs reside in `/etc/pam.d`.

Key Terms

Before going on to the next chapter, be sure you're familiar with the following terms:

> key
>
> LDAP
>
> maps
>
> NIS
>
> PAM
>
> TCP wrappers

Additional Sources of Information

For further information on restricting access to primary network services, see:

- The LDAP documentation, /usr/doc/openldap-*, and the LDAP Web site, www.openldap.org

- *NET-3-HOWTO*, by Terry Dawson and Alessandro Rubini, /usr/doc/HOWTO/NET-3_HOWTO

- *NIS HOWTO*, by Thorsten Kukuk, /usr/doc/HOWTO/NIS-HOWTO

- The PAM documentation files, /usr/doc/pam-*

Review Questions

1. Which of the following are configuration files used to configure TCP wrappers?

    A. /etc/allow

    B. /etc/hosts

    C. /etc/hosts.allow

    D. /etc/tcpwrapper

2. Which of the following options should generally be set for the UDP services specified in inetd.conf?

    A. nowait

    B. stream

    C. udp

    D. wait

3. Which of the following /etc/hosts.allow entries permits access to the FTP service by only the local host, assuming that /etc/hosts.deny forbids all access?

    A. ftpd: LOCAL

    B. ftpd: LOCAL ONLY

    C. in.ftpd: LOCAL

    D. in.ftpd: LOCAL ONLY

4. Which of the following is a reasonable /etc/hosts.allow directive?

    A. imapd: 192.168.1.1

    B. imapd: www.example.net

    C. portmap: 192.168.1.1

    D. portmap: www.example.net

5. Which of the following presents a secure environment for management of network information?

   A. LDAP with SSL

   B. NIS

   C. NIS+

   D. SSL

6. What is the name of the RPM package that should be installed to implement LDAP?

   A. `ldap`

   B. `ldapis`

   C. `ldapssl`

   D. `openldap`

Answers to Review Questions

1. C. The files /etc/inetd.conf, /etc/hosts.allow, and /etc/hosts.deny configure TCP wrappers.

2. C, D. UDP services should generally receive the wait option in addition to the udp protocol option.

3. C. The FTP service is known to inetd as in.ftpd. The LOCAL keyword specifies access to the local host.

4. A, B, C. The portmap service should not be specified with a host name that requires DNS resolution.

5. A, C. NIS is not a highly secure service. SSL does not provide management of network information, though it can be used with LDAP to do so.

6. D. The openldap package contains support for LDAP.

Chapter
23

Understanding Secondary Network Services

RHCE PREPARATION TOPICS COVERED IN THIS CHAPTER:

✓ Be familiar with secondary network services supported under Red Hat Linux, such as DHCP, IPX, lpd, Internet news, squid, and time synchronization.

In addition to the primary network services covered in Chapter 21, Red Hat Linux supports many additional services. This chapter explains several of the most important and commonly used secondary network services. The Red Hat, Inc. study points for the Red Hat Certified Engineer exam require only conceptual familiarity with these secondary network services. This chapter, therefore, focuses on basic concepts related to secondary network services; however, it also includes practical hints intended to help you install, configure, and use the services.

Dynamic Host Configuration Protocol (DHCP)

A *Dynamic Host Configuration Protocol (DHCP)* server can help you manage your network's IP address space. The Red Hat Linux DHCP server is compatible with the older *BOOTP* protocol still used in some Unix shops. DHCP is particularly helpful if your network includes computers that are intermittently connected or that move from location to location, such as laptops.

When a host running a DHCP client boots, it contacts a DHCP server. The DHCP server can assign such host-related information as the following:

- IP address
- Host and domain names
- Network IP address
- Broadcast IP address
- Default gateway IP address
- DNS server IP address
- WINS server IP address

A DHCP server can be configured to provide static or dynamic information, or both. A static configuration provides a client with a fixed IP address based on the Media Access Control (MAC) address assigned to the client's network interface and the subnet address of the client's point of network connection. Thus, the combination of host identity and location determine the assigned configuration.

A dynamic configuration arbitrarily assigns IP addresses from one or more ranges. This conserves IP addresses, because only hosts that are active have an associated IP address. However, the IP address associated with a host may be different each time the host boots. A DHCP configuration can be both dynamic and static, providing designated hosts with a static configuration and other hosts with a dynamic configuration.

Installing DHCP

The DHCP server is contained in the dhcp package. To install DHCP, move to the directory containing the package and issue the command

```
rpm -Uvh dhcp-*.rpm
```

DHCP requires the associated network interface to support and be configured for broadcast and multicast operation. To determine if a network interface is properly configured, issue the command

```
ifconfig -a
```

The output pertaining to a typical network interface should resemble the following:

```
eth1 Link encap:Ethernet  HWaddr 00:A0:CC:25:8A:EC
     inet addr:192.168.1.1  Bcast:192.168.1.255
➥Mask:255.255.255.0
     UP BROADCAST RUNNING PROMISC MULTICAST  MTU:1500
➥Metric:1
     RX packets:4648466 errors:0 dropped:0 overruns:0
➥frame:0
     TX packets:679303 errors:0 dropped:0 overruns:0
➥carrier:0
     collisions:33062 txqueuelen:100
     Interrupt:11 Base address:0x6000
```

Note the keywords BROADCAST and MULTICAST, which appear in the third line of the output. If these keywords are not present, DHCP will not operate correctly. To resolve the problem, you may need to do any or all of the following:

- Reconfigure the interface by using the ifconfig command.

- Replace the network interface with a card that supports MULTICAST.

Configuring DHCP

The DHCP configuration file is /etc/dhcpd.conf. Here's a typical configuration, which includes both dynamic and static information:

```
default-lease-time 64800;
max-lease-time 64800;

option subnet-mask 255.255.255.0;
option broadcast-address 192.168.1.255;
option routers 192.168.1.1;
option domain-name-servers 192.168.1.1;
option domain-name "azusapacific.com";

subnet 192.168.1.0 netmask 255.255.255.0 {

        server-identifier 192.168.1.1;

        host sara {
                hardware ethernet 00:50:04:d2:3f:15;
                fixed-address 192.168.1.33;
                default-lease-time 2592000;
        }

        range 192.168.1.20 192.168.1.29;
}

subnet 192.168.100.0 netmask 255.255.255.0 {
}
```

The configuration assigns the IP address 192.168.1.33 to the interface with MAC address 00:50:04:d2:3f:15. Other DHCP clients are assigned an IP address in the range 192.168.1.1 to 192.168.1.29. For more information on the contents of the /etc/dhcpd.conf file, see the man page dhcpd.conf.

Before starting the DHCP service, you must create the file /var/state/dhcp/dhcpd.leases; otherwise, the DHCP server will terminate immediately after it's started. To create the file, issue the following command

```
touch /var/state/dhcp/dhcpd.leases
```

Some releases of Red Hat Linux require you to place the dhcpd.leases file in /etc.

Once the DHCP service starts, it stores the assignments it makes—called *leases*—in the dhcpd.leases file, which you can view by using, for example, the more command or a text editor. Here is an example of such leases:

```
lease 192.168.1.20 {
        starts 6 2000/02/12 09:20:15;
        ends 2 2000/05/09 13:58:16;
        hardware ethernet 00:e0:98:77:08:40;
        uid 01:00:e0:98:77:08:40;
        client-hostname "OEMComputer";
}
lease 192.168.1.24 {
        starts 0 2000/03/12 18:20:23;
        ends 0 2000/03/12 18:20:23;
        hardware ethernet 00:50:56:be:01:03;
}
lease 192.168.1.23 {
        starts 6 2000/03/11 21:52:29;
        ends 6 2000/03/11 23:52:29;
        hardware ethernet 00:50:56:a0:01:03;
}
lease 192.168.1.22 {
        starts 6 2000/03/11 21:46:24;
        ends 6 2000/03/11 23:46:24;
        hardware ethernet 00:50:56:b9:01:03;
}
lease 192.168.1.21 {
        starts 6 2000/03/11 18:17:53;
        ends 6 2000/03/11 18:18:39;
        hardware ethernet 00:50:56:a7:01:03;
}
```

Leases are assigned for a finite time, specified in /etc/dhcpd.conf, after which they must be renewed by the client.

To start the configured DHCP server, issue the command

```
/etc/rc.d/init.d/dhcpd start
```

When using DHCP with a Microsoft Windows client, DHCP should add a route to host 255.255.255.255; the route is needed to communicate with Microsoft DHCP clients. Check the system log for messages indicating the status of DHCP. You can do this by issuing the command

```
tail /var/log/messages
```

The result should resemble the following:

```
May  9 07:18:45 www dhcpd: Internet Software Consortium
➥DHCPD $Name:
  V2-BETA-1-PATCHLEVEL-6 $
May  9 07:18:45 www dhcpd: Copyright 1995, 1996, 1997, 1998
➥The Internet Software Consortium.
May  9 07:18:45 www dhcpd: All rights reserved.
May  9 07:18:45 www dhcpd: Listening on
➥Socket/eth1/192.168.1.0
May  9 07:18:45 www dhcpd: Sending on
➥Socket/eth1/192.168.1.0
May  9 07:18:45 www dhcpd: Listening on
➥Socket/eth0/192.168.100.0
May  9 07:18:45 www dhcpd: Sending on
➥Socket/eth0/192.168.100.0
May  9 07:19:33 www dhcpd: dhcpd shutdown succeeded
```

The DHCP Client

The standard Red Hat Linux DHCP client is a program called pump, contained in a package having the same name. The pump package is part of the standard base installation of Red Hat Linux.

To configure a Red Hat Linux host to use DHCP to determine its network configuration, launch linuxconf and choose Config ➢ Networking ➢ Client Tasks ➢ Basic Host Information. Select the paragraph or tab corresponding to the network interface (adapter) you want to configure. Set the following options:

- Enabled

- Config Mode = DHCP

Select Accept ➢ Quit ➢ Activate Changes to install the new configuration. Figure 23.1 shows the relevant linuxconf screen in graphical mode.

FIGURE 23.1 The linuxconf Host Basic Configuration screen

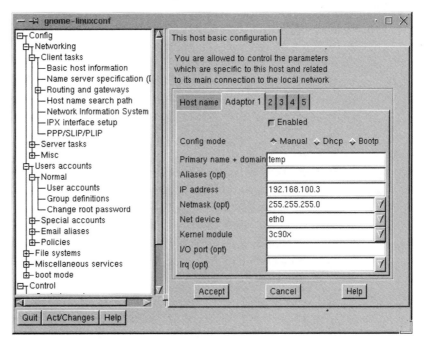

You can check the status of pump by issuing the command

```
/sbin/pump -s
```

To force immediate renewal of a lease, issue the command

```
/sbin/pump -i eth0 -R
```

More Information on DHCP and *pump*

For more information on DHCP, see

- The DHCP Web page at www.isc.org

- The *DHCP mini-HOWTO* by Vladimir Vuksan, which resides in /usr/doc/dhcp-*

- The DHCP documentation in /usr/doc/dhcp-*

For more information on pump, see its man page.

The IPX Protocol

Red Hat Linux includes the mars-nwe package. This package provides file and printer sharing for Novell networks, which are based on the IPX protocol. The related ipxutils package includes useful IPX utilities. If you're working with an IPX-based network, you should install both packages.

The mars-nwe package lets you mount IPX file systems by using the ncpmount command or by using a mount command specifying file system type ncp. You can also specify IPX file systems in the /etc/fstab file.

The mount command reports the file system type as ncpfs; but, you can specify ncp or ncpfs as an argument to the mount command and in the /etc/fstab file.

For more information on using IPX under Linux, see the mars_nwe documentation in /usr/doc/mars-nwe-* and the ipxutils documentation in /usr/doc/ipxutils-*. Also see the following man pages:

- ipx_cmd
- ipx_configure
- ipx_interface
- ipx_internal_net
- ipx_route
- ncopy
- ncpmount
- ncpumount
- nprint
- nsend
- nwauth
- nwbocreate
- nwbols
- nwboprops
- nwborm
- nwbpadd
- nwbpcreate

- nwbprm
- nwbpset
- nwbpvalues
- nwclient
- nwdir
- nwfsctrl
- nwfsinfo
- nwfstime
- nwgrant
- nwmsg
- nwpasswd
- nwpurge
- nwrevoke
- nwrights
- nwsfind
- nwtrustee
- nwuserlist
- nwvolinfo
- pqlist
- pqrm
- pqstat
- pserver
- slist

Remote Printer Access via *lpd*

You can easily access a Red Hat Linux printer remotely. Of course, you must first configure the server and client systems. To configure the server system, list each client host in `/etc/hosts.lpd`. If the client host is under the same administrative control as the server, you can list the host in `/etc/hosts.equiv`, if you prefer. Also, be sure the host name of the client host can be resolved to an IP address; add a line to `/etc/hosts`, if necessary.

To configure the client, add an entry in the following form to the client's `/etc/printcap` file:

```
remlp:\
  :lp=:rm=host:rp=printer:sd=dir
```

In this entry, *host* is the host name of the server, *printer* is the name by which the target printer is listed in the server's `/etc/printcap` file, and *dir* is the spool directory to be used on the client. The spool directory is usually a subdirectory of `/var/spool`.

Once the server and client are configured, you should be able to access the server's printer by issuing commands on the client host. For example, you can print a file by using the `lpr` command, and you can check the print queue by using the `lpq` command.

Internet News

The `inn` package provides `innd` and other programs that support the *Network News Transfer Protocol (NNTP)* and Internet news. Internet news transmits and receives postings to Internet newsgroups, which were the dominant method of multi-way user-to-user interaction before the advent of the Web. Today, Web forums provide a simpler way of supporting multi-way user-to-user interaction. However, Internet news remains a popular service, even though it's complicated to work with and requires significant resources. You can use `inn` to support local newsgroups or to provide access to Internet newsgroups. To adequately support Internet newsgroups, the host system must have multiple gigabytes of free hard disk space and a high-speed Internet connection.

Like e-mail, Internet news has become a means of transmitting spam. To suppress spam news articles, you can install the `cleanfeed` package.

Synchronizing Time

Red Hat Linux provides two ways to synchronize system time:

- rdate, which synchronizes to the clock of another host

- xntp3, which synchronizes to Universal Coordinated Time (UTC)

The rdate program, contained in the rdate package, is the older and less sophisticated method of synchronizing time. To synchronize the local host's clock to that of another system, issue a command in the form

```
rdate -p -s host
```

where *host* is the host name of the remote host. Often, a command such as this is placed in the /etc/rc.d/rc.local file, so that it will be executed when the system boots. Once synchronized, the clocks are apt to drift apart; the rdate command makes no provision for continual synchronization.

The xntpd program, which is contained in the xntp3 package, continually synchronizes the system clock to a precise estimate of UTC, based on time data obtained from remote servers. You can configure the xntpd service to run at desired runlevels. Alternatively, you can use the cron facility to regularly run ntpdate, another program in the xntp3 package; when invoked, ntpdate adjusts the system clock and then terminates. Both xntpd and ntpdate use the *Network Time Protocol (NTP)*, described in RFC 1305. Typically, a host is configured to synchronize with multiple hosts, so that synchronization can continue even if a host cannot be contacted.

NTP hosts are arranged in a hierarchy. Servers near the top of the hierarchy—called *stratum* 1 servers—receive time information from a highly accurate, terrestrial source, such as radio signals sent from an atomic clock. Servers in stratum 2 synchronize to one or more stratum 1 servers, and so on.

NTP continually adjusts the system time, usually to millisecond precision. NTP never adjusts the clock backward; if necessary, it slows the clock until real time catches up with the errant clock.

The man pages for ntpdate, the primary NTP command, and other NTP programs are absent in some releases of the xntp3 package. Here's a man page for ntpdate:

```
ntpdate - set the date and time via NTP
SYNOPSIS
ntpdate [ -bdos ] [ -a key# ] [ -e authdelay ] [ -k
➥keyfile ]
  [ -p samples ] [ -t timeout ] server ...
DESCRIPTION
Ntpdate sets the local date and time by polling the Network
```

Time Protocol server(s) on the host(s) given as arguments to determine the correct time. It must be run as root on the local host. A number of samples are obtained from each of the servers specified and the standard NTP clock filter and selection algorithms are applied to select the best of these. Typically, ntpdate can be inserted in the /etc/rc.local startup script to set the time of day at boot time and/or can be run from time-to-time via cron(8). Note that ntpdate's reliability and precision will improve dramatically with greater numbers of servers. While a single server may be used, better performance and greater resistance to insanity on the part of any one server will be obtained by providing at least three or four servers, if not more.

Time adjustments are made by ntpdate in one of two ways. If ntpdate determines your clock is off by more than 0.5 seconds it will simply step the time by calling settimeofday(2). If the error is less than 0.5 seconds, however, it will by default slew the clock's time via a call to adjtime(2) with the offset. The latter technique is less disruptive and more accurate when the offset is small, and works quite well when ntpdate is run by cron (8) every hour or two. The adjustment made in the latter case is actually 50% larger than the measured offset since this will tend to keep a badly drifting clock more accurate (at some expense to stability, though this tradeoff is usually advantageous). At boot time, however, it is usually better to always step the time. This can be forced in all cases by specifying the -b switch on the command line. The -s switch tells ntpdate to log its actions via the syslog(3) facility rather than to the standard output, a useful option when running the program from cron(8) .

The -d flag may be used to determine what ntpdate will do without it actually doing it. Information useful for general debugging will also be printed. By default ntpdate claims to be an NTP version 2 implementation in its outgoing packets. As some older software will decline to respond to version 2 queries, the -o switch can be used to force the program to poll as a version 1 implementation instead.

The number of samples ntpdate acquires from each server can be set to between 1 and 8 inclusive using the -p switch. The default is 4. The time it will spend waiting for a response can be set using the -t switch, and will be rounded to a

multiple of 0.2 seconds. The default is 1 second, a value
suitable for polling across a LAN.

Ntpdate will authenticate its transactions if need be. The
-a switch specifies that all packets should be authenticated
using the key number indicated. The -k switch allows the
name of the file from which the keys may be read to be
modified from the default of /etc/ntp.keys. This file should
be in the format described in xntpd(8) . The -e option
allows the specification of an authentication processing
delay, in seconds (see xntpd(8) for details). This number is
usually small enough to be negligible for ntpdate's purposes,
though specifying a value may improve timekeeping on very
slow CPU's.

Ntpdate will decline to set the date if an NTP server
daemon (e.g. xntpd(8)) is running on the same host. When
running ntpdate on a regular basis from cron(8) as an
alternative to running a daemon, doing so once every hour or
two will result in precise enough timekeeping to avoid
stepping the clock.

FILES
/etc/ntp.keys contains the encription keys used by ntpdate.

Other NTP commands, in addition to xntpd and ntpdate, include:

- /usr/sbin/ntpdate
- /usr/sbin/ntpq
- /usr/sbin/ntptime
- /usr/sbin/ntptrace
- /usr/sbin/tickadj
- /usr/sbin/xntpd
- /usr/sbin/xntpdc

For additional information, see the man pages for these NTP commands.
The main configuration file for NTP is /etc/ntp.conf. Here are the contents of a typical /etc/ntp.conf file:

```
# Undisciplined Local Clock. This is a fake driver intended
# for backup and when no outside source of synchronized time
# is available. The default stratum is usually 3, but in
# this case we elect to use stratum 0. Since the server line
```

```
# does not have the prefer keyword, this driver is never
# used for synchronization, unless no other other
# synchronization source is available. In case the local
# host is controlled by some external source, such as an
# external oscillator or another protocol, the prefer
# keyword would cause the local host to disregard all other
# synchronization sources, unless the kernel modifications
# are in use and declare an unsynchronized condition.

server  128.173.14.71    # vt.edu
server  140.247.60.28    # harvard.edu
server  165.227.1.1      # scruz.net
server  131.216.16.9     # unlv.edu
server  127.127.1.0      # local clock
fudge   127.127.1.0 stratum 10

restrict   default ignore
restrict   199.184.237.129
restrict   128.173.14.71
restrict   140.247.60.28
restrict   165.227.1.1
restrict   131.216.16.9
restrict   192.168.0.0 mask 255.255.0.0
restrict   127.0.0.0   mask 255.255.255.0

# Drift file.  Put this in a directory which the daemon can
# write to. No symbolic links allowed, either, since the
# daemon updates the file by creating a temporary in the
# same directory and then rename()'ing it to the file.

driftfile /etc/ntp/drift

#multicastclient                          # listen on default
➥224.0.1.1
#broadcastdelay 0.008

# Authentication delay.  If you use, or plan to use
# someday, the authentication facility you should make the
# programs in the auth_stuff directory and figure out what
# this number should be on your machine.

authenticate no

# Keys file.  If you want to diddle your server at run
# time, make a keys file (mode 600 for sure) and define the
# key number to be used for making requests.
```

```
# PLEASE DO NOT USE THE DEFAULT VALUES HERE. Pick your own,
# or remote systems might be able to reset your clock at
# will.

#keys           /etc/ntp/keys
#trustedkey     65535
#requestkey     65535
#controlkey     65535
```

For more information on NTP, see the documentation in /usr/doc/ xntp3*. Also see the NTP Web site at www.ntp.org.

 Take care when choosing NTP servers with which to synchronize. One study found that a significant number of NTP servers were badly configured and, therefore, reported erroneous time values.

The *squid* Proxy Server

The squid proxy server is a caching proxy server compatible with FTP, HTTP, and SSL. It directly handles HTTP and FTP requests and can forward SSL requests to another server or proxy. It can, for example, be used to:

- Reduce bandwidth demands due to multiple requests for popular Web pages.

- Control access to external Web sites by means of Access Control Lists (ACLs).

- Accelerate an HTTP server.

The proxy works by caching HTTP data requested through it and serving the cached response rather than repeatedly retrieving popular data from a remote server. It intelligently forwards requests for dynamic content to remote servers; so CGI (Common Gateway Interface) pages, for example, are properly handled.

To accelerate an HTTP server, the proxy typically runs on port 80, the usual HTTP port. It then forwards requests not found in its cache to a Web server running on another port or system.

An instance of the proxy can participate in a hierarchy of cache sites known as the Harvest Cache. The motivation behind the Harvest Cache project is a 1993 study showing that NFSNET backbone FTP traffic could be reduced by 44 percent by means of several well-placed caches. For more information on the Harvest Cache, see the project's Web site at ircache.nlanr.net.

The proxy is contained in the package squid-2.2.STABLE4-8.i386.rpm, along with a 1900-line default version of its main configuration file, /etc/squid/squid.conf. The default configuration file is adequate for many applications, so squid is often ready to go immediately following installation. To start the service, issue the command

```
/etc/rc.d/init.d/squid
```

To configure a Web browser to use squid, set the browser's proxy host to the host name of the system running squid and set the proxy port to the port on which squid is running, generally 3128.

For more information on squid, see the documentation files in /usr/doc/squid-* and the information on the squid Web site at squid.nlanr.net.

Services Using Encryption

U.S. export laws restricting the export of software that uses encryption stronger than 56 bits have recently been somewhat relaxed. But, several important encryption algorithms are covered by patents. Therefore, Red Hat Linux does not contain some popular software that uses strong encryption. In particular, ssh (a more secure substitute for telnet and rsh) and scp (a more secure substitute for rcp) are not included.

You can obtain RPM packages for popular applications that use strong encryption from the Web site www.zedz.net.

From these sites, you can also obtain the GNUPG program, gnupg, a GNU implementation of the popular Pretty Good Privacy (PGP) program. GNUPG is particularly useful, because Red Hat, Inc. signs RPM packages it creates by using its GNUPG public key. Thus, you can use GNUPG to authenticate the origin of RPM packages alleged to have been built by Red Hat, Inc. Red Hat Linux 6.2 includes GNUPG as part of the standard distribution.

At one time, Red Hat, Inc. signed RPM packages by using the PGP program. However, packages are now signed by using GNUPG.

To authenticate the origin of RPM packages, you must download the GNUPG package. Move to the directory containing the package, and install the package by issuing the following command

```
rpm -Uvh gnupg-*.rpm
```

Then, generate a key pair by issuing the following command

```
gpg --gen-key
```

The dialog that ensues will resemble the following:

```
gpg (GnuPG) 1.0.1; Copyright (C) 1999 Free Software
Foundation, Inc.
This program comes with ABSOLUTELY NO WARRANTY.
This is free software, and you are welcome to redistribute
it under certain conditions. See the file COPYING for
details.

Please select what kind of key you want:
   (1) DSA and ElGamal (default)
   (2) DSA (sign only)
   (4) ElGamal (sign and encrypt)
Your selection? 1
DSA keypair will have 1024 bits.
About to generate a new ELG-E keypair.
                 minimum keysize is  768 bits
                 default keysize is 1024 bits
    highest suggested keysize is 2048 bits
What keysize do you want? (1024) 1024
Requested keysize is 1024 bits
Please specify how long the key should be valid.
         0 = key does not expire
      <n>  = key expires in n days
      <n>w = key expires in n weeks
      <n>m = key expires in n months
      <n>y = key expires in n years
Key is valid for? (0) 0
Key does not expire at all
Is this correct (y/n)? y

You need a User-ID to identify your key; the software
constructs the user id from Real Name, Comment and Email
Address in this form:
    "Heinrich Heine (Der Dichter) <heinrichh@duesseldorf.de>"

Real name: Bill McCarty
```

```
Email address: bmccarty@azusapacific.com
Comment:
You selected this USER-ID:
    "Bill McCarty <bmccarty@apu.edu>"

Change (N)ame, (C)omment, (E)mail or (O)kay/(Q)uit? o
You need a Passphrase to protect your secret key.
thisisatest
We need to generate a lot of random bytes. It is a good
idea to perform some other action (work in another window,
move the mouse, utilize the network and the disks) during
the prime generation; this gives the random number generator
a better chance to gain enough entropy.
+++++.+++++......++++++++++...+++++.......+++++
+++++.++++++++++...+++++......+++++..+++++....+++++
+++++.+++++..........++++++++++.........+++++.......+++++
+++++......+++++..+++++..+++++.+++++.....+++++...+++++
+++++.................+++++
public and secret key created and signed.
```

You must also download and install the public key used by Red Hat, Inc. to sign RPM packages. This key is available at www.redhat.com/about/contact.html. Download the key into the file redhat2.asc, then install it by issuing the command

```
gpg --import redhat2.asc
```

The command output will resemble the following:

```
gpg (GNUPG) 0.4.0; Copyright (C) 1998 Free Software
Foundation, Inc.
This program comes with ABSOLUTELY NO WARRANTY.
This is free software, and you are welcome to redistribute
it under certain conditions. See the file COPYING for details.

gpg:redhat2.asc: key DB42A60E: public key imported
```

To verify the signature of an RPM package, issue a command in the following form

```
rpm -K package_file
```

You could, for example, issue the following command to verify the signature of the basesystem package

```
rpm -K basesystem-6.0-4.noarch.rpm
```

If the signature matches, the output will resemble the following:

```
basesystem-6.0-4.noarch.rpm: md5 gpg OK
```

For more information on GNUPG, see the GNUPG Web site, `www.gnupg.org`.

Summary

In this chapter, you learned about secondary network services. The most important topics covered are:

Dynamic Host Configuration Protocol (DHCP)   DHCP lets you configure clients to obtain their network configuration information during system start up. The DHCP configuration file is `/etc/dhcpd.conf`. A DHCP server can be configured to provide fixed information to a given host, which the server identifies by the host's Media Access Control (MAC) address. Alternatively, a DHCP server can provide an available configuration from a pool.

DHCP Clients   The Linux DHCP client is named `pump`. Using `linuxconf` or `netconf`, you can configure a Linux system to obtain its network configuration at system start up via `pump`.

The IPX Protocol   The IPX protocol is the native protocol of Novell NetWare systems. The Red Hat Linux `mars-nwe` package provides file and printer sharing compatibility with Novell's IPX protocol.

Remote Printer Access   Red Hat Linux remote printer access is provided by the `lpd` service. To define a remote printer, you can use `printtool` or modify the `/etc/printcap file`. To enable printer access for a remote host, list the remote host in the `/etc/hosts.lpd` or `/etc/hosts.equiv` file.

Internet News   Internet news is provided by the `inn` package. Internet news is relatively difficult to configure and requires a relatively large amount of computing resources, particularly disk space.

Time Synchronization   You can synchronize system time by using `rdate` or `xntp3`. The `xntp3` facility, which uses Network Time Protocol (NTP), is the more sophisticated of the two facilities and provides more precise time synchronization. The facility's main configuration file is `/etc/ntp.conf`.

The **squid** Proxy Server   The `squid` proxy server is a caching proxy server that is compatible with FTP, HTTP, and SSL. It can be used to:

- Reduce bandwidth demands due to multiple requests for popular Web pages

- Control access to external Web sites by means of Access Control Lists (ACLs)

- Accelerate an HTTP server

Encryption Software   U.S. law restricts the export of software that uses strong encryption; that is, encryption via a key longer than 56 bits. Several popular Unix and Linux programs use strong encryption and are therefore not included in the Red Hat Linux distribution. You can download RPM packages for popular programs that use strong encryption from `www.zedz.net`.

Key Terms

Before going on to the next chapter, be sure you're familiar with the following terms:

BOOTP

Dynamic Host Configuration Protocol (DHCP)

Network News Transfer Protocol (NNTP)

Network Time Protocol (NTP)

stratum

Additional Sources of Information

If you'd like further information about the topics presented in this chapter, you should consult the following sources:

- The DHCP Web page, `www.isc.org`

- The *DHCP Mini-HOWTO*, by Vladimir Vuksan, `/usr/doc/dhcp-*`

- The DHCP documentation in `/usr/doc/dhcp-*`

- The `mars_nwe` documentation in `/usr/doc/mars-nwe-*`

- The `ipxutils` documentation in `/usr/doc/ipxutils-*`

- The `squid` documentation files in `/usr/doc/squid-*`

- The GNUPG Web site, `www.gnupg.org`

Review Questions

1. Which of the following can be supplied by a DHCP server?

   A. Host name

   B. DNS server IP address

   C. IP address

   D. WINS server IP address

2. The packages commonly used to support NNTP are:

   A. `cleanfeed`

   B. `inn`

   C. `rdate`

   D. `xntp3`

3. Which of the following programs synchronizes time continually?

   A. `ntpdate`

   B. `rdate`

   C. `setclock`

   D. `xntpd`

4. What is the port on which `squid` is usually run?

   A. 80

   B. 3128

   C. 8080

   D. Not applicable: `squid` does not require a port

5. Red Hat, Inc. signs RPM packages by using:

    A. GNUPG

    B. MD5

    C. PGP

    D. RPMSIGN

6. Which of the following is the most accurate stratum of synchronized time?

    A. Stratum 0

    B. Stratum 1

    C. Stratum 2

    D. Stratum 3

Answers to Review Questions

1. A, B, C, D.   A DHCP server can supply essentially all the elements of a complete network configuration.

2. A, B.   The inn package provides the NNTP daemon, innd; the cleanfeed package provides a spam filter useful when running innd.

3. D.   The rdate and ntpdate programs set the time only once, when either is executed.

4. B.   The squid proxy can run on any available port; but, by default, it runs on port 3128.

5. A.   Red Hat, Inc. formerly used PGP to sign RPM packages but now uses GNUPG.

6. B.   Stratum 1 is the highest level of the synchronization hierarchy; stratum 0 does not exist.

Chapter
24

Administering Logs

RHCE PREPARATION TOPICS COVERED IN THIS CHAPTER:

✓ Understand and be able to administer system logs.

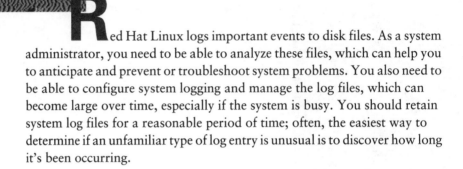

ed Hat Linux logs important events to disk files. As a system administrator, you need to be able to analyze these files, which can help you to anticipate and prevent or troubleshoot system problems. You also need to be able to configure system logging and manage the log files, which can become large over time, especially if the system is busy. You should retain system log files for a reasonable period of time; often, the easiest way to determine if an unfamiliar type of log entry is unusual is to discover how long it's been occurring.

System Logging Processes

A Red Hat Linux system has two system logging processes:

syslogd   The main system logging process

klogd   The process that logs kernel messages

The following subsections describe these processes.

The *syslogd* Process

The main system logging process is `syslogd`. The `syslogd` process is started at system boot time by the initialization script `/etc/rc.d/init.d/syslog`.

When an important event occurs and an application needs to log a message, it sends the message to `syslogd`, which logs the message. Generally, logging the message entails writing it to the file `/var/log/messages`. However, `syslogd` can take a variety of other logging actions. For example, `syslogd` can log the event to a file other than `/var/log/messages`, display the message on the system console, send a message to a logged on user, and so on. The `syslogd` configuration file is `/etc/syslog.conf`. The section "Configuring System Logging" explains how to configure the `syslogd` process.

The *klogd* Process

Another important system logging process is klogd, which handles kernel messages. The klogd process generally passes received messages to syslogd, which logs them in the usual manner. However, by specifying appropriate command line arguments, you can configure klogd to log kernel messages to a designated file, if you prefer. The klogd process is started by the same /etc/rc.d/init.d/syslog script that starts the syslogd process.

System Log Files and Entries

By default, most message types are logged to the file /var/log/messages, the system log file. You can view the most recent entries in the system log file by issuing a command of the form

```
tail -n /var/log/messages
```

where *n* is the number of lines you want to view. The system log typically contains a wide variety of message types. Here are some typical entries:

```
May 10 15:09:59 www named[474]: listening on [127.0.0.1].53
➥(lo)
May 10 15:09:59 www named[474]: listening on [192.168.100.2]
➥.53 (eth0)
May 10 15:09:59 www named[474]: listening on [192.168.1.1]
➥.53 (eth1)
May 10 15:10:00 www named[474]: Forwarding source address
➥is [0.0.0.0].1024
May 10 15:10:00 www named: named startup succeeded
May 10 15:10:00 www named[475]: Ready to answer queries.
May 10 15:10:00 www sshd[481]: log: Server listening on
➥port 23.
May 10 15:10:00 www sshd[481]: log: Generating 768 bit RSA
➥key.
May 10 15:10:01 www xntpd: xntpd startup succeeded
May 10 15:10:01 www xntpd[496]: xntpd 3-5.93e Wed Apr 14 20
➥:23:29 EDT 1999 (1)
May 10 15:10:01 www xntpd[496]: tickadj = 5, tick = 10000,
➥   tvu_maxslew = 495, est . hz = 100
```

```
May 10 15:10:01 www xntpd[496]: precision = 13 usec
May 10 15:10:02 www xntpd[496]: read drift of -94.732
➥ from /etc/ntp/drift
May 10 15:11:49 www dhcpd: DHCPREQUEST for 192.168.1.90
➥ from 00:e0:98:77:08:40 via eth1
May 10 15:11:49 www dhcpd: DHCPACK on 192.168.1.90 to 00:e0
➥:98:77:08:40 via eth1
May 10 15:17:26 www lpd[11305]: www.azusapacific.com
➥requests printjob lp
May 10 15:17:27 www kernel: parport0: PC-style at 0x3bc
➥[SPP,PS2]
May 10 15:17:27 www kernel: parport0: Printer, Hewlett-
➥Packard HP LaserJet 2100 Series
May 10 15:17:27 www kernel: lp0: using parport0 (polling).
➥  (serial 2000050901)
May 11 11:34:05 sbmserver lpd[22139]: sbmserver.azusapacific
➥.com requests printjob lp
May 11 13:15:09 sbmserver ftpd[22243]: ACCESS DENIED (not
➥in any class) TO usr57-dialup119.mix2.Atlanta.cw.net
➥[166.62.189.121]
May 11 13:15:09 sbmserver ftpd[22243]: FTP LOGIN REFUSED
➥  (access denied) FROM usr57-dialup119.mix2.Atlanta.cw
➥.net [166.62.189.121], anonymous

➥May 11 13:15:10 sbmserver ftpd[22243]: FTP session closed
May 11 23:01:56 sbmserver ftpd[21811]: FTP LOGIN FROM
➥  pool1209.dialup.earthlink.net [209.179.138.189], jczarnec
May 11 23:05:29 sbmserver ftpd[21811]: FTP session closed
```

Each entry has the general form

time_stamp host application[process_ID]: message

where

- *timestamp* is the date and time at which the message was received

- *host* is the name of the host that originated the message

- *application* is the name of the application that sent the message

- *process_ID* is the process number of the application that sent the message

- *message* is the message contents

Some common message types include:

- Authorization failures
- Failed su commands
- Hardware errors, such as timeouts
- Logins via FTP, SSH, and TELNET
- Mail activity
- Startups and shutdowns of processes and services

If you're looking for a particular type of log message in a large log file, you may find the grep command handy. Issue a command in the form

```
grep string /var/log/messages | more
```

where *string* is a string of text common to log messages of the type you're interested in. The grep command will display only those log entries that contain the specified text.

Now, take a few minutes to complete Exercise 24.1, which will further acquaint you with the system log.

EXERCISE 24.1

Examining the System Log

To gain experience in working with the system log, perform the following steps:

1. Use the more command to display each line of the system log file.

2. Study each line to discern its meaning and significance.

3. Often, a study of the system log will expose previously unknown problems that require attention. If you find problems, seek to resolve them.

You can look back to this book or consult other documentation for help in completing this exercise. But before taking the RHCE exam, be sure you can work with the system log without consulting such help.

Configuring System Logging

The file /etc/syslog.conf contains the system logging configuration. Each entry in the file specifies a class of log messages and a corresponding logging action. Entries have the general form

```
facility.priority [; facility.priority ...] action
```

where

- *facility* specifies the class of application that originates the messages. You can specify multiple facilities by separating each facility from the others with a comma (,).

- *priority* specifies the priority associated with the messages.

- *action* specifies the action to be taken with respect to messages from the given facility and having the given priority.

Table 24.1 summarizes the keywords used to refer to facilities that originate log messages. Table 24.2 summarizes the keywords and symbols used to refer to message priorities. Table 24.3 summarizes the keywords and symbols used to designate logging actions.

TABLE 24.1   Facilities and Their Designations

Facility Designation	Description
auth	Messages from user authorization facilities
authpriv	Messages from privileged user authorization facilities; ordinary users should not see these messages
cron	Messages from the cron facility
daemon	Messages from daemons and TCP services
kern	Messages from the kernel
lpr	Messages from the printer facility
mail	Messages from the mail facility
news	Messages from Internet news

TABLE 24.1 Facilities and Their Designations *(continued)*

Facility Designation	Description
syslog	Messages from system logging
user	Messages from user-defined facilities
uucp	Messages from the Unix-to-Unix Copy Program (UUCP)
local0– local7	Messages from locally defined facilities
*	Messages from any facility

TABLE 24.2 Message Priority Designations

Message Priority	Priority	Description
debug	1	Log debug messages and messages of higher priority.
info	2	Log info messages and messages of higher priority.
notice	3	Log notice messages and messages of higher priority.
warning	4	Log warning messages and messages of higher priority.
err	5	Log err messages and messages of higher priority.
crit	6	Log crit messages and messages of higher priority.
alert	7	Log alert messages and messages of higher priority.
emerg	8	Log emerg messages and messages of higher priority.
*	N/A	Log all messages, irrespective of priority.

TABLE 24.2 Message Priority Designations *(continued)*

Message Priority	Priority	Description
=priority	N/A	Log messages of only the specified priority.
! *priority*	N/A	Ignore messages of the specified priority and higher.
!= *priority*	N/A	Log all messages except those of the specified priority.

TABLE 24.3 Logging Action Designations

Action Designation	Description
absolute path	Log messages to the specified file.
/dev/console or /dev/tty*n*	Log messages to the specified terminal.
@*host*	Log messages to the remote host.
userid	Send messages to the specified user, if the user is logged in. You can specify multiple user IDs by separating each user ID from the others with a comma.
*	Send messages to all logged in users via the wall command.

Here are the contents of a typical /etc/syslog.conf file:

```
# Log all kernel messages to the console.
# Logging much else clutters up the screen.
#kern.*
➥/dev/console

# Log anything (except mail) of level info or higher.
# Don't log private authentication messages!
*.info;mail.none;authpriv.none
➥/var/log/messages
```

```
# The authpriv file has restricted access.
authpriv.*
➥/var/log/secure

# Log all the mail messages in one place.
mail.*
➥/var/log/maillog

# Everybody gets emergency messages
*.emerg *

# Save mail and news errors of level err and higher in a
# special file.
uucp,news.crit
➥/var/log/spooler
```

Notice that authpriv messages are sent to the file /var/log/secure, which is readable only by root.

Linux remote logging is useful for duplicating logs and centralizing log files for convenient analysis. However, remote logging is somewhat buggy.

To experiment a bit with system logging, complete Exercise 24.2.

EXERCISE 24.2

Configuring System Logging

To learn more about system logging, temporarily reconfigure logging of authorization messages (auth) to see the effects of some unusual logging methods. Set the system to runlevel 3, and perform the following operations:

1. Configure system logging to send authorization messages to the file /var/log/authlog. Verify that the configuration works.

2. Configure system logging to send authorization messages to the system console. Verify that the configuration works.

3. Configure system logging to send authorization messages to the root user. Verify that the configuration works. To receive the messages, you'll need to log in as root rather than merely issue the su command to obtain root privileges.

4. Configure system logging to send authorization messages to all users. Verify that the configuration works.

5. Restore the original system logging configuration.

You can refer to outside help while working on this exercise. But before taking the RHCE exam, be sure you can perform operations such as these without recourse to books, notes, or other help.

Boot Log

When the Linux kernel boots, it displays boot messages on the system console. These messages are stored in the kernel ring buffer, which is overwritten when full. You can view the kernel ring buffer by issuing the command

    dmesg

To prevent the loss of potentially important boot messages, the initialization scripts save the contents of the kernel ring buffer in the file /var/log/dmesg, the boot message file, which can be viewed by issuing the command

    more /var/log/dmesg

Here is typical output of the command:

```
Linux version 2.2.5-15 (root@porky.devel.redhat.com) (gcc
➡version
egcs-2.91.66 19990314/Linux (egcs-1.1.2 release)) #1
➡   Mon Apr 19 23:00:46 EDT 1999
Detected 548955270 Hz processor.
Console: colour VGA+ 80x25
Calibrating delay loop... 547.23 BogoMIPS
Memory: 64152k/66556k available (996k kernel code, 412k
➡reserved, 936k data, 60k init)
VFS: Diskquotas version dquot_6.4.0 initialized
```

CPU: AMD AMD-K7(tm) Processor stepping 02
Checking 386/387 coupling... OK, FPU using exception 16
➥error reporting.
Checking 'hlt' instruction... OK.
POSIX conformance testing by UNIFIX
mtrr: v1.26 (19981001) Richard Gooch
(rgooch@atnf.csiro.au)
PCI: PCI BIOS revision 2.10 entry at 0xfdb01
PCI: Using configuration type 1
PCI: Probing PCI hardware
PCI: Enabling I/O for device 00:00
Linux NET4.0 for Linux 2.2
Based upon Swansea University Computer Society NET3.039
NET4: Unix domain sockets 1.0 for Linux NET4.0.
NET4: Linux TCP/IP 1.0 for NET4.0
IP Protocols: ICMP, UDP, TCP, IGMP
Initializing RT netlink socket
Starting kswapd v 1.5
Detected PS/2 Mouse Port.
Serial driver version 4.27 with MANY_PORTS MULTIPORT SHARE_
➥IRQ enabled
ttyS00 at 0x03f8 (irq = 4) is a 16550A
pty: 256 Unix98 ptys configured
apm: BIOS version 1.2 Flags 0x03 (Driver version 1.9)
Real Time Clock Driver v1.09
RAM disk driver initialized: 16 RAM disks of 4096K size
VP_IDE: IDE controller on PCI bus 00 dev 39
VP_IDE: not 100% native mode: will probe irqs later
    ide0: BM-DMA at 0xffa0-0xffa7, BIOS settings: hda:DMA,
➥hdb:pio
    ide1: BM-DMA at 0xffa8-0xffaf, BIOS settings: hdc:pio,
➥hdd:DMA
hda: Maxtor 92048D8, ATA DISK drive
hdd: CD-ROM Drive/F5B, ATAPI CDROM drive
ide0 at 0x1f0-0x1f7,0x3f6 on irq 14
ide1 at 0x170-0x177,0x376 on irq 15
hda: Maxtor 9204, 19531MB w/1024kB Cache, CHS=2489/255/63
hdd: ATAPI 48X CD-ROM drive, 128kB Cache
Uniform CDROM driver Revision: 2.54

```
Floppy drive(s): fd0 is 1.44M
FDC 0 is a post-1991 82077
md driver 0.90.0 MAX_MD_DEVS=256, MAX_REAL=12
raid5: measuring checksumming speed
raid5: using high-speed MMX checksum routine
   pII_mmx    :   1444.752 MB/sec
   p5_mmx     :   1559.052 MB/sec
   8regs      :    734.949 MB/sec
   32regs     :    639.318 MB/sec
using fastest function: p5_mmx (1559.052 MB/sec)
scsi : 0 hosts.
scsi : detected total.
md.c: sizeof(mdp_super_t) = 4096
Partition check:
 hda: hda1 hda2 < hda5 hda6 hda7 hda8 hda9 hda10 hda11 >
autodetecting RAID arrays
autorun ...
... autorun DONE.
VFS: Mounted root (ext2 filesystem) readonly.
Freeing unused kernel memory: 60k freed
Adding Swap: 538140k swap-space (priority -1)
Creative SBLive! detected
```

The system boot log is particularly helpful in troubleshooting problems related to device drivers. If a hardware device is not functioning properly, check the system boot log to see whether the driver loaded and initialized without error.

Log Rotation

If a system is busy, its log files can quickly grow large and cumbersome to work with. To control the size of system logs, the cron facility runs a daily job that rotates log files, /etc/cron.daily/logrotate. The contents of the logrotate script, as distributed in Red Hat Linux, are as follows:

```
#!/bin/sh
/usr/sbin/logrotate /etc/logrotate.conf
```

The `logrotate` command can manipulate log files in several ways. For instance, it can do the following tasks:

- Rotate log files

- Compress log files to minimize disk space used

- Mail log files to a specified user

Rotating a log file involves establishing a series of log files. When the current log file reaches a specified age, it is renamed rather than deleted. So, the current log file is always a manageable size. By using *log rotation*, several generations of log files can be retained for convenient access. The `logrotate` configuration file is `/etc/logrotate.conf`. By default, logs are rotated weekly, and four weeks of logs are retained in addition to the current log. Here are the contents of a typical `/etc/logrotate.conf` file:

```
# see "man logrotate" for details
# rotate log files weekly
weekly

# keep 4 weeks worth of backlogs
rotate 4

# send errors to root
errors root

# create new (empty) log files after rotating old ones
create

# uncomment this if you want your log files compressed
#compress

# RPM packages drop log rotation information into this
# directory
include /etc/logrotate.d

# no packages own lastlog or wtmp -- we'll rotate them here
/var/log/wtmp {
    monthly
    create 0664 root utmp
```

```
        rotate 1
}

/var/log/lastlog {
    monthly
    rotate 1
}

# system-specific logs may be configured here
```

Red Hat Linux also uses the `logrotate` utility to maintain logs other than the system log. The relevant configuration files reside in `/etc/logrotate.d`; the name of this directory is specified in the `/etc/logrotate.conf` file.

Now complete Exercise 24.3, which asks you to study some actual log rotation schemes.

EXERCISE 24.3

Configuring *logrotate*

It's seldom necessary to tweak the default log rotation scheme used by Red Hat Linux. But, you won't know whether the scheme needs tweaking unless you know its particulars. To get acquainted, examine the `logrotate` configurations for each of the following applications that are installed on your system: apache, FTP, samba, squid, sudo, and `syslog`.

The *swatch* Utility

When a system is busy, log files can rapidly become large and, therefore, too time-consuming to examine manually. The `swatch` utility, distributed as part of the Red Hat PowerTools collection, monitors log files and can take specified action when a given type of event message is logged. For example, `swatch` can send an e-mail message, call a pager, and so on.

A similar utility, `logwatch`, is also distributed as part of the Red Hat PowerTools collection. The `logwatch` utility can process Samba logs as well as system logs.

Summary

In this chapter, you learned about system logging. The most important topics covered are:

System Logging Processes   The system logging processes are klogd, the kernel logging process, and syslogd, the system logging process. By default, klogd uses syslogd to handle its log requests. The system logging configuration file is /etc/syslog.conf.

System Log Files   The system logging process sends most log entries to /var/log/messages. Messages that contain information that might compromise user account or system security are sent to /var/log/secure, which is readable only by the root user. Log files can be viewed using familiar Linux commands, such as tail. Boot messages are logged to /var/log/dmesg.

Log Entry Contents   A log entry contains the following information:

- The date and time at which the message was received

- The name of the host that originated the message

- The name of the application that sent the message

- The process number of the application that sent the message

- The message contents

Log Entry Types   Common log entry types include the following:

- Authorization failures

- Failed su commands

- Hardware errors, such as timeouts

- Logins via FTP, SSH, and TELNET

- Mail activity

- Startups and shutdowns of processes and services

Log Rotation   Log rotation controls the amount of disk space consumed by log files. The configuration of the logrotate utility, which is stored in /etc/logrotate.conf, determines how long log files are retained and what action is taken when a log file reaches a specified age or size.

The swatch Utility   The swatch utility can help you automate the regular review and analysis of system logs.

Key Terms

Before going on to the next chapter, be sure you're familiar with the following term:

log rotation

Additional Sources of Information

If you'd like further information about the topics presented in this chapter, you should consult the following sources:

- The `syslog.conf`, `klogd`, `sysklogd`, `syslogd`, and `logrotate` man pages
- Documentation files in `/usr/doc/sysklogd*`

Review Questions

1. Which of the following is the main system logging process?

   A. klogd

   B. linuxlog

   C. syslog

   D. syslogd

2. Which of the following is the main configuration file for system logging?

   A. /etc/klog.conf

   B. /etc/klogd.conf

   C. /etc/syslog.conf

   D. /etc/syslogd.conf

3. The command used to view the kernel ring buffer is which of the following?

   A. bootmesg

   B. dmesg

   C. logmesg

   D. sysboot

4. Which of the following operations is built into the logrotate command?

   A. compression

   B. deletion

   C. rotation

   D. sending via mail

5. Which of the following is a useful utility for analyzing log files?

    A. `logman`

    B. `logrotate`

    C. `logwatch`

    D. `swatch`

6. By default, Red Hat Linux retains system logs for how long?

    A. 1 day

    B. 1 week

    C. 4 weeks

    D. 16 weeks

Answers to Review Questions

1. D. The main system logging process is syslogd; the klogd process logs kernel messages, generally by passing them to syslogd.

2. C. The /etc/syslog.conf file is the configuration file for the syslogd process.

3. B. The dmesg command displays the contents of the kernel ring buffer.

4. A, B, C, D. During rotation, the oldest log file is deleted.

5. C, D. The swatch and logwatch tools are distributed as part of the Red Hat PowerTools collection. Neither logman nor logrotate analyze log files.

6. C. The logrotate program rotates log files weekly, keeping four generations of log files in addition to the current log file.

Chapter

25

Administering Security

RHCE PREPARATION TOPICS COVERED IN THIS CHAPTER:

✓ Understand basic security issues and be able to protect a system against common security threats.

A stand-alone computer that is kept in a locked office to which only the user has a key is highly resistant to security threats. However, few users are content to relinquish network access in exchange for improved security. And as a system administrator, you're probably responsible for both workstations and servers, which, by their very nature, must be connected to a network. Protecting networked multiuser systems requires skill and diligence. This chapter explains computer security fundamentals and gives guidance on how to avoid and recover from common security threats.

Security Fundamentals

The challenge of computer security is that a system is only as secure as its weakest point. Vigilance, therefore, is paramount; it matters little that the front door is double-bolted and chained if the back door stands open. However, vigilance must be joined with insight and skill. Even a vigilant system administrator must possess insight that properly directs vigilance; for, misdirected vigilance comes to nothing. Likewise, the vigilant system administrator must posses skill that leads to appropriate action in the face of potential and real threats, for inaction in the face of danger leads to catastrophe.

Computer security can be viewed from many perspectives. One useful perspective focuses on what's at risk. A security breach can lead to the loss of such things as:

- Tangible property, such as computer equipment

- Information

- Service, as in the inability to access a mail server

Protecting tangible property is more of a familiar function than protecting information or service, since most of us have homes and cars and understand how locks and keys can be used to protect them. Protecting tangible property is a prerequisite to protecting information and service: If an intruder can access a system's console, it's likely that the intruder can manage to boot the system into single-user mode and obtain privileged access.

Another way of looking at security is to consider the issue of intent. A security breach can be either unintentional or intentional. An unintentional security breach is particularly serious when logged in as root. It's easy to mistype a command and thereby lose data. For example, suppose you want to delete files having names beginning with *a*. You intend to type

```
rm -f a*
```

but instead you type

```
rm -f a *
```

The space between the *a* and the asterisk causes the command to delete all files, not just those having names beginning with *a*.

Intentional security breaches arise from two sources: authorized users and unauthorized users. Often, great effort is devoted to preventing unauthorized system access; but security can be breached by trusted, authorized users even more easily than by the unknown cracker. Effective security must restrict even authorized users from performing operations that compromise information or service.

The security bulwark of a Linux system is the system of password-protected user accounts and the related ability to restrict user access to files and directories which have been assigned permissions. If passwords or user accounts are compromised, security is soon breached. However, perfect security is an illusion: Experience shows that no amount of effort or expenditure can guarantee the security of a system. Instead of aiming at perfection, a security policy should aim at effectiveness. An effective security policy imposes costs on the would-be intruder that outweigh the benefits the intruder might enjoy by breaching security. At some point a rational intruder will decide that a secure system will require more effort to crack than it's worth and will seek a more vulnerable target. However, some would-be intruders are not economically motivated; for example, they may see cracking as a fun way of passing time. Excluding such intruders requires a more sophisticated security policy than that which is required to exclude the economically motivated cracker.

A good security policy must balance the costs of security mechanisms against the benefits the mechanisms provide, for security mechanisms generally inconvenience users, at least to some degree.

The following sections of this chapter address system and network security in more detail, with a focus on preventing security breaches. The final section of the chapter focuses on detecting and recovering from security breaches. Although physical security is fundamental to computer security, this chapter does not address it; the RHCE exam does not test your knowledge of physical security.

System Security

System security begins with the installation of the system from distribution media known to be authentic. Prudent system administrators are wary of network installations, which present a would-be intruder with an opportunity to introduce malicious software. Prudent Red Hat Linux system administrators monitor the Red Hat Linux mailing lists and other lists that transmit information on security fixes and promptly install applicable fixes to close publicly known vulnerabilities. They're also cautious about installing software downloaded from untrusted sites. Such software can include vulnerabilities or even malicious code, leading to a security breach.

The *root* Account

If not properly managed and used, the root account can provide an intruder with the means to breach your security. To avoid a security breach, you should use the root account only when necessary. Don't, for example, continuously leave open a terminal window logged in as root. Likewise, when logged in as root, be aware whether the current terminal window is a root or non-root session, and use a window associated with a non-root session whenever possible. By default, the root user receives the special command-line prompt #, whereas non-root users receive $ as a command-line prompt.

Be very careful when issuing commands as root. It's altogether too easy, as shown earlier, to mistype a command and suffer unintended consequences.

Generally, it's best for only one user to know and use the root account of a system. Likewise, it's generally best not to use programs like sudo, which let non-root users temporarily gain root access. By restricting access to the root account, you can ensure that the individual who has access to the root account is aware of the current system configuration and is able to evaluate proposed configuration changes for possible effects on system security.

Good practice includes specifying only standard system directories such as /bin, /sbin, /usr/bin, and /usr/sbin in the PATH of the root user. In particular, the current directory and home directory should not be included in the PATH. Omitting these directories from the PATH helps to avoid unknowing execution of malicious code planted by an intruder. Similarly, the default PATH of non-root users should omit the current directory and home directory or place them at the end of the PATH, so that ls, for example, will refer to /bin/ls, rather than a Trojan horse planted by an intruder in the user's home directory.

User Accounts and Passwords

When installing a new system, you should enable the shadow passwords facility, which prevents ordinary users from reading the encrypted passwords associated with user accounts. Otherwise, a would-be intruder can use a program such as crack to discover passwords.

By default, the Plugable Authentication Module (PAM) is configured to enforce rules that prevent users from choosing passwords that are particularly easy to guess or crack. Generally, you should not relax or disable this facility; rather, you should consider imposing further restrictions on passwords. See the information on the cracklib PAM module in the /usr/doc/pam-*/txts/pam.txt file.

You should also regularly purge unused user accounts, which may present opportunities for breaching security. The contents of the home directories of such accounts should be erased or archived and erased, because they may contain malicious code, files, or directories that are world-writable.

setuid and *setgid* Files and Directories

Files can be setuid or setgid. When a user executes a setuid file, the program runs with the effective user ID of the file's owner, rather than that of the user. Similarly, when a user executes a setgid file, the program runs with the effective group ID of the file's group owner, rather than that of the user.

To enable `setuid` or `setgid`, issue a command in the form

```
chmod u+s files    # enable setuid
chmod g+s files    # enable setgid
```

To disable `setuid` or `setgid`, issue a command in the form

```
chmod u-s files    # disable setuid
chmod g-s files    # disable setgid
```

Directories can also be `setgid`. The command to enable or disable `setgid` for a directory is the same as that to enable or disable `setgid` for a file. When a user creates a file in a non-`setgid` directory, the group owner-ship of the file is set to the user's group ID. However, when a user creates a file in a `setgid` directory, the group ownership of the file is set to the group owner of the directory.

Red Hat Linux exploits `setgid` behavior to facilitate sharing of files and directories. Unlike most other UNIX-like operating systems, Red Hat Linux assigns each user to a *user private group* that has the same name as the user's account; as the term suggests, the user is the only member of the user's private group. Also, the `/etc/profile` script distributed with Red Hat Linux assigns ordinary users a default `umask` of 002 rather than the more common 022. A `umask` value of 002 yields a default permission of 775, which implies that the members of the group who own the file can not only read and execute, but also write newly created files. However, since the user is the only member of the user's private group, write access is not unreasonably extended.

The point of the user private group and unusual `umask` value is evident when users must share write access to files or directories. Here's a procedure for implementing sharing:

1. Create a group that represents the department, project, or organization whose members need to share write access.

2. Place each affiliated user in the group.

3. Create a directory to hold the shared files and directories.

4. Set the group ownership of the directory to the group created in step 1.

5. Enable `setgid` for the directory.

When a member of the group creates a file in the directory, the group owner of the new file is set to the group owner of the directory. And, since the user's `umask` value is 002, the file permissions are set to 775. So, members of the group can read, write, and execute the file. However, nonmembers of the group can only read and execute the file. Of course, the user can issue the chmod command to restrict or loosen access permissions as desired; in particular, the user can change the file's permissions to exclude access by nonmembers of the group.

Now, take the time to actually create a shared directory by completing Exercise 25.1.

EXERCISE 25.1

Establishing a Shared Directory

Red Hat's shared directory convention is a point of pride within the Red Hat community. So, you should be familiar with the convention before taking the RHCE exam. To gain some practical experience with a shared directory, perform the following steps:

1. Create a shared directory for the group writers, which includes the users tolstoy and hemingway.

2. Verify that members of the group can write the shared files and that other users cannot.

While working on this exercise, look back to this book and consult other help as the need arises. But, before taking the RHCE exam, be sure you can perform operations such as these without resource to help of any sort.

Choosing User IDs for Services

As a rule, daemon processes should run using either an ordinary user account or the special user account nobody. They should generally not run as root, because a vulnerability in the process may provide a would-be intruder with the means to execute a command as root. If the process runs as an ordinary user, the intruder may compromise the user account. If, however, the process runs as root, the intruder may compromise the root account, which compromises the entire system.

The /etc/passwd file contains several user accounts that have been created to avoid running a process using the root account. Here are the contents of a typical /etc/passwd file:

```
root:x:0:0:root:/root:/bin/bash
bin:x:1:1:bin:/bin:
daemon:x:2:2:daemon:/sbin:
adm:x:3:4:adm:/var/adm:
lp:x:4:7:lp:/var/spool/lpd:
```

```
sync:x:5:0:sync:/sbin:/bin/sync
shutdown:x:6:0:shutdown:/sbin:/sbin/shutdown
halt:x:7:0:halt:/sbin:/sbin/halt
mail:x:8:12:mail:/var/spool/mail:
news:x:9:13:news:/var/spool/news:
uucp:x:10:14:uucp:/var/spool/uucp:
operator:x:11:0:operator:/root:
games:x:12:100:games:/usr/games:
gopher:x:13:30:gopher:/usr/lib/gopher-data:
ftp:x:14:50:FTP User:/home/ftp:
nobody:x:99:99:Nobody:/:
```

In particular, the nobody account has no associated home directory or shell and, therefore, cannot log in to the system. The httpd process, for example, runs using the nobody account. An intruder who compromises the nobody account can cause significant harm—for example, by killing processes—but far less harm than possible via a compromised root account.

Network Security

If a computer system is connected to a network, you should consider the following additional security measures in addition to those described in the preceding section.

As a start, you should not run telnet, rcp, rexec, rlogin, or rsh servers; instead, you should install an ssh server. Unlike ssh, the telnet, rcp, rexec, rlogin, and rsh servers send passwords over the network in clear text. Unless you use ssh, someone running a packet sniffer can easily obtain important system passwords and use them to compromise your system. For the same reason, unless you need it, you should not install an FTP server, particularly an anonymous FTP server. If you need the functions provided by FTP, but don't require FTP as such, you may be able to use scp, which is based on ssh.

You should remove unneeded services from /etc/rc.d/rc?.d and /etc/inetd.conf and configure TCP wrappers to protect services that remain in /etc/inetd.conf. By removing an unneeded service from /etc/inetd.conf, you eliminate the possibility that the unneeded service can be used to compromise your system. Generally, it's also a good idea for you to remove finger, netstat, and systat, which can provide a would-be intruder with potentially useful information about your system. On the other hand, you should run identd, which can help track an intruder by confirming the identity of the user account used to request a TCP service.

Finally, you should remove any information that identifies your system's hardware and software configuration from /etc/issue.net. A would-be intruder could use this information to determine what vulnerabilities might exist.

Chapter 30, "Configuring a Firewall Using ipchains," explains why and how to construct a firewall that will help to protect your system against attacks mounted across the network.

Detection and Correction

Preventing a security breach is better than coping with a security breach. But, it's not always possible to prevent a breach. Therefore, it's necessary to know how to detect a breach and recover from it.

Detecting a Breach

A good way to detect a real or attempted breach is to regularly review system logs. Unusual log entries or gaps in recorded information may point to a breach. However, keep in mind that a clever intruder may tamper with system logs, erasing evidence of the breach.

The Red Hat Linux RPM facility can help you to detect a breach. You can use it to verify the file size, modification date, permissions, and MD5 checksum of files owned by an RPM package. However, for this approach to be effective, you must protect the RPM database, /var/lib/rpm, against tampering. Unless the database is small, it won't fit on a standard floppy disk. However, you can copy the files in the RPM database to offline media, such as a ZIP disk. It's often more convenient to copy the files to another host on the local network; but if that host is compromised, the intruder may still tamper with the RPM database. So, it's best to keep an offline copy of the database.

Several applications provide a more sophisticated facility for detecting actual and potential security breaches. Among these are the following:

- AIDE, www.cs.tut.fi/~rammer/aide.html, which is licensed under the GNU General Public License

- COPS, www.fish.com/cops, which is free and open source

- Gog&Magog, www.multimania.com/cparisel/gog, which is free and open source

- Tripwire, www.tripwiresecurity.com, which is a commercially licensed product that can be freely used under certain circumstances

These applications can detect changes to files in much the same way as the RPM facility, but they can also monitor files that are not part of an RPM package. The COPS application also checks the system configuration for common errors and omissions that can lead to a security breach. The use of such an application is highly recommended.

Recovering from a Breach

The safest way to recover from a breach is to restore a backup that predates the breach. However, the system may quickly be compromised again if the original vulnerability is not found and fixed. Moreover, it's difficult to determine reliably that a given backup does not contain an image that has been comprised; worse yet, restoring a backup entails loss of data that was added or changed after the backup was made.

So, recovering from a breach often involves a "recovery in place" in which you attempt to find and fix the original vulnerability and any Trojan horses, trap doors, or other malicious code left by the intruder. Here are some considerations to keep in mind:

- You should remove the compromised host from the network; otherwise, the intruder may be able to thwart your recovery efforts.

- You should consider the possibility that the intruder has compromised the security of other hosts on your network.

- You should retain copies of log files and other evidence that might be helpful in identifying the intruder or the extent of the breach.

- You should determine the means used to compromise the system so that you can determine the scope of damage and eliminate the vulnerability.

- You should reinstall the operating system from trusted media.

- You should study every file that is owned by root, especially files that are setuid. Ensure that none of these files have been tampered with; if you're unsure, delete and replace the file.

- You should notify administrators of hosts the cracker may have used in breaching your system. You should also contact security organizations with which you or your organization are affiliated.

Summary

In this chapter, you learned about system and network security. The most important topics covered are:

Security Breaches   Security breaches can be committed by authorized and unauthorized users. Breaches can be intentional or unintentional and can lead to loss of the following:

- Tangible property

- Information

- Service

System Security   System security rests on good password security, proper use of the root account, controlled use of `setuid` and `setgid` binaries, and proper choice of user ID for services.

Network Security   Network security rests on the elimination of unneeded services, avoidance of insecure servers, and use of a properly configured firewall.

Detection and Correction   No security policy can prevent every breach. Therefore, it's important to have mechanisms for detecting a security breach and facilities for recovering from such a breach.

Key Terms

Before going on to the next chapter, be sure you're familiar with the following terms:

security policy
user private group

Additional Sources of Information

If you'd like further information on the topics presented in this chapter, you should consult the following sources:

- The *Linux Security HOWTO*, by Kevin Fenzi and Dave Wreski, `/usr/doc/HOWTO/Security-HOWTO`

- *The Linux Administrator's Security Guide*, by Kurt Seifried, `www.securityportal.com/lasg`

- The Root Shell Web site, `rootshell.com`, which features news and information on security vulnerabilities and exploits

Review Questions

1. Which types of security breaches should systems and networks be protected against?

    A. Breaches by authorized users

    B. Breaches by unauthorized users

    C. Intentional breaches

    D. Unintentional breaches

2. Which of the following is true of security policy?

    A. Perfect security is essential.

    B. Perfect security is impossible.

    C. Security exacts a cost in convenience.

    D. Security should be effective.

3. Which of the following is true of the root account?

    A. An available terminal window should always be logged in to the account.

    B. Generally, only one user should have access to the account.

    C. Programs like sudo improve system security.

    D. The account is associated with the special prompt symbol %.

4. Which of the following is true of password security?

    A. You should disable PAM.

    B. You should enable shadow passwords.

    C. You should leave unused user directories in place after purging the associated accounts.

    D. You should regularly purge unused user accounts.

5. When a `setuid` executable is loaded, the effective user ID of the process is which of the following?

A. The group ID of the group that owns the executable file

B. root

C. The user ID of the user who owns the executable file

D. The user ID of the user who ran the program

6. Which of the following TCP services should generally not be used?

A. rcp

B. rlogin

C. rsh

D. telnet

Answers to Review Questions

1. A, B, C, D. Security policies should attempt to protect against the full range of threats.

2. B, C, D. No security policy can preclude every potential threat. Security consumes resources, so considerations of security must be balanced against other considerations, such as convenience.

3. B. Ideally, the root account should be used only when necessary, and only by one user. The account is associated with the special prompt symbol #.

4. B, D. You should consider using PAM to strengthen password security. You should enable shadow passwords and MD5 encryption. You should regularly purge unused user accounts and the associated files and directories.

5. C. The setuid permission causes the process to run using the user ID of the file's owner, which may be root or another user.

6. A, B, C, D. You should generally use ssh instead.

X Window System
Administration

Chapter 26

Installing and Configuring X

RHCE PREPARATION TOPICS COVERED IN THIS CHAPTER:

✓ Understand X in general and the XFree86 X servers in particular.

✓ Be able to install and configure X.

he X Window System, or X, is the graphical user interface distributed with Red Hat Linux. There are a variety of X implementations; the implementation distributed with Red Hat Linux was produced by the XFree86 Project, Inc. Their implementation of X, known as XFree86, is freely redistributable. This chapter explains basic X operation, installation, and configuration. The following two chapters explain how to configure and use more advanced X capabilities, including window and desktop managers and remote X clients.

Basic X Concepts

X includes X servers and X clients; however, in the context of X, the terms have unusual meanings. An *X server* is a video driver for a particular set of video devices. An *X client* is a program or application that uses the graphical user interface provided by an X server. The service that an X server provides is video output.

X servers and clients communicate through the appropriately named X protocol. X is a distributed client/server system: An X client need not run on the same host as the associated X server. For example, an X server can host X clients running on multiple hosts. Similarly, a host can run X clients associated with X servers on several remote hosts.

In addition to servers and clients, X features window managers. A *window manager* works with an X server, providing a standardized graphical appearance and interface behavior to all clients using the server. For example, the window manager draws window title bars and provides an appropriate response when the user clicks a window's close box. The window manager also provides methods of moving, resizing, iconizing, and raising windows.

X also features desktop managers. A *desktop manager* works with a window manager to provide a set of basic capabilities and features needed by most users. For example, a typical desktop manager provides desktop icons, a file manager, a task bar, and so on. The most commonly used Linux desktop managers are KDE and GNOME.

By itself, X is not useful; starting X generally entails starting a window manager and one or more clients. If you launch X without a window manager or clients, all you'll see is a featureless screen.

Installing X

To install X, you must install a set of packages that include:

- An appropriate X server

- The font server and a set of suitable fonts

- Common X code

- An X configuration tool

- Libraries

- The `xinitrc` script

In addition, you'll generally choose to install:

- A window manager

- A desktop manager

- One or more X clients

The easiest way to install X is to install it during system installation. This lets you specify the X components that you want to install, rather than the individual packages. Specifying components is more convenient and accurate than specifying individual packages.

If you prefer, you can install X after system installation is complete. However, without help, you may find it somewhat cumbersome to identify and install the proper packages. Installing X after system installation is a two-step process:

1. Determine the proper X server.

2. Install the proper packages.

The next two subsections describe the procedure for installing X after system installation.

To determine what packages are included in a given installation component, consult the file RedHat/base/comps on the Red Hat Linux distribution CD-ROM.

X Server Selection

If you like, you can install every X server available on the distribution media, even though a system requires only one. XFree86 includes only 15 servers, and each associated RPM file is only about 1MB in size, so installing unneeded servers won't waste a great deal of disk space. Regardless of the number of servers you install, you must determine which server is appropriate for your system's video device.

Determining the proper X server is sometimes problematical, because there may be none. Although XFree86 is regularly updated, it often lacks support for the latest video hardware. However, some video hardware vendors have begun to distribute XFree86-compatible X servers for their products.

For a list of video devices compatible with Red Hat Linux, see www.redhat.com/corp/support/hardware/index.html. For a list of video devices supported by XFree86, see the XFree86 Video Card and X Server List at xfree86.org/cardlist.html. Over 500 video devices are currently supported. Moreover, many video devices that are not fully supported by XFree86 can be run in SVGA, VGA, or monochrome mode by using the appropriate XFree86 server. Of course, the best possible video resolution and color depth may fall short of the full capabilities of the device if this is done.

Table 26.1 summarizes the X servers currently distributed as part of XFree86. Consult the table to determine the server that supports your video device.

TABLE 26.1 X Servers

X Server RPM Package Name	Description
XFree86-3Dlabs	Server for devices built around 3Dlabs GLINT and PERMEDIA chipsets, including the GLINT 500TX with IBM RGB526 RAMDAC, the GLINT MX with IBM RGB526 or IBM RGB640 RAMDAC, the PERMEDIA with IBM RGB526 RAMDAC, and the PERMEDIA 2a, 2v, and 2 Classic.

TABLE 26.1   X Servers   *(continued)*

X Server RPM Package Name	Description
XFree86–8514	Server for the IBM 8514 video cards and compatibles, such as those made by ATI.
XFree86–AGX	Server for the AGX video card.
XFree86–FBDev	Server for the generic frame buffer device.
XFree86–I128	Server for devices such as the Number Nine Imagine 128.
XFree86–Mach32	Server for devices built around the Mach32 chip.
XFree86–Mach64	Server for devices built around the Mach64 chip.
XFree86–Mach8	Server for devices built around the Mach8 chip.
XFree86–Mono	Generic monochrome server that works with nearly all VGA devices.
XFree86–P9000	Server for devices built around the Weitek P9000 chip.
XFree86–S3	Server for devices built around the S3 chip, including most Number Nine cards, many Diamond Stealth cards, Orchid Fahrenheits, the Miro Crystal 8S, most STB cards, and some motherboards with built-in graphics accelerators, such as IBM ValuePoint PCs.
XFree86–S3V	Server for devices built around the S3 ViRGE chip.
XFree86–SVGA	Server for simple frame buffer SVGA devices, including cards built from ET4000 chips, Cirrus Logic chips, Chips and Technologies laptop chips, Trident 8900 and 9000 chips, and Matrox chips. It also works for Diamond Speedstar, Orchid Kelvins, STB Nitros and Horizons, Genoa 8500VL, most Actix boards, and the Spider VLB Plus. It works with many other SVGA devices as well.
XFree86–VGA16	Generic 16-color server that works with nearly all VGA devices.

TABLE 26.1 X Servers *(continued)*

X Server RPM Package Name	Description
XFree86-W32	Server for devices built around ET4000/W32 chips, including the Genoa 8900 Phantom 32i, the Hercules Dynamite, the LeadTek WinFast S200, the Sigma Concorde, the STB LightSpeed, the TechWorks Thunderbolt, and the ViewTop PCI.
XFree86-Xvfb	X Virtual Frame Buffer server that runs without display hardware and input devices.

Installing the Packages

Once you know the name of the package that contains the proper X server for your system, you're ready to install X. During installation, you should also install the following additional packages:

- freetype, which contains a library that renders TrueType fonts
- gtk+, which contains a library used by X clients
- X11R6-contrib, which contains many useful X clients
- Xconfigurator, which contains the Red Hat Linux program for configuring X
- XFree86-libs, which contains the main XFree86 libraries
- XFree86, which contains XFree86 common code
- XFree86-75dpi-fonts, which contains the standard Western European fonts for use with X
- XFree86-xfs, which contains the X font server
- xinitrc, which contains a script used to start a window manager

Don't attempt to install the packages one by one. Several of the packages depend on other packages, so installation is likely to fail owing to unsatisfied dependencies. Instead, move to the directory containing the packages, and issue a single rpm command that installs all of the packages. The command should have the form

```
rpm -Uvh freetype-*.rpm gtk+-*.rpm X11R6-contrib-*.rpm \
    Xconfigurator-*.rpm XFree86-libs-*.rpm XFree86-*.rpm \
```

```
XFree86-75dpi-fonts-*.rpm XFree86-xfs-*.rpm \
xinitrc-*.rpm XFree86-server-*.rpm
```

where *XFree86-server* is the name of the package containing the proper X server.

If you like, you can install additional fonts. Table 26.2 summarizes other font packages distributed with Red Hat Linux.

TABLE 26.2 Additional Font Packages

Package Name	Description
urw-fonts	Free versions of the 35 standard Adobe Postscript fonts
XFree86-100dpi-fonts	Fonts for high-resolution 100 dpi displays
XFree86-cyrillic-fonts	Cyrillic fonts
XFree86-ISO8859-2-Type1-fonts	Central European Type1 (scalable) fonts
XFree86-ISO8859-7-Type1-fonts	Greek Type1 (scalable) fonts
XFree86-ISO8859-2-75dpi-fonts	Central European 75 dpi fonts
XFree86-ISO8859-7-75dpi-fonts	Greek 75 dpi fonts
XFree86-ISO8859-9-75dpi-fonts	Turkish European 75 dpi fonts
XFree86-ISO8859-2-100dpi-fonts	Central European 100 dpi fonts
XFree86-ISO8859-7-100dpi-fonts	Greek I European 100 dpi fonts
XFree86-ISO8859-9-100dpi-fonts	Turkish European 100 dpi fonts

You may find the quite extensive XFree86 documentation helpful. The package requires a little over 11MB of disk space. To install it, move to the directory containing the packages, and issue the command

```
XFree86-doc-*.rpm
```

Configuring X

The main X configuration file is /etc/X11/XF86Config. You can manually edit this file; however, most system administrators prefer to configure X by using a tool. Popular tools include the following:

Xconfigurator   The Red Hat Linux X configuration tool, which can be used during a text-based installation and after a text-based or graphical installation

XF86Setup   The XFree86 X configuration tool

xf86config   A text-based X configuration tool

This section explains the use of these tools. In addition, this section describes two other useful tools:

SuperProbe   A text-based tool that helps you obtain information about your system's video card

xvidtune   A text-based tool that helps you tune X to yield the best possible image

Xconfigurator

Most Red Hat Linux administrators seem to prefer Xconfigurator to other X configuration tools. One reason for the preference is familiarity: Xconfigurator is used in the text-based Red Hat installation procedure, so many Red Hat Linux administrators are comfortable using the tool. Xconfigurator supports more cards and monitors than XF86Setup—currently, over 600 cards and 900 monitors.

To launch Xconfigurator, issue the command

```
Xconfigurator
```

Xconfigurator can be used in a special noninteractive "kickstart" mode, in which it probes for information, attempting to configure a card without human intervention. To use kickstart mode, issue the command

```
Xconfigurator --kickstart
```

Alternatively, Xconfigurator can be used in expert mode, in which the user has the ability to override probed values. To use expert mode, issue the command

```
Xconfigurator --expert
```

The following step-by-step explanation assumes that you're using Xconfigurator in ordinary mode—that is, neither kickstart nor expert mode.

Figure 26.1 shows the Xconfigurator Welcome screen that appears when you launch Xconfigurator. Xconfigurator does not support the use of a mouse. Instead, you communicate with the program via the keyboard. The following keys have special meaning:

- Tab, Up, Down, Right, and Left are used to navigate from field to field; the current field is the one that's highlighted.

- The spacebar is used to toggle a radio button or check box.

- Enter is used to click the highlighted button.

FIGURE 26.1 The Xconfigurator Welcome screen

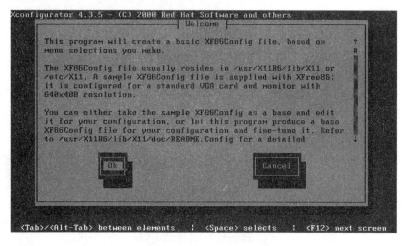

To proceed with the configuration, use the navigation keys to highlight the OK button, and press Enter to click it. The Choose a Card screen, shown in Figure 26.2, will appear.

FIGURE 26.2 The Xconfigurator Choose a Card screen

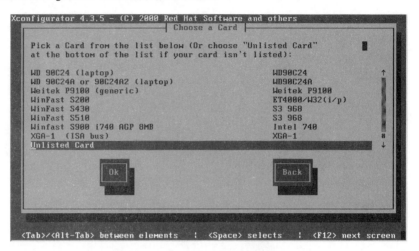

You can choose a card from the list and click the OK button, or you can choose the final entry, Unlisted Card. Xconfigurator will try to determine the proper X server for the selected card. If it cannot, it will display the Pick a Server screen, shown in Figure 26.3.

FIGURE 26.3 The Xconfigurator Pick a Server screen

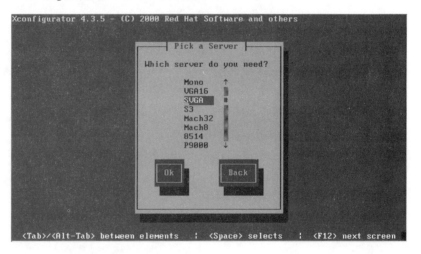

Use the navigation keys to highlight the proper server; then click the OK button. If you're unsure which server to choose, consider choosing SVGA, VGA16, or Mono because these servers support a variety of cards. However, these servers provide limited resolution and color depth; using a generic server may not take full advantage of the capabilities of the system's video device. When you've made your choice, click the OK button. The Monitor Setup screen, shown in Figure 26.4, will appear.

FIGURE 26.4   The Xconfigurator Monitor Setup screen

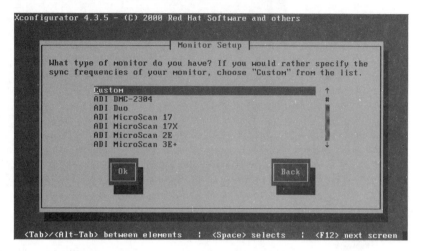

Use the navigation keys to highlight the proper monitor; if you can't find your monitor, choose Custom. Click the OK button.

The monitor make and model selection should exactly match those of your monitor. *Don't choose a monitor that's merely similar to, not identical to, your monitor.* Often, similarly numbered models have quite different operating characteristics. You can permanently damage your monitor by selecting an incorrect monitor. If in doubt, choose Custom and enter the operating parameters directly.

If you chose Custom, the Custom Monitor Setup screen, shown in Figure 26.5, will appear; otherwise, the Screen Configuration screen, shown in Figure 26.8, will appear. Click the OK button to proceed. The Custom Monitor Setup (Continued) screen, shown in Figure 26.6, will appear.

FIGURE 26.5 The Xconfigurator Custom Monitor Setup screen

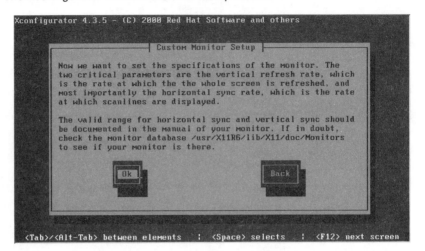

 As the Custom Monitor Setup screen informs you, the horizontal sync rate and vertical refresh rate are critical parameters. Entering an incorrect value for either parameter can permanently damage a monitor. Obtain these values from a reliable source, such as the owner's manual or the manufacturer's Web site. Modern multi-sync monitors are more resistant to damage than older monitors; however, they are not immune. In any case, don't allow a monitor to display a garbled image any longer than necessary; immediately turn off power and reconfigure the operating parameters.

FIGURE 26.6 The Xconfigurator Custom Monitor Setup (Continued) screen

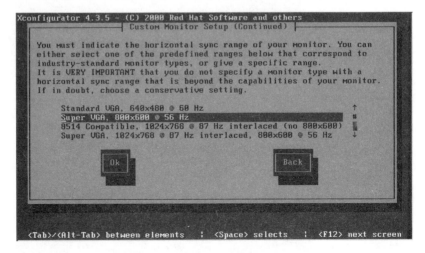

Select an appropriate *horizontal sync rate* for your monitor. If in doubt of the proper value, choose conservatively in order to avoid damaging the monitor. When you've highlighted the proper sync rate, click the OK button. A second Custom Monitor Setup (Continued) screen, shown in Figure 26.7, will appear.

FIGURE 26.7   The Xconfigurator Custom Monitor Setup (Continued) screen

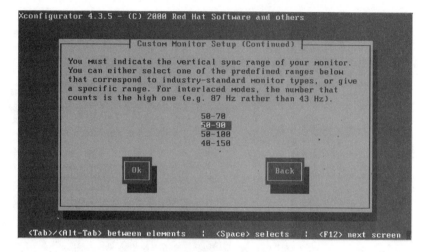

Select an appropriate *vertical refresh rate* for your monitor. If in doubt of the proper value, choose conservatively in order to avoid damaging the monitor. When you've highlighted the proper sync rate, click the OK button. The Screen Configuration screen, shown in Figure 26.8, will appear.

FIGURE 26.8   The Xconfigurator Screen Configuration screen

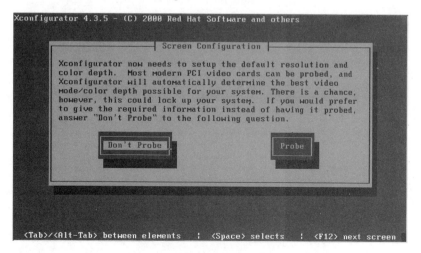

The screen lets you avoid probing the video card, because probing can sometimes hang a system. Generally, you should select Probe and let Xconfigurator probe the card; if you experience a problem, you can restart Xconfigurator and skip the probe.

If you select Probe and click the OK button, a dialog box will confirm your action and ask you to click OK to proceed. If the probe is successful, the Probing to Begin screen, shown in Figure 26.13, will appear. If you select Don't Probe or if the probe fails, you're prompted for the needed information. For example, the Video Memory screen, shown in Figure 26.9, may appear.

FIGURE 26.9 The Xconfigurator Video Memory screen

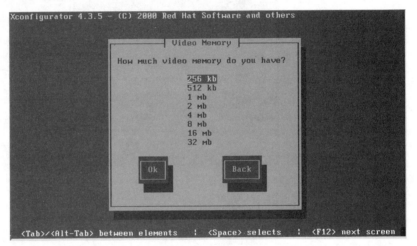

Select the amount of video RAM available on your video device, and click the OK button. The ClockChip Configuration screen, shown in Figure 26.10, will appear.

FIGURE 26.10   The Xconfigurator ClockChip Configuration screen

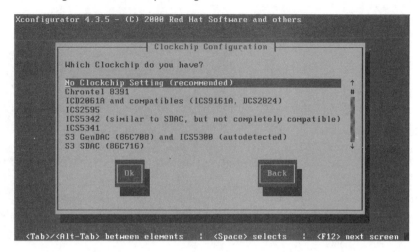

Generally, you should select the No ClockChip setting because the X server can probe to determine the ClockChip setting. However, some cards cannot successfully probe; this screen lets you work around this problem. When you've selected the proper ClockChip setting, click the OK button. If you selected No ClockChip, the Probe for Clocks screen, shown in Figure 26.11, will appear; otherwise, the Select Video Modes screen, shown in Figure 26.12, will appear.

FIGURE 26.11   The Xconfigurator Probe for Clocks screen

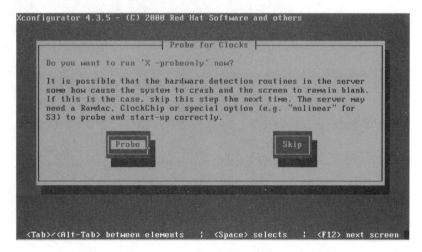

In the Probe for Clocks screen, click the OK button to begin the probe. The Select Video Modes screen, shown in Figure 26.12, will appear.

FIGURE 26.12 The Xconfigurator Select Video Modes screen

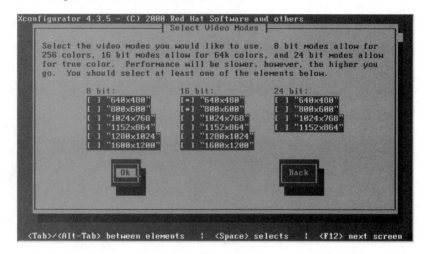

Select one or more desired resolutions and color depths. If you select multiple modes, you can use Ctrl+Alt++ to cycle among them during X operation. However, you must use the + key on the numeric keypad; the ordinary + key will not function for this purpose. When you've selected the desired modes, click the OK button. The Probing to Begin screen, shown in Figure 26.13, will appear.

FIGURE 26.13 The Xconfigurator Probing to Begin screen

Click the OK button to test your X configuration. If the configuration is a good one, you'll see a small dialog box asking "Can you see this message?" If you can see the dialog box, click the Yes button. A second dialog box will

ask if you want to configure the system to start X at boot time. Click the Yes or No button, according to your preference.

If you can't see the small dialog box, Xconfigurator will return you to the configuration procedure after several seconds. You can specify different operating parameters and try again to start X.

Laptops are notoriously difficult to configure for X. One reason is that seemingly identical laptops may contain very different video hardware. For help on configuring Linux laptops, see the Linux Laptop Web page, www.cs.utexas.edu/users/kharker/linux-laptop.

Now complete Exercise 26.1 to gain experience using Xconfigurator.

EXERCISE 26.1

Using *Xconfigurator*

You may sometimes find it necessary to install X after installing Linux. This exercise gives you practice in doing so. Perform these steps:

1. Install X and the X-related packages that are required to use Xconfigurator.

2. Configure X by using Xconfigurator. Verify that the configuration works.

3. Configure X by using Xconfigurator's quickstart facility. Verify that the configuration works.

For assistance in completing this exercise, you may refer to this book and other documentation. However, before taking the RHCE exam, be sure you can install X by using Xconfigurator without recourse to help.

XF86Setup

The XFree86 Project distributes its own X configuration tool, XF86Setup. Some administrators prefer the tool to Xconfigurator because it allows use of the mouse. To do so, it uses the facilities of the VGA16 server, which is supported by a wide range of video devices.

To use XF86Setup, you should install the following packages in addition to those identified in the preceding subsection:

- glib10, a library of utility functions, some of which are used by the tool

- tcl, a scripting language used by the tool

- tk, a widget set used by tcl

- XFree86-VGA16, the VGA16 server

- XFree86-XF86Setup, the tool itself

To install these packages, move to the directory containing them and issue the command

```
rpm -Uvh glib10-*.rpm tcl-*.rpm tk-*.rpm \
    XFree86-VGA16-*.rpm XFree86-XF86Setup-*.rpm
```

To launch XF86Setup, issue the command

```
XF86Setup
```

The XF86Setup introduction screen, shown in Figure 26.14, will appear.

FIGURE 26.14   The XF86Setup Introduction screen

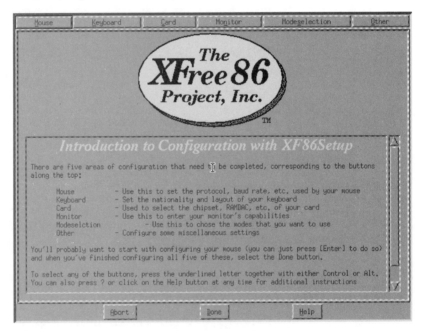

The screen provides six buttons across its top:

- The Mouse button lets you configure the mouse.

- The Keyboard button lets you configure the keyboard.

- The Card button lets you configure the video device.

- The Monitor button lets you configure the monitor.

- The Mode Selection button lets you configure the color depths and video resolutions.

- The Other button lets you configure several X options.

To configure the mouse, click the Mouse button. A help screen will appear, explaining various mouse-related options. After you've perused the information, click Dismiss to close the window. The Mouse screen, shown in Figure 26.15, will appear.

FIGURE 26.15   The XF86Setup Mouse screen

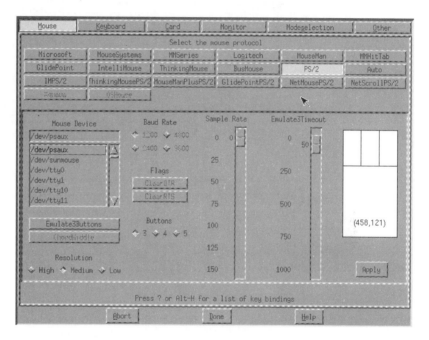

Select the desired mouse options. Click the Apply button to immediately apply the mouse configuration. When the mouse is working properly, click the Keyboard button. The Keyboard screen, shown in Figure 26.16, will appear.

FIGURE 26.16 The XF86Setup Keyboard screen

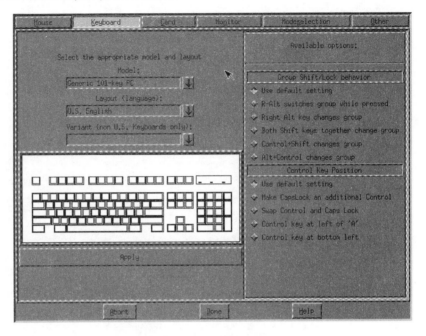

Select the desired keyboard options. Click the Apply button to immediately apply the keyboard configuration. When the keyboard is working properly, click the Card button. The Card screen, shown in Figure 26.17, will appear.

FIGURE 26.17   The XF86Setup Card screen

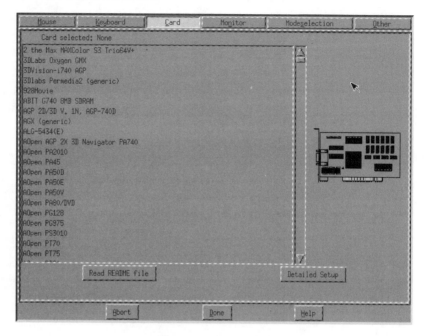

Select the proper card from the list. If the card is not listed, click the
Detailed Setup button to enter the configuration manually. The Detailed
Card screen, shown in Figure 26.18, will appear.

FIGURE 26.18 The XF86Setup Detailed Card screen

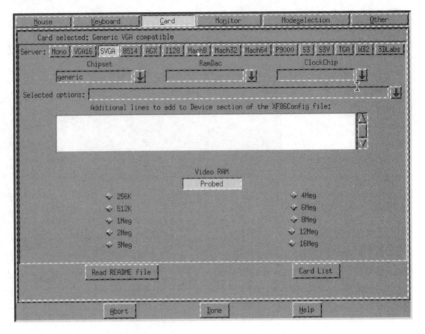

Select the proper configuration for the card. If you prefer, you can click the Card List button to return to the Card screen. When the configuration is properly set, click the Monitor button. The Monitor screen, shown in Figure 26.19, will appear.

FIGURE 26.19   The XF86Setup Monitor screen

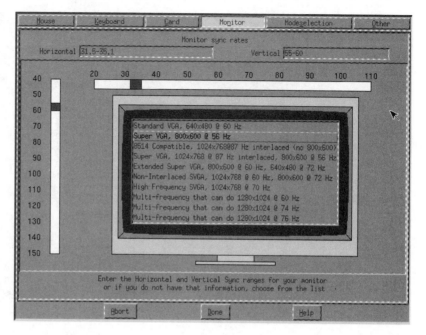

Enter the horizontal sync rate and vertical refresh rate for the monitor. Or, if you prefer, select the list item that corresponds to the characteristics of the monitor. Click the Mode Selection button. The Mode Selection screen, shown in Figure 26.20, will appear.

FIGURE 26.20 The XF86Setup Mode Selection screen

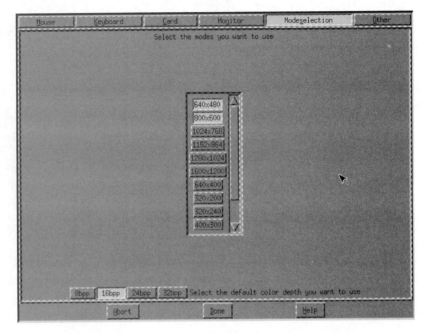

Select the mode or modes and the color depth you prefer. Select only values supported by the video device. When you've made your selections, click the Other button. The Other screen, shown in Figure 26.21, will appear.

FIGURE 26.21   The XF86Setup Other screen

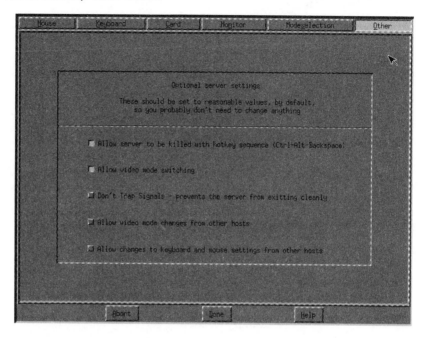

The Other screen lets you enable and disable several X options. When you've selected the configuration you prefer, click the Done button. XF86Setup builds the configuration you've specified and stores it in the /etc/X11/XF86Config file.

For more information on XF86Setup, see its man page.

Now complete Exercise 26.2 to gain experience with XF86Setup.

EXERCISE 26.2

Using *XF86Setup*

The XF86Setup tool gives you greater control over the X configuration than does Xconfigurator. To gain experience using XF86Setup, perform these steps:

1. Install X and the X-related packages required to use XF86Setup.

2. Configure X by using XF86Setup. Verify that the configuration works.

For assistance in completing this exercise, you may refer to this book and other documentation. However, before taking the RHCE exam, be sure you can install X by using XF86Setup without recourse to help.

---

xf86config

The third X configuration tool, xf86config, is a text-based tool that uses a prompt/reply dialog to configure X. As such, the tool is somewhat cumbersome to use. But it is highly flexible and is contained in the XFree86 package. Thus, xf86config may work where other tools require installation of additional packages.

The steps in the xf86config dialog resemble those of Xconfigurator and XF86Setup, because all gather essentially the same information. The basic steps are:

1. Introduction

2. Mouse configuration

3. Keyboard configuration

4. Monitor configuration

5. Card configuration

6. Server selection

7. Mode selection

8. Configuration file generation

Now complete Exercise 26.3 to gain experience using xf86config.

EXERCISE 26.3

Using *xf86config*

The xf86config tool has a less sophisticated user interface than Xconfigurator or XF86Setup, but it gives you a great degree of control over the X configuration. To gain experience using xf86config, perform these steps:

1. Install X.

2. Configure X by using xf86config. Verify that the configuration works.

For assistance in completing this exercise, you may refer to this book and other documentation. However, before taking the RHCE exam, be sure you can install X by using xf86config without recourse to help.

SuperProbe

The SuperProbe tool can help you determine the type and operating characteristics of a video device. The tool is contained in the XFree86 package. To run SuperProbe, issue the command

```
SuperProbe
```

The output should resemble the following:

```
SuperProbe Version 2.18 (22 December 1998)
    (c) Copyright 1993,1994 by David Wexelblat
    ➥<dwex@xfree86.org>
    (c) Copyright 1994-1998 by The XFree86 Project, Inc

    This work is derived from the 'vgadoc2.zip' and
    'vgadoc3.zip' documentation packages produced by Finn
    Thoegersen, and released with all appropriate permissions
    having been obtained. Additional information obtained
    from 'Programmer's Guide to the EGA and VGA, 2nd ed', by
    Richard Ferraro, and from manufacturer's data books

Bug reports are welcome, and should be sent to
XFree86@XFree86.org. In particular, reports of chipsets
that this program fails to correctly detect are
appreciated.

Before submitting a report, please make sure that you have
the latest version of SuperProbe (see http://www.xfree86
.org/FAQ).

WARNING - THIS SOFTWARE COULD HANG YOUR MACHINE.
          READ THE SuperProbe.1 MANUAL PAGE BEFORE
          RUNNING THIS PROGRAM.

          INTERRUPT WITHIN FIVE SECONDS TO ABORT!
First video: Super-VGA
    Chipset: Matrox Millennium (PCI Probed)
    RAMDAC:  TI ViewPoint3026 24-bit TrueColor DAC w/cursor,
      pixel-mux,clock (with 6-bit wide lookup tables (or in
      6-bit mode)
```

Notice that the tool warns that it may hang some systems. You can type Ctrl+C to interrupt the program before the probe is initiated.

Now practice using SuperProbe by completing Exercise 26.4.

EXERCISE 26.4

Using *SuperProbe*

SuperProbe is a useful, but not infallible, tool. To gain experience with it, run it on your system. Does the output correctly state the type and characteristics of your system's video device?

---

xvidtune

The xvidtune tool can help you fine-tune an X configuration. It lets you interactively adjust video modes and scan rates for optimal performance. The tool is part of the XFree86 package.

If you improperly specify a scan rate, the xvidtune tool can damage a monitor. Be careful to provide only correct values.

Important X Directories and Files

The /usr/X11R6/bin directory contains X binaries. For X programs to operate correctly, the /usr/X11R6/bin directory should appear on the program path, stored in the PATH environment variable.

Another important X directory is /etc/X11. This directory and its subdirectories contain the X configuration. The symbolic link /etc/X11/X points to the currently selected X server, which resides in /usr/X11R6/bin.

The /etc/X11 directory also contains the XF86Config file, the main X configuration file, which is generally built by using Xconfigurator or XF86Setup. For more information about the /etc/X11/XF86Config file, see the XF86Config man page.

Now complete Exercise 26.5, which asks you to study the main X configuration file.

EXERCISE 26.5

Examining the */etc/X11/XF86Config* File

Because of variation in video characteristics, the X configuration is likely to vary significantly from system to system. Compare the XF86Config file of a properly configured X installation with the configuration shown in this subsection. What similarities and differences do you find?

Summary

In this chapter, you learned about the installation and configuration of X. The most important topics covered are:

The X Window System (X)   X provides the graphical user interface used with Red Hat Linux. Implementations of X are available for a variety of Unix and non-Unix platforms. The version of X distributed with Red Hat Linux is published by the XFree86 Project.

Servers and Clients   The X program that manages a user interface is called an X server. An application or other program that uses a user interface is called an X client.

Installing X   Installing X involves installing several packages. One of the most important is the package containing the X server, which must be chosen to suit the type of video adapter installed in a system.

Configuring X   You can configure X using a variety of tools, including the following:

- Xconfigurator
- XF86Setup
- xf86config
- SuperProbe
- xvidtune

X Directories and Files   The /usr/X11R6/bin directory contains X binaries. The /etc/X11 directory and its subdirectories contain the X configuration. The symbolic link /etc/X11/X points to the currently selected X server. The /etc/X11 directory also contains the XF86Config file, the main X configuration file.

Key Terms

Before going on to the next chapter, be sure you're familiar with the following terms:

desktop manager

horizontal sync rate

vertical refresh rate

window manager

X client

X server

Additional Sources of Information

If you'd like further information about the topics presented in this chapter, you should consult the following sources:

- The XFree86 FAQ, www.xfree86.org/FAQ

- The XFree86 documentation in the XFree86-doc package

- *The Official Red Hat Linux Reference Guide*

Review Questions

1. Which of the following is the component of X responsible for interfacing with the video hardware?

   A. The client

   B. The desktop manager

   C. The server

   D. The window manager

2. Which of the following X servers supports the greatest number of video device types?

   A. XFree86-AGX

   B. XFree86-S3

   C. XFree86-SVGA

   D. XFree86-W32

3. Which of the following methods of configuring X is most popular in the Red Hat community?

   A. vi

   B. Xconfigurator

   C. xf86config

   D. XF86Setup

4. To avoid damaging a monitor, what should you specify accurately?

   A. The color depth

   B. The horizontal sync rate

   C. The resolution

   D. The video RAM amount

5. Which of the following is the directory that holds X binaries?

    A. /etc/X11

    B. /etc/X11R6/bin

    C. /usr/X11R6

    D. /usr/X11R6/bin

6. Which of the following is true of the currently configured X server?

    A. It resides in the same directory as other X binaries.

    B. The link /etc/X11 points to it.

    C. The link /etc/X11/X points to it.

    D. The link /etc/X11/XServer points to it.

Answers to Review Questions

1. C. The server acts as a device driver, providing graphics service on behalf of applications, which are known as clients.

2. C. The SVGA server supports many SVGA devices. Only the VGA16 and Mono servers support more.

3. B. The Xconfigurator program was written by Red Hat, Inc. and is invoked as part of the text-based installation procedure. Both xf86config and XF86Setup are distributed by the XFree86 Project, Inc. as part of XFree86.

4. B. The horizontal sync rate—and to a lesser degree, the vertical refresh rate—are critical operating characteristics.

5. D. The X binaries reside in /usr/X11R6/bin.

6. A, C. The X server resides in /usr/X11R6/bin with other X binaries. The link /etc/X11/X points to it.

Chapter

27

Understanding and Using Window Managers and Desktops

RHCE PREPARATION TOPICS COVERED IN THIS CHAPTER:

✓ Be familiar with the window manager and desktop environments available under Red Hat Linux, and know how to select them.

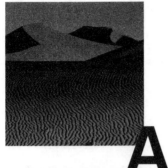

A suite of programs cooperates to provide the X environment. These include:

- The *window manager*, which draws borders, title bars, menu bars, and window manipulation buttons

- The *desktop manager*, which provides the desktop environment, including the file manager, help system, and virtual desktop

- X clients, the applications you run

In addition, if you log in via X, a *display manager* authenticates your identity by using the PAM facility. This chapter introduces you to window, desktop, and display managers, explaining how to select and configure them.

Desktop Environments

Red Hat Linux lets you choose between two primary desktop environments:

- GNOME

- KDE

By default the GNOME environment includes the GNOME desktop manager and the Enlightenment window manager. The KDE environment includes the KDE desktop manager and the KWM window manager. This section describes these desktop environments, explains how to choose between them, and explains how to configure them to work with alternative window managers.

The GNOME Desktop Manager

The open-source GNOME desktop environment is written using CORBA (Common Object Request Broker Architecture) and the GIMP (GNU Image Manipulation Program) toolkit (GTK+). Development of GNOME has been graciously funded by Red Hat, Inc. through RHAD Labs. Figure 27.1 shows a typical GNOME desktop.

FIGURE 27.1   The GNOME Desktop Manager

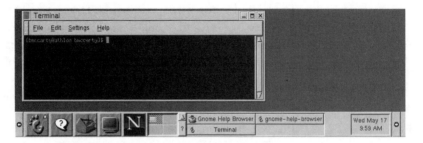

GNOME-compliant applications are session aware, meaning that they save their state when you exit GNOME. When you reenter GNOME, session-aware applications reopen documents that were previously open, reposition the cursor to its original position, and generally help you resume work where you left off. GNOME developers plan to eventually offer a capability that resembles Microsoft's Object Linking and Embedding (OLE), through CORBA.

GNOME is often used with the Enlightenment window manager, which was specially designed for use with GNOME. However, it can also be used with other window managers. Several window managers have been revised to work better with GNOME, including Window Maker and IceWM, which are considered GNOME-compliant. Authors of other window managers, including AfterStep and FVWM, are generally working toward GNOME compliance. See the GNOME FAQ, `www.gnome.org/gnomefaq`, for the latest information.

GNOME includes many useful features and facilities, such as:

- A file manager, `gmc`, that supports drag-and-drop operations

- Desktop icons that represent programs and directories

- A virtual desktop that can exceed the size of the physical screen

- A pager that lets you navigate the virtual desktop

- A panel that provides functions similar to those provided by the Microsoft Windows taskbar

- Launchers that let you launch applications by clicking the mouse

- Themes that let you choose a coordinated visual appearance

For more information on GNOME, see the GNOME Web site, www.gnome.org. For information on GNOME themes, see gtk.themes.org; Enlightenment has its own themes site, e.themes.org.

The KDE Desktop Manager

The KDE desktop manager provides features and facilities similar to those provided by GNOME. Unlike GNOME, which uses the separate Enlightenment window manager, KDE has its own window manager, KWM, which is the most popular window manager for use with KDE; however, KDE is also compatible with such window managers as AfterStep, Enlightenment, and WindowMaker. Figure 27.2 shows a typical KDE desktop.

FIGURE 27.2   The KDE Desktop Manager

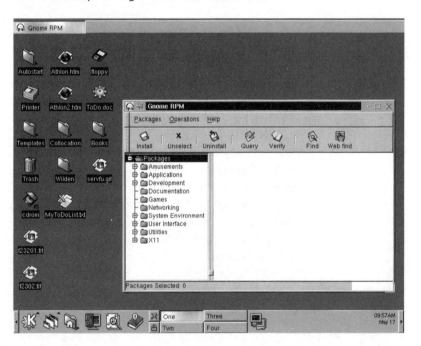

KDE was written using the Qt toolkit, authored by Troll Tech, a Norwegian software development company. Originally the Qt toolkit had a somewhat restrictive license, which slowed acceptance of KDE by the open source community.

Recently, the Qt license restrictions have been lifted and KDE has found a much wider following.

KDE's file manager is known as KFM. KDE includes a wealth of useful desktop applications. For further information on KDE, see the KDE Web site, www.kde.org.

Switching Desktop Managers

To specify the desired desktop manager, use an xterm to invoke the switchdesk utility by issuing the command

    /usr/bin/switchdesk

The program presents a small dialog box, which is shown as Figure 27.3. Select the desired desktop manager, and click the OK button. The following desktop managers are supported:

- GNOME

- KDE

- AnotherLevel, a desktop manager that resembles the desktop manager once used in the NeXTStep operating system

The change does not have immediate effect. You must exit X and reenter it to load the specified desktop manager.

FIGURE 27.3   The switchdesk Utility

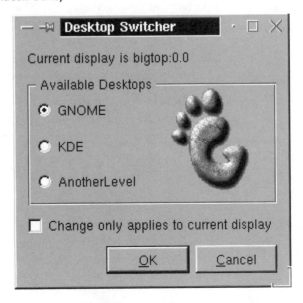

When switchdesk is run, it creates two configuration files—which are actually scripts—that reside in the home directory of the running user:

- .Xclients, which invokes .Xclients-default or a special .Xclients file that pertains to a specific host

- .Xclients-default, which launches the window and desktop managers

Here are the contents of a typical .Xclients script:

```
#!/bin/bash

# Created by Red Hat Desktop Switcher

if [ -e "$HOME/.Xclients-$HOSTNAME$DISPLAY" ]; then
    exec $HOME/.Xclients-$HOSTNAME$DISPLAY
else
    exec $HOME/.Xclients-default
fi
```

Now, practice choosing a desktop manager by completing Exercise 27.1.

EXERCISE 27.1

Choosing a Desktop Manager

Choosing a desktop manager is straightforward. See for yourself by performing these steps:

1. If either GNOME or KDE is not installed, install it.

2. Under X, use switchdesk to specify GNOME as the desktop manager. Exit and reenter X to verify that your selection works properly.

3. Use switchdesk to specify KDE as the desktop manager. Exit and reenter X to verify that your selection works properly.

The next subsection explains how window managers are selected.

Choosing a Window Manager

As explained, the window manager supplies borders, title bars, menu bars, window manipulation buttons, and other visual elements. Some popular window managers include:

- AfterStep, which resembles the GUI formerly used by the NeXTStep operating system.

- Enlightenment, the window manager favored by GNOME. Enlightenment is a feature-rich window manager that requires considerable system resources.

- FVWM, a rather old and yet very efficient window manager that can mimic Windows 95 or Motif. FVWM was developed for Linux use and remains popular.

- Sawfish, formerly known as Sawmill, a new and largely GNOME-compliant window manager noted for its low resource requirements in comparison to Enlightenment. In Red Hat Linux 6.2, it's distributed as the `sawmill` and `sawmill-gnome` packages.

- WindowMaker, a popular and efficient window manager that resembles the NeXTStep GUI.

If the `~/.Xclients` script exists, it determines which window manager is run. If no `~/.Xclients` script exists, the `/etc/X11/xinit/Xclients` script determines which window manager is run. Here are the contents of the standard `/etc/X11/xinit/Xclients` script:

```bash
#!/bin/bash
# (c) 1999, 2000 Red Hat, Inc.

# check to see if the user has a preferred desktop
PREFERRED=
if [ -f /etc/sysconfig/desktop ]; then
    if [ -n "`grep -i GNOME /etc/sysconfig/desktop`" ]
    then
        PREFERRED=gnome-session
    elif [ -n "`grep -i KDE /etc/sysconfig/desktop`" ]
    then
        PREFERRED=startkde
    elif [ -n "`grep -i AnotherLevel
➥/etc/sysconfig/desktop`" ]
```

```
        then
            PREFERRED=AnotherLevel
        fi
fi

if [ -n "$PREFERRED" -a "$PREFERRED" != "AnotherLevel" ] \
   && which $PREFERRED >/dev/null 2>&1; then
      PREFERRED=`which $PREFERRED`
      exec $PREFERRED
fi

# now if we can reach here, either they want AnotherLevel
# or there was no desktop file present and the PREFERRED
# variable is not set.

if [ -z "$PREFERRED" ]; then

    GSESSION=gnome-session
    STARTKDE=startkde

    # by default, we run GNOME.
    if which $GSESSION >/dev/null 2>&1; then
        exec `which $GSESSION`
    fi

    # if GNOME isn't installed, try KDE.
    if which $STARTKDE >/dev/null 2>&1; then
        exec `which $STARTKDE`
    fi
fi

# Last, try AnotherLevel

# these files are left sitting around by TheNextLevel.
rm -f $HOME/Xrootenv.0
rm -f /tmp/fvwmrc* 2>/dev/null
```

```
# First thing - check the user preferences
if [ -f $HOME/.wm_style ] ; then
    WMSTYLE=`cat $HOME/.wm_style`
    case "$WMSTYLE" in
        Afterstep | AfterStep)
        exec /usr/X11R6/bin/RunWM --AfterStep
        ;;
        WindowMaker | Windowmaker | WMaker | wmaker)
        exec /usr/X11R6/bin/RunWM --WindowMaker
        ;;
        Fvwm95 | fvwm95)
        exec /usr/X11R6/bin/RunWM --Fvwm95
        ;;
        Mwm | MWM | Lesstif)
        exec /usr/X11R6/bin/RunWM --FvwmMWM
        ;;
    esac
fi

# Argh! Nothing good is installed. Fall back to fvwm2
# (win95-style) or twm
/usr/X11R6/bin/RunWM --Fvwm95 || {
    # gosh, neither fvwm95 nor fvwm2 is available;
    # fall back to failsafe settings
    xclock -geometry 100x100-5+5 &
    xterm -geometry 80x50-50+150 &
    if [ -f /usr/bin/netscape \
      -a -f /usr/doc/HTML/index.html ]
    then
        netscape /usr/doc/HTML/index.html &
    fi
    if [ -f /usr/X11R6/bin/fvwm ]; then
        exec fvwm
else
        exec twm
    fi
}
```

The script checks for a `~/.wm_style` file containing the name of the window manager to be run and launches the specified window manager. If that file is not present, the script launches the FVWM95 window manager. If the script cannot launch the FVWM95 window manager—perhaps because it is not installed—the script launches FVWM or TWM, a very small and efficient window manager installed as part of the XFree86 package.

Now perform Exercise 27.2, which asks you to choose a window manager.

EXERCISE 27.2

Choosing a Window Manager

As explained, the `~/.wm_style` file specifies the name of your window manager. Perform these steps to experiment with changing the window manager:

1. If FVWM95 is not installed, install it.

2. Use `~/.wm_style` to specify FVMW95 as your window manager. Exit and reenter X to verify that your selection operates properly.

You can consult this book or other documentation to help you in completing this exercise. But, before taking the RHCE exam, be sure you can choose a window manager without consulting books or notes.

Display Managers

Red Hat Linux lets you choose among three display managers:

- GDM, a display manager associated with GNOME
- KDM, a display manager associated with KDE
- XDM, a display manager distributed as part of XFree86

All three display managers can be used with a variety of desktop environments. For example, you can use the GDM display manager with AnotherLevel, GNOME, or KDE. Both GDM and KDM are highly configurable. The XDM display manager is not highly configurable, but it is more robust than GDM or KDM when used to support remote X logins, which are explained in Chapter 28, "Configuring and Using Remote X Servers and Clients."

To select the display manager, revise the /etc/sysconfig/desktop file as follows:

- For the GDM display manager, specify GNOME.

- For the KDM display manager, specify KDE.

- For the XDM display manager, specify AnotherLevel.

Now complete Exercise 27.3 to gain experience choosing a display manager.

EXERCISE 27.3

Choosing the Display Manager

Under Red Hat Linux 6.2, choosing a display manager is straightforward. Try your hand at choosing a display manager by performing the following steps:

1. Configure a system to use the gdm display manager. Log in to verify that your selection works properly.

2. Configure a system to use the kdm display manager. Log in to verify that your selection works properly.

3. Configure a system to use the xdm display manager. Log in to verify that your selection works properly.

For help in completing this exercise, you can consult this book or other documentation. But before taking the RHCE exam, be sure you can choose a display manager without consulting books or notes.

Starting X

You can set a system to provide a console login or an X login. The /etc/inittab file contains the line:

```
id:n:initdefault:
```

where *n* is the default runlevel. Set *n* to 3 to provide a console login; set *n* to 5 to provide an X login. The X startup process depends on the runlevel you specify.

If you specify runlevel 3, you should start an X session by issuing the command

```
startx
```

X will source the file `~/.xinitrc`, if it exists; otherwise, X sources the file `/etc/X11/xinit/xinitrc`. In turn, this file sources `~/.Xclients` if it exists and `/etc/X11/xinit/Xclients` otherwise. Under Red Hat Linux 6.2, this file also sources all scripts in `/etc/X11/xinit/xinitrc.d`.

If you specify runlevel 5, X will display a login prompt. When you log in, X will source `~/.xsession`, if it exists. The `~/.xsession` file can be revised by the user and therefore may start an alternative window or desktop manager. If `~/.xsession` does not exist, X will source `~/.Xclients` if it exists and `/etc/X11/xinit/Xclients` otherwise.

Now complete Exercise 27.4, which asks you to tailor the X environment.

EXERCISE 27.4

Setting the X Environment

Because the operation of X is based on scripts, you can tailor the operation of X essentially any way you like. To gain experience setting the X environment, configure X to start GNOME by default for all users, but KDE for some particular user.

You can consult this book or other documentation to help you in completing this exercise. But, before taking the RHCE exam, be sure you can perform operations such as the one required by this exercise without consulting books or notes.

Using X Clients

When launching an X client, you can specify options that determine the client's appearance. Some of the most useful options are summarized in Table 27.1. For example, to launch an X terminal having green text on a black background, issue the command

```
xterm -foreground green -background black
```

TABLE 27.1 Popular Options for X Clients

Option	Description
-background *color* or -bg *color*	Set the color of the window background.
-bordercolor *color*	Set the color of the window border.

TABLE 27.1   Popular Options for X Clients *(continued)*

Option	Description
`-borderwidth` *width*	Set the width of the window border (in pixels).
`-display` [*server*]:*n.m*	Set the display, where *server* is the host, *n* is the display number, and *m* is the screen number. The first display and screen are designated 0.0.
`-font` *font*	Set the default font used in the window.
`-foreground` *color* or `-fg` *color*	Set the color of the window foreground.
`-geometry` *widthxheight+x+y*	Set the size and location of the window (in pixels), where *width* is the window width, *height* is the window height, *x* is the horizontal offset of the top left corner of the window, and *y* is the vertical offset of the top left corner of the window.
`-title` *string*	Set the window title.

You can control the operation of X by entering a control sequence from the keyboard. Table 27.2 describes several of the most useful control sequences.

TABLE 27.2   Useful Control Sequences

Control Sequence	Description
Ctrl+Alt++	Switch video mode (must use + key on numeric keypad).
Ctrl+Alt+Backspace	Exit X.
Ctrl+Alt+F*n*	Switch to a text-mode virtual terminal, *n*=1 to 6.
Ctrl+Alt+F7	Switch from a text-mode virtual terminal to X.

Summary

In this chapter, you learned about X window managers, desktop managers, and display managers. The most important topics covered are:

Desktop Environment   A typical desktop environment provides desktop icons, a menu for launching programs, a menu for selecting windows, a file manager, a help facility, and a variety of other features. Red Hat Linux lets you choose either of two desktop environments, one provided by the GNOME desktop manager and another provided by the KDE desktop manager. You can choose the desktop environment during or after system installation.

Window Managers   A window manager controls the appearance and behavior of windows. You can use a variety of window managers with either desktop environment supported by Red Hat Linux. However, most users prefer to use a window manager that is closely integrated with their chosen desktop environment: Enlightenment with GNOME or KWM with KDE. You can choose a new window manager by modifying the `~/.wm_style` configuration file.

Display Managers   A display manager manages access to an X server and presents an X-based login. Red Hat Linux supports three display managers: XDM, GDM, and KDM. Users who work with remote windows may find XDM more robust than the other two display managers.

X Logins   A system that has a default runlevel of 5 will automatically present an X-based login. To suppress the X-based login, set the default runlevel to 3.

X Clients   X clients support a variety of arguments that let you tailor their appearance and behavior.

Keyboard Control Sequences   You can use keyboard control sequences to transition from X to a virtual console or from a virtual console to X.

Key Terms

Before going on to the next chapter, be sure you're familiar with the following terms:

desktop manager

display manager

window manager

Additional Sources of Information

If you'd like further information about the topics presented in this chapter, you should consult the following sources:

- The man page for X
- The XFree86 documentation, /usr/doc/XFree86-*
- The GNOME documentation, /usr/doc/gnome-*
- The GNOME and KDE Web sites, www.gnome.org and www.kde.org

Review Questions

1. Which of the following are primary Red Hat Linux desktop environments?

   A. AfterStep

   B. FVWM

   C. GNOME

   D. KDE

2. Which window manager was the first GNOME-compatible window manager?

   A. AfterStep

   B. Enlightenment

   C. FVWM

   D. WindowMaker

3. Which window manager is generally used with KDE?

   A. AfterStep

   B. FVWM

   C. KWM

   D. WindowMaker

4. The utility used to specify the desktop manager is:

   A. `control-panel`

   B. `switchdesk`

   C. `xdm`

   D. `xinitrc`

5. If X is started via `startx`, X will attempt to source which of the following files?

A. `~/.startx`

B. `~/.xinitrc`

C. `~/.xrc`

D. `~/.Xsession`

6. To specify that an X client should display red text, which of the following options should be specified?

A. `-background red`

B. `-bordercolor red`

C. `-font red`

D. `-foreground red`

Answers to Review Questions

1. C, D. GNOME and KDE are the primary Red Hat Linux desktop environments.

2. B. Enlightenment was the first GNOME-compatible window manager; several other window managers are now more or less GNOME compliant.

3. C. KDE is generally used with KWM.

4. B. The `switchdesk` utility lets you specify the desktop manager.

5. B. If X is started via `startx`, it will source the file `~/.xinitrc`, if the file exists.

6. D. The `-foreground` option sets the color of text.

Chapter

28

Configuring and Using Remote X Servers and Clients

RHCE PREPARATION TOPICS COVERED IN THIS CHAPTER:

✓ Understand and be capable of configuring and using the remote capabilities of X, including remote clients and remote logins.

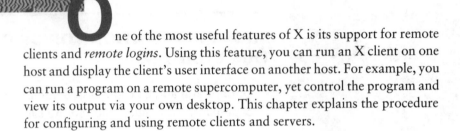

One of the most useful features of X is its support for remote clients and *remote logins*. Using this feature, you can run an X client on one host and display the client's user interface on another host. For example, you can run a program on a remote supercomputer, yet control the program and view its output via your own desktop. This chapter explains the procedure for configuring and using remote clients and servers.

X Security

X implements a simple *host-based security* scheme that prevents unauthorized hosts from accessing an X server. More sophisticated, user-based authentication schemes are also supported.

Host-based X security is configured via the xhost command. You can view the current security settings by issuing the following command:

```
xhost
```

The command will report whether access control is currently enabled or disabled and list the hosts on the access list. For example, the following output indicates that access control is currently disabled and that, if access control were enabled, only the hosts dale and roy could connect:

```
access control disabled, clients can connect from any host
INET:dale
INET:roy
```

You can issue the xhost command to query a local or remote X server. Issuing the command remotely lets you verify that the local host has permission to access the remote server, which is identified by the value of the DISPLAY environment. For example, the following commands check the permission of the local host to access the X server running on the host bigger:

```
export DISPLAY=bigger:0.0
xhost
```

Other forms of the xhost command must be executed locally—that is, on the host running the X server. To enable host-based security, issue the command

```
xhost -
```

To disable host security, so that all hosts can access the local X server, issue the command

```
xhost +
```

To extend permission for a client to access the local X server, issue a command of the form

```
xhost +client
```

where *client* is the IP address or host name of the client. To deny permission for a client to access the local X server, issue a command of the form

```
xhost -client
```

where *client* is the IP address or host name of the client. The X server stores the IP addresses of hosts, rather than host names, on the access list. Therefore, DNS must be able to perform forward and reverse lookups on any host name you specify.

Launching a Remote Client

Launching a remote client is simple and can be accomplished in any of several ways. One way is to use the display argument provided by most X clients. For example, the following command launches the X client xeyes so that it runs using the X server on the host bigger:

```
xeyes -display bigger:0.0 &
```

Figure 28.1 shows the xeyes client, which displays a pair of eyes that follow the movement of the mouse, in operation.

FIGURE 28.1 The xeyes Client

 The xeyes program doesn't do much. But, for exactly that reason, it's useful for testing and troubleshooting X.

The general form of the command for launching a remote X client is

xclient -display server[:m[.n]] [xclient_args])

where:

- xclient and xclient_args are the client and its optional arguments.
- server is the host name or IP address of the X server.
- m is the optional server display number (by default, 0).
- n is the optional server screen number (by default, 0). This argument is used in the somewhat unusual situation of a server that has multiple screens associated with a single display.

If you plan to launch several X clients, you may find it more convenient to set the DISPLAY environment variable. Subsequently, when you launch an X client, the value of the DISPLAY environment variable determines the X server that is used. For example, the following sequence of commands launches xeyes and xclock to run using the X server on the host bigger; it also launches a second instance of xeyes to run on biggest:

```
export DISPLAY=bigger:0.0
xeyes &
xclock &
xeyes -display biggest:0.0 &
```

If the X server's host authentication feature is active, the client host must be authorized to access the X server. Otherwise, the client program fails with a message such as the following:

```
Xlib: connection to "bigger:0.0" refused by server
Xlib: Client is not authorized to connect to Server
Error: Can't open display: bigger:0.0
```

Follow the command to launch an X client with an ampersand (&) if you want the shell to immediately return a new prompt.

Suppose you're currently logged into the host workstation and you want to run a program—say, xterm—on the host server but receive its output locally on the host workstation. The following sequence of commands accomplishes that goal:

```
[user@workstation]$ xhost +server
[user@workstation]$ telnet server
(log in dialog omitted)
[user@server]$ export DISPLAY=workstation:0.0
[user@server]$ xterm &
```

Now complete Exercise 28.1, which gives you experience working with host-based X security.

EXERCISE 28.1

Configuring X Security for Remote Clients

Host-based X security does not give a fine degree of control over remote clients, but it's simple to configure and use. To gain experience working with host-based X security, perform the following steps:

1. On a server, enable host-based X security so that it excludes some client host.

2. From the client host, attempt to log in to the server or open an X window on the server. What happens?

3. Without disabling host-based security, extend the client permission to connect to the server.

4. From the client host, attempt to log in to the server or open an X window on the server. What happens?

You can perform this exercise on a single computer by running two instances of X. However, you'll likely find it far simpler to use two computers. You can consult this book and other documentation to help you complete this exercise. But, before taking the RHCE exam, be sure you can perform operations such as these without help.

Configuring Remote Login

In addition to running X clients remotely, you can remotely log in to a host that is running an X display manager. The display manager will display a dialog box, such as that shown in Figure 28.2, that lets you specify the login username and password. Some display managers will provide dialog boxes that let you specify the desired window manager or other options.

FIGURE 28.2 An X Login dialog box

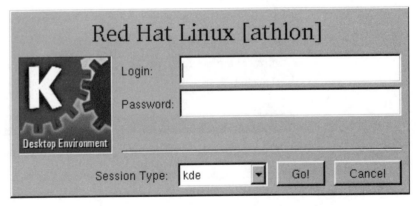

Logging In Remotely

To log in to a host running an X display manager, issue a command of the form

    X -query *server*

where *server* is the host name or IP address of the host running the display manager. To log in to an arbitrary host on the local network, issue the command

    X -broadcast

Some hosts are configured to provide a *chooser*, a special menu that lets you select the host you want to log in to. Figure 28.3 shows a typical chooser. To request a chooser, issue a command of the form

    X -indirect *server*

where *server* is the host name or IP address of the host configured to provide a chooser.

FIGURE 28.3 A Chooser

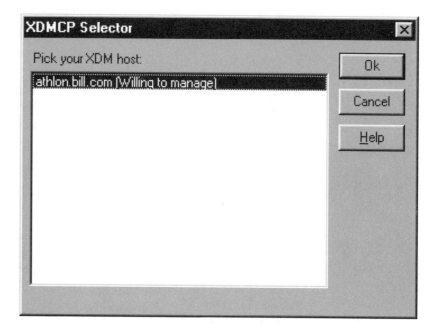

Choosing a Display Manager

As explained in Chapter 27, "Understanding and Using Window Managers and Desktops," Red Hat Linux lets you choose one of three X display managers:

- XDM, the display manager distributed by the XFree86 Project
- GDM, the display manager distributed with GNOME
- KDM, the display manager distributed with KDE

If you want to be able to provide a chooser, you should configure XDM as the preferred display manager; both GDM and KDM have some peculiarities that limit their ability to work with choosers. For example, GDM doesn't respond to chooser messages and therefore won't appear on the chooser menu. The KDM display manager responds to chooser messages, but sometimes won't provide a chooser.

Configuring *xdm* to Provide a Chooser

To configure XDM to provide a chooser, you must modify the xdm configuration file, /etc/X11/xdm/Xaccess, by adding one or more chooser directives. These directives have the following format:

```
client CHOOSER server_list
```

where *client* specifies the client hosts to whom a chooser will be provided, and *server_list* specifies the servers that will appear in the chooser.

The client hosts can be specified by using wildcards. Consider the following example configuration:

```
workstation         CHOOSER server1 server2
*.azusapacific.com CHOOSER server3
*                   CHOOSER server4
```

The first line specifies that the host workstation will be provided a chooser that shows hosts server1 and server2. The second line specifies that all hosts in the azusapacific.com domain will be provided a chooser that shows host server3. The final line specifies that all hosts will be provided a chooser that shows host server4. If the name of a host matches several CHOOSER lines, the line appearing first is used. In the example configuration, the host workstation.azusapacific.com would be provided a chooser that shows server1 and server2 even though the host name matches lines 2 and 3 as well as line 1.

You can specify the list of servers dynamically by using the keyword BROADCAST. For example, consider the following directive:

```
* CHOOSER BROADCAST
```

The BROADCAST keyword causes the display manager to assemble a list of X servers on the local network by sending a special broadcast message. All servers that respond to the broadcast message will be included in the chooser.

By default, XDM ignores chooser requests. To configure XDM to respond, you must comment or remove the last line in /etc/X11/xdm/xdm-config:

```
DisplayManager.requestPort:      0
```

If you prefer to use KDM as a display manager and want it to provide a chooser, you can configure KDM using the same procedure used for XDM. To configure gdm to provide a chooser, you must set Enable=1 in the [xdmcp] section of the /etc/X11/gdm/gdm.conf file and force gdm to reread the file by issuing the command killall-HUP gdm.

Now, complete Exercise 28.2 to gain experience configuring X remote logins.

EXERCISE 28.2

Configuring X Remote Logins

To practice configuring remote X logins, perform the following steps:

1. On a server, configure XDM as the preferred display manager and configure XDM to provide a chooser to any host on the local network.

2. From a client host, log in to the server by means of the chooser. What happens?

3. On a server, configure GDM as the preferred display manager.

4. From a client host, attempt to log in to the server by means of the chooser. What happens?

5. On a server, configure KDM as the preferred display manager.

EXERCISE 28.2 *(continued)*

6. From a client host, attempt to log in to the server by means of the chooser. What happens?

You can consult this book and other documentation to help you complete this exercise. But, before taking the RHCE exam, be sure you can perform operations such as these without help.

The *Xnest* Program

Sometimes it's useful to run multiple X servers on a single host that has only a single video adapter. For example, you may want to test a new window manager or log in via X to a remote server while already running a local X server. The Xnest program provides an X server that runs in a window owned by the currently running X server. You can run multiple instances of Xnest and use each X server it provides just as you would an ordinary X server. For example, to create a second X server by using Xnest, issue the following command:

```
Xnest :1 &
```

Similarly, to create a third X server by using Xnest, issue the following command:

```
Xnest :2 &
```

To create a second X server and use it to log in to a specified host, issue a command of the form

```
Xnest -query server :1 &
```

where *server* is the host name or IP address of the host you want to log in to. Similarly, you can use Xnest to log in to an arbitrary host or to obtain a chooser:

```
Xnest -broadcast :1 &          # log in to any host on the
                               # local network
Xnest -indirect server :1 &    # log in via chooser
                               # provided by server
```

WARNING Xnest will fail unless both the Xnest system and the remote system have identical fonts installed. This significantly limits the applicability of Xnest.

Now complete Exercises 28.3 and 28.4 to gain experience using Xnest.

EXERCISE 28.3

Using *Xnest*

One common use of Xnest is to run multiple X servers on a single host. Perform these steps to experiment with such a configuration:

1. Start an X session, and then use Xnest to create a second X server on the same host.

2. Launch an X client—such as xeyes–that uses the second X server.

You can consult this book and other documentation to help you complete this exercise. But, before taking the RHCE exam, be sure you can configure Xnest without help.

EXERCISE 28.4

Running Multiple Window Managers

Another common use of Xnest is to run multiple desktop managers on a single host. Try this firsthand by using Xnest to run GNOME and KDE simultaneously on a single host.

X Font Server

By default, each system configured to run Red Hat Linux runs its own copy of the X *font server*, xfs, which provides access to locally stored fonts, including True Type fonts. However, you can reconfigure a system to access a remote X font server, if you prefer.

To do so, modify the FontPath directive of the /etc/X11/XF86Config file of each client system. By default, the directive has this form:

```
FontPath "unix/:-1"
```

To access a remote font server, revise the directive to have the form:

```
Font Path "tcp/server:7100"
```

where *server* is the host name or IP address of the host running the font server. You must also modify the /etc/rc.d/init.d/xfs file. Change the line

```
daemon xfs -droppriv -daemon -port -1
```

to read

```
daemon xfs -droppriv -daemon -port 7100
```

By default, an X font server listens on port 7100. However, you can assign another port, if you prefer. To do so, modify the font server configuration file, /etc/X11/fs/config, and the font server SysVInit file, /etc/rc.d/init.d/xfs. See the xfs man page for details.

Now, configure a remote font server by completing Exercise 28.5.

EXERCISE 28.5

Configuring a Client to Use a Remote X Font Server

To test your understanding of xfs, configure a client host to use the X font server running on a remote server.

You can consult this book and other documentation to help you complete this exercise. But, before taking the RHCE exam, be sure you can configure a remote X font server without help.

Summary

In this chapter, you learned about configuring and using remote X servers and clients. The most important topics covered are:

X Security   X implements a simple host-based security system. You can configure which hosts are allowed to access an X server by using the xhost command.

Remote X Clients   The DISPLAY environment variable specifies the X server, which can reside on a remote host.

Remote X Logins   You can log in to a remote host via X in several ways:

- You can specify the host name or IP address of the login host.

- You can broadcast a message to the local network and log in to whichever host first responds.

- You can query a host configured to provide a chooser, which lets you choose from a menu of login hosts.

The Xnest Program   The Xnest program lets you run an X server that's associated with a window rather than a video adapter. Xnest lets you run multiple X servers on a system with only a single video adapter.

The X Font Server   X can obtain fonts from a local hard drive or from a font server accessed via the network. The FontPath directive of the X configuration specifies the source for X fonts.

Key Terms

Before going on to the next chapter, be sure you're familiar with the following terms:

chooser

font server

host-based security

remote logins

Additional Sources of Information

If you'd like further information about the topics presented in this chapter, you should consult the man pages for X, including X, XF86Config, XFree86, xauth, xdm, xfs, and xhost.

Review Questions

1. To disable host-based X security, which of the following commands should be issued?

   A. xhost +

   B. xhost -

   C. xhosts +

   D. xhosts -

2. Which of the following commands launches the xclock client to run on display 0 of server?

   A. xclock -display server

   B. xclock -display server:0

   C. xclock -display server:0.0

   D. xclock -display server:0:0

3. To log in to the X server on the host server, which of the following commands should be issued?

   A. X -broadcast server

   B. X -indirect server

   C. X -query server

   D. X server

4. To log in to an X server via a chooser, which of the following commands should be issued?

   A. X -broadcast server

   B. X -indirect server

   C. X -query server

   D. X server

5. To use Xnest to create a second X server, which of the following commands should be issued?

   A. Xnest &

   B. Xnest :0 &

   C. Xnest :1 &

   D. Xnest :2 &

6. To specify that a host should access the X font server on the host server rather than a local font server, which directive should be specified?

   A. FontPath tcp/server

   B. FontPath tcp/server:5100

   C. FontPath tcp/server:7100

   D. FontPath tcp/server:9100

Answers to Review Questions

1. A. The xhost + command lets any host access the X server.

2. A, B, C. The display argument has the syntax *server:m.n*, where *server* is the host name or IP address of the server, *m* is the display number (which defaults to 0), and *n* is the screen number (which defaults to 0).

3. C. The –query option lets you specify the login host.

4. B. The –indirect option requests that the specified host provide a chooser.

5. C. The first server is associated with display 0; therefore, the second server is associated with display 1.

6. C. By default, the X font server listens on port 7100.

Network
Administration

Chapter

29

Configuring a Linux Router

RHCE PREPARATION TOPICS COVERED IN THIS CHAPTER:

✓ Be familiar with configuration issues associated with using Red Hat Linux as a router, including routing options, IP forwarding, and kernel configuration.

Red Hat Linux is a capable router, as well as server or workstation. Among the router-related features of Red Hat Linux are:

- Support for WAN protocols such as X.25, frame relay, and PPP

- Support for LAN functions such as IP forwarding, firewalling, and masquerading

- Advanced routing capabilities such as quality of service, policy-based routing, and transparent proxying

This chapter explains the routing function and the configuration of static routing. A conceptual understanding of dynamic routing is adequate preparation for the RHCE exam.

Routing Basics

Only hosts with multiple network addresses can perform routing. The most basic routing operation is *forwarding*, which forwards packets received on one network interface to another network interface. *Routing* is the process of forwarding packets based on the packet source address, the packet destination address, and other relevant information. A *route* is the path taken by a packet. A *router* is a host or device that performs routing. A Red Hat Linux host can function as a dedicated router or it can perform routing in addition to functioning as a server or workstation. Figure 29.1 shows a typical router configuration that routes packets incoming on a network interface to one or another of two network interfaces. Routers are often used in this fashion to join networks and subnetworks.

FIGURE 29.1   Packet forwarding and routing

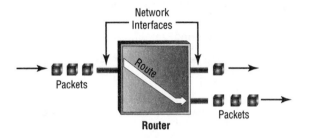

Red Hat Linux can perform both *static* and *dynamic routing*. In static routing, the rules that govern the paths taken by packets are fixed and can only be adjusted manually. In dynamic routing, the rules are adjusted automatically. Networks that feature dynamic routing can sometimes continue to function when one or more network components fail; the remaining components automatically adjust their routing rules to bypass the failed components. Of course, if the only connection to a given host fails, then it's not possible to access the host. Therefore, dynamically routed networks generally feature hosts and networks having redundant routes; if one route fails, routing rules can be adjusted to use a remaining operational route.

Static Routing

Static routing is simpler to configure and use than dynamic routing. Most small networks of a few score hosts are configured to use static routing. To set up static routing, you must enable IP forwarding and properly configure the routing tables. In addition, the kernel must be configured to support the desired routing options. The standard Red Hat Linux kernel supports the most commonly used routing options. However, you may choose to recompile the kernel to enable additional options or suppress unneeded options.

IP Forwarding

Unless you enable IP forwarding, a host will not forward IP packets. The likely result is that network operations fail with the message "host unreachable."

You can enable IP forwarding in any of several ways. The simplest is to use `linuxconf` (or `netconf`). Select Config ➢ Networking ➢ Client Tasks ➢ Routing and Gateways ➢ Defaults from the `linuxconf` menu. The Routing Defaults screen, shown in Figure 29.2, will appear. To enable IP forwarding, click the Enable Routing button; then click the Accept button.

FIGURE 29.2   The Routing Defaults screen

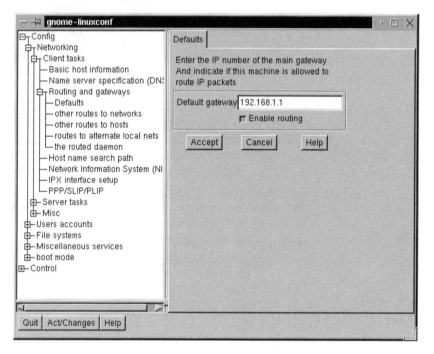

In early releases of Red Hat Linux 6.2, `linuxconf` does not properly update the /etc/sysctl.conf file. Therefore, under such releases, you cannot use `linuxconf` to enable packet forwarding.

If you prefer, you can enable IP forwarding by editing the file /etc/sysctl.conf to include the line

    net.ipv4.ip_forward=1

Another way to enable IP forwarding is to manipulate the /proc file system. Issue the command

```
echo "1" >/proc/sys/net/ipv4/ip_forward
```

The drawback of this method is that you will have to reissue the command each time you reboot the system.

Routing Configuration

To configure routing requires the route command, which is contained in the net-tools package automatically installed during the standard installation procedure. You can use the route command directly; but many Red Hat Linux system administrators prefer to configure routing by using linuxconf, which invokes route based on information you supply by using dialog boxes.

Conceptually, the routing configuration consists of a table that contains routing rules. Each rule has two or three components:

- A destination IP address, which can refer to a host, subnetwork, or network.

- An interface, which refers to a network adapter.

- An optional gateway IP address, which refers to a host that routes packets to the specified destination. If the gateway IP address is omitted, the destination IP address is assumed to be directly reachable via the specified interface.

PPP and SLIP devices always act as gateways. You don't need to—and shouldn't—specify a gateway address for a destination reachable via PPP or SLIP.

Using *linuxconf* to Specify Routing Rules

To specify routing rules for accessing a network by using linuxconf, select Config ➤ Networking ➤ Client Tasks ➤ Routing and Gateways ➤ Other Routes to Networks from the linuxconf menu. The Route to Other Networks screen, shown in Figure 29.3, will appear. Specify the destination IP address and (optionally) the network mask of the network. Also specify the IP address of the gateway host on the local network that provides access to the network.

FIGURE   29.3   The Route to Other Networks screen

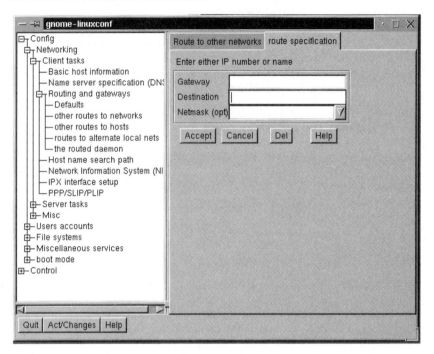

You can similarly specify routing rules for accessing a host. Select Config ➢ Networking ➢ Client Tasks ➢ Routing and Gateways ➢ Other Routes to Hosts from the linuxconf menu. Unless a host is the only host on its network that you want to access, it's generally more convenient to specify a routing rule for the network than to specify a routing rule for each of the network's hosts.

 The file /etc/sysconfig/static-routes holds the network and host routes entered via linuxconf. You can edit this file directly, if you prefer.

Using *route* to Specify Routing Rules

Rather than use linuxconf to establish routing rules, you can issue the route command. However, when you reboot the system, you must re-establish routing rules created by using route. Therefore, it's generally much more convenient to use linuxconf.

To specify a network routing rule by using route, issue a command of the form

```
route add -net ip_address netmask mask_address interface
```

where *ip_address* is the IP address of the network, *mask_address* is the network mask address of the network, and *interface* is the network device by which to access the network. For example, the command

```
route add -net 192.168.1.0 netmask 255.255.255.0 eth0
```

adds a routing rule for the network 192.168.1.0, accessible via interface eth0.

To specify a host routing rule, issue a command of the form

```
route add -host ip_address interface
```

where *ip_address* is the IP address of the host and *interface* is the network device by which to access the host.

Disabling Dynamic Routing

When using static routing, you should disable the routed daemon. To do so, launch linuxconf and select Config ➢ Networking ➢ Client Tasks ➢ Routing and Gateways ➢ The Routed Daemon from the linuxconf menu. The Routed Daemon screen, shown in Figure 29.4, will appear. Click the Does Not Export Any Routes (Silent) button, and click the Accept button.

FIGURE 29.4   The Routed Daemon screen

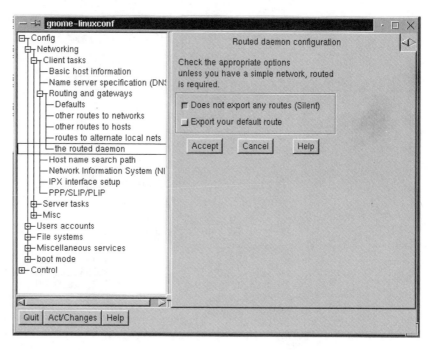

An Example Network

Figure 29.5 shows an example network, which consists of two subnetworks joined to one another and the Internet by a router. The route commands corresponding to the example network are:

```
route add -net 192.168.1.0 netmask 255.255.255.0 eth0
route add -net 192.168.100.0 netmask 255.255.255.0 eth1
route add -net 1.1.1.0 netmask 255.255.255.0 eth2
route add default gw 10.1.1.2 eth2
```

FIGURE 29.5   A typical network

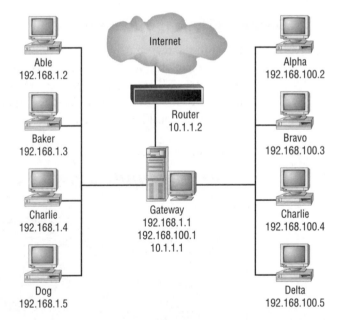

If you issue the route command without arguments, it reports the current routing rules. Here is the output corresponding to the example network:

```
Kernel IP routing table
Destination   Gateway Genmask         Flags Metric Ref Use Iface
192.168.1.1   *       255.255.255.255 UH    0      0   0   eth0
192.168.100.1 *       255.255.255.255 UH    0      0   0   eth1
10.1.1.1      *       255.255.255.255 UH    0      0   0   eth2
192.168.1.0   *       255.255.255.0   U     0      0   0   eth0
192.168.100.0 *       255.255.255.0   U     0      0   0   eth1
default       router  0.0.0.0         UG    0      0   0   eth2
127.0.0.0     *       255.0.0.0       U     0      0   0   lo
```

The Flags field can contain such values as:

- U, which indicates that the network link is up

- H, which indicates that the destination address refers to a host rather than a network

- G, which indicates that the routing rule specifies a gateway

The Metric, Ref, and Use fields are irrelevant except when using dynamic routing.

Now complete Exercise 29.1 to gain practical experience with network configuration.

EXERCISE 29.1

Network Configuration

If you have access to three hosts connected to a network, configure one as a router that joins the two remaining hosts. Then, experiment by using linuxconf and route to specify various routing rules until you feel comfortable manipulating the routing table.

Refer back to this chapter and other resources when completing this exercise. But, be prepared to perform similar operations without help when taking the RHCE exam.

Kernel Configuration

The Linux kernel provides a variety of network-related options. You can see most of these in Figure 29.6, which shows the top part of the make menuconfig page that includes the network-related options. Table 29.1 summarizes the most important options. Two especially important options optimize Red Hat Linux for use as a router: IP: advanced router and IP: optimize as router not host, which is not visible in Figure 29.6. If a Linux system is used primarily—or exclusively—as a router, you should specify these options and recompile its kernel.

FIGURE 29.6 Kernel networking options

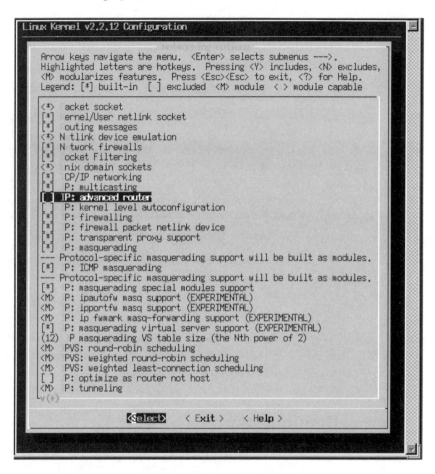

TABLE 29.1 Kernel Networking Options

Typical Value	Option	Description
Y/N	IP: advanced router	Specify Y if the host is used mostly as a router.
Y	IP: aliasing support	Includes support for assigning multiple IP addresses to a single network interface; commonly used to support multihosting, virtual domains, or virtual hosting.

TABLE 29.1   Kernel Networking Options *(continued)*

Typical Value	Option	Description
N	IP: ARP daemon support	Includes support for a user-space ARP daemon that can maintain a table large enough to handle a very large switched network (more than several hundred hosts).
M	IP: autofw masquerade support	Includes support for masquerading of protocols that lack their own protocol helpers.
Y/N	IP: broadcast GRE over IP	Includes support for using Generic Routing Encapsulation (GRE) to construct a broadcast WAN, which operates like an ordinary LAN.
Y	IP: firewall packet netlink device	Includes support that lets you create a character special file that receives a copy of packets that match specified criteria; used to monitor network traffic and detect possible attacks.
Y	IP: firewalling	Includes kernel support for firewalling and masquerading.
M	IP: GRE tunnels over IP	Includes support for GRE, allowing encapsulation of IPv4 and IPv6 packets over IPv4. This support is more compatible with Cisco routers than that provided by the IP: tunneling option.
Y	IP: ICMP masquerading	Includes support that enables a firewall to translate ICMP packets that originate from the local network and are destined for a remote host to appear as though they had originated from the firewall host. Used, for example, to allow hosts that have only private IP addresses to access the Internet.

TABLE 29.1 Kernel Networking Options *(continued)*

Typical Value	Option	Description
M	IP: ipmarkfw masquerade support	Includes support for Firewall Mark Forwarding, a facility similar to port forwarding.
N	IP: kernel level autoconfiguration	Enables automatic configuration of IP addresses of network interfaces and the routing table during kernel boot; used to support diskless hosts that boot via the network.
Y	IP: masquerading	Includes support that enables a firewall to translate UDP and TCP packets that originate from the local network and are destined for a remote host to appear as though they had originated from the firewall host. Used, for example, to allow hosts that have only private IP addresses to access the Internet.
Y	IP: masquerading special modules support	Includes support for modules that can modify masquerade rules; used by such modules as ipautofw and by port forwarding.
M	IP: masquerading virtual server support	Includes support that lets you build a virtual server that consists of two or more real servers.
12	IP: masquerading VS table size	Specifies the size of the hash table used to manage active connections; the actual table size is 2^n, where n is the value specified.
N	IP: multicast routing	Includes support for routing multicast IP packets—that is, packets that have multiple destination addresses.

TABLE 29.1 Kernel Networking Options *(continued)*

Typical Value	Option	Description
N	IP: Multicasting	Includes support for addressing packets to multiple computers—used, for example, by hosts connected to the MBONE, a high-speed audio-video network.
Y/N	IP: optimize as router not host	Disables support for copy and checksum operations that improve host performance but degrade router performance.
Y	IP: TCP syncookie support	Includes support for cookies that protect against a SYN flood denial-of-service attack.
Y	IP: transparent proxying	Includes support that enables a firewall to redirect packets that originate from the local network and are destined for a remote host to a local server (a transparent proxy server).
M	IP: tunneling	Includes support for encapsulating packets having one protocol within packets of another protocol.
M	IPL ipportfw masquerade support	Includes support for port forwarding, which lets you forward packets that originate outside the local network and are destined for a specified port of the firewall host to a specified port of a host on the local network.
M	IPVS: round-robin scheduling	Specifies that the virtual server will use round-robin scheduling.
M	IPVS: weighted least-connection scheduling	Specifies that the virtual server will use weighted least-connection scheduling.
M	IPVS: weighted round-robin scheduling	Specifies that the virtual server will use weighted round-robin scheduling.

TABLE 29.1 Kernel Networking Options *(continued)*

Typical Value	Option	Description
Y	Kernel/User netlink socket	Includes support for communication between the kernel and user processes via character special files.
Y	Netlink device emulation	A backward compatibility that will soon be removed.
Y	Network firewalls	Includes support for packet filter-based firewalling and masquerading.
Y	Packet socket	Includes support for the packet protocol, which is used by programs such as tcpdump to communicate directly with network devices.
Y	Routing messages	Includes support for the special file /dev/route, which lets you read network-related information.
Y	Socket filtering	Includes support that lets user programs filter packets, except TCP packets.
Y	TCP/IP networking	Includes support for the TCP/IP protocols.
Y	Unix domain sockets	Includes support for Unix domain sockets, which are used even by hosts not connected to a network.

Dynamic Routing

Red Hat Linux provides two daemons that support dynamic routing. If you want dynamic routing, you should install and configure one or the other. The routed daemon provides basic dynamic routing via the Routing Information Protocol (RIP). The more sophisticated gated daemon supports a variety of routing protocols such as:

- RIP and RIP-2

- Intermediate System to Intermediate System (IS-IS)

- Open Shortest Path First (OSPF-2)

- Exterior Gateway Protocol (EGP)

- Border Gateway Protocol (BGP-4)

RIP, IS-IS, and OSPF-2 are *interior routing protocols*, suitable for use within a network or autonomous set of networks. RIP is a *distance-vector routing protocol*, one that merely informs its neighbors of its routing table. IS-IS and OSPF-2 are *link-state routing protocols*, protocols that require each routing host to maintain a map of the network. When the status of a network link changes, broadcast messages notify routers of the change. RIP is suitable for managing LANs; OSPF-2 is suitable for managing very large networks.

EGP and BGP-4 are *exterior routing protocols,* suitable for use between autonomous networks. In particular, BGP-4—which is a distance-vector protocol—is the protocol used on the Internet and is, therefore, much used by ISPs. EGP is a rather old protocol that is no longer popular.

Table 29.2 summarizes these protocols.

TABLE 29.2   Routing Protocols Supported by Red Hat Linux

Protocol	Interior/Exterior	Type
BGP-4	exterior	distance-vector
EGP	exterior	distance-vector
IS-IS	interior	link-state
OSPF-2	interior	link-state
RIP, RIP-2	interior	distance-vector

Summary

In this chapter, you learned about configuring a Linux router. The most important topics covered are:

Routing   Routing forwards packets from one network host to another. The most basic routing operation is forwarding, which accepts a packet incoming on a network interface and resends it via the proper network interface. To enable routing, use `linuxconf` to set the IP forwarding network configuration option.

The Routing Table   The Linux kernel maintains a routing table that specifies the network address of each local interface and the networks and hosts accessible via that interface.

Static and Dynamic Routing   In static routing, the routing table is established and maintained manually. In dynamic routing, the routing table is automatically updated to accommodate changing conditions, such as equipment malfunctions.

Configuring Routing   Routing can be configured via `linuxconf` or via the `ifconfig` and `route` commands.

Configuring Kernel Options for Routing   The Linux kernel supports a variety of routing options. To configure a system to function as a router rather than a server or workstation, enable the kernel options `IP: advanced router` and `IP: optimize as router not host`.

Key Terms

Before going on to the next chapter, be sure you're familiar with the following terms:

distance-vector routing protocol

dynamic routing

exterior routing protocols

forwarding

interior routing protocol

link-state routing protocol

route

router

routing

static routing

Additional Sources of Information

If you'd like further information about the topics presented in this chapter, you should consult the following sources:

- *The Linux IP Masquerade HOWTO,* `members.home.net/ipmasq,` by David Ranch and Ambrose Au

- *The Linux IP Masquerade Resource,* `ipmasq.cjb.net`

- *The NET-3-HOWTO,* `/usr/doc/HOWTO/NET-3-HOWTO,` by Terry Dawson and Alessandro Rubini

- *The Linux Networking Overview HOWTO,* `/usr/doc/HOWTO/Networking-Overview-HOWTO,` by Daniel Lopez Ridruejo

- The man pages for `ifconfig`, `netstat`, and `route`

- *Linux Network Servers 24seven,* by Craig Hunt (Sybex, 1999)

Review Questions

1. Which of the following is true of a Red Hat Linux host configured as an IP router?

   A. The host can act as a server or workstation as well as a router.

   B. The host forwards packets.

   C. The host has more than one IP address.

   D. The host performs dynamic routing.

2. Which of the following must be a part of every routing rule?

   A. A destination IP address

   B. A gateway IP address

   C. A source IP address

   D. An interface

3. Which of the following commands could establish a network route?

   A. `route add -host 192.168.100.0 \`
      `netmask 255.255.255.0 eth0`

   B. `route add -net 192.168.100.0 \`
      `netmask 255.255.255.0 eth0`

   C. `route -add host 192.168.100.0 \`
      `netmask 255.255.255.0 eth0`

   D. `route -add net 192.168.100.0 \`
      `netmask 255.255.255.0 eth0`

4. Which of the following kernel options might be beneficial if a host is used primarily as a router?

    A. IP: advanced router

    B. IP: no host

    C. IP: optimize as router not host

    D. IP: router

5. Which of the following options are required for operation as a router?

    A. IP: advanced router

    B. IP: firewalling

    C. TCP/IP networking

    D. Unix domain sockets

6. Which of the following are link-state protocols?

    A. BGP-4

    B. IS-IS

    C. OSPF-2

    D. RIP

Answers to Review Questions

1. A, B, C. A router must forward packets and can act as a server or workstation in addition to performing routing. In order to forward packets, the host must have more than one IP address. The host may perform static routing rather than dynamic routing.

2. A, D. A routing rule never contains a source IP address. A routing rule may, but need not, contain a gateway address.

3. B. The –net argument specifies that the rule is a network rule rather than a host rule. The add flag must be specified as add not –add.

4. A, C. The options IP: no host and IP: router do not exist.

5. C, D. The IP: advanced router and IP: firewalling options are not required, though they are often useful. A host cannot be connected to an IP network unless the TCP/IP networking option is enabled. A host—even a host not connected to a network—cannot perform essential functions such as logging unless the Unix domain sockets option is enabled.

6. B, C. RIP and BGP-4 are distance-vector protocols.

Chapter

30

Configuring a Firewall Using *ipchains*

RHCE PREPARATION TOPICS COVERED IN THIS CHAPTER:

✓ Be able to use ipchains to implement basic firewall policies.

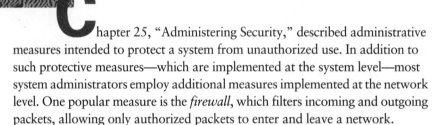

Chapter 25, "Administering Security," described administrative measures intended to protect a system from unauthorized use. In addition to such protective measures—which are implemented at the system level—most system administrators employ additional measures implemented at the network level. One popular measure is the *firewall*, which filters incoming and outgoing packets, allowing only authorized packets to enter and leave a network.

Many sites purchase dedicated hardware units that function as firewalls or firewall/routers. However, Red Hat Linux lets you configure a router that runs on a PC or other platform supported by Red Hat Linux. This chapter explains basic Linux firewall concepts and how to implement simple firewalls.

Firewall Concepts

A firewall blocks unauthorized packets from entering or leaving a network. Version 2.2 of the Linux kernel includes support for the `ipchains` facility, which can be used to construct an IP firewall—that is, a firewall that filters TCP/IP packets. Some earlier versions of the Linux kernel supported the `ipfwadm` facility, a less flexible facility that is now obsolete. Figure 30.1 shows a typical firewall configuration. In the example configuration, all packets entering and leaving the protected local network must transit the Linux firewall. Based on a set of *firewall rules*, the firewall blocks suspicious and unauthorized packets.

FIGURE 30.1 A typical firewall

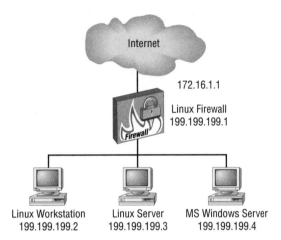

To support a firewall, the Linux kernel must be compiled with the appropriate options:

- `Network firewalls`
- `IP: firewalling`
- `/proc` filesystem

The standard Red Hat Linux kernel supports these options. To determine whether a kernel supports the necessary options, check for the file `/proc/net/ip_fwchains`; if this file exists, the options are supported.

Some firewall documentation states that the kernel option `IP: always defragment` must be configured. This option can now be enabled dynamically by including the line `net.ipv4.ip_always_defrag=1` in the file `/etc/sysctl.conf`.

Masquerading

Masquerading is closely related to firewalling, and often a Red Hat Linux system is configured to provide both functions. In masquerading, packets leaving a protected network are rewritten to appear as though they originated from the firewall host. Similarly, related packets arriving from outside the protected network are rewritten by the firewall host to specify the actual destination host. Masquerading is often used to conceal the identity of hosts within the protected network. For example, hosts within the network can be assigned private IP addresses—such as those on the 192.168.1.0 Class C network—and yet have access to external networks including the Internet. Figure 30.2 shows a typical masquerading firewall.

FIGURE 30.2 A masquerading firewall

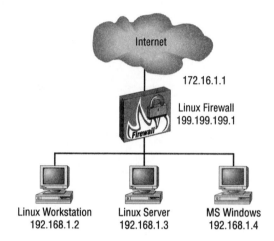

The kernel of a masquerading Linux host should be compiled with the following options in addition to those required to support firewalling:

- `IP: transparent proxy support`
- `IP: masquerading`
- `IP: masquerading special modules support`
- `IP: ipportfw masq support`

The standard Red Hat Linux kernel includes these options.

The *ipchains* Facility

The ipchains facility lets you control the progress of IP packets through the Linux kernel. Figure 30.3 shows the kernel packet path.

FIGURE 30.3 The kernel packet path

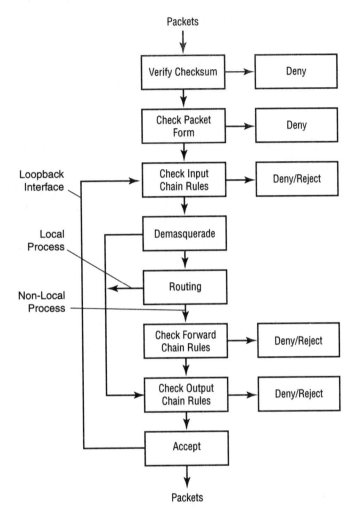

The `ipchains` facility lets you specify rules that can block, divert, or rewrite IP packets. The rules can distinguish packets based on:

- Source host or network IP address
- Source port
- Destination host or network IP address
- Destination port
- Protocol
- Connection type (SYN)

Three classes of filters, referred to as *chains*, are implemented by default:

- The input chain, which controls what packets are received

- The output chain, which controls what packets are sent

- The forward chain, which controls what packets are forwarded to a another network interface

Implementing a Firewall by Using *ipchains*

A firewall is comprised of three sets of ipchains *packet filter* rules, one set for each packet chain: input, output, and forward. To implement a firewall by using the ipchains facility, specify filter rules by issuing the ipchains command, which has the general form

```
ipchains command chain [rule] [target]
```

The *command* argument lets you

- Add a rule to the specified chain

- Delete a rule from the specified chain

- Delete all rules from the specified chain

- List the rules in the specified chain

- Specify a default policy for the specified chain

For example, to list the rules associated with the input chain, issue the command

```
ipchains -L input
```

Similarly, to flush the rules associated with the output chain, issue the command

```
ipchains -F input
```

Table 30.1 summarizes the values that can be specified for the *command* argument.

TABLE 30.1   ipchains Commands

Command	Description
-A	Appends the specified rule to the end of the specified chain.
-D	Deletes the specified rule from the specified chain.
-L	Lists rules in the specified chain.
-F	Deletes all rules from the specified chain.
-P	Sets the default policy of the specified chain to the specified target.
-h	Displays command help.

Table 30.2 summarizes the values that can be specified for the `target` argument. To specify that the default policy for packets on the input chain is DENY, issue the command

```
ipchains -P input DENY
```

It is generally good practice to set the default policy to DENY. If a packet does not match a rule that specifies some other target, the packet will be denied—that is, discarded. Any omission from the rule set will therefore cause a packet to be discarded; the discarding of packets will likely be noticed and the rule set fixed. If the default policy were ACCEPT, an omission from the rule set would allow inappropriate packets to transit the firewall, possibly leading to a security breach.

TABLE 30.2   ipchains Targets

Target	Description
ACCEPT	Admits the packet.
DENY	Denies the packet without sending an error message to the sender.

TABLE 30.2 ipchains Targets *(continued)*

Target	Description
REJECT	Denies the packet and sends an error message to the sender.
MASQ	Outgoing packets are rewritten to appear as though they originated from the firewall host. Incoming packets are reverse masqueraded—that is, rewritten to have the proper destination host.
REDIRECT	Incoming packets are redirected to a port, regardless of the specified packet destination.
RETURN	For a built-in chain, packets are handled using the default rule for the chain. For a user-defined chain, the packet is sent back to the calling chain.

Table 30.3 summarizes the form of the `rules` argument. Addresses can be specified by using any of several forms. For example, you can specify the source host IP address:

`-s 192.168.1.0`

or the destination network IP address:

`-d 192.168.1.0/24`

The /24 specifies that the network mask consists of 24 bits; the associated network address is therefore a Class C network address having a network mask value of 255.255.255.0.

TABLE 30.3 ipchains Rules

Rule	Description
-d *address* [*port*]	Specifies the destination IP address or address and port.
-i *interface*	Specifies the interface at which an input packet was received or to which an output packet is directed.
-j *target*	Specifies the target action.

TABLE 30.3 ipchains Rules *(continued)*

Rule	Description
-p *protocol*	Specifies the protocol (TCP, UDP, ICMP, or ALL).
-s *address* [*port*]	Specifies the source IP address or address and port.
-y	Specifies a TCP SYN packet, which is used to initiate a connection with a server.

You can specify a port or range of ports with the address. For example, the rule

```
-d 192.168.1.0/24 25
```

specifies a packet destined for port 25—the SMTP port—of hosts on the 192.168.1.0 network. The more general rule

```
-d 192.168.1.0/24 0:1023
```

specifies a packet destined for any privileged port of a host on the 192.168.1.0 network.

Several special values can be specified in rules. For example, the value any refers to any IP address, as does the value 0/0. Also, you can precede a rule with ! to negate the meaning of the rule. For example, the rule ! -y refers to a packet other than a TCP SYN packet.

You can combine several rules to form a compound rule. For example, the command

```
ipchains -A input -d 192.168.1.0/24 -p UDP -j DENY
```

includes a rule that refers to UDP packets destined for a host on the 192.168.1.0 network; moreover, it specifies that such packets should be discarded. Most ipchains rules include a –j argument that specifies the associated target action.

The ipchains command logs packets if the rule matching the packet includes the –l flag. The log entries have the source kern (referring to the kernel) and the priority info. So, by default, they're sent to /var/log/messages. For further information on the ipchains command, see its man page. For a complete example of an ipchains firewall, see the next section.

Implementing Masquerading by Using *ipchains*

Masquerading is a form of Network Address Translation (NAT), which is commonly used to translate private (RFC 1918) IP addresses to the address of the firewall host, so that hosts behind the firewall can access exterior networks, including the Internet.

To specify masquerading by using `ipchains`, add one or more entries specifying the MASQ target to the forward chain. For example, suppose that the 192.168.1.0/24 network is a protected local network and that the interface eth2 is an external interface of the network's firewall host—that is, an interface connected to exterior networks. The command

```
ipchains -A forward -i eth2 -s 192.168.1.0/24 -j MASQ
```

establishes a forwarding rule that masquerades packets originating from the protected network (192.168.1.0/24) and appearing on the external interface (eth2).

Special kernel modules support masquerading of commonly used protocols. You should load the necessary modules so that the protocols operate properly. These modules and their associated protocols are:

- `ip_masq_cuseeme` (CUSEEME)
- `ip_masq_ftp` (FTP)
- `ip_masq_irc` (IRC)
- `ip_masq_quake` (Quake)
- `ip_masq_raudio` (Real Audio)
- `ip_masq_vdolive` (VDO Live)

Red Hat provides an example firewall service script, which you can view on the Web at www.redhat.com/support/docs/tips/firewall/firewallservice.html. The script is distributed under the terms of the GNU General Public License, so you can freely use and redistribute it. The script does not suit every firewall situation, but you can use it as a starting point for creating your own firewall.

Saving and Restoring *ipchains* Rules

Many system administrators create an /etc/rc.d/rc.firewall script that issues ipchains commands and other commands. Generally, they modify the /etc/rc.d/rc.local script to invoke /etc/rc.d/rc.firewall. This technique for implementing a firewall lets you intersperse comments with the ipchains command, making it easier to understand and modify the firewall.

However, if you prefer, you can use the ipchains-save and ipchains-restore commands to implement a firewall. The ipchains-save command dumps the current firewall rules to stdout and the ipchains-restore command loads the firewall from stdin. By redirecting stdout to a file, you can cause ipchains-save to dump the current firewall rules to a disk file. The Red Hat Linux 6.2 script /etc/rc.d/init.d/ipchains tests for the existence of a file named /etc/sysconfig/ipchains; if the file exists, the script runs ipchains-restore against the file.

Now try your hand at constructing a firewall by completing Exercise 30.1.

EXERCISE 30.1

Constructing a Basic Firewall

Configure a simple firewall that masquerades a protected network. Allow only HTTP and FTP traffic to flow into and out of the protected network. Within the protected network, allow unrestricted flow of packets.

You can consult this book and other helps while working on this exercise. But, before taking the RHCE exam, be sure that you can construct a basic firewall without consulting external help.

Summary

In this chapter, you learned about constructing a firewall using ipchains. The most important topics covered are:

Firewalls   A firewall blocks unauthorized packets, which it discerns by consulting a set of rules that match unauthorized packets and specify their disposition.

Masquerading   Masquerading is a facility that rewrites packets so that they appear to have originated from or be destined to a specified host. Masquerading is used in many ways. One of the most common is to provide Internet access to hosts that have been assigned private IP numbers. Masquerading is also used to enhance network security by concealing the structure of a network from outsiders.

The `ipchains` Facility   The `ipchains` facility lets you specify rules that the kernel applies to packets on its input, output, and forward TCP/IP chains. The facility also lets you work with user-defined chains. The `ipchains` rules can identify packets by the following characteristics:

- Source host or network IP address
- Source port
- Destination host or network IP address
- Destination port
- Protocol
- Connection type

Matching packets are handled as specified by the rule. Possible dispositions include accepting the packet, blocking the packet, or redirecting the packet to a specified port.

Saving and Restoring a Firewall Configuration   The `ipchains-save` and `ipchains-restore` commands can be used to save a rule set to a disk file and restore a rule set from a disk file. However, many system administrators prefer to code `ipchains` rules as a script file, which can include explanatory comments that facilitate understanding and maintaining the firewall.

Key Terms

Before going on to the next chapter, be sure you're familiar with the following terms:

chains

firewall

firewall rules

masquerading

packet filter

Additional Sources of Information

If you'd like further information about the topics presented in this chapter, you should consult the following sources:

- *The Firewalling and Proxy Server HOWTO*, /usr/doc/HOWTO/ Firewall-HOWTO, by Mark Grennan

- *The IPCHAINS HOWTO*, /usr/doc/HOWTO/IPCHAINS-HOWTO, by Paul Russell

- *The Linux IP Masquerade Mini HOWTO*, /usr/doc/HOWTO/mini/ IP-Masquerade, by Ambrose Au and David Ranch

- The ipchains man page

Review Questions

1. The Red Hat Linux firewall facility is implemented by using which command?

   A. The `firewall` command

   B. The `ipchains` command

   C. The `ipfwadm` command

   D. The `ipportfw` command

2. To support FTP from a masqueraded network, you should load which of the following modules?

   A. `ip_masq`

   B. `ip_masq_all`

   C. `ip_masq_ftp`

   D. `ip_masq_tcp`

3. To list the rules associated with the input chain, which of the following commands should you issue?

   A. `ipchains -A input`

   B. `ipchains -F input`

   C. `ipchains -L input`

   D. `ipchains -P input`

4. To purge all rules associated with the output chain, which of the following commands should you issue?

   A. `ipchains -A output`

   B. `ipchains -F output`

   C. `ipchains -L output`

   D. `ipchains -P output`

5. To block packets that attempt to establish an incoming TELNET connection to hosts of the 199.199.199.0/24 network, with which of the following `ipchains` commands should be issued?

A. `ipchains -A forward -p tcp \`
   `-d 199.199.199.0/24 23 -j DENY`

B. `ipchains -A forward -p tcp`
   `! -d 199.199.199.0/24 23 -j DENY`

C. `ipchains -A input -p tcp \`
   `-d 199.199.199.0/24 23 -j DENY`

D. `ipchains -A input -p tcp`
   `! -d 199.199.199.0/24 23 -j DENY`

6. To discard a packet and send an error message to the sender, which target should be specified?

A. DENY

B. REDIRECT

C. REJECT

D. RETURN

Answers to Review Questions

1. B. The `ipfwadm` command was supported by some earlier versions of the Linux kernel.

2. C. None of the other listed module names correspond to actual modules.

3. C. The –L argument instructs `ipchains` to list the rules associated with the specified chain.

4. B. The –F argument instructs `ipchains` to flush the rules associated with the specified chain.

5. C. Such packets would be on the input chain and destined for port 23.

6. C. The DENY target sends no error message; the remaining targets do not discard the packet.

The RHCE Exam (RH302)

Chapter

31

The RHCE Exam

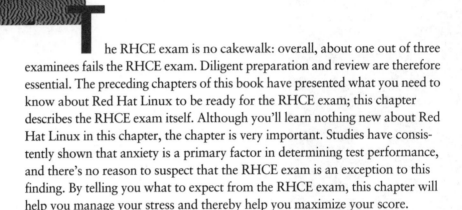

The RHCE exam is no cakewalk: overall, about one out of three examinees fails the RHCE exam. Diligent preparation and review are therefore essential. The preceding chapters of this book have presented what you need to know about Red Hat Linux to be ready for the RHCE exam; this chapter describes the RHCE exam itself. Although you'll learn nothing new about Red Hat Linux in this chapter, the chapter is very important. Studies have consistently shown that anxiety is a primary factor in determining test performance, and there's no reason to suspect that the RHCE exam is an exception to this finding. By telling you what to expect from the RHCE exam, this chapter will help you manage your stress and thereby help you maximize your score.

The RHCE Exam

The RHCE exam has three parts:

- The multiple-choice exam (1 hour)
- The Server Install and Network Services Setup exam (2 $1/_2$ hours)
- The Debug exam (2 $1/_2$ hours)

This section describes the RHCE exam generally, including the structure of the exam and the exam protocol. The following three sections describe the three components of the exam.

Structure of the RHCE Exam

Each of the three parts of the RHCE exam is scored on a 100-point scale. To pass the exam, you must score a total of 240 points, an average of 80 points on each part of the exam. Moreover, you must score at least 50 points on each part of the exam.

The multiple-choice exam resembles exams you had in high school or college. You have one hour to answer 40–50 technical questions. Some of the questions may require a true/false response; others may require you to identify which responses in a set are correct or to choose the best response from among a set of responses.

The remaining two parts of the exam are performance-based, requiring you to install, configure, or troubleshoot an actual system. If you've never taken a performance exam, you may be anxious. However, your anxiety is unwarranted. Unlike a written exam, a performance exam includes no trick questions. You'll be asked to perform the same sort of system administration tasks that system administrators perform on the job. If you have the requisite experience and expertise, you can master the performance exam.

Red Hat, Inc. states that many examinees score well on the multiple-choice exam but do poorly on the performance-based exams, thereby failing the test. This leads some to believe that the performance-based exams are more difficult than the multiple-choice exam. This may be so. But, it's possible that the unfamiliar format of performance-based exams and apprehension arising from a significant failure rate hamper student performance. By learning more about the RHCE exam and its performance-based exams in particular, you can minimize test anxiety and increase your likelihood of passing the exam.

Exam Protocol

The RHCE exam requires about seven hours. The three parts of the exam require a total of six hours. Another hour is allocated as a lunch break.

You should plan to arrive early in order to avoid arriving late due to unforeseen circumstances such as traffic. Bring at least two forms of identification, including a photo ID. Otherwise, bring a minimum of belongings: During the exam, you're not allowed to use materials other than those provided by the exam proctor. You can expect to receive such items as:

- Pen or pencil

- Blank paper

- A non-disclosure agreement

Immediately prior to the relevant part of the exam, you can expect to receive such items as:

- Task assignments for the performance-based exams

- Rescue disk for the Debug Exam

- Installation media for the Server Install and Network Services Setup Exam

You must execute the non-disclosure agreement, in which you agree not to divulge information about the RHCE exam; if you don't, you will not be permitted to take the exam.

The non-disclosure agreement is intended to safeguard the integrity of the examination process. Because the value of RHCE certification rests on accurately assessing the knowledge and skills of examinees, it is in your interest, as well as that of Red Hat, Inc., to comply with the terms of the non-disclosure agreement.

The examination room will be equipped with PCs. The proctor will assign you to a PC, which you will use to take the exam.

The exams are timed; as the proctor will announce, you are not to open materials or begin the exam until the proctor instructs you to do so.

The three parts of the exam will be given in an order chosen by the proctor. For example, the proctor might choose the following schedule:

10:00 - 12:30	Server Install and Network Services Setup exam
12:30 - 1:30	Lunch
1:30 – 2:30	Multiple-choice exam
2:30 – 5:00	Debug exam

Do not communicate—or attempt to communicate—with another examinee during the exam. If you breach this or other protocols explained by the exam proctor, you will immediately fail the exam.

The Multiple-Choice Exam

The multiple-choice exam tests your knowledge of Red Hat Linux, Linux, and Unix. Items address topics such as Linux commands, command redirection, and system administration. You cannot consult computer-based documentation or other resources, such as notes or books, during the exam.

You're allowed a maximum of one hour to complete this exam, which consists of about 50 items. An item may require you to respond by

- Classifying the item as true or false

- Identifying correct responses among a set of responses

- Identifying the best response from among a set of responses

Be sure you clearly understand the sort of response appropriate for each item.

In taking the exam, you'll probably notice items that were not addressed in this book or in the RH300 course, if you took it. Bear in mind that the purpose of the exam is to certify readiness to function as a Red Hat Linux system administrator. Red Hat, Inc.'s description of the exam is intentionally general and vague, in order to avoid certifying as RHCEs persons who are knowledgeable of the exam but not knowledgeable of system administration. Contrary to statements by some, the exam is not littered with trick questions. Rather, it is a good faith effort by Red Hat, Inc. to identify and certify examinees who possess Red Hat Linux system administration skills. If you have the proper experience and have prepared diligently, you should expect to pass the exam.

Here are some hints that can improve your score on the multiple-choice exam:

- If you have trouble recalling information you suspect may be on the test, review the information before taking the test. When you're allowed to begin, immediately write as much of the information as you can recall on the blank paper provided by the proctor. Then, you can refer to your notes during the exam.

In order to avoid a mistaken accusation of cheating, you should put the proctor on notice that you intend to use the blank paper in this fashion. Make sure it's clear that you haven't smuggled a crib sheet into the exam room.

- Be sure to read each question carefully; you may find it worthwhile to read each question twice.

- Be sure to read each response. Don't mark the first response that seems correct, because another response may be better. This is perhaps the most important exam hint of all.

- Read the responses carefully. Little words such as *not* are easily overlooked but significantly change the meaning of a response.

- Quickly eliminate any responses that are obviously incorrect and focus on the remaining responses, seeking the best response.

- If you can't confidently identify the best response, make a note of the question number and move on. Don't waste too much time pondering a single question until you've answered the straightforward questions.

- After completing the straightforward questions, return to those you noted as problems. With luck, some other question has jogged your memory and questions that initially seemed difficult are now clear. If, however, you're still unable to eliminate all the distractor responses, make your best guess.

The Practice and Bonus exams on the CD-ROM that accompany this book are excellent preparation for the multiple-choice exam. Be sure to take the Practice and Bonus exams before sitting for the RHCE exam; if possible, do so under conditions approximating those of the RHCE exam. That is, time yourself and don't allow yourself to access notes or other help.

The Server Install and Network Services Setup Exam

The 2 $1/2$-hour Server Install and Network Services Setup exam requires you to install and configure a Red Hat Linux system that satisfies a provided set of requirements. Many of the exercises in this book resemble requirements you may find on the Server Install and Network Services Setup exam. For example, you can expect to be asked to:

- Install Red Hat Linux

- Compile and install a kernel that is configured to support specified options

- Set up user accounts

- Install and configure network services, such as Apache, NFS, and Samba

- Configure the user environment

- Establish security measures that restrict access to files or services

The proctor will use an automated script to verify your work, so completeness and accuracy are important to scoring well. You shouldn't expect curveballs or odd requirements on the Server Install and Network Services Setup exam. So, your score will depend largely on your use of time and careful checking of your work.

If you plan your work well, you can anticipate a surplus of time. Before starting work, spend a few minutes carefully reading the requirements. Then decide:

- Which requirements you expect will be easy to satisfy and which requirements you expect will be hard to satisfy

- The sequence in which you'll complete the requirements

Chances are, you'll find some requirements that must be completed before you begin work on others. For example, you must establish user accounts before you can give users specified file-access privileges. You may find that some requirements involve tasks that take significant time, such as compiling a kernel; you may be able to work toward completing other requirements while these are ongoing.

While reading the requirements, you may find it useful to jot down reminders that keep you on track when implementing the requirements.

Once you begin work, don't get bogged down attempting to meet a difficult requirement unless completing it is prerequisite to meeting other requirements. Instead, make a note of the problem and move on to satisfy the remaining requirements. Later, time permitting, you can return to the problem requirement, resolve the problem, and complete the requirement.

You'll be allowed free access to man pages and other online documents during the Server Install and Network Services Setup exam, so be sure to install any documentation packages that you expect you may find useful.

Check off requirements as you complete them so that you don't inadvertently fail to complete a requirement. When you've satisfied all the requirements, spend the remainder of the allotted time checking and rechecking your work. Don't cease work until you're confident that you've correctly completed each requirement.

The Debug Exam

Like the Server Install and Network Services Setup exam, the Debug exam is a 2 $\frac{1}{2}$-hour performance-based exam. You're given a series of 2–4 exercises that cannot be completed unless you first identify and resolve one or more system configuration problems. For example, you may be asked to configure the system to boot to runlevel 5, but the system may not boot at all or the /usr file system may not mount.

When you complete an exercise, the exam proctor will verify your work and provide you with the next exercise. You're required to keep a log of the steps you took in solving the exercise and should be prepared to explain your procedure in case it's unclear that you've properly completed the exercise.

You're allowed to consult documentation installed on the system, but, as on other parts of the exam, you cannot refer to books or notes. And you won't be allowed to fix problems by reinstalling packages. For some exercises, you'll be provided with a system rescue disk.

The Debug exam is potentially the most stressful of the three exams, because you can't map out your procedure in advance. Instead, you must follow a problem-solving process that distinguishes symptoms and problems:

- Identify the symptoms.

- Discover the problem or problems causing the symptoms.

- Fix the problem or problems.

- Perform any requested configuration changes.

Here is a general procedure that you can tailor to fit the demands of specific exercises, especially those that involve boot-related problems:

1. Boot the system. If the system will not boot normally, you may have to boot it in single-user mode or by using a rescue disk.

2. Mount the required file systems. You may need to inspect /etc/fstab or use fdisk to check the partition table in order to identify the partitions and file systems. You may need to run fsck to check or repair file systems.

3. Perform repairs and make configuration changes as needed.

4. Prepare the system for rebooting. You may need to reinstall the lilo boot map or unmount file systems before rebooting. Under some circumstances, you may need to use the sync command to flush output buffers to disk.

5. Reboot the system and check your work.

It's especially important to remain calm during this exam. With the permission of the proctor, use hard candy or other relaxation aids. If the system doesn't perform as you expect, consider the resources available to you; use your imagination to devise a way of working around the problem.

For More Information

For more information on the RHCE exam, see the Red Hat, Inc. Web site, `www.redhat.com/services/training/training.html`. For opinions and commentary concerning the RHCE exam and RHCE certification, see various Internet newsgroups and forums, such as `www.slashdot.org`.

Appendix A

Practice Exam

1. What is the maximum number of partitions that can be defined on a single hard disk?

    A. 4

    B. 12

    C. 15

    D. 16

2. Which of the following mount points must be present in a Linux system?

    A. /

    B. /boot

    C. /usr

    D. /var

3. To print the file data, which Red Hat Linux command do you enter?

    A. lp data

    B. lpr data

    C. pr data

    D. print data

4. To make the value of environment variable *x* accessible outside of the immediate local environment, which command do you enter?

    A. assign *x*

    B. export *x*

    C. global *x*

    D. import *x*

5. Which service provides fonts for the X Window System?

    A. xf

    B. xfonts

    C. xfontserver

    D. xfs

6. Which of the following statements applies to the IP address 192.168.0.1?

A. It can be freely assigned to a host on a private network.

B. It cannot be assigned to a host that accesses the Internet.

C. It is designated for multicast transmission.

D. It is reserved.

7. What is the GNU General Public License (GPL)?

A. A form of copyright

B. A device used to copyleft software

C. A device that prevents software from being copied

D. A device that prevents software from being copyrighted

8. Which of the following are components of the Linux operating system?

A. The kernel originally created by Linus Torvalds

B. The GNU utilities and programs

C. The MINIX utilities and programs

D. The UNIX utilities and programs

9. Which of the following is true of the Red Hat Linux text-based installation procedure?

A. It is easier for beginners to use than the graphical installation procedure.

B. It is faster than the graphical installation procedure.

C. It is more reliable than the graphical installation procedure.

D. It requires fewer system resources, such as RAM, than the graphical installation procedure.

10. Which of the following image files are needed to start a Linux installation from CD-ROM on a system that has a PCMCIA network adapter?

   A. `autoboot.bat`

   B. `boot.img`

   C. `bootnet.img`

   D. `pcmcia.img`

11. Which of the following is true of MD5 passwords?

   A. They improve system security.

   B. They pose a security hazard.

   C. They should be used with NIS.

   D. They should not be used with NIS.

12. Which of the following is the program used by the installation procedure to configure X?

   A. `Xcfg`

   B. `Xconfig`

   C. `Xconfigurator`

   D. `Xconfiguration`

13. How should you install Linux from CD-ROM on a computer that has a PCMCIA network card?

   A. You should use the network boot disk.

   B. You should use the PCMCIA boot disk.

   C. You should use the PCMCIA supplementary disk.

   D. You should use the standard boot disk.

14. How must you perform a kickstart installation?

   A. You must boot by using the network boot disk.

   B. You must create a script by using `mkkickstart`.

   C. You must specify the `ks` argument at the boot prompt.

   D. You must store the distribution media on an FTP server.

15. Which of the following runlevels corresponds to multi-user operation without networking?

   A. 1

   B. 2

   C. 3

   D. 4

16. Which of the following programs is used to enable MD5 password encryption?

   A. md5conv

   B. md5unconv

   C. pwconv

   D. None of the above

17. Which of the following files establishes the user's path?

   A. /etc/bashrc

   B. /etc/profile

   C. ~/.bashrc

   D. ~/.bash_profile

18. Which of the following methods can be used to modify group membership?

   A. The groupmod command

   B. The linuxconf command

   C. The useradd command

   D. The userconf command

19. Which of the following commands activates user quotas?

A. quotaon -a

B. quotaon -ag

C. quotaon -au

D. quotaon -aug

20. Which of the following operations should be performed first?

A. Create the quota files

B. Set default quotas

C. Set individual quotas

D. Turn on quotas

21. Which of the following commands will replace package xyz if that package is already installed?

A. rpm -i xyz

B. rpm -f xyz

C. rpm -F xyz

D. rpm -U xyz

22. When you issue the rpm -bb command, what kind of file must be specified as the argument?

A. A binary RPM file

B. A package file

C. A SPEC file

D. A TAR file

23. Where might modules associated with a release of version 2.2 of the Linux kernel reside?

A. /lib/2.2.15

B. /lib/modules/2.2.15-2

C. /modules/2.2.15

D. /modules/2.2.15-2

24. Which of the following files can be used to identify installed PCI devices?

A. /proc

B. /proc/ioports

C. /proc/devices

D. /proc/pci

25. Which of the following commands should you issue to restart the lpd service?

A. /etc/rc.d/init.d/lp restart

B. /etc/rc.d/init.d/lp start

C. /etc/rc.d/init.d/lpd restart

D. /etc/rc.d/init.d/lpd start

26. Which of the following commands should you issue to specify that the gpm service should be executed at runlevel 3?

A. chkconfig --level 3 gpm

B. chkconfig --level 3 gpm on

C. chkconfig --levels 3 gpm

D. chkconfig --levels 3 gpm on

27. Which of the following commands will halt the system?

A. init 0

B. halt

C. shutdown -h now

D. telinit 0

28. Which of the following commands should you issue to inform the init process that its configuration file has changed?

A. `init q`

B. `init -q`

C. `kill -HUP init`

D. `killall -HUP init`

29. Which of the following is true when you modify the file `/etc/crontab`?

A. `cron` immediately recognizes the change.

B. You must reboot the system immediately thereafter.

C. You must issue the touch command to update the modification time of the `/var/spool/cron` directory.

D. You must restart the `cron` system.

30. Which of the following `cron` jobs are executed daily?

A. `logrotate`

B. `makewhatis`

C. `rmmod`

D. `slocate.cron`

31. Which `/etc/conf.modules` line specifies that default module path information is to be retained?

A. `default-path`

B. `hold`

C. `keep`

D. `retain`

32. Which of the following commands correctly creates an initial ramdisk for use during system boot?

A. `mkinitrd /boot/initrd-`*version*

B. `mkinitrd /boot/initrd-`*version* *version*

C. `mkinitrd /boot/initrd-`*version*`.img`

D. `mkinitrd /boot/initrd-`*version*`.img` *version*

33. Which of the following files contains the dynamic loader's cache?

    A. `/etc/ld.so.cache`

    B. `/etc/ld.so.conf`

    C. `/lib/ld.so.cache`

34. To start a system in runlevel 1 without initial processes, what should be typed in response to the boot prompt?

    A. `linux`

    B. `linux emergency`

    C. `linux s`

    D. `linux single`

35. Which of the following are Apache configuration files that must exist?

    A. `access.conf`

    B. `httpd.conf`

    C. `modules.conf`

    D. `srm.conf`

36. Which of the following programs is not PAM-aware?

    A. `in.ftp`

    B. `in.rlogin`

    C. `in.telnetd`

    D. `login`

37. Which file should list a host in order to permit the host to access a printer remotely?

    A. /etc/hosts

    B. /etc/hosts.equiv

    C. /etc/hosts.lpd

    D. /etc/printcap

38. By default, what type of logging messages are sent to the file /var/log/secure?

    A. alert

    B. auth

    C. authpriv

    D. emerg

39. How many members does the default group of a newly created ordinary user contain?

    A. 1

    B. 2

    C. 4

    D. 8

40. Which of the TCP services should *not* generally be used?

    A. finger

    B. identd

    C. netstat

    D. sysstat

41. Which flag should be used to invoke Xconfigurator non-interactively?

    A. --auto

    B. --expert

    C. --kickstart

    D. --probe

42. Which of the following programs can damage a monitor?

   A. SuperProbe

   B. xf86config

   C. xinitrc

   D. xvidtune

43. Which of the following is the file that specifies a user's window manager when using the AnotherLevel desktop environment?

   A. ~/.wm_style

   B. ~/.wmanager

   C. ~/.Xclients

   D. ~/.Xsession

44. Which of the following key sequences typically switches from a virtual console to X?

   A. CTRL-ALT-F1

   B. CTRL-ALT-F3

   C. CTRL-ALT-F7

   D. CTRL-ALT-F8

45. Which of the following attempts to log in to an arbitrary X server on the local network?

   A. X -all

   B. X -broadcast

   C. X -indirect

   D. X -query

46. Which of the following directives configures xdm to provide any requesting host with a chooser that includes server1 and server2?

A. `* CHOOSER server1 server2`

B. `server1 server2 CHOOSER *`

C. `ALL CHOOSER server1 server2`

D. `server1 server2 CHOOSER ALL`

47. Which of the following are ways to disable dynamic routing?

A. `echo "0" > /proc/sys/net/ipv4/dynamic_routing`

B. Editing `/etc/sysconfig/network-scripts`

C. The `linuxconf` Gated Daemon screen

D. The `linuxconf` Routed Daemon screen

48. Which of the following protocols is a popular exterior protocol?

A. BGP-4

B. EGP

C. OSPF-2

D. RIP-2

49. Which of the following kernel options are required to support masquerading?

A. `IP: firewalling`

B. `IP: masquerading`

C. `IP: masquerading special modules support`

D. `IP: transparent proxy support`

50. Which of the following commands could be used to masquerade packets originating from a local protected network?

A. ipchains -A forward -i eth0 \ -s 192.168.1.0/24 -j MASQ

B. ipchains -A input -i eth0 \ -s 192.168.1.0/24 -j MASQ

C. ipchains -A local -i eth0 \ -s 192.168.1.0/24 -j MASQ

D. ipchains -A output -i eth0 \ -s 192.168.1.0/24 -j MASQ

Answers to Practice Exam

1. D. A hard disk can have four primary partitions and 12 logical partitions. However, only three of the primary partitions and the 12 logical partitions can hold file systems. See Chapter 2 for more information.

2. A. The /boot partition is not required if the hard disk is small, if the / partition is small, or if the system BIOS is not subject to addressing restrictions. The /usr and /var partitions are never required. See Chapter 2 for more information.

3. B. The Red Hat Linux command to print a file is lpr. See Chapter 3 for more details.

4. B. The export command marks an environment variable as accessible outside of the local environment. See Chapter 3 for more details.

5. D. The X font server is named xfs. See Chapter 4 for more information.

6. A. You can assign this IP address to a host on a private network and use network address translation to enable the host to access the Internet. See Chapter 4 for more information.

7. A, B. The GPL is a form of copyright—known as a copyleft—that guarantees rights to use, modify, copy, and redistribute software. See Chapter 5 for more information.

8. A, B. Linux, sometimes called GNU/Linux, is the combination of Torvalds's kernel and the GNU utilities and programs. See Chapter 5 for more information.

9. B, C, D. The graphical installation procedure is generally easier for beginners to use, but it requires more resources and, therefore, may not run as quickly as the text-based installation procedure, particularly on a system that has limited RAM. The text-based installation procedure is more likely to recover from problems and requires fewer system resources. See Chapter 6 for more information.

10. B. The file boot.img contains an image suitable for installation from a CD-ROM disk or a local hard drive partition that contains the installation files. The image in the file pcmcia.img is needed only if PCMCIA devices are used during installation. See Chapter 6 for more information.

11. A, C. MD5 passwords improve security and should generally be used. See Chapter 7 for more information.

12. C. The installation program uses Xconfigurator to configure X. See Chapter 7 for more information.

13. D. The PCMCIA boot disk is needed only if PCMCIA devices are accessed during installation. The PCMCIA supplementary disk no longer exists. See Chapter 8 for more information.

14. C. You can boot using the standard boot disk, so long as the ks.cfg file and distribution media are on local devices. You can create the kickstart script by hand. You cannot perform a kickstart installation by using an FTP server; only NFS is supported. See Chapter 8 for more information.

15. B. Runlevel 1 is single-user mode. Runlevel 3 is multi-user mode with networking. Runlevel 4 is essentially the same as runlevel 3. See Chapter 9 for more information.

16. D. You cannot conveniently enable MD5 password encryption using any of these tools; the authconfig program lets you enable MD5 passwords. See Chapter 9 for more information.

17. A, C. See the listings and descriptions presented in Chapter 10 to verify that the /etc/bashrc and ~/.bashrc files set the path. See Chapter 10 for more information.

18. B, C, D. The groupmod command can be used to change the name of a group. See Chapter 10 for more information.

19. A, C, D. The –a option activates user and group quotas unless –g or –u is given, in which case it activates only the specified type of quotas. See Chapter 11 for more information.

20. A. You must create the quota files before quotas can be set or turned on. See Chapter 11 for more information.

21. C, D. The -i command installs the package if the package is not already installed; the -f flag has no valid meaning in this context. See Chapter 12 for more information.

22. B. The command `rpm -bb` builds a binary RPM from a source RPM. See Chapter 12 for more information.

23. A, B. The modules reside in a subdirectory of /lib/modules that is named for the kernel version and build with which they're associated. See Chapter 13 for more information.

24. C. The /proc/pci directory identifies installed PCI devices. See Chapter 13 for more information.

25. C. The service is named lpd and the `restart` argument is appropriate. See Chapter 14 for more information.

26. B. The flag is level, not levels, and the on argument is required. See Chapter 14 for more information.

27. A, B, C, D. Any of the alternatives will work. See Chapter 15 for more information.

28. A. The init command is used; its q argument must not have a preceding dash (-). See Chapter 15 for more information.

29. A. The cron system tracks the modification time of the /etc/crontab file and knows when the file has been changed. See Chapter 16 for more information.

30. A, B, D. The rmmod job is executed every 10 minutes. See Chapter 16 for more information.

31. C. The keep line specifies that path information in /etc/conf.modules supplements default information. See Chapter 17 for more information.

32. D. You should specify the img extension and the kernel version and extraversion code. See Chapter 18 for more information.

33. A. The cache file is /etc/ld.so.cache; the configuration file is /etc/ld.so.conf. See Chapter 19 for more information.

34. B. The responses `linux emergency`, `linux s`, and `linux single` all start the system in runlevel 1. But, only `linux emergency` omits the initial processes. See Chapter 20 for more information.

35. A, B, D. All three Apache configuration files must exist; however, directives can be placed in any file. See Chapter 21 for more information.

36. C. The `in.telnetd` program need not be, and is not, PAM-aware since it invokes the PAM-aware `login` program to establish a login session. See Chapter 22 for more information.

37. B, C. If the remote host is under the same administrative control as the local host, the remote host can be listed in `/etc/hosts.equiv`; otherwise, it should be listed in `/etc/hosts.lpd`. The host name must be resolvable, but the host need not be listed in `/etc/hosts`; for example, the host name could be resolved by DNS or NIS. See Chapter 23 for more information.

38. C. By default, `authpriv` messages are sent to `/var/log/secure`, so that ordinary users cannot view them. See Chapter 24 for more information.

39. A. Red Hat Linux places each ordinary user in a user private group having 1 member. See Chapter 25 for more information.

40. A, C, D. These services can reveal useful information to a cracker. The `identd` service can help you verify user identities across your network. See Chapter 25 for more information.

41. C. The `--kickstart` flag specifies non-interactive operation to the extent possible. The `--expert` flag lets you override probed information. See Chapter 26 for more information.

42. B, D. The `xvidtune` and `xf86config` tools let you set invalid operating characteristics that can damage a monitor. In the case of `xf86config`, any damage will occur after the tool is run, since the tool itself operates only in text mode. See Chapter 26 for more information.

43. A. The `~/.Xclients-default` script checks the contents of the `~/.wm_style` file. See Chapter 27 for more information.

44. C. Virtual console 7 is associated with X. See Chapter 27 for more information.

45. B. The –broadcast keyword causes X to send a broadcast message and provide a login screen to a responding server. See Chapter 28 for more information.

46. A. You can use a wildcard to specify the client hosts. The servers are specified following the CHOOSER keyword. See Chapter 28 for more information.

47. D. The /proc file system does not provide an option for disabling gated, and /etc/sysconf/network-scripts is a directory, not a file. See Chapter 29 for more information.

48. A. OSPF-2 and RIP-2 are interior protocols. EGP is no longer popular. See Chapter 29 for more information.

49. A, B, C, D. Each listed option is required to support masquerading. See Chapter 30 for more information.

50. A. To masquerade a local network, append the proper rules to the forward chain. See Chapter 30 for more information.

Index

Note to the Reader: Throughout this index **boldfaced** page numbers indicate primary discussions of a topic. *Italicized* page numbers indicate illustrations.

G

J

K

N

T

V

W

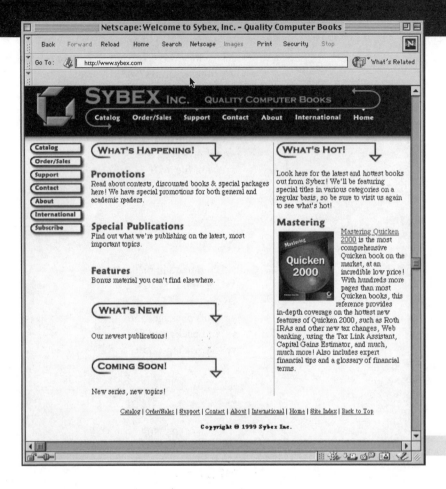